A WOMAN'S PLACE

A Woman's Place

To Pat

REX DENVER BOROUGH

July 8, 1992

AMERICAN WEST BOOKS
P.O. BOX 693
ALBUQUERQUE, N.M. 87103
U.S.A.

A Woman's Place is a work of fiction.
The characters and in it have been invented by the author,
and any resemblance to actual persons living or dead,
is purely coincidental. The story is also fictitious.

Published by American West Books,
Post Office Box 693,
Albuquerque, New Mexico, U.S.A. 87103

Library of Congress Cataloging-in-Publication Data

A Woman's Place / Rex Denver Borough

Library of Congress Catalog Card Number
91-078122

ISBN
1-880988-00-3

Manufactured in the United States of America

First Edition

This book is dedicated to the national women's organizations of America whose commitment to the principles of our democracy has been a guiding force in bringing women into the mainstream of our country's interests.

Founded:

1881	American Association of University Women
1890	General Federation of Women's Clubs
1890	Daughters of the American Revolution
1897	National League of American Pen Women
1917	Altrusa International
1919	National Federation of Business and Professional Women's Clubs
1919	Zonta International
1920	League of Women Voters of the United States
1921	Pilot International
1921	American Federation of Soroptimist Clubs
1938	National Federation of Republican Women
1949	American Business Womens Association
1966	National Organization of Women (NOW)
1969	National Women's Hall of Fame
1971	National Women's Political Caucus
1972	National Federation of Democratic Women
1979	American Society of Professional and Executive Women
1984	National Political Congress of Black Women

...and the many women's clubs in the nation's communities, and women's groups at Universities.

About the Author...

Rex Denver Borough is a native New Mexican
whose grandparents homesteaded on the plains of eastern
New Mexico before it became a state.
He was born about an hour's drive from where
Caprock City would be if it were a real town.
He is grateful for his upbringing in the pioneer country.

Mr. Borough lives in Albuquerque, New Mexico.

Acknowledgments...

For their great help and insight which encouraged me so much during the creation of *A Woman's Place*, I sincerely thank Eileen Stanton, Paula Paul, Happy Shaw, Edith Flaherty, John Bender, Michelle Lommasson, Elana Willey, Jan Fehrman, Arnold Baron, Dixie René Colvin, V.A.L. Lewis, Neal Singer, Sandra Richardson, Jesse Price and Peter Vogel.

Kathleen Herbison and Tom Perry get my special gratitude for their selfless contributions and skillful editing, and many thanks to Clayton Newman for helping me to unravel the mysteries of computers.

I also thank the many readers of the manuscript in its various stages, whose enthusiasm for the story has been very inspiring: Dorothy Sess, Marcie Allen, Virginia Mitchell, Nancy Bowra and Steve, Katha Brady, Georgene and Hayes Keeler, Carolyn Barnes, Kitty Sadock, Bea Bragg, Bill and Marilynn Heckman, Jack McMains, Gene and Mac Buescher, Margo Gordon, and Dr. Sherry A. Perry.

And, to Jane, who couldn't keep from helping.

Thank you so very much,
Rex Denver Borough

*All of the action in this story
takes place from about the
fourth of July through the
first Tuesday in November
of a presidential election year.*

1

Even in July it's cool in the pre-dawn hours in Albuquerque. Katy Jenkins pulled the blanket around her shoulders, pushed herself up against the massive headboard and, although puzzled by such an early morning call, confidently picked up the phone. The bedside clock glowed—4:30 A.M.

"Katy, it's Margaret," said the distressed voice at the other end. "It must be the middle of the night out there. But I just had to catch you."

"Margaret, what's wrong?"

"I'm in bad trouble, Katy, and with me the entire Coalition party. Everything I've worked for is going down the drain."

"Why, Margaret? What's going on?"

"Someone's trying to destroy me and stop the Coalition." Margaret's voice regained some of its characteristic firmness. "There's something weird about the whole thing. I can't find out who's behind all this. It just hit the Grand Jury out of the blue and they ran with it."

"I don't understand. What's the Grand Jury got to do with you?"

"Eric's construction business. The City Prosecutor is indicting him next week for fraud on city building contracts. Somebody, or several somebodies, fed the Grand Jury some trumped-up evidence. It's vicious, Katy. They're using my son to go after me."

Katy pulled the blanket up to her chin. She ran a slender finger behind her ear, dragging with it short wisps of her shining blond hair. Now the receiver fit.

"You?" she exclaimed. "What have the charges against Eric

got to do with you?   Are the allegations based in fact at all?"

"Hell no, the allegations aren't true, Katy. Don't you get it?
It's blackmail! They'll drop the whole thing if I refuse to run. If
I don't get out, they'll put the boots to Eric and me along with
him.   There goes the American Coalition party right down the
tubes, with me pulling the plug."

"Can't you isolate yourself from Eric's business?"

"That's just it, I can't. I put some money into the business.
That's what his father would have done and I felt I had to do it in
his place. I'm tied to it, damn it, because I'm on the board—an
officer, too. They're filing criminal charges as well as civil. As
well as wrecking his business, Eric could land in jail. That's the
gun they're holding to my head. And you know damned well what
the press will do with this. They'll crucify me!"

Katy had followed the remarkable growth of the American
Coalition party. She knew Margaret was one of the founders and
the party leader.   But, as the senior Congresswoman from her
state, she had given no endorsement or support to Margaret's
efforts, except that of a friend encouraging another in a valiant
struggle.

Deep anguish came through in Margaret's voice as she
continued. "You know how I've worked the past four years to
make this party what it is today. The foundation is laid. We
depended on a groundswell from the women of the nation to
launch me into the presidential race." She paused briefly. "This
thing is ruining me," she said grimly. "I can't run."

Katy thought back on their years as colleagues in the U.S.
Congress.   Their friendship was unusual considering the
differences between their political philosophies and backgrounds.
Margaret, a champion of women's rights, a Doctor of American
History from Columbia University, stood in contrast to Katy
Jenkins, the first woman governor of her state, but still a
self-confessed country girl from Caprock City, New Mexico. Katy
was a "born" Democrat, but her ideals were sometimes considered
conservative.

Margaret had authored a forthright and powerful feminist book
during an earlier hiatus from elected office. Katy made little
distinction between women's rights and the rights of any other
group. But many times the Congresswomen had found themselves

on the same side of the fence, battling together for causes they believed in, respecting each others strategies and principles, their friendship growing over the years.

Katy seethed inwardly for her friend. "There must be a way!" She tried to think of an angle—some way to help. But she knew Margaret was right. No matter what the facts were in Eric's case, the damage would be done.

Margaret sounded more like herself now. "I worked damn hard for this party. Got us on the ballot in all fifty states. God, I was so close I could smell the victory. I wanted it bad...damned bad." She hesitated a moment as if she were reluctant to say what she had to say next. "Katy, I want you to take my place on the ticket."

Katy caught her breath. She sat bolt upright in bed. "You mean run for president in your place?"

Margaret's voice lost its desperate tone, but the urgency remained. "You're the one person I know who could land on her feet running. Please, just come to our convention."

"Margaret! I don't know if it would be best for you, me, or your party. What about Andy Barker? He's one of the founders and a party mainstay, isn't he?"

"Sure, and he'll be at the convention. But we don't want a male candidate. There's really no one else with the backing and experience you have. You would bring us into the mainstream."

Margaret continued, leaving no room for Katy's objections. "Katy, the convention starts Thursday, at the Brown Palace Hotel in Denver. This may be our best chance to elect a woman president. Just come to the Convention; that's all I ask."

Katy collected her thoughts. "Margaret, I appreciate your confidence in me, believe me I do, but I'm not so sure. You know I'm tagged a conservative, and even though the label doesn't always fit, it's still my image. Your people might not approve. And you know what I have to lose. My political career could end up in ashes after nineteen years of hard work. Margaret, let me give this some thought. It intrigues me, but I never quite imagined myself as a candidate for president. I'll get back to you after I've had a chance to think about it."

"You're the only woman I know who can do it," Margaret said quietly.

Katy replaced the receiver in its cradle. She noticed the numbness in her fingers and realized how tightly she had gripped the phone. Congresswoman Jenkins, the decisive, intrepid woman whose confidence never faltered, lay in bed, limp as a rag doll.

Run for President of the United States!

She tossed back the covers and stood beside the bed. Her knees shook, threatening to give out beneath her.

What would I be getting myself into? She turned on the water in the shower and let it run for several minutes as she stood in thought. Finally she remembered to step into the shower under the flowing water.

Toweling herself dry, she brushed her short-cut hair quickly into place, pulled on a bright yellow terry robe and stepped from the bedroom into the spacious living area.

The enormous, tightly woven Navajo rugs felt good beneath her bare feet. The wall lamps with hand-wrought tin shades shed a warm glow on the southwestern decor. Her suite in the famous old downtown La Posada Hotel was her home in Albuquerque. When a Santa Fe hotelier restored the hotel to its original southwestern elegance, this suite had been designed for her, with a rooftop garden.

Relaxed now, she paused at the blue and yellow Mexican tile trimmed fireplace, let her gaze rest a moment on the painting above it, then returned to the bedroom. She settled into the rocking chair in the corner by her bed, and rocked gently as her mind shifted into gear to confront Margaret's proposition.

Her political intuition flashed warnings of danger and disaster ahead. Margaret Kincaid, although brilliant, able, and a good friend, was still looking into the wrong end of the telescope, zeroing in on women's concerns rather than seeing women as part of the broad spectrum. Andy Barker—a likable fellow, great family background, seasoned campaigner, but a liberal straight out of the sixties. She knew that all the laws of probability would have to be repealed to win that election with the little upstart American Coalition party. But the sheer adventure of running for president of the United States might make it worthwhile.

Danger signals flashed again. The Women's Movement—she had read in the paper that they were putting up a million dollars seed money for the Coalition party campaign. The contributions, collected from almost 100,000 members, averaged only eleven dollars each. Grass roots support! But the Movement, with its many organizations, could be pure hell on a candidate.

And there was another, greater threat. For twenty-seven years now she had kept a secret—a secret that could ruin her career. If she were a man it might not have mattered, but a woman is vulnerable in ways a man is not. If she ran for president, she would be subjected to intense scrutiny by her enemies as well as the press. And if the secret of her past were revealed, it would not only ruin her and her candidacy, it could damage women's stature throughout the political world.

Well, she'd have to face that when, and if, the time should ever come.

2

Katy felt a quiver of expectant joy deep inside as she anticipated Johnny's impending visit. Even Margaret's call in no way altered the high priority for this Saturday morning. The tall young man who called her "sis" was twenty-seven now. His tennis career, including two years on the circuit, had delayed his graduation. A few more credits next year and he would graduate from the University of New Mexico. Katy hadn't met his new girlfriend, Gloria, but Johnny's enthusiasm for her came through in his phone calls.

She pulled the curtains apart and peeked outside. The Sandia mountains, barely revealed in earliest dawn light, gave Katy a sense of comfort by their very existence.

She tucked in her western cut blouse and cinched the narrow leather belt around her slim waist. The soft leather boots, her favorites, gleamed from years of careful polishing. Because of the frequent trips between Washington, D.C., and Albuquerque, Katy kept one complete wardrobe in Georgetown and another at La Posada. She made a quick appraisal in the full length mirror, approved of what she saw, then rushed through the patio, past the rose bushes and flowering trumpet vine, to peer over the garden wall. Down on the street Johnny was pulling the Jaguar up to the curb. The car she had driven when she was at the University suited him well. Uncle Cliff had restored the Jag as Johnny's high school graduation gift.

"Johnny!" Katy called. "Gloria! Hi! Come on up."

Johnny waved up at her, smiled broadly, and hopped over the closed driver's door with the grace and fluid motion of a fine athlete. Gloria, a willowy young woman, whose auburn hair billowed around her face on a sudden updraft, clasped Johnny's hand as he helped her out of the convertible.

The scene made Katy's breath catch in her throat. Images overwhelmed her, the images of the summer so many years ago when the young couple emerging from the Jaguar could have been John Van Dorn and herself. Memories of that summer, the summer she fell in love, flooded into her mind. They have the look of a couple physically comfortable with each other, she mused.

She wondered when they would tell her.

Before going to the mezzanine landing, she flipped the collection of local and eastern newspapers onto the foyer table. Normally, she would have spent the early morning poring over them. But between her thinking about Margaret Kincaid's call and anticipating Johnny's visit, they now lay completely forgotten.

She reached the stairway just as Johnny and Gloria came leaping up the red-tile steps two at a time. Laughter bounced off the stairwell walls. Johnny took two long strides ahead of Gloria and enfolded Katy in his arms.

"Hi ya, sis. You're looking good!" He let her go. "Say, did you shrink?"

"Watch it, kid, or I'll have to beat you arm wrestling one more time."

Johnny pulled Gloria to his side and introduced her. "It's about time I got you two together. You both know everything about one another. Well...almost everything."

"Ah! I thought so," Katy smiled. "You two moved in together."

"We sure did," he said as he hugged Gloria. "Cuts the overhead and we're as happy as two prairie dogs in a burrow."

"Johnny, you're embarrassing me."

Katy noted the sudden color in the young woman's cheeks. "Oh, I'm happy for you both. But Gloria, can he cook?"

Gloria quickly warmed up to Katy as they joked about Johnny's culinary skills, which left him a diet of popcorn and beer.

"Johnny, show Gloria around while I get organized."

"Oh, this is an original Von Hassler," Gloria said, scrutinizing the artist's signature on one of the oil paintings. Gloria marveled aloud at the skill of the painter as she contemplated the high valley settlement of the weavers of Chimayo. Autumn cottonwoods shaded an old Spanish adobe village. The Sangre de Cristo mountain range rose behind the village to a forever blue sky accented by fleecy white clouds.

Johnny touched her arm and pointed to another painting hanging over the fireplace.

"This one's by Beatien Yazz, a Navajo who never had formal art training. He has this impressionist style all his own." A young buck leaped side-by-side with his doe, suspended within a wintry landscape. Katy watched the young couple admire the watercolor depiction of the sacred spirits of the deer in joyous pairing. She perceived the lovely union of two kindred souls—a union she had known briefly with John Van Dorn.

"They seem to leap across the universe," Gloria remarked.

They drank from white ironstone mugs outside in the garden. The azure sky contrasted with dawn's dusty pinks and yellows which earlier had nudged their way into the eastern skyline.

"What a wonderful place for our Senator to live," Gloria said.

"That's Congresswoman," Katy chuckled. "Thank you anyhow."

"Oh sure, the House of Representatives." Gloria's cheeks tinged again with a hint of red.

Katy's mind wandered at the mention of Congress. What would her constituents and backers in New Mexico think if she bolted the party? Especially H.B. McGee, her political mentor whose backing had helped put her into the Governor's office and five terms in the U.S. Congress? And Uncle Cliff? And Pop? The list went on. As far as they were concerned, she was at the pinnacle of success. But Katy felt frustration as she watched the nation's economy go sour, with the political system unable to cope because of its self-indulgence and lack of leadership.

"I'll be going up to Santa Fe later this afternoon to see Uncle Cliff and Aunt May. You want to join me?"

Johnny looked disappointed. "Gee, I play a seeded position at the Tennis Club today. I hoped you could come."

"Oh, I'd like nothing better than to watch you play. Maybe...no, I've got to see Uncle Cliff, and I promised to drop in on the Ortega wedding party at La Fonda. You know, Johnny, these choices are worse than any I have to make in Washington."

"Don't worry about it, sis. Maybe we'll head up there later tonight. We're about due for a visit to Aunt May's wonderful kitchen."

Gloria laughed, "He can always eat."

Katy rose, collecting the coffee cups. "Let's go downstairs for breakfast."

She felt exuberance as she descended the stairs with Johnny and Gloria.

*　*　*

Katherine Jenkins was a striking woman at forty-seven. She inherited her strong features from the Viking ancestry of her father's side of the family, which also accounted for her natural blond hair. Although slightly taller than the average woman, she moved with grace and self-assurance. Her deep blue eyes twinkled as if she had just heard a good story, or was about to tell one.

"Hello Katy," rang out as Katy made her appearance in the lobby, "welcome home!" The familiar greetings always accompanied her in a public place. As Katy visited her way across the lobby, Johnny guided Gloria, arm around her waist, to the fountain at the center. The lobby rose two stories above them to a high-beamed ceiling. A fine Mexican tiled basin held a beautiful fountain of cascading water. The young couple took in the atmosphere of the hotel as they made their way to the entrance of the coffee shop, arriving just as Katy got there.

After the usual round of greetings in the coffee shop, Katy relaxed over breakfast with Gloria and Johnny. "You ought to sell off some of that herd of ours, Johnny, and get your tuition put away for Harvard. I'd like to see an MBA behind your name, and I'm sure Pop would welcome the pasture room."

"We already did, sis. Pop smelled the drought coming, and we sold off a bunch before prices dropped."

Katy thought a moment. The drought must be serious. To Johnny she said, "Sounds like Pop."

"Say sis, look who's here." Johnny nodded toward the door. She turned to see Dick Donovan—a small man, frail with age and white-haired, but as feisty as ever. Ever since Katy answered the hand written ad from the university's job opportunities board, she had taken the direct track with Dick. She remembered their first meeting in his office. Fresh out of law school, she was looking for a place to land.

"I'm here about the notice posted at the university," she had said.

He looked at her, eyes wide. "I hadn't expected a girl."

"Why not?" Katy shot him the question.

"Why not indeed!" he exclaimed. "If I had a proposition that wouldn't guarantee you a thin dime, just a chance to have your own office, would you still be interested?"

"Yes, I would," she answered. The three words launched her career and began a lasting friendship with Dick.

Now, as Dick made his way in from the lobby, he pulled off his hat with the colorful feather stuck in the hatband. Before he got halfway across the room Katy was up to meet the old gentleman with a loving hug.

"You never lose your vim and vigor, do you gal? 'Bout time you returned to the roost. Not that I'd ever miss that blond head of yours."

Katy hugged him again. "Oh Dick, it's good to see you."

"Katy, let a man breathe. Now, who is this pretty young woman seated at your table?" Donovan extended a friendly hand to Gloria. "Obviously, you have atrocious judgment of character if you choose to associate with the likes of this young man."

Johnny stood and grasped Dick's hand in warm greeting as the old man took the seat between Gloria and Katy.

"Weren't you Governor of New Mexico, Mr. Donovan?" Gloria asked.

"Too far back for you to remember—I held the office of Lieutenant Governor back in the fifties." Then he added, "Stow the Mr. Donovan, gal. A man like me needs affection more than formality."

Dick ordered a poached egg when the waitress brought him his usual coffee and toast.

"Any big news on the political front, Katy?"

She squirmed a bit as Margaret's call leaped back into her thoughts. "Well, there's one thing I need to talk with you about, but it'll wait."

Dick's attention settled back on Gloria. "Have you been to Caprock City yet?"

The young couple shared the events of their trip. Johnny bragged like a new father about the herd of grade cows he and Katy ran at the home place. Gloria commented that she saw the great Angel Fire, Johnny's prize bull. Dick took it all in, then leaned to Katy's ear and whispered, "For the money Johnny paid for him, that bull ought to have gold-plated balls!"

Time slipped by until the match was but an hour away.

"You still making the big bucks playing tennis?" Dick asked.

"Oh, no," laughed Johnny. "A couple of years on the circuit was enough for me to fully appreciate the value of an education. I still get into the draw when a good tournament comes to the Club, though; I like the competition."

As Katy's brother and Gloria rose to leave, Dick posed one more question. "Johnny, can you still get the Jaguar to do a hundred in fourteen seconds?"

"On a good day, I can beat that."

"You better not!" countered Katy. "Good luck with your match, Johnny. Please, drive sanely." Katy hugged Gloria and gave Johnny a kiss on the cheek. "Take care."

Katy's love for Johnny ran deeper than anyone might have guessed. The five people who knew the likeness of blood that ran between her and the young man had kept the secret safe from the day he entered her parent's family as an infant. Elizabeth, Katy's cousin and best friend, knew. Uncle Clifford and Aunt May, Elizabeth's parents, knew. Katy's parents knew. None of them shared their knowledge with any other. The veil concealing Johnny's identity was drawn, never to be removed.

* * *

Alone now, Katy told Dick her news. "Margaret Kincaid called me this morning."

"I saw yesterday's New York Times. The DA's office is making some ugly threats. They're really going to ride her 'til she quits," Donovan said.

"She can't run. That's pretty obvious." Katy kept her voice

steady.

"It is. What's the party going to do now—run Andy Barker?"

"That's not what Margaret has in mind."

"Well, why not? Andy's a good man, despite his party choice. He's got a lot of backing in the east. And he has the finances to conduct a campaign."

"They want a woman."

"Is there another woman in that party with Margaret's drawing strength?"

"No, there isn't. They're thinking of someone outside the party."

"Well, this likely means the end of the American Coalition party. Who else could they get?"

"Me!" Katy blurted.

Dick sat back. His high tenor voice pierced the dining room from end to end. "Jesus! Katy, are you serious? Is that what Margaret wanted?"

"What do you think?" Katy asked.

Dick's next words were measured. "Katy, you have been the 'fair-haired girl' in New Mexico. You've practically owned the press. They all loved Steve, and with him missing in Vietnam they looked after you." His brow furrowed. "But Katy, this is the big league. Going against the national tickets means trouble. The Democrats, and the Republicans even more so, will chop you to bits. The national press will lie in wait. And if you make one goof, they will pounce on you and eat you alive."

"I can take it, Dick."

"Oh, I know that, Katy. But this thing that happened to Margaret sounds sinister to me. How do you know they won't go after you? And the Right Reverend Thomas 'right-to-life' Atwood will burn you at the stake if he can."

"I know." Katy looked at Dick appreciatively. She could depend on him to lay it on the line. "You're the only one I've told, Dick."

"Are you going to mention this to H.B.?"

"Why bring it up? I'm sure he wouldn't approve."

Dick's thin eyebrows rose. "That's putting it mildly."

"Don't worry. I'm not going to do anything rash. But I may drop in at their Convention in Denver this weekend." Katy looked at her watch. "I've got to get over to the office now. See what's piled up. Maria is coming in and maybe H.B. Want to tag along?"

Dick declined the invitation and they parted in the lobby. Dick shook his head, not daring to believe what he felt was certain to happen.

As she walked the few blocks to her office in the Federal Building, Katy felt another light come on—not flashing, not warning. Instead, this light furnished a flood of understanding. She suddenly realized she could no longer stay with the Democratic party when so much of its current doctrine was in direct opposition to her own convictions. Nor could she stand the philosophy of the Republicans, part of which violated her sense of fair play. Spend and get re-elected! This was the Congressional code. Crazy bills were passed, cutting painfully into the paychecks of millions of workers. The situation outraged her concept of what government should be.

The light was all-encompassing now. Her shoo-in reelection for two more years in the Congress suddenly lost its attraction. Her heart pounded. Now she knew. *She had to go to that Convention.*

3

Manuel Garcia, bell-captain at La Posada, brought Katy's car around for her drive to Santa Fe. He held the door for her and watched as she slid into the driver's seat. *This handsome lady is no passing cactus flower*, he thought, *to bloom for a day and wither away*. Aloud he said, "Katy, your Cadillac is purring like a kitten."

Katy agreed as she pressed the gas pedal ever so slightly. "Still as smooth as ever. Thank you, Manuel."

A few blocks from the hotel she turned onto Interstate 25 north. Only an hour's easy drive lay between her and Santa Fe. Soon the last of the highway hotels and industrial parks slipped by the windows, giving way to the Sandia Pueblo Indian Reservation lands with their centuries old Indian villages. Next would be San Felipe, then Santo Domingo.

Fiercely protective of her Native American constituency in the pueblo villages, she worked side by side with the pueblos to obtain government financing and engineering for community water systems. No rural community attained that by themselves. But, at the risk of her own popularity, she encouraged them to reject food stamps. She reasoned that they owned the best land and water rights on the Rio Grande, giving them the opportunity to be self-sufficient.

The old highway had run alongside the pueblos nestled near the Rio Grande. But the new Interstate climbed through the high barren mesas, its only purpose to support the smooth continuous flow of traffic between Albuquerque and Santa Fe. From the valley below, the road seemed set apart from civilization, giving it a desolate sort of charm and a sense of determined arrogance.

The Jemez range loomed off to the northwest. Other jagged peaks jutted toward the sky directly ahead. To either side of the highway spread the prairie, with vegetation so sparse that it took sixty acres to graze one cow.

Katy, unconscious of the miles, thought how comforting a talk with Elizabeth was sure to be.

Elizabeth had shared lots of Katy's important life moments. So many of their private slumber parties turned into sleepless nights of endless talk, with hours of stifled giggles. School vacations found them together again either in Caprock City or Santa Fe. After high school, they gravitated together to the University of New Mexico.

God, thought Katy, what would we have done without each other? We've shared our best and our worst times. Elizabeth was bound to be astonished by Katy's news.

Katy sighed as she thought back to twenty-eight years ago, when she and Elizabeth shared a small cottage on Silver Avenue two blocks from campus. They fixed it up themselves, and to them it was a palace. Elizabeth dated Harold O'Connor—everyone called him Hank—all through their sophomore year.

It was then Katy got caught up in a romance with handsome John Van Dorn. She met John at the first session of Professor Radcliffe's political science seminar. They were aware of each other from the moment they both entered the room. It was as if the dozen other people didn't exist. As their eyes stole bold, bright glances at each other, Katy saw the magnetic sort of man for whom a woman might give up her chance at heaven.

John saw a delightfully wholesome young woman with a sensual fullness he appreciated, even though the lovely, lithe young body looked so untouchable.

At the end of the session, Katy introduced herself, and invited John to go with her to see the century plant blooming in the cactus garden at Zimmerman Library.

"The century plant blossoms in its own time," she said. "This one is shooting up a stalk so fast you can almost see it grow. It may go twelve feet high; then it will bloom in all its glory, and die."

"I'd love to see it," John said.

While walking toward Zimmerman Library, John took Katy's hand in his. Katy felt excitement spread through her body unlike anything she had experienced before. John seemed to feel it too. Neither spoke as they continued, hand in hand, toward the garden.

* * *

She remembered the first time John and she made love.

Barely a week from the day they met at Ms. Radcliffe's seminar, John accepted her invitation to go to Santa Fe with her to visit Elizabeth's family, Uncle Clifford and Aunt May.

It was a glorious day, Katy remembered.

They drove up North 14, the Turquoise Trail, and turned off at the junction to Sandia Crest for a nature trail hike. John picked a wild flower.

"You're not supposed to do that up here in the National Forest."

John chuckled, "Maybe I'm not supposed to do this either, but I am." And he kissed her right on the lips. She felt the warmth flood through her belly and down to the soles of her feet.

The drive continued through the ghost towns of Golden, Madrid, and Cerillos—all once bustling mining boom towns, now sleeping under the summer sun.

At the King's sprawling adobe mansion off Hyde Park Road in the foothills north of Santa Fe, they sipped drinks and lounged around the pool with Elizabeth and Hank. Clifford made drinks. Afterwards, Aunt May served a scrumptious dinner of her special chimichangas and Indian sweet bread.

If ever there was an enchanted evening, that was it. And we kept the magic going all the way home, Katy reminisced.

She remembered her cocky assurance as she pulled her little VW off the highway in a secluded spot. The memory of their kiss on the Crest lingered on her lips and she had to have another. John's warm response made her a little giddy; she quickly pulled back onto the road.

As the little car approached Albuquerque, she drove past Corrales Road, Candelaria, and Indian School Road. "Didn't you pass the turn-off to my place?" John asked. "The University Inn is on Yale Boulevard."

"I thought we'd go on to Central Avenue and up to my place for coffee royals. You do like coffee royals, don't you?"

"I'm not sure what a coffee royal is, but it sounds good."

As Katy pulled into the driveway, she was glad she'd cleaned house the day before. She had left a table lamp on, and the little house looked inviting as they entered. She told John how she and Elizabeth found the place and redecorated it themselves. "We love it," she said as she gave him a quick tour, turning on lights as she went. She flicked on the all-music radio, returned to the kitchen, and made coffee royals for them both: hot coffee laced with Irish whiskey, topped with whipped cream.

They had their first taste in the kitchen at the dinette. She noticed John had slipped off his sweater. "Katy, this has been one of the best days I can remember," he said.

"It has for me, too." They went into the living room for their second coffee royal. John sat on the day bed, and Katy sat in the rocking chair.

"You're a lovely person, Katy," John said. "I have a little present for you." Katy watched as he pulled a small paper sack from his pocket. "It's the turquoise ring you liked up at the Sandia Crest House." It tumbled out of the sack.

"John? You got it for me?" She moved over to the daybed and sat by his side, extending her left hand to him. He slipped the ring onto her third finger.

"It's beautiful! And it fits! When did you get it? I didn't see you shopping."

"The fellow running the place saw you admiring it when we had coffee. When we went back in after the trail walk he pointed it out to me, and I approved. Do you like it?"

She stood up, admiring it on her hand. "I love it, John. Thank you." She stooped and gave him a quick kiss on the lips.

"I love you, Katy." He said it simple and straight.

She looked at him sitting among the colorful daybed pillows. She kissed him again. His arms came around her—and she was beside him. She felt a strange wild heat rise within her as she gasped his name, "John ..."

He responded, "Katy," questioningly, almost desperately -- and in a moment she was learning for the first time the new and exotic language of the body. There was no pretense about it. She belonged to him and was glad.

They took their time removing the last shreds of clothing. He caressed her gently, exploring her with his hands and his mouth. She was returning every lovely touch. The passion that mounted in them was tempered only by the tenderness they shared. She was as close to heaven as mortals can get.

The rest of the summer with John at the university spread out before her like a new carpet woven of one thread. They lived each single day with a wholeness of spirit only those in love attain.

* * *

As Katy approached Santa Fe the landscape changed character. Rolling hills with scatterings of piñon trees gradually replaced the mesa lands. The Sangre de Cristo mountains loomed straight ahead. At seven thousand feet elevation, two thousand feet higher than Albuquerque, breezes blew cooler and the landscape stayed greener.

The dirt road, almost obscured by piñon trees, wound past several houses before reaching the O'Connor's adobe block home. Katy pulled the De Ville parallel to the front portal. Elizabeth waited there for her.

"I've got lemonade ready," Elizabeth said hugging her close. "Come on back to the studio; I'm dying to show you something."

An unfinished landscape rested on the floor easel. New works covered the walls letting little blank space show. A particularly dramatic landscape stirred Katy's emotions.

"Oh, I like this," she said, admiring the scene of golden aspens. "Hyde Park?" she asked.

"That's the one I wanted to show you," Elizabeth responded. "It's yours," she added.

Always embarrassed by Elizabeth's generosity, Katy protested, although she dearly loved the painting at first sight.

"Let me pay you for this one. I'd like to," she said.

"How could I sell you something that's already yours? I knew that one was yours the minute I started painting it."

She poured cold lemonade into Katy's glass and without

warning leaped right to her next question.

"Katy, are you going to run for president?"

A sudden rush, akin to being found while playing hide and seek, flooded through Katy's body.

"How in blazes did you get wind of that? I've only mentioned it to Dick Donovan," she said.

Elizabeth smiled. "Harriett Lansdale."

"Harriett?" Katy's voice was filled with puzzlement.

"Sure," Elizabeth said and continued in her usual rush of conversation, "Harriett's really stumping for the American Coalition party. She's passionate about it. She came to see me this morning. What a horrible thing Margaret Kincaid is going through! It has Harriett pretty upset. She was behind Margaret's candidacy all the way. From what she told me about Margaret, I wouldn't be in politics for the crown jewels of England."

As soon as Elizabeth seemed ready to take a breath Katy asked the question gnawing at the base of her skull. "What did she say?"

"Well, she never came right out and said so, but I think she wanted me to convince you to accept the offer. I like Harriett very much, and I was afraid I'd hurt her feelings. But I finally told her what I thought of the idea."

"And what do you think?" Katy shoved her question into Elizabeth's flow of conversation.

"I hate to think about it. What an awful life politics makes you live. Six cities in three days, burnt coffee and smoke polluted meeting rooms. No sleep and always rushing to meet some appointment or another. And you'd be the target of every crackpot in America."

Her pace slowed. "But I'm not so certain you shouldn't do it. I got to thinking how little attention most women give to the issues. Including me. Women need you. There isn't anybody who has your background—governor, representative, and all those committees you've been on in the Congress. Trouble is you're not just my cousin, you're my best friend."

Katy noticed Elizabeth's pause. "What is it, Elizabeth?"

Her cousin spoke deliberately now. "I really do hate the idea of you exposing yourself and your career to danger. But, with credit due Margaret Kincaid, I think you'd be a better candidate. You just seem to rise above the petty, ugly things that snag the rest of us."

"Elizabeth, I love you. Does your dad know about this?"

"Uh, uh. I don't think so. Say, he'll be here in a bit to take you to the Ortega wedding reception at La Fonda. You and I can talk more tonight. You'll be wanting to call Harriett."

* * *

Clifford King drove a Lincoln Continental, always had. The car looked too long as it wound through the narrow streets. Originally all streets in Santa Fe took the line of least resistance, skirting arroyos and piñon trees, but always winding up at the plaza. Katy settled back comfortably in the leather seat, letting all the tensions of the past few days drain from her mind, as Uncle Clifford negotiated the sudden inclines and tight turns.

Maybe now is a good time to tell him about Margaret's call, she thought. But the idea seemed out of place in old Santa Fe, against a backdrop of earthy two hundred year old buildings with their lush gardens and cozy patios hidden from the street by thick adobe walls.

In La Fonda's parking garage a spindly sign on a pedestal blocked the way. "Full," it read. An attendant sprang from the collection booth, rolled the sign away and waved the familiar car inside. Uncle Clifford dropped the keys into the smiling young man's hand.

"Thanks, Pablo," Clifford said, pressing cash into his hand. "I can always count on you to make a space for this tank of mine."

Tall, angular, white-haired, with a carefully trimmed goatee, Clifford stood erect as a general in a reviewing stand. Katy tucked her hand under his arm, fully confident that their grand entrance into La Fonda was captivating the gathered revelers.

"Good evening, Governor." The greeting rang out time and again as they crossed the lobby. "And good evening, Ambassador."

It was a repeat of many an entrance the pair had made at the various social and political functions during Katy's governorship. Santa Feans still fondly preferred "Governor" to any other style of address for Katy.

From the ballroom came the rhythmic sound of the mariachi band brass and strings. It was a tune Katy loved: "La Malaguena Salerosa." Two cornets were blowing tight, loud staccato phrases in passionate harmonies. Violins' melodic cry played on in thirds, while the guitars underlaid the harmony of four male voices. In the pause between measures, the lead singer's lamenting call—"Aiii Yi Yi Yi"—rang out above everything.

Uncle Cliff excused himself to greet friends and Katy did the same, winding through the crowded ballroom, soaking up the atmosphere. Many people, faces glowing from drink and lively dancing, made happy and boisterous greetings as she passed through the gathered crowd. Young couples, men elegantly attired in pastel blue satin-trimmed tuxedos with matching ruffled shirts, women adorned in formal lacy gowns and patent leather dancing slippers, talked gaily among themselves. Katy made her way past the heavily laden buffet tables to the host and hostess, knowing it would be impolite to linger with the guests before making her greetings to them. The men at the head table rose and greeted her.

"Doña Katy, como está política?"

"Estoy bien, Don Luis," she said to the father of the bride, Luis Ortega—the mayor of Socorro and an active politician.

"Por favor," he said, "to make the acquaintance of the mother of the bride, this is my beloved wife and mother of all my children, Estrella Lourdes Ortega. Be pleased also to know the mother of the groom, Christina Esmerelda Peralta and her husband, the father of the groom, Antonio Patricio. You call them Star, Christine, and Tony, for you are now all friends.

"My gathered family, new and old, it is my pleasure to introduce, the former governor and now congresswoman, la señorita, Katy Jenkins.

"Soon," he continued to Katy, "you will go listen to the women's gossip; but first allow me to get the bride and groom for you to meet."

By the time Don Luis located the couple, the mariachis, strolling through the throng of guests, moved closer to play in her honor. Gold braid ran down their tight waistcoats and pants, multi-colored embroidered ruffles spilled out from between the jacket lapels. And on their heads rested great sombreros covered with gold decorations and dazzling sequins.

As the mariachis played, Katy gave her blessing to the newlyweds.

"May your life be blessed with happiness and as many children as you desire," she said to the bride. And to the groom she added, "And you, handsome young man that you are, take care to treat her well. I pray prosperity and health will mark your life together."

The lithe young girl, wedding gown cut to display the attributes of her youthful figure, smiled graciously as she received Katy's warm hug and returned with her raven-haired husband to the dance floor.

Katy chatted with the other women at the head table until Uncle Clifford arrived, making a second round of full greetings and introductions necessary. As they left the reception, Katy asked, "Uncle Cliff, could we go somewhere private and talk?"

"We'll have to head for the house. There's not a single spot in Santa Fe that's private for the likes of us," he said.

Clifford King was a former ambassador to the Kingdom of Saudi Arabia. As a farmer's son in Oklahoma, he might have left school early to take over the family business, but his father insisted on education. Katy remembered her grandfather's oft-repeated phrase, "A man's got to amount to something."

After high school uncle Cliff had worked roustabout in the oil fields until he scraped together enough cash for college. Later he worked for Phillips Petroleum, combining his masters in petroleum geology with his intuitive ability to locate new areas for drilling. The entrepreneurial spirit led him to become a successful freelance oil lease broker. His farming background endeared him to the old homestead farmers, and he was pleased to make them richer than they ever expected to be. The years never subdued his exuberant personality.

In the car, Katy broke the silence. "Did you read the New York Times this morning?"

Clifford ran a hand along the side of his head to smooth the snow white hair stirred by the air conditioning.

"No," he said. "I only read the Sunday edition anymore. What did I miss?"

"Oh, just Margaret Kincaid's son Eric being indicted by the Grand Jury on charges of financial corruption and charged by the New York city attorney's office. Margaret's involved in Eric's construction company. It seems the New York Democrats have gone so far as to suggest the indictment won't proceed if she backs out of the race for president on the National Coalition party ticket."

"That's a helluva state of affairs," he said.

At the King home, a pair of massive doors opened from the front terrace into a large entryway at the Clifford home, the ceiling of which rose a full twenty feet. The way left led to a library filled not only with books, but with paintings, many of which were Elizabeth's. Two overstuffed chairs sat in front of the stone fireplace and Katy sat down in one of them.

"How's your congressional campaign going?" Clifford asked.

"H.B. is sure we need your 'Republicans for Katy' more than ever. According to him, we're in for a real fight this time."

"Of course you can count on us. In fact, I've been working on it for the past few months. The money's there and we are all set to go." He paused. "What's got you bothered, Katy girl? You don't get that look on your face over nothing."

"What would you think if I ran for president?"

"President, of what?"

"Of the United States. On the American Coalition ticket. Margaret called me at 4:30 this morning. She's asked me to consider it. She says the nomination is as good as mine—if I want it. Harriett Landsdale is ecstatically for it. I spoke to her this afternoon. Their aim is to get a woman in the presidency."

Clifford was obviously caught by surprise. But he, first of all, was a diplomat. Katy knew that he must know more about this before he would show any emotion.

"What about money?" Cliff began. "I can't say either of the major parties have a wholly appealing candidate. But you could be headed for a debacle. It takes a powerful amount of backers to overcome the taint of party disloyalty. They'll call you an opportunist like they did the Kennedy that ran for New York's Senate seat."

"I know. But he won."

"Go say hello to your Aunt May. She's still up, the light's on.

I'll make us some decaf and we'll talk some more on this."

Cliff punched in the New York number as soon as Katy left. He knew the number by heart.

"Hello, John. I know it's the middle of the night back east, but this is something we've got to discuss right now. Katy is here—back talking to May. She dropped a bombshell! I thought I should call you. Margaret Kincaid, you know who she is, the Coalition party, wants Katy to run on their ticket for president." Cliff explained the situation, then listened to John's unexpectedly quick reaction.

"...I agree," said Clifford. "You're quite ready to do that? Well, fine, no, no, that's just between us...Don't worry, I'll keep in touch."

By the time Katy got back to the library, two cups of decaf waited on the low marble topped table in front of the fireplace.

"Katy, let's talk about that convention in Denver." Clifford seemed quite relaxed as he posed his first question to Katy. "Have you made any commitment to Kincaid?"

"Just that I will go to the convention. It's next weekend."

"The proposition just came out of the blue, huh?"

"Margaret's call, that's it. I talked to Harriett Landsdale from Elizabeth's. She knows too."

"Who're they considering for vice president?"

"Maybe someone from the Women's Movement. The Movement is putting up the first million dollars for the campaign. All from small contributions, thousands of them."

"An all-female ticket, huh?"

"Probably, but I don't know for sure."

Clifford spoke out with an interest and conviction that surprised Katy. "The trouble with the whole Coalition party set-up is that it's too women-oriented. I've told Harriett that all along. They've got to broaden their base or they'll just sputter around some and fizzle out."

"I know."

Clifford set his cup down and looked straight at Katy. "Their platform isn't bad though. It's short—only twenty-five pages, more thematic than specific. You could run on it as much as any candidate can run on any platform."

Katy put her cup down too. She listened carefully to Uncle Cliff. She valued his seasoned wisdom. "I'm glad to hear that," she said quietly. "Women are really being kicked around on this abortion thing with state and church ganging up on them. I think it's a shame that in the land of the free so many people want to impose their beliefs on others."

"Hey, you feel strongly about this."

"Yes, I do. And I resent a president making 'anti-choice' a part of the Republican philosophy just to garner votes. I had high hopes for the president. So many of his policies made sense to me. But he is wrong as far as women are concerned." Katy caught her breath. "And the incestuous relationship he fosters between fundamentalist churches and state is an affront to anyone who can read history. I don't think any political party should condone this intolerance." Katy caught her breath. "Maybe it is time for women to get into serious politics in this country."

"One thing about you, gal," Clifford said, "you don't pull your punches. You never did. At least you have something in common with the Women's Movement and the American Coalition party." He looked at Katy gravely. "But I doubt if they can ever elect a president. The question is, Katy, do you want to get involved with the Coalition party? Apparently the pressure is on. You're going to the Convention. You will have to decide."

"I'm staying at Elizabeth's tonight. Tomorrow Harriett is going to brief me on the Coalition party. She is chair of their platform committee. It may be more than a briefing. She's asked me to plan for at least a couple of hours."

Uncle Clifford rose, standing ramrod straight as always. "I better get you on over to Elizabeth's. She's dying to talk to you about Gloria and Johnny and the rest of the tribe, and about the gossip at the 'hungry five' hen parties."

In a gesture rare for Clifford, he put his arm around Katy and kissed her gently on the cheek. "Good luck to you, honey. You know I'll back you all the way, whatever you do—but this one scares the hell out of me."

4

Jet engines droned a steady one note song, lulling Katy into a world of memories. Denver was still forty-five minutes away.

She thought about Steve. It was during her first session in the State Legislature that she met Steve Wilson. He wrote a syndicated political column called "The Tactless New Mexican." They became constant friends. By the session's end they tumbled into a companionable marriage, deciding abruptly to tie the knot. Attending the wedding were Elizabeth and Hank and their three children, Uncle Cliff and Aunt May, Mom and Pop, Jim, Jack, and Johnny. They squeezed into the Chapel of Loretta along with as many press and friends and fellow legislators as could fit. The ceremony took a scant twenty minutes and the crowd gaily celebrated the union as guests of Uncle Cliff and Aunt May at their home in the foothills north of Santa Fe.

The urgency of Steve's political reporting assignments and Katy's pressing responsibilities in her law practice made a honeymoon trip impractical. Neither of them saw the need to change living arrangements and so they commuted between Katy's Albuquerque apartment and Steve's Santa Fe condo, enjoying a string of little honeymoons through the time they had together. Katy didn't change her name, preferring to keep Jenkins since she had carried the name with her that far into her law business and budding political career.

Their happy lifestyle dissolved into the tragedy that was Vietnam. Steve joined the Press Corps, staying close to the fight with the frontline troops, but managed to send off a weekly column to the "New Mexican." The hilarious account of the long delayed honeymoon Katy and Steve enjoyed on his R&R in Hawaii held the last of his irreverent opinions on life. His writings soon descended into the dark gloom of depression as the war ground hopelessly toward stalemate.

Katy worked fervently to support her husband's efforts and managed to convince her fellow legislators to pass a resolution imploring the President, as Commander-in-Chief, to allow America to win the war.

Then came a day when no more columns would arrive. Two military men appeared at her door. She wondered how their manners could seem so perfect when their words were so terribly wrong.

"Mrs. Steven R. Wilson?" asked one of the men.

"Steve Wilson is my husband," she said.

"I'm sorry to inform you..."

Katy paled. "Steve's dead, isn't he?"

"No ma'am. Missing in action," said the other.

And with those words Katy plunged into the terrible frustrating whirlpool of "not knowing." Hopes, built on quicksand foundations, consumed in despair, only to be rebuilt on shreds of news, new leads, and unrelenting denial. After seven years, Steve Wilson found official death in the courts, but hope still lingered in Katy's mind that her husband's jubilant sense of living had not really been squandered in an impossible war.

Katy drowned out the intolerable pain of waiting for news with fresh endeavors. She joined the Albuquerque Little Theatre group on a tour to London.

She gravitated to the political scene in England. The traditional majesty of Parliament stirred her blood. The speeches seemed so much more eloquent pronounced with British accent and surrounded by so much history. Margaret Thatcher impressed her most, speaking out against the malaise the unions had brought on England.

The theatre group returned to the States without Katy. With pain still too acute, she extended her trip, visiting the capitals of Europe. East Berlin's alarming contrast with free and prosperous West Berlin frightened and appalled her. The Wall marked a terrible division between living and existing. The dreariness of communism haunted her.

In Rome, Katy abruptly realized summer had slipped by. It

was almost September, and her campaign for a third run in the State Legislature waited, dormant.

She rushed back to Albuquerque and made a last minute blitz, but on election night, as she sat with a group of friends and supporters watching the returns, she was dismayed at the crushing defeat handed to her. "I blew it this time," she admitted. "It was all too last minute...and not enough when we did get going." Her efforts to be cheerful about the whole thing failed. Defeat caught her unawares and it hurt. What was to be a victory celebration broke up early, ending with a toast from a law associate.

He raised his glass and said:

> "Here's to Katy our friend,
> and Legislator of late,
> who lucked out tonight,
> in a queer turn of fate."

How prophetic he was, Katy thought.

As if to fulfill the prophecy, it was H.B. McGee who provided the spark which enlivened her dejected spirit. Everybody knew H.B. He was "Mr. Democrat" in New Mexico. His down-home ways made friendship easy, but few would have guessed from visiting his storefront insurance office in downtown Albuquerque the kind of political clout he wielded. H.B. came to Katy's office the second morning after her defeat, greeting Katy with a hug.

"You got a minute to talk?" he asked.

"Sure." She sat at her desk and H.B. took the chair alongside the desk.

"Katy," he said, "you were running for the wrong office. You ought to be governor."

This got Katy's attention. The absurd idea gained credibility as she considered it.

So when H.B., Mr. Democrat himself, asked Katy to join him at lunch with some of the state Party leaders, she accepted. The next day Katy found herself in a clandestine meeting with the Democrat "Bull Ring." They were intrigued. Why not run a woman for governor?

What a campaign that was. Little did the opposition know how their "girl wonder" label, meant to be sarcastic, would work to her benefit. She quoted them time after time in her campaign speeches. They grew to regret the label they had given her.

Katy smiled to herself as she relived the excitement of nomination day and the thrill of a new challenge achieved. The memories tumbled over one another in her mind.

She listened and observed and questioned, and became a hands-on governor. She was especially successful in handling the fiscal affairs of the state. Starting with a deficit, she left the state budget with a surplus. As governor she made her mark. And she enjoyed the sense of personal achievement. She had succeeded. And a warm glow of success came from within her.

According to state law at that time, the governorship could only be hers for one term. Sometime in the last year of her term, there was H.B. sitting across the desk.

"I've got a proposition for the purr-tiest governor this side of the Mississippi," he said.

Katy leaned forward and clasped her hands beneath her chin. "And what could that be?" she asked.

"Continued employment in politics, gal."

"I certainly don't mind steady work. Out with it, H.B."

"The party wants you to run for the First Congressional District seat."

Challenge exhilarated Katy, and she drew energy from each private quest. How her territory had expanded! From the small town of Caprock City to the entire nation, from junior Congresswoman to a true "insider."

Those years, she thought, were marred only by the nagging heartache of being unable to find out anything about Steve. Through Wives of Missing Military she met J. Ross Temple, a southern gentleman made wealthy by his own business acumen, who had a penchant for helping those who defended the nation. His efforts to bring home Vietnam war prisoners and locate those missing in action became an American legend.

At a meeting for wives whose husbands were missing in action at his palatial home in Dallas, he was openly impressed by Katy's keen mind and dedication to the project. After the meeting he proposed she become a consultant for him on the MIA project.

"Governor Jenkins, may I ask your input on a regular basis?"

"On the one condition that you call me Katy."

He quickly agreed, and Katy became a working partner with him on the MIA undertaking. Their friendship grew over the years.

The MIA issue took her to Washington several times, on military transport, for briefings at the Pentagon and receptions by the president in the Rose Garden. And twice she went on foreign missions, organized and financed by J. Ross Temple, one of them into Saigon where progress was made on the release of American prisoners. But they found no trace of Steve.

The stewardess was gathering empty cups and mugs. The throaty hum of the jet engines slowed in preparation for landing at Denver. Next stop, the Brown Palace Hotel, headquarters for the American Coalition Party Convention.

5

As her cab pulled up to the Fremont Street entrance of the Brown Palace, Katy wondered how it would feel to go inside. Her mind filled with memories of an earlier stay.

"Place ain't changed a bit, lady. It's the same Brown Palace it was twenty or even forty years ago—well, almost."

The cab driver's cheerful commentary went almost unnoticed. Katy stared at the Ship Tavern sign tucked into the corner of the hotel.

Barely twenty, she thought, and like a young colt in the pasture, running wild, frolicking and prancing with head high. I was reveling in the sheer joy of living.

No matter the anguish that followed, she would never lament that youthful time. A few steps into the hotel, she let her gaze drift upward, pausing at each of the six tiers of balconies with their artful cast iron railings, and focused on the beauty of the stained glass ceiling eight stories above the lobby.

Still grand, she thought.

The bellman checked her room assignment and took the luggage up, so Katy could slip into the Ship Tavern for a late lunch.

"Ship Dip sandwich, and a seven-up, please." she told the waitress as she surveyed the richly paneled room replete with artifacts and replicas of early American clipper ships.

Twenty-eight years ago she drank ginger ale in the same room. John sat across from her dressed in his usual sport jacket. He suggested a cocktail for her, but she insisted on ginger ale. She grinned, remembering.

Now she sat comfortably in the oak captain's chair and

watched busboys clear the previous customers' cluttered tables. Only two other people occupied the tavern.

Good, Katy mused, we'll be certain of privacy. Andy would be there by 2:30.

"Is everything all right?" the waitress inquired as she brought Katy's sandwich.

"Looks to be," Katy replied. "When the party I'm expecting arrives, will you please bring us two coffees. And I'd appreciate it if you'd help us have our meeting in private."

"Oh, why yes, of course." The waitress winked a kind of knowing understanding. "A little afternoon delight is good for the soul."

Katy nodded her thanks, suppressing a laugh at the thought of Andy and herself as bedfellows. She had seen him amid a crowd of Coalition delegates as the group moved, much like an amoeba, from the Palace Arms restaurant through the lobby. She recognized Ruth Silverton, Chair of the Women's Movement, Ellen Steele who founded the Voice of the Feminine Majority after her term as head of the Movement, Dorothy Hastings, new president of the Women Voters Caucus, and Jean Porter, national president of Feminist Writers, and Harriett Landsdale and Charlotte Greenberg from Santa Fe.

An illustrious group, Katy thought.

The Brown Palace Hotel. *What a name for a place which seems to have a pivotal significance in my life.* Perhaps the hotel's own charm and elegance was partly responsible for the rapture that had swallowed her whole twenty-eight years ago. Perhaps it was the cause of her impulse to escape here in the Ship Tavern today before checking into her room. So many memories!

"Well Katy, I'm glad you made it." Andy Barker stood at the edge of the table. He looked young in his late forties, with a heavy stand of dark hair; very nearly the look of John Kennedy. Katy smiled and indicated the chair across from her.

"I'm glad to be here, Andy. What's been going on?"

Andy seemed to hedge. "Not much action yet except delegates arriving from just about everywhere." Katy felt his gaze. Perhaps he was trying to read for clues. "There's a meeting in Margaret's suite at four. V.I.P.'s only. You're expected of course. She's formally announcing her withdrawal."

"I know. Since I spoke with her last week, I've thought of little else."

She absently tapped her spoon against the tablecloth. Coffee arrived, and after the waitress was well away from the table, she continued.

"Are you certain Margaret's decision is final?"

Andy became more animated. "She's out. No doubt about it." Damn, Katy thought. Somebody, somehow, deprived the country of one good candidate. Andy continued, "She made a deal for the sake of her son and for the sake of the Coalition. She'll continue to work for the party, support the ticket it chooses. But her candidacy is impossible."

"I'm sure you're right. So where does that leave you?"

"Up the creek. Ruth Silverton and Ellen Steele both came here expecting to be nominated for vice president. They're uptight."

"Have they or anyone else made any overtures toward running in Margaret's place?"

"Not yet. I've been approached, but I refused. It would defeat the whole purpose to nominate me. We want a woman candidate."

"You're right, Andy," Katy said. "The Silverton-Steele problem needs defusing. Hasn't the Movement already pledged a million dollars for the campaign chest—and promised more? They've got to come to terms. They're indispensable."

Andy sat back in his chair. He looked directly into Katy's eyes. "Katy, you won't believe the organization we have in place! We're on the ballot in all fifty states and Puerto Rico. No small feat. But that's just the beginning. There's been delegate conventions in every state, too. Some were small grass roots deals. A few had respectable numbers, two hundred or more participants. A majority of the state chairpeople are crossovers from the dominant political parties. Delegates from every state will stand on the floor of the first American Coalition Convention to nominate the presidential candidate, altogether 216 registered delegates. Every state represented. Every state!"

Katy raised her hand slightly.

"Good Andy, very good. What percentage of the delegates are

men? What percentage women?"

"One hundred and sixty-seven women. Forty-nine men."

Katy worked to control her excitement. "You'll want to keep the men up front for the media. Emphasize the visual."

Andy set his coffee cup in its saucer and looked at her. "Good suggestion, I'll pass the word along right away."

"Who else is here, other than delegates?"

"Well, as I said, Silverton, Steele, and little Betty Rudlen, grand dame of the activists, as feisty as ever and—oh yes, this is something you'd be interested to know—Ms. Arnold, the P.R. genius from D.C., is here, too; she's been poking around asking questions. I got her a press card. Then there's Jane Ellsworth, former U.N. ambassador. Margaret arranged for her to give the keynote address tomorrow."

Katy released a low appreciative whistle, "What a coup that is! Pretty respectable group." She glanced at her watch. A thin film of perspiration glistened on her upper lip. My timing has to be right. The cold knot tightened in her stomach. Andy was saying something about the party being qualified for matching funds in every state. The little voice inside her head said, "Wait, not yet." She relaxed.

"Whoa, Andy, look at the time. 3:15." She rose abruptly. "I've got to freshen up before Margaret's meeting."

"You look fresh as a crocus in spring."

"I'll see you in Suite 824," she said, heading for the door.

* * *

As she entered Suite 824 and crossed the threshold between the bedroom and sitting room, Katy realized that she had been in this very same suite before. The expansive corner room, complemented with window-boxes hanging over the street, was furnished like an exclusive townhouse. Katy caught her breath as her gaze drifted to the majestic grand piano which fit comfortably in the space allotted to it. *Looks just the same as it did twenty-eight years ago*, she thought. Memories flooded her mind. The lingering remembrance of John's hands on her body, the fresh scent of his hair, the sight of him standing at the balcony window framed against the late sun filled her senses. For one moment he stood there, and in the next she shook the vision from her mind. Of all the risks she had taken in her life, none were as great as the ones she faced in Suite 824.

The furniture had been re-arranged to accommodate the fifteen or so people now standing or sitting in small groups. Katy glanced across the room at Andy, his face alive with a genuine smile as he shook hands all around.

The last man with whom she had entered this room consumed her young passions. Her love for John Van Dorn had bubbled through her blood like wine and carried her beyond thought of the consequences of her decision. John accepted her gift of love and then left her. Yet here she was about to give herself away again.

"Katy!" Margaret Kincaid seemed to be charging at her. "I want you to know everyone here."

Katy snapped back to reality. "Margaret. Yes, I know almost everyone here except the three gentleman over there."

"That's Andy's brother talking to Andy, Harrison P. Barker. He runs E.F. Woods, the Philadelphia-based publishing company. The family founded the company in the 1890's. But you'll meet him later. The other two helped start the American Coalition party. The heavy-set gentleman is Judge Gordon Cosgrove from Seattle, and the other is Tom Bennett, attorney in Orlando.

Margaret guided Katy around the room seeming to observe a self-dictated hierarchy of presentation. Silverton and Steele, both seeming to patronize her simply because she was under Margaret's invisible protection, clearly had hidden agendas they wished to make known. Katy carefully noted the nuances of their speech and the innuendos behind their meaningful smiles. *The two of them need to return to their favorite arena: the women's organizations,* Katy thought. *That's where they would most benefit the Coalition.*

Katy nodded to and briefly chatted with the people around the room before Margaret left her at the refreshment table talking with Harriett Landsdale and Ms. Arnold. She catalogued names and faces in appropriate mental niches. Although deep in conversation, another part of her brain was busy rerunning the gamut of Margaret's social strategy.

She caught notice of Harrison Barker as he shifted from one

foot to the other and uneasily continued a hushed conversation with Andy. The family publishing executive seemed to be trying to convince his brother of something. Suddenly, Harrison's gaze met Katy's, and, as abruptly, he looked away. Andy picked up on the exchange and had Harrison by the elbow, guiding him toward Katy. Before they could reach her, however, the late and apologetic arrival of Jane Ellsworth, former Secretary-General of the United Nations, signaled the onset of the meeting.

Margaret gained silence simply by standing still at the center of the room. The color drained from her face as she began to speak.

"Each of you has helped to nurture and support the birth and growth of the American Coalition party in his and her own special way. Up until ten days ago, I thought my place was at the head of the party." Tears sprang from the glistening edges of her eyes. "Due to the events of the last week, it is clear I will best serve the Coalition by withdrawing my name from consideration as your presidential candidate."

Margaret played their natural behaviors to her advantage. Small groups of two and three talked briefly among themselves as Margaret paused. Conversation ceased as she resumed speaking.

"I am not faint-hearted in the face of a mighty contest as some of you might think." A murmur of negative response fluttered through the room. "Unfortunately, if this David brings down her Goliath, the Coalition can only falter as a result of the aftershock."

Heads nodded in agreement. Katy intently watched Margaret's effect. She could learn from her.

Margaret brought the focus of her speech away from herself and on to the problems of the fledgling party.

"We have a secret weapon, a power against those who would see us fail. We can survive this attempt of sabotage. Remember the big boys fight dirty when they're scared. So, what characteristics do we need in a viable candidate?"

Replies rang out from all corners of the room.

"Someone of unshakable integrity."

"Who can't be bought."

"Or threatened."

Margaret continued guiding the group process. "The Coalition candidate must possess a vision equal to our own. The candidate must have a persona and natural charm..."

"Political savvy," Andy Barker added.

"And experience in a major office," Jane Ellsworth injected.

Katy found herself standing alone in the center of a thoughtful group. She heard Andy whisper, "I knew it!" to Jean Porter. Silverton and Steele moved closer to one another. Betty Rudlen looked askance at first, but seemed to be reconsidering. Margaret came to stand near Katy as she continued to speak.

"I've introduced you all to Katy Jenkins. What I haven't told you is my impression of her." She carefully made her case. "Katy and I worked together in the U.S. Congress. For her, people and principles came before party line. I worked with her on many bills, and we served on some of the same committees. Katy made her mark on Agriculture, on which I didn't serve, Energy, Foreign Affairs, and now the Armed Forces and Ways and Means.

"Before she came to Washington, Katy sat in the New Mexico State Legislature for two terms. She is an ex-governor of the state and New Mexico's First Congressional District sent her to Washington five times in a row."

Margaret turned to Katy and smiled, "You probably wore out three sets of luggage traveling back and forth in your ten years of office. If I heard it once I heard it a thousand times: 'I'm off to inform my constituents.'"

Margaret turned back to her audience. "Isn't that what we're about? Isn't that what the Coalition wants for America? Informed decisions based on caring about people. What do we want? A paternally custodial autocracy or a government directed by an aware, educated people? The answer is clear to all of us. And so we must make our choice based on these ideals.

"I believe the American Coalition party has its candidate for the office of president and her name is Katy Jenkins."

Andy led the applause. "Speech! Speech!"

Katy looked around the room and knew that these people held the keys to her future. What she said now would be the most important words in her political career. A tiny smile played around her lips as she began to speak.

"I've never thought of myself as a radical feminist," she began, hesitant.

"Nor have I," Betty Rudlen heckled good-naturedly from across the room. The tension dissipated with laughter.

Katy relaxed and continued in a conversational tone. She smiled at Rudlen who winked back at her, grinning widely. "And you're right, Betty, but I do consider myself a genuine humanist. And having won, and lost, at the polls, I've become a political realist."

She saw a few nods of encouragement. Her tone became confidential. "I have a confession to make. I'm not a very good Democrat these days. I'm disillusioned with Democratic party philosophy. The Democrats have controlled the House of Representatives for fifty years and the Senate, too, for most of that time. And during all of that time we still haven't figured out how to pay the bills. We're borrowing a billion dollars a day, that's a thousand million dollars every day—and we're still letting people sleep on the streets!

"But I'm also disenchanted with the Republicans; they are a disservice to America through their pandering to the fundamentalists on the abortion issue just to get votes. They preach less government interference in people's lives but all the while, they push for more. They seem to be very interested in democracy and political, economic, and religious freedom for other peoples of the world, while neglecting their own country.

Margaret's nod of approval, and the general concurrence of the people in the room, was not lost on Katy. She had counted on this. She chose her words carefully for what she had to say next.

"I have had an aisle seat in the Congress for ten years, and I am appalled at what I see there—on both sides of the aisle. Our bloated Congress is in trouble. Congressional aides have multiplied like rabbits, from maybe 2,000 staffers in 1947 to some 12,000 today. This new army not only costs a fortune in pay, benefits, and expenses, it deprives us of our elected Senators and Representatives when they turn their work over to 'staff.'"

Katy slowed her pace. "You can see why I'm dissatisfied with the direction that the Republican and Democratic parties are taking. I welcome a new political party in America. I think we need new blood, new leadership, new ideas." She looked at Margaret and exclaimed, "We need a new voice in America. Maybe the time has come to elect our first woman president!"

Margaret bounced out of her seat and stood alongside Katy. "Do you think Katy could do some good Republican and Democrat bashing?" She asked with such enthusiasm that she answered her own question. "I think we all need a break, some space to consider what Katy has said. Let's have coffee."

When the group around Katy thinned out, she casually looked around for Harrison P. Barker. Andy responded immediately and escorted Katy over to meet his brother.

The conversation was light. But they hit it off well. She learned the "P" in his name stood for Putnam, of the "see the whites of their eyes" Putnams of the American Revolution.

Ms. Arnold turned off her tape recorder and surveyed the situation. Mostly she liked what she saw. There was excitement and tension in the air. Katy was emerging as the leader. But Ms. Arnold could see that it wasn't unanimous. Ellen Steele spoke intently to Betty Rudlen, and Betty listened too carefully to suit Ms. Arnold.

An awkward lull in the conversations gave Dorothy Hastings, of the Women's Voter Caucus, a chance to ask the question on everybody's mind.

"Katy, are you available as a candidate?"

The tension nettled at the base of Katy's neck. This is it. Time to drop the bombshell. It has to be done right, for their sake and mine.

"You know," she said, "it takes two to make a ticket, president and vice president." She looked around the room and made a quick decision. She thought about saying something about how many vice-presidential possibilities there were in the room. But that might muddy the waters. She considered mentioning that the decision was the hardest she had encountered in her life. But that was personal and had no place here. Finally, she decided to just be her usual straightforward self.

"I would like to be the Coalition party candidate for president *if* Andy Barker will run with me as vice-presidential candidate."

This sudden announcement took everyone by surprise. Ellen Steele looked stricken, her hopes dashed. Ruth Silverton showed no emotion even though she likely had designs on the spot just suggested for Andy. Dorothy Hastings beamed approval; the

Women Voters Caucus was bound to be more active in the election process if Andy Barker was on the ticket.

It was Ms. Arnold who broke the silence. "Wonderful," she said above the rising volume of the group, ignoring the questioning glances. "That's the ticket! We'll have a true coalition, and it will be the voters' dream come true."

Andy evidenced the least reaction. All eyes were on him. His comment sounded casual, off-hand.

"Harrison, here, came all the way from Philadelphia to offer me a big job with the publishing house. I think he feels my talents are wasted in the political arena. I've already agreed to go back to the family business. I've had my political fling as governor of Pennsylvania."

Harrison cleared his throat and showed as little reaction as Andy. "There's not one of us Barkers who wouldn't like to have Andy back in the publishing business," he said. "And I did come here with a carrot in both hands to lure Andy back to Philadelphia. But this is an unexpected development." He looked sternly at Andy. "If you ever tell Dad I said this, I'll deny it. But maybe this is an opportunity you should consider. The publishing business will survive another four years without you." He looked at Andy with the love of an older brother. "Of course, it's up to you, Andy."

Andy showed less surprise than he felt. His eyes darted to Harrison with a look of thanksgiving. His voice was firm and enthusiastic as he spoke. "Damn well, yes, I'll run with Katy Jenkins if the Convention wants us."

Margaret was quick to respond. "Then it's Katherine Jenkins and Andrew Barker—unless there are other suggestions." She waited expectantly, but there were none.

It was that quick. Katy realized she had reached the point of no return. She had a gut feeling that bubbled up from inside allowing no room for misgivings: she was going to do everything in her power to become President of the United States of America.

* * *

A phone call was made from Denver about an hour later that same evening. This call wasn't made from the Brown Palace; it went out from an old commercial hotel down the street.

"Kincaid is out for sure," the voice said.

"Good," grunted Joe Domino. "But you better stick around 'til it's over. Make sure she isn't playing games."

"Will do, boss."

Joe Domino didn't ordinarily take a personal hand in politics. Wasn't necessary. The Union took care of that. No politician who knew enough to come in out of the rain would go against the Union. It would be easier to go against God and Motherhood. But in the Kincaid affair, he made the necessary arrangements directly.

Smug satisfaction spread through his mind as he thought about it. Joe Domino had come a long way when the most powerful "family" in New York came to him for an operation like that. He grunted his satisfaction. He had put the skids to Kincaid in a very professional way, slick as a whistle. His building trade connections in New York came through with an iron-clad case. They put the screws on; she caved in—and nobody knew how it happened.

He grinned. Owning a Senator proved useful, too.

Not bad for a Jersey City street kid who doesn't even know who his own mother is.

6

Following the meeting in Suite 824, Katy invited Ruth, Ellen, and Harriett to dinner in the Palace Arms dining room. Word had filtered out about Margaret's meeting, so the invitation carried with it a certain amount of prestige. Other delegates would see them there and recognize their importance. This worked out just as Katy planned; it seemed as if half the people in the dining room stopped by their table. In between visits the four discussed strategy for the campaign. Katy returned to her room late that evening with the feeling that everything was under control.

Another incident occurred immediately following the meeting which aroused Katy's curiosity. She thought about it as she arrived at her room. Ms. Arnold had waited for her in the hallway outside 824. "Are you still the early bird, Katy?" she asked.

"Yes..." Katy answered warily.

Ms. Arnold pushed on. "You and I need to get together early tomorrow, where we can have some privacy." Katy hesitated. "You're going to need all the help you can get," Ms. Arnold insisted.

Katy agreed. "Okay," she said, "how about breakfast?" When the time and place was set, Katy retreated to her room, picked up the phone and requested an early call, then collected her thoughts. She decided the next order of business was to make some phone calls. The first call was to Caprock City.

"Hi Mom. I'm calling from Denver."
"Katy, honey, you're in Denver?"
"Yes. I have to talk with you and Pop."

Pop Jenkins picked up the extension questioning; "Katy, what are you doing in Denver?"

"Are you sitting down.?"

"Your Mom is. I can take whatever it is standing up. What you up to?"

"I had to tell you first."

"Tell us what, honey?" Mom's voice cracked with curiosity.

"Watch TV tomorrow evening. The network news."

"What's goin' on?" Pop asked.

"Have you ever heard of the American Coalition party?"

"Sure, I've heard of it. We have some of them here. Matter of fact, your first grade teacher, Mrs. Bayze heads the group down here. Mostly women libbers, I think."

Mom broke in. "Katy, what are you trying to tell us?"

"It looks like I'm going to be nominated for president by the Coalition party."

"You're going to run for president? Of the United States?" The questions burst simultaneously from the two of them.

"Could be!" responded Katy. "But, whatever happens here, I wonder if Jack or Jimmy can come up to Denver in the Cessna and take me back to Caprock early Monday morning?"

"Why, sure," Pop said. "But Katy, are you sure you know what the hell you are doing?"

"Time will tell," said Katy airily. "I'll see you Monday. Love you both."

"We love you, too, Katy," said Mom.

Her next call was to Maria Romero, the fiery little brunette with sparkling brown eyes and lovely dark complexion, who put all her energies into managing Katy's Albuquerque Congressional office. A veteran of Katy's campaign for Governor and all the campaigns since, Maria was Katy's confidant in political matters.

The phone rang several times before Maria answered.

"Katy," Maria said as she gasped to get her breath. "I was watching Washington Week."

"Guessed as much. Listen, I'm in Denver at the Coalition Convention."

"Harriett got you to go?"

"You might say that. Anyhow, Margaret can't run. She, Harriett, and some of the other party leaders want me to take Margaret's place on the ticket."

"Run for president? Oh, Katy!"

"It may work out that way. Nothing definite yet, but you had better alert key staff, you know, confidential."

Maria had caught her breath and her enthusiasm began to mount. "You gotta do it, Katy. When is the nomination?"

"Tomorrow afternoon! Watch the evening news."

"I'll handle everything here with the staff. Don't worry. But what about H.B.?"

Katy knew Maria's concern was one she'd have to deal with, but she would have to give it more thought.

"I'll have to call him, and soon," Katy said.

"Hi, sis. How's it going up there?"

"Oh, Johnny, I have news you wouldn't believe."

"I know all about it, Katy. Dick told me. You know, I always get a kick out of that guy. I was downtown and I dropped in on him. The way he told me was funny."

"That's typical. What did he tell you?"

"He said you're going to run for president. And he said old H.B. was going to be fit to be tied when he found you had bolted the party."

Before Katy had a chance to respond he said, "Good luck, sis. Here's Gloria."

"I can't believe what I'm hearing. A woman for president. And it's you!"

Katy smiled to herself thinking about Johnny and Gloria in their snug apartment, mulling over the possibility of being houseguests at the White House. Johnny came back on the line.

"Sis, go for it!"

Ten o'clock, Katy thought. Not too late to call H.B. What am I going to say to him? Don't have to ask his advice. I know it won't coincide with my plans. This won't be easy.

Uncle Cliff had surprised her with his easy acceptance. Dick Donovan tilted in favor, with reservations. Maria was enthusiastic. How was H.B. going to take it? There was only one way to find out.

"Hello?" His voice was sluggish.

"Were you asleep?"

"Katy? Oh no, I was reading. Where in blazes have you disappeared to? Got a helluva speaker for the fund raiser: Harry Stone, no less. We're gonna make a big bash of it."

The pit of her stomach went queasy as Katy groped to find a way to tell H.B. She wondered if this is the way a traitor feels when he betrays his country. H.B., with his single-minded concentration, was her mentor; without his skills she might still be handling divorces and settling estates.

"H.B., I'm in Denver at the American Coalition party Convention."

"I think that outfit will hurt the Republicans more than us. But Katy, we don't need to get mixed up with them. What are you doing there?"

"Margaret Kincaid invited me, and I thought I'd check it out. She's not running, and that's strictly confidential."

"Well, hell, they haven't got a candidate."

The space of silence made Katy wonder if H.B. suddenly realized why she was here. He changed the subject back to the fund-raiser. "We're thinking big on this dinner. I'm considering booking the Convention Center."

"H.B., I have to tell you, they're asking me to be their candidate." She was relieved that she had said it.

"Hell, gal, don't do anything stupid. We have a Congressional race to win. Maybe I should take the red-eye up there."

"You needn't come up. I'll stay in control of myself."

"Well, I hope so." Katy felt the distress in H.B.'s voice. After wishing him good night, she hung up. The thought that H.B. wouldn't be her friend and backer in this campaign haunted her.

She was startled by the sharp ring of the phone. On the line was the reporter from the Denver Post who had interviewed Margaret at great length earlier in the evening.

At first, he pumped her about Margaret. Katy added nothing to what Margaret had told him. He changed his tack, "What are your views on women's rights?"

Katy's answer was quick and direct. "Same as they are for every American regardless of sex, race, or creed: freedom and opportunity are the greatest treasures a nation can give its people—and women should not be excluded from either."

The reporter repeated her words as he wrote them down, but, he obviously wasn't satisfied with her answer. "Come on, Miss Jenkins, you must have something more than that."

Katy let down her guard for a minute. The emotional strains of the day left her vulnerable to this insistent reporter. She gave him a generalized answer which she hoped would placate him. "Women have won the war—now we must win the peace." She explained in some detail what she meant. Surprisingly, this seemed to satisfy him.

"Thank you," he said and hung up.

One more call—to her Washington office manager. She wouldn't tell him much, just that she was in Denver and would be dropping in on the American Coalition party convention. No one could be trusted in the city that gorged itself on rumor and speculation. But, she would ask him what he knew about Ms. Arnold.

* * *

The humidity weighed down on Joe Domino like a liquid albatross. Too bad he loved his estate and the view of the Hudson too well to abandon it for the coast of Maine. It surely was cooler there.

His mind was captured by the memories of racking up balls and stacking beer in the coolers in his father's pool hall. As a kid, he lived with the smell of sour beer, the noise of billiard balls clacking on the green felt tables, and the smoke that lingered even when the place was closed.

The old man had a head for business which he drowned in the bottle, shutting out his son without really meaning to. The customers, blue-collar types, had lives built on hard labor punctuated by lay-offs and strikes. The Union meetings held their spirits for ransom. Dumb clucks all of them. They always had enough for beer and a rack.

At fourteen, Joe had his own numbers racket. The net proceeds went punctually and accurately to the newsstand on the corner. Best to stay on the good side of the Syndicate—the nameless men whose necks were larger than his two thighs and who could snuff out his life for nothing more than grunts of approval from their bosses. Cops were either the kind you could trust or the kind you couldn't buy. The ones who couldn't be paid off were the crazy ones—one day rounding up all the whores at the Savoy and the next few weeks walking right by like they were lamp posts. Crazy cops screwed up business. Crazy cops were no damn good.

His thoughts were interrupted by the phone call from Denver.

"Kincaid is out for sure," the voice on the other end said. "But you're not gonna like what they're talking about."

"Yeah, so spill it. I ain't got time for guessing games," Joe said irritably.

"Remember that Congresswoman, the one who was governor down in New Mexico when they put ol' Woody away for bringing a little grass in from Chihuahua, the one that damn near got the liquor license laws changed, and upset everything at the race tracks with her meddling?"

"That bitch. Yeah, I remember her. What of it?"

"Well, Kincaid is pushing her to be their candidate."

Joe didn't have to think about it. *That loud-mouthed dame is a wild card nobody wants. That just won't wash.*

To the caller he said, "Well, it ain't a problem unless we let it be one. You know what to do: get something on her."

Suddenly, the heat wave lost its oppression. He grinned. Joe Domino would enjoy knocking out the Jenkins woman. It would be easy enough and she'd never know what hit her.

7

Wiley Smith, political reporter for the Denver Post, hung up the courtesy phone in the Brown Palace lobby after talking to Katy Jenkins. Dissatisfaction showed on his face. He had tried to pry more information from her, but couldn't. Margaret Kincaid's withdrawal was a story in itself; but his reporting instinct told him there was a better story, if he could just unearth it.

His face lit up as Ellen Steele, headline maker, approached him on the mezzanine. He introduced himself casually enough, well aware that she probably already knew who he was. "How's it going?" he asked. Then he listened.

Ellen advised him how well the Convention was going, and that Katy Jenkins would be an outstanding candidate.

Wiley Smith could see that she wasn't putting out anything either. At the same time he sensed tension behind her casual remarks. "Oh well," he said, "women have already won the war; now all you have to do is win the peace."

"Who says so?" snapped Ellen.

"The new candidate we just spoke of," he said casually.

"She did?" The question fairly burst from her lips.

"Sure she did. Don't you agree?"

Three short minutes later Wiley Smith had his story and was on his way to his typewriter. He wasn't the least bit concerned that his story would set the Coalition Convention on end. He knew from long experience that the public is far less interested in the programs of a candidate than a good fight on the floor of the convention.

* * *

On Saturday morning streaks of first light pierced the darkness as Katy stepped out onto Fremont Street. The only street traffic at that hour was the food suppliers' trucks. Some stood idling at the curb, with doors flung open allowing the sweet smells of their contents to waft into the street. Stout delivery men called to each other as they carted crates of milk, racks of bread, and boxes of fresh produce into the hotel and other Fremont Street eateries.

Ms. Arnold had suggested they meet at the Civic Center coffee shop. At 6:30 A.M., the thought of a short stack with some crisp bacon on the side and steaming cup of coffee made Katy's mouth water. A country girl's breakfast, she thought.

Steam obscured the coffee shop windows. Clattering noise of flatware and china plates being set out on the formica-topped counters filled Katy's ears as she pushed the door open. Orders in short-order lingo shot through the room. Banks of fluorescents flooded the place making it impossible to discern the features of the silhouetted figures hunched at the counters.

A couple departed from the third low-slung booth along the wall, so she seated herself as the busboy scooped the dirty dishes into his deep plastic tray.

What a place for a private conference, Katy mused. Looks like the whole world is here for breakfast, but I'll bet it's more private than anywhere else. I wonder why Ms. Arnold wants to meet?

Ms. Arnold held no official position related to the convention, yet she helped in every way she could. It wasn't a bad idea to have the head of one of D.C.'s most prestigious public relations organizations working in your corner. Katy reviewed the profile notes she had made last night. First name, Lucille—never used. Known only as Ms. Arnold. Estimated six figure personal income. Fluent in two foreign languages, French and Spanish. Taught in Philadelphia before working full-time for the Smithsonian as historical researcher. Possibly three marriages, two while abroad. Single at present. Opened public relations firm ten years ago. Political affiliation unknown. Drives a late model prestigious car. Katy smiled to herself as she deciphered her own handwriting. "A woman of big proportions and big intellect." Not a shred of scandal nor dishonor clouded this flamboyant adventure-seeking woman's background. Katy slid the notes back into her purse as she noticed Ms. Arnold heading her way.

"Good morning, Katy Jenkins," said Ms. Arnold. "You and I have one thing in common—we like an early start."

"It's a habit I started young while living on the farm."

"Well, I never had that growing up in Philly. But I discovered early on you can get more done in a couple of hours before eight in the morning than you can the rest of the day."

The waitress appeared for their breakfast order. Ms. Arnold said, "I was glad to see you dining with Steele and Silverton,—oh, and Harriett Landsdale—last evening."

"Well, after the meeting in 824, it seemed the first order of business," Katy said.

"And getting Andy Barker as running mate? That was a stroke of genius."

"It had to be," Katy commented.

"And lucky—you've got to get some breaks to survive in this business."

"The dinner went well," Katy advised. "Silverton, as head of the Women's Movement, has agreed to be the national coordinator for forty-two of the nation's leading women's organizations. She is a good executive. And Steele tentatively agreed to be the field coordinator for the women's organizations. It's just her style. Harriett will be liaison to the state party organizations. She's all set."

"Well done, Katy," Ms. Arnold whistled appreciatively. "Smart moves, all of them."

Katy noted a twinge of her own surprise realizing how much information she willingly shared and felt no need to add the usual "and this is strictly confidential" comment. The waitress broke in with their plates of food and refills for the coffee. Conversation turned to small talk as they ate. Ms. Arnold took a long slow sip of coffee and leaned back in the booth. "I'm going to work for you, Katy."

Katy's mind groped for just a moment. What did she say? Did I hear correctly? "I'm afraid we're not ready for a public relations firm. And I doubt if we could afford you. Besides, the convention hasn't nominated me yet."

"Oh, you'll be nominated all right. No question there. It will be fact before this day is over. I figure to get you on TV for the early news in half the country and definitely on the late news, also front page of the Sunday papers. More press will be here this afternoon. Hell, I had to get more. You don't have enough media here to launch a campaign for mayor!

"Listen, keep the speeches between you and Andy down to thirteen and a half minutes if you can, in case I can get someone to air the entire program. I'm leaving it to Margaret to get you nominated and ready to accept by five o'clock. Make your speech the prettiest ever."

Katy nodded, "That's all great thinking. I'll work it out just as you say. Perhaps tomorrow we can discuss your joining the campaign."

"Katy, you don't understand what I'm saying—I've already gone to work for you, no price tag. 'Pro bono' as you lawyers might say; only consider me an executive-on-loan. I suspect I know more about what you need at this point than you do and one of those things is me."

Katy's thoughts ran computer speed. Do I need help? Positive. Decide now? Positive. Any negative responses? Negative. Ms. Arnold sat quietly. "Okay," Katy said, "I accept your help."

"Good! Then we're in business. I'm just a passionate student of history," she said. "Can't pass up this chance to help make some."

"That answers my only remaining question. Well, for better or for worse, we'll put a few pages in future history books." Katy toasted Ms. Arnold with the last of the coffee.

"The first woman president," said Ms. Arnold. "Should make a good read."

* * *

"Where have you been, Katy?" Margaret's voice was raspy. "Have you seen this morning's Denver Post?"

"Just a glimpse of it," Katy responded, wondering why Margaret seemed so upset. She and Ms. Arnold had picked up a copy of the newspaper on the street corner as they returned to the Brown Palace, but Ms. Arnold took the paper and headed straight for the news room on the mezzanine. Katy had crossed the lobby to talk to Margaret.

"Ellen is throwing a fit." Katy's bewilderment registered on Margaret. "It's this story in the Post. They quoted you about women having 'won the war' and something about now 'winning the peace.'" Margaret had lowered her voice. "I missed your line of reasoning myself."

Katy's heart sank. She dropped into the nearest lobby chair. She scanned the newspaper Margaret had thrust at her. Prominent front-page story. Headline okay. "KINCAID OUT AS Coalition party CANDIDATE." Details followed. Typical political story with plenty of innuendo and speculation. Her eyes raced down the double-column story:

Katy Jenkins, Democratic Congresswoman from New Mexico, and former governor of that state, is purportedly frontrunner to replace Kincaid at the head of the ticket. Jenkins is known as more moderate on women's issues than Kincaid. "Women have won the war—now all they have to do is win the peace," states Jenkins.

Ellen Steele, former president of the Women's Movement organization, which is highly visible in the Coalition party activities, disagrees. "We've won a few battles, but we've lost some, too. The war isn't over. They're trying to crucify women on abortion—make them breeding animals controlled by male masters. Women working for poor pay and at the same time taking care of kids, doing double duty, and doing it all without decent, affordable child care. Katy Jenkins just doesn't know how the other half lives. "What progress women have made, we've had to fight for every inch of the way. I doubt if Jenkins has ever

led a demonstration or even been on a
picket line. If we've won the war, as
Jenkins says, I'd hate to see what we'd
get in the peace. Women would be back
in the dark ages."

"Well, thank you Denver Post," Katy muttered. She tried to
explain to Margaret that she had given the reporter specific details
of what she meant by winning the peace, but he had conveniently
replaced it with Steele's pithy comments. Margaret looked
unconvinced.

"I have to admit Steele's words were more earthy than mine."
Ordinarily Katy would have laughed, or at least grinned, as she
made the admission, but not now.

"Anyhow," Margaret continued, "Steele is up in arms. She's
ready to recommend that the Movement withdraw support and put
on their own campaign."

Katy winced. "I'll do my best to straighten this out," she said
defensively. "But I'll need some time. Do you think you can hold
her off?"

"By God, I've got to. The Convention opens in forty-five
minutes. Keynote speech. I'm not going to have this messed up.
I'll soften Steele up. Try to get her to button her lip until this
afternoon when the Convention takes up the Platform Committee
report. I'll promise her the floor then. You will have to be
there—and we'll see who wins this round."

8

Katy's apprehensions dissipated as she and Margaret arrived on the mezzanine amid the bedlam of activities. Delegates converged on Margaret, giving Katy an opportunity to appraise the situation. Other conventioneers were either clustered in groups, or making their way to the passageway above the street leading to the convention hall in the hotel annex. All of the meeting rooms off the mezzanine buzzed with various activities.

Ms. Arnold dominated the press room and was tantalizing the media with hints of a major suprise to come. Katy marveled; the woman seemed capable of being in three places at once, not counting the phone. Wire service reporters hovered at the computer terminals. Television newscasters clogged the aisles. Ms. Arnold moved out onto the crowded mezzanine, stopping to speak to as many people as she could.

Where is Ellen Steele?, wondered Katy.

She moved toward the passageway to the convention hall, falling in easily with people going the same way, greeting friends and making new acquaintances. She gasped as she entered the hall itself. The walnut paneled walls and luxuriously carpeted floors didn't resemble any convention hall she had ever seen. The seating area reminded her of the Congress. Arranged in a semi-circle, long narrow tables flanked by ten chairs faced the speaker's platform. Sections were indicated for every state delegation, some as few as one or two seats, but California and New York each took a complete table for ten. A giant American flag hung in back of the speakers' platform.

Ruth Silverton moved in beside Katy. They moved forward together, skirting the traffic. Harriett Landsdale appeared as if on cue. "Ellen is going to make her move first thing this afternoon when the platform comes up," Harriett said in a whisper. "She's going to move that the 'women's rights' plank be made more inclusive and specific, and that it be made the first item on the platform. She's drumming up a following. As chair of the platform committee, I'll be giving the report. How do you want it handled?"

Katy thought fast. "Main thing is to put a time limit on the debate, or this could develop into a marathon fight." She glanced around. They still had some privacy. "Why not give Ellen and her backers thirty minutes total, and the same for me?"

"Good strategy," Ruth said quietly. "We'll work it out. And I will speak for you if you like."

Katy felt secure with Ruth. She knew Ruth resented Ellen's contentious radicalism. She responded without hesitation, "I'll call on you, maybe first." She looked at Harriett. "Can you be prepared to speak—maybe last?

"Can do!" said Harriett.

"We're organized," Katy said as Andy came up.

Andy cordially greeted Ruth and Harriett, then lowered his voice. "Katy, you have a little problem."

"I know," she said quickly. "Let's you and I find a quiet corner for a minute during the coffee break."

* * *

Margaret Kincaid opened the meeting. "The first National Convention of the American Coalition party will come to order," she boomed. Silence hung like a curtain for a moment, only to be shattered by rising thunderous applause. Shivers ran up and down Katy's spine as a chant filled the room. "Margaret! Margaret!"

Cheers reverberated through the hall despite Margaret's outstreched arms signalling for quiet. She smiled and accepted the expression of support. She had worked with every one of them in their home states. Now they all knew she couldn't be their candidate, and this was their way of showing appreciation for the gigantic effort she had made. Delegates clapped in unison as they rose to give her a standing ovation.

Brushing at her eyes, Margaret finally gained the delegates' attention. The proceedings took on a fluid smoothness, the best orchestrated meeting Katy had ever witnessed. Rules accepted. Dorothy Hastings, president of the Women Voters Caucus, elected permanent chair of the Convention. The Chair then called on Andy Barker, former governor of Pennsylvania, to introduce Jane Ellsworth, keynote speaker. Andy's introduction conveyed his high regard for Ellsworth as he reviewed the milestones in her career, capped by her achievements as secretary general of the United Nations. The solid applause as she arrived at the podium expressed the assembly's pleasure at having her.

Katy noticed several large TV cameras and a bevy of reporters moving in close. Ellsworth's speech launched the Convention on a high note of optimism for America and the world.

Wonderful start, thought Katy. Chairwoman Hastings declared a twenty minute recess. "Roll call and treasurer's reports from each state when we re-convene," announced Hastings.

Katy fervently hoped the press and television would feature Ellsworth's address rather than the confrontation on the women's plank coming up in the afternoon.

Katy never left the main hall during the recess. One mini-conference after another kept her attention. As the delegates were re-assembling, Harriett Landsdale made a beeline for Katy. "You'll never guess who's here." She didn't wait for an answer. "H.B. McGee—and he's all over the place."

"Oh boy," said Katy, "the fat's in the fire." She took a seat alongside Harriett on the outside aisle of the front row. This strategically located seat gave her a view of the entire assembly, affording her a chance to study the delegates as they spoke.

The Chair called the Convention to order, and asked that state chairpersons or treasurers limit their reports to one minute. "Happy Moultrie is here from Alabama. You're on, Happy."

"Well, we don't have a million dollars to talk about like I understand the Women's Movement will report, but we do have a thousand in our treasury, and a state-wide organization with over five hundred members, and..."

That's the way it went for the next hour and a half. There were some clowns who put fun into their reports. Madge Bloomfield from Texas made the most glowing accounting. She estimated ten-thousand members and almost forty-thousand dollars in the bank account. Although California had reported much less, Lila Stanford from California asked to be recognized again after the Texas report; she vowed to beat Texas in fund-raising before the campaign was over.

Harriett nudged Katy. "Isn't this something," she exclaimed as the last report was made.

"Let's all stand and stretch a minute, while Margaret comes up here," Dorothy Hastings said. "I see her, way in the back. But don't go away, Margaret is going to bare her soul telling us how this all started. I've heard the story and I think you'll enjoy it."

Margaret arrived at the podium, addressed the Chair and the assembly. She launched into her story with a casualness that belied her enthusiasm.

"After my book was published, Women Shakers and Movers, I was a celebrity. Interviewed on TV shows, featured in the book reviews—the whole routine. Then I received a very special invitation. I was invited to attend a re-union of a unique group of writers that had organized themselves at Berkeley, U.C., in the sixties. Berkeley was a vanguard of any campus movement whether philosophical, artistic, or political. The group was started by Andy Barker—who was a student there, as I was. It was secretly called the 'Literary Shakers and Movers of America.' Nothing modest about us!"

She was interrupted by exclamations of surprise, good-natured cat-calls, and scattered applause.

"Where do you make more life-long friends than in the formative college years?" She didn't wait for an answer.

"Anyhow, there were thirty-six of us at the reunion, about equally divided as to men and women. Every one of those attending had made his or her mark somewhere. Newspaper editors, the president of a publishing company, a famous novelist, a state governor and a Congresswoman. Oh yes, and a woman who has become a big-time PR personality in D.C.

"At the final dinner, a Kangaroo Court was organized, and I was tried for the crime of plagiarism—for using part of the organization's name for my book title. Judge Cosgrove from Seattle presided. He appointed one of the attorneys in the group as counsel for the defense and the other to prosecute the case.

Whereas one witness eloquently called the act 'nefarious,' another proclaimed it a 'patriotic gesture.' The verdict was 'guilty as charged.' Whereupon the judge ordered that as retribution I should buy a round of after-dinner drinks for everyone. As we drank, Sam Pickens from Texas spoke up. He was easily the most affluent person in the room—you know him—Texas Electronics. We called him 'Slim' then.

"All six-feet-four inches of him towered over one end of the table. 'We're a bunch of smug fat cats here tonight,' he said, 'but we still haven't elected a woman president. Remember Johnson was president when we started meeting, then Carter. We looked at politics with a jaundiced eye, and decided maybe we needed a real change—a woman president.

"'Well, things haven't changed for the better. Democrat or Republican, they seem determined to spend the country into bankruptcy. Maybe we were right about electing a woman president. But, we haven't done a damned thing about it.'

"'Why not elect Margaret?' someone piped up.

"'Good idea,' said Andy Barker with conviction that only a few drinks could have inspired."

Margaret's tone became confidential. "The upshot of the discussion was that everyone there wrote a thousand dollar check, made out to the American Coalition party, a name dreamed up on the spot, nothing more than a figment of imagination. They gave me the checks and said, 'Get started.' That was four years ago.

"Back in New York the next day I toyed with the idea of sending the checks back to their makers. I counted and found only thirty-five. Then I realized that my own was missing. I wrote out my check for a thousand and put it on the stack. I was committed!

"And here we are today! Twenty-eight of the thirty-six people who were at the re-union are here today, and we have wires and phone calls or letters pledging support from most of the others."

People were frantically pointing toward Sam Pickens who had just come into the room.

"Welcome, Slim Pickens," Margaret continued, "I just told the delegates about you at the Berkeley re-union, and how you fathered all this." She immediately wanted to bite her tongue. She had just remembered reading something about Sam being involved in a paternity suit with a twenty-six year old secretary.

But Sam wasn't perturbed. He grinned sheepishly. "Seems like I'm being accused of being a father quite often these days. This one I admit, but if I'm the father of the party, then Margaret must be the mother. It's possible. I admit I don't recall everything that went on that last night of the re-union."

Margaret blushed. A roar of laughter surged through the assembly.

"Anyhow," Margaret said as the laughter subsided and she regained her composure, "Sam Pickens is here. He's chairman of the party's finance committee for Texas. We just heard what a job he has done.

Katy sat in rapt attention as Margaret's story unfolded. So Harriett Landsdale had been in on it from the beginning. And Andy Barker. And Mrs. Arnold, too. She had heard bits about some illustrious party founders, but nothing about "Shakers and Movers." Now the pieces are fitting together, she thought.

More of the pieces would soon fall into place. The Chair called on Ruth Silverton. "Want to tell us about the Million Dollar Club? It was your inspiration."

Ruth took the floor. "I'll tell you the historical role the Women's Movement played.

"Margaret must have called me at the Movement office the same day she put her thousand dollar check with the others. We met the next afternoon in Philadelphia, checked into a downtown hotel, and talked. We talked some more over dinner at the old Bookbinder's Restaurant. From the hotel that evening and the next morning I made phone calls to a dozen key people in the Movement. Believe me, I was excited. Elect a woman president! The thought was electrifying. We decided to start the Million Dollar Club. We would raise a million dollars in donations of five, ten, twenty-five, fifty and one hundred dollars from the members. We quietly sent out letters to our entire membership."

Ruth peered over her glasses at the people in the room with a triumphant look. "We did it. A few months later we put a million dollars into trust accounts in various banks earmarked exclusively to help elect a woman president. Thousands of contributors became members of the Million Dollar Club. The average contribution was only eleven dollars!

"Next week in Washington, D.C., on the steps of the nation's capital with the American flag flying above, we will make a public presentation of the million dollars to the American Coalition party to help elect our party's first president."

A roar of approval went up from the crowd.

"Now Ellen has an announcement," Ruth said as she sat down.

Ellen strode up the aisle to the front microphone to speak. "Now," she said, "I know why the rich get richer. That million dollars sitting in the banks for the past three years has earned us $200,000 in interest." She paused for this to register. "We are planning to use this windfall to launch the 'Second Million Club' in a direct mail appeal to the women of the nation with the goal of raising an additional million dollars. Sample mailings have already gone out, and the response indicates we will reach this goal."

The solid hand-clapping continued for some time.

Ellen hesitated. She was scheduled to tell how the same mailings that would build the 'Second Million Club' were also aimed at inspiring a hundred thousand new grass-roots workers for the Coalition campaign. She didn't. With all of the frustrations she felt the last two days with Margaret Kincaid withdrawing, and her own chance to be the vice-presidential candidate scuttled, the street-fighter in her emerged.

Her voice became fierce. "But I don't have much stomach for raising any more money for the American Coalition party if their candidate is so far removed from reality that she thinks women have won their war." She shouted the question that followed. "Does anyone in this room think that women have won the war?"

Reporters and cameramen snapped to life.

"Let's see a show of hands." She looked hard at the assembly. A chill went through the room. No hands went up.

"Thank you," Ellen said. Without another word she returned to her seat.

Dorothy Hastings rose to the occasion. "Thank you for the report, Ellen," she said. "And you raised a provocative issue." Addressing the Convention she announced they would recess for lunch, and re-assemble at 1:30 p.m. sharp, at which time the platform committee report would be the first order of business.

As Ellen made her way triumphantly back to her seat, Katy saw H.B. McGee standing at the entryway to the Convention Hall. He must have seen Ellen's performance, she thought.

Immediately after Dorothy banged her gavel, recessing the Convention, Katy yielded to her urge to get out of there. She made a beeline for H.B. She would have welcomed one of his bear hugs right then, but there was none. He did the next best thing, however, and put his arm around her shoulder as they walked across the corridor to the hotel.

"You sure you want to get mixed up with this bunch of felines?" H.B.'s voice was gentle. Katy was glad for that.

"I may not be mixed up with them after the 1:30 meeting," Katy said without feeling.

"You sure as hell opened up a can of worms," he said. "I heard about it on the plane coming up here first. And from the time I came into the hotel, that's been the main topic of conversation. Even Ms. Arnold wanted to talk about it."

"You know her?" Katy questioned.

"Not until I got here. But she's on your side, that's for sure. And so is Harriett."

"You talked to Harriett?"

"First one I talked to. She was always on our side, remember, until this crazy thing came up." H.B. waved his hand taking in the mezzanine and meetings rooms, all evidence of the "crazy thing" he referred to. Ms. Arnold came up behind them. H.B. stepped back as Ms. Arnold moved in close to talk to Katy. "That's just sour grapes from Ellen," she said.

"Yeah, maybe a million dollars worth." Katy said it before she saw the reporter trailing behind Ms. Arnold. She hoped he hadn't heard their bits of conversation. She could imagine the lead for his column: "Million dollars worth of sour grapes splits Coalition Convention." Neither Ms. Arnold nor H.B. understood why Katy chuckled aloud, but the tension eased.

H.B. noticed the big television camera coming across the passageway on coasters, looking self-propelled and dangerous. "I better get out of here," he said to Katy and Ms. Arnold. "I don't want my picture on TV this time." To Katy he had a surprising comment. "Keep your chin up! I'll be back for the main event at 1:30 if I can squeeze in."

"I'll make you a place, H.B." Ms. Arnold said, "so you can watch Katy clobber her."

9

"Look at this crowd. I hope the fire marshall doesn't show."
Ms. Arnold's remark was partly to herself, and partly to H.B.
She had managed to squeeze in an extra chair for him at one of the
back tables. Along the walls, people were standing two and three
deep.

Excitement crackled in Dorothy's voice as she called the
Convention to order and promptly called on Harriett Landsdale for
the report of the platform committee.

Harriett stood tall at the lectern as she addressed the group.
"The first meeting of the Platform Committee was held in Santa Fe
last spring. The members came as my guests. For three days we
enjoyed the invigorating climate of Santa Fe, and the just as
invigorating task of putting together a platform for the first new
major political party in America since Teddy Roosevelt's Bull
Moose Party in 1912." She put in a quick aside. "Incidentally,
he didn't get elected, but they did defeat Taft which resulted in
Woodrow Wilson's election." She resumed her vibrant official
tone.

"Yesterday in the Prospector's Room off the mezzanine in the
hotel, we did our final revisions; a copy is at each delegate's
place, and there are additional copies available if anyone doesn't
have one. Let's take five minutes to look at the suggested
platform; then we will have discussion."

None of the delegates left their seats during the five minutes.
They studied the platform, and spoke in low tones. Then Dorothy
came back to the lectern and called the meeting to order. Harriett
would remain at the podium for questions.

"I have a question." It was Ellen Steele.

"The Chair recognizes Ellen Steele."

"There are a couple dozen planks here," Ellen began. "Most all of them I agree with—in principle, at least. I think the Federal Government should have more fiscal responsibility; military spending should be cut; environment, education—all good planks! But my question is about the women's plank. Why is it buried down near the end? And why doesn't it include an Equal Rights Amendment—ERA? It comes straight out for 'freedom of choice,' but why bury it?"

Dorothy motioned Harriett to move to the mike.

"That's a mouthful," began Harriett, "two questions in one. I think I will take the last one first. ERA is past tense. We had our 'day in court.' The committee decided we should move on to new frontiers rather than rattle skeletons from the past." She moved on quickly to the remaining question. "As to the placement of the women's rights plank, the committee felt that although it is as important as any in the entire platform, we wanted the platform to cover a large spectrum of issues."

Ellen interrupted. "So you buried it!" she exclaimed impatiently. "All right, I want to make a motion that the women's rights plank be strengthened, and be made number one."

The sharpness of Harriett's voice was the only indication that she was perturbed. "I cannot accept a motion. That will be up to the Chair. I'm sure your motion will be accepted in due course." She dismissed Ellen. "Are there other questions regarding the platform?" She handled the questions which followed from the delegates. Then she returned control of the meeting to the Chair.

Dorothy rose, thanked Harriett and members of the platform committee for all the work they had done. Then she said, "The Chair recognizes Ellen Steele."

The suddenness of her recognition caught Ellen by surprise. She was slow responding as she collected her thoughts.

"Do you have a motion, Ellen?" the Chair prompted her.

"Oh, yes, I do."

"Use the mike there in the center aisle."

Static crackled as she adjusted the mike. Then loud and clear she made her motion. "I move that the women's rights plank be strengthened, and made number one."

Two "seconds" rang out from across the room.

She has her backers all right, Katy thought.

"May I speak to my motion now?" Ellen inquired.

"In just a minute," the Chair said. Addressing the assembly, she asked if there would be others to speak for the motion. Three or four hands went up.

"Will someone speak against the motion?"

Katy rose. "I'd like to speak against."

"Are there others who would like to speak against the motion?" Another three or four hands went up.

"Point of order!" Margaret's voice rang out.

"The Chair recognizes Margaret Kincaid."

"This discussion seems to be basic as far as Coalition party policy is concerned," Margaret began, "but the discussion could get out of hand. I'd like to move that a time limit of one hour be put on the discussion."

Ellen's face showed her displeasure.

"The motion to limit debate takes priority and is not subject to debate," the Chair announced. "The only question is do you want to limit the discussion of the motion to one hour."

"Question," someone shouted.

"Okay. All in favor of the motion to limit the debate on the motion before the house to one hour, say AYE." The "AYEs" rang out.

"Opposed, NO." The "NOs" were obviously the minority.

"The "AYEs" have it. Debate will be limited to one hour. Will you act as 'chair' *for* the motion, Ellen?"

"Yes."

"Will you act as 'chair' *against* the motion, Katy?"

"Yes."

"Ellen, will you please come up to the front mike? You will have thirty minutes."

Ellen strode to the microphone.

"I'd like to call on Gladys Moore from Chicago to speak for the motion. You can use the mike there nearest you."

Gladys, a small black woman wearing glasses, spoke out with surprising force. "I live on Chicago's south side where women have such a tough time the people in this room wouldn't believe it. You can't imagine the poverty and degradation suffered there.

When a woman and her kids are forced onto relief, there's no way out from then on. They're stuck in poverty.

"If they get some sort of job, right then their payments and food stamps stop. And when the job peters out, maybe not their fault at all, they can't get their checks, or food stamps, or anything else goin', and they face starvation. Do you think they try to get another job?" She let this soak in.

"We need somethin' to get women so they can take a job, any kind they can get, and still get their support, so they can afford to take the job. We need somebody in Washington who will come to my district, and hold their nose long enough to see what goes on. The old political parties are bogged down. We need understanding. And I hope the Coalition party doesn't leave us out, or put us so far down on the platform that we're the forgotten people."

Ellen made no comment. She paused for the careful applause, and pushed on with another speaker, and then two more. All of them were worthy spokespersons, and made their points. They spoke from their hearts about child care, abortion, equality in the workplace, and in the home. Ellen knew they made a good case. Now she would be the final speaker.

"Well," she asked, "does it sound like women have won the war? Does it sound like our new political party should look the other way, pretend all's well in women's world? What about some states criminalizing women and doctors for abortion, even in the first thirteen weeks when the 'human life' they talk about is really just a fertilized egg? The human being is the woman. It is *her* freedom of choice they are taking away. I say we haven't won any war. Does it sound like we should present the nation with a milquetoast women's plank buried down in the bottom part of the platform?"

She reviewed the history of women's struggle, naming the heroines in the battle for the suffrage to vote, and heroines of battles won and lost—winding up with Margaret Kincaid. The applause was genuine, spontaneous.

Ellen warmed to her conclusion. "We're faced with a major decision today in this convention. It goes far beyond the wording in a plank, or placement in the platform. We must make the right decision on this, of course, and your votes for my motion will do that. But, beyond that, we must ask ourselves who should be our leaders, and specifically, who should be our candidates for president and vice president?"

She looked directly at Margaret. "We knew Margaret. We knew she was our candidate. We knew what she stood for. We could have poured our hearts and our funds into Margaret's campaign. But how about her candidate-designate, Katy Jenkins? Now don't get me wrong. I like Jenkins personally, but her background isn't ours. She comes from a wealthy farm and ranching family away down in eastern New Mexico—a state, incidentally, with *five* electoral votes." The scorn at five electoral votes came through in her voice. "Are we going to have a practical political party, or just a political farce?" There was a moment of quiet.

"I disagree with Jenkins. I don't think women have won the war. And neither do the people in this room. When I asked for a show of hands a while ago as to how many here think women have won the war, not one was raised. That says it all. The Jenkins philosophy is not that of this Convention. I ask that you pass my motion to strengthen the women's plank and move it to the top of the platform, and get this Convention back on track."

"Katy Jenkins will lead the speakers in opposition to the motion," the Chair announced matter-of-factly. As Katy made her way to the podium, she gained confidence and reassurance with every step.

Her first words were a surprise to the audience.

"I agree with Ellen and the others who have spoken," she began. Her manner was deliberate.

"I agree women still have a way to go to achieve equality in the workplace. I agree we need more and better child care and that freedom of choice for abortion remains threatened. And I agree that women's issues are among the things which must be addressed by the American Coalition party.

"When I spoke to the Denver Post reporter, I said women had 'won the war' in the sense of recogizing all of the progress we have made. What the writer didn't report was that I told him 'winning the peace' will come in winning equality and equal opportunity for all."

Katy's usual good humor surfaced as she continued.

"Usually when I make a goof, not everyone gets upset about it. But this time, I guess I hit the jackpot. From all I've heard, the verdict is unanimous—women have not 'won the war' from anyone's perspective."

Katy smiled wryly. "I yield. I'll continue fighting the unwon war. And you know what? I'll not have to change my philosophy or tactics. Only the words. We have won some battles, and I hope I can help win more."

Katy paused to look around at as many of the people in the audience as possible, then listed some of the gains made by women in the professions and the workplace.

"Certainly there's more to be done," she said. "Fortunately, there's opportunity for women out there still." Her voice reflected the excitement she felt.

"Sure, it's a tough, competitive world for women. But it is for men, too. Don't forget that."

Her eyes sought out Gladys.

"As you know, Gladys, I've been to your area and worked for two days with one of your social workers. Conditions *are* deplorable. I was appalled. I went straight back to Washington to see what could be done to keep providing support while women make the transition from welfare to employment. I got assurance at the Cabinet level that 'something would be done about it.' But I also was warned, as usual, that, 'It will take some time.' We're still waiting. Save us from bureaucrats!

"I saw the sad plight of women in your area. All too often black women have a painfully hard lot."

Katy changed pace with a question. "You know who I also feel sorry for? Black men and boys. Without jobs, they lose their self-respect and identity. Finally they despair.

"It is my hope," she continued, "that the American Coalition party will be a party of compassion. It is just as important also that it be an intelligent party, dedicated enough to wipe out these blights on America. Simply passing another appropriations bill will not suffice. We must come up with answers, new solutions to old problems. And no political party can justify itself before the electorate as a single issue party.

"I believe that fiscal responsibility is our main concern. If the nation goes broke, we cannot solve any problems and democracy itself will be sorely threatened."

Katy's gaze searched the room and found Ruth. "For another viewpoint, I would like to yield some time to Ruth Silverton."

A hush fell over the room. What would Ruth say? She was not the orator Ellen was, or Katy. She came to the lectern looking more like a schoolteacher than the president of the Women's Movement. She adjusted her glasses and spoke in a conversational tone. "For many years, most of my working hours have been devoted to women's causes. I am dedicated to the proposition that women have been discriminated against long enough, and that we must insist on more fairness. We must pursue this goal in every possible direction, including the political process."

Ruth adjusted her glasses and continued. "For this reason, I especially welcome the American Coalition party. I am pleased that the Women's Movement has been, and will continue to be, an integral part of this new party. I do not believe, however, for one instant that we should in any way dominate the party or impose our will upon it.

"In my opinion, we are fairly represented in the party platform. Two members of the platform committee are very active in our organization. The committee did an excellent job." One final adjustment of her glasses, and Ruth looked out over the convention. "In conclusion, it would be my preference to see the platform adopted as submitted by the platform committee."

Ellen slid down in her seat, obviously disappointed in Ruth's stand.

Katy returned to the lectern and immediately called on Andy Barker. He bounded to the podium, peremptorily addressed the Chair and delegates, and launched into his remarks. "Katy's too smart to call on me if she wasn't pretty sure I would take her side on this. I agree with the previous two speakers that we have a good platform. Anything we'd try to do to it here would be anti-climactic. We can all support this platform. It covers the waterfront. I'd say let it be." He was gone as quickly as he had appeared.

"That was short and sweet," commented Katy. "Would anyone else like to speak against the motion?" No one spoke up.

"Harriett, since you are chair of the platform committee, would you like to have the last word?"

"Thank you, Katy. May I speak from here." She was at one of the aisle microphones.

"Go ahead. We can hear you fine."

"I appreciate the public comments, and also the side remarks I've heard. I appreciated the input yesterday, too. We listened to every suggestion, and did our best to incorporate them. We think it is the best platform for the American people that has been written by a political party. We would like to see it approved."

Dorothy Hastings moved to the lecturn. "Thank you Ellen and Katy," she said, "and all the other participants." She casually looked over the assembly to see if anyone was trying to get her attention. Discovering none, she announced the question, restated the motion and asked for the vote. "All in favor of the motion, say 'AYE'." There were scattered "AYEs." "All opposed 'NO'." The room reverberated with "NOs."

Margaret Kincaid rose, and was recognized. "I move the platform be adopted by the Convention."

"Second," rang out from several delegates.

The vote was overwhelmingly in favor. "Motion carried. The platform is adopted. We will have a fifteen minute recess, then have other committee reports, resolutions, and finally, the most important order of business—the nominations of our candidates for president and vice president of the United States of America."

* * *

H.B. waited for Katy outside the door of the Convention Hall. "Katy, you finessed that hand! And you've got the Convention with you now; you're nominated."

"Can you stay?" She posed the question tenuously.

"Naw, I've got no more business here; I'll head on back to Albuquerque, and start trying to put the pieces back together."

"I'm sorry, H.B. I know I'm messing you up."

"You sure as hell are. But you could no more have passed this up than you could fly." Ms. Arnold approached, beaming. H.B.

had one parting thought as he took off.   "Good luck to you anyhow, Katy."   He was gone; Katy felt the finality of his departure even as she turned her attention to Ms. Arnold.

"We have a TV monitor set up in suite 824 for you, Katy. You can go on up there and watch the proceedings for the next couple hours. I think we can get you on the six o'clock network news, live! Don't let any reporters or anybody else in. I'll put a hold on all calls." Katy could hear the excitement in Ms. Arnold's voice. "Your next appearance will be as the nominee!"

In the suite, Katy watched the proceedings with one eye as she made her acceptance speech notes. At five o'clock Chairwoman Hastings called for nominations. Two "favorite daughter" candidates were offered up in respectable speeches by state chairpeople. Both individuals politely withdrew their names from consideration.

"The Chair recognizes Margaret Kincaid," rang out from the podium. Dorothy stepped back from the battery of microphones and moved out of the spotlight, as Margaret moved in. With a flourish she nominated Andy Barker for vice president. The seconding speech by Harvey Fletcher of Pennsylvania preceded Andy's selection by acclamation.

The mounting excitement had been forged into a steel arrowhead whose target was the presidential nomination.

Again Margaret approached the lectern. Katy's breath caught in her throat. Her mouth went dry. There was the nomination, her mind was racing so fast she almost missed it. Deep breath once. Deep breath again. Composure regained, she watched as Andy, in an unusual arrangement of procedure, made the seconding speech for Katy and switched into accepting his own nomination.

"...and I will be proud to be the American Coalition party vice president nominee when you select Katy Jenkins as your presidential candidate."

As the shouts of approval rose over the roaring applause on the television, Katy turned to the grand piano. She sat on one side of the bench, leaving room for John's ghost to sit beside her. With two fingers she tentatively began to tap out 'chopsticks.' Softly at first, the notes chased their echoes of twenty-eight years before, then with increasing speed and urgency the music took her back in time to that glorious 4th of July weekend at the Brown Palace: the Saturday drive to Estes Park village in the shadow of Long's Peak; the Jaguar, top down, her hair blowing in the wind as they drove above timberline in Rocky Mountain National Park, on top of the world; to magnificent Grand Lake; back to Denver, talking and singing and touching as they traveled; dinner in the Palace Arms; the giddy feeling from the wine; Suite 824; 'chopsticks' side by side at the grand piano; John sweeping her into his arms and carrying her into the bedroom.

Her heart pounded as if to keep time to the wild rhythm of the chords. The remembering held her.

Her youthful world orbited around John Van Dorn. *We lived and loved each day as if it might be our last—and one day, it was.*

That day, late in August, started out like the others. She breakfasted with John in the University Inn Coffee Shop. Later she dropped him off at the tennis Club and took the Jaguar to run some errands. They would meet at the little house after John's session at Hibben's anthropology class in the afternoon.

She drove to the little house that afternoon, and was glad to see Elizabeth's car in the driveway.

"Elizabeth," she called out as she burst into the house, "is John here?"

"Haven't seen him, but I've just been here a few minutes."

"He should have been here by now. He was coming over here after anthropology. Even if he stayed after class he should be here by now. I wonder what could be keeping him?"

When John didn't show that afternoon, she figured he must have gone to the hotel to freshen up. Strange, though. His Jaguar sat in the driveway—she decided to make a quick trip to University Hilton.

"I'll be back with John in a little while," she called to Elizabeth.

"Then I'll make dinner for us," Elizabeth said. "But first I'll need to get something to cook. The cupboard is bare. What do you do for food when I'm not here to take care of you?"

"Dine out like rich folks," Katy grinned. She gave her cousin a loving hug and let the screen door slam behind her. "I won't be long."

The clerk at the hotel registration desk told her before she could ask. "John was trying to get you on the phone right up until the time he had to leave."

"He left?" Katy questioned. The blood rushed out of her face.

"Oh, don't worry; he left this note for you," the clerk said. He handed her an envelope. It was hotel stationery with the University Inn logo in the upper left corner. Brown ink. Raised letters.

Katy tore it open. In a quick scrawling hand it read:

> Emergency at home. Dad. Sounds serious. Hibben told me and took me to airport. Hold onto the Jag. I signed the title. Will be in touch.
>> As always, John.

The car title was folded inside the envelope.

She drove around for awhile. There was something so final about his leaving the title to the Jag. She pictured the end of a western movie with the hero riding off into the sunset—alone. No, the note had said he would "be in touch." Elizabeth would be her comfort tonight and John would be calling her.

When she returned to the little house, it was strangely dark in the growing twilight. She entered the front room, missing the smell of dinner cooking, noticing the blouse Elizabeth had worn, lying on the floor. A single shoe sat in the hallway. This was not like Elizabeth, Katy thought—herself maybe, she just couldn't be tidy—but not Elizabeth. She picked up the blouse. It was torn and smudged.

"Elizabeth!" she screamed. "Where are you?" She heard water running. She ran for the bathroom and shouted through the locked door, "Elizabeth, are you all right?"

The lock came free, the door opened and Elizabeth fell into Katy's arms. Her face already had traces of purplish bruises. She sobbed in gulps, half gurgling, uttering small moans as she tried to speak. Tears mingled with the water dripping down her face from still soapy hair. "Raped. Katy, he raped me," she gasped.

"Who? Who did this to you?" Katy said. She rocked her cousin in her arms.

"Short. Heavy set. Mask. He wore a mask. I don't know. I don't know," cried Elizabeth.

Blinding rage seethed inside Katy as she helped settle her cousin in the big rocking chair. A clear recollection of the day they had bought the rocker came to her in a bizarre calm spot at the center of her fury. What fun it had been then. How long ago it seemed now.

She had run out the front door, out into the street, searching in the gathering darkness for some clue. No one anywhere. She picked up a large rock from the edge of the flower bed and circled the house with murderous intent. She found nothing. The rapist had vanished.

Back in the house, she helped Elizabeth.

"Katy, I feel so dirty. I can't wash him out of my mind."

With clean pajamas and freshly untangled hair, Elizabeth was still distressed.

"Let me call Aunt May," Katy said. She wanted to call the police too, but Elizabeth was in no condition for their tedious interrogation.

"Oh no, please. I couldn't face anyone. I feel so dirty, I would just rather crawl out of my skin." Almost child-like, she pleaded, "Can I take another bath?"

Katy took complete control. While Elizabeth washed again, she collected the scattered clothes and checked for any sort of clues the rapist might have left behind. Nothing. She went directly into the bedroom and laid out good traveling outfits for Elizabeth and herself, packed a bag for them both and announced, "Listen. We're getting out of this town right now. Dry off. Let's go as far from here as we can get."

The flight away from their shattered dreams took them into Arizona. They stayed in a nondescript roadside motel for a few hours. Elizabeth couldn't rest, so they headed into Tucson.

The giant cacti first attracted them and they finally settled in at the Saguaro Resort. For a few days only their mothers knew of their whereabouts. Katy tried to reach John, but never managed to get past the help. When she called the LAND & SEA office, the switchboard operator said he wasn't there. And when she called his home on Long Island, she was cut off. Finally she realized she had to face a new reality. John was gone.

* * *

Suddenly, Katy realized the phone was ringing. Quickly she looked at the TV monitor. Still pandemomium down in the convention hall. She moved toward the phone and let it ring one more time before lifting the receiver from its cradle.

"Katy? Katy, you're the nominee." Margaret's voice was vibrant. "...on the first ballot. Meet us on the mezzanine. Andy and I will escort you to the podium. Can you hear Ms. Arnold's band? The Convention is going wild."

"I'll be right down," said Katy.

10

Katy walked into the convention hall to face the wildest and most enthusiastic crowd she had ever seen. She moved through the noisy congratulations of a surging group of well-wishers, to make her way to the lectern. There she was confronted by a bank of microphones. Television cameras, whose gleaming red lights focused on her every change of expression, connected her to millions of people all over America. Speech was impossible in the roaring welcome and for a time she just stood there, waving, smiling, enjoying the exuberance of the people and listening to the fast-paced upbeat music straining to make itself heard above the tumult.

"Thank you," she shouted. "Thank you so very much."

As the crowd quieted she began to speak.

"I want you to know that this is the proudest moment of my life. And I thank all of you for making it possible."

Katy lowered her voice, speaking firmly and deliberately. "I want you to know also that I am most happy to accept your nomination to be the American Coalition party's first candidate for president of the United States."

She paused for the cheers and applause of the delegates to die down. Smiling broadly, Katy said, "And it is my distinct pleasure to be campaigning with Andy Barker as our candidate for vice president." Again the hall erupted into bedlam. It was a while before Katy could make herself heard again.

"We are a new party with new ideas," she paused briefly, "but we are dedicated to the old, enduring principles which have made America the greatest country in the world." Applause and shouts of approval interrupted her once more. When the noise died down, she continued.

"Freedom, democracy, free enterprise, education for all, equality of opportunity—all of these are our heritage and we cherish them. At the same time, we realize that changing times require new responses to the challenges embodied in our ideals. New responses that will bring the meaning of America into the lives of everyone without diminishing our commitment to the foundation stones upon which this country is built.

"As you, and Andy and I—all of us—embark on this great adventure, let us dedicate our efforts to the idea that this is a crusade—a Crusade to Renew America."

Again the din of applause, whistles and cheers filled the hall.

Katy began to let herself believe it was working. She felt easier, more confident.

"Only a new political party, the American Coalition party, made up of people in every state, from every occupation and ethnic group, devoted to solving our nation's problems can accomplish this job of renewal. The old parties have been running things for too long. They've grown set in their ways, cemented to those particular special interests which have kept them in the driver's seat for so long."

The crowd loved her words and showed it by the loud response.

"Republicans and Democrats are no longer flexible enough to meet the challenges of our society. They've had their chance and what is the result? We all know—a sputtering economy, a national debt out-of-control, enormous trade imbalance, shaky financial institutions and unbelievably costly bailouts, deteriorating schools and a shameful illiteracy rate; an intolerable lack of child care, hundreds of thousands homeless, and the devastation of drug abuse and its companion, violent crime."

Katy stopped and looked over the crowd while her words hit home. Then she continued. "The politicians who let these things happen on their watch will not renew America. They've had the opportunity and the power. But they have only entrenched themselves in office. The exciting, new alternative is the American Coalition party!"

She was interrupted by a roar of approval. When she resumed, she touched on many of the themes she would carry throughout the election drive: government borrowing, and a new approach to tax and budget reform, more value for the dollar in Pentagon spending with emphasis on building a strong anti-missile defense, an energy plan, and Social Security solvency. Katy saw surprise and anger on faces as she explained how the Social Security trust fund is being milked by Congress and the Administration in order to spend billions 'off budget.'"

Her manner changed. "You gave Andy and me a great platform on which to build a campaign. There is nothing in it that will not help renew America. As the campaign progresses we will make our positions abundantly clear to all Americans on the issues that must be dealt with *now*. We believe they will agree."

The effusive reaction of the delegates let Katy know she was in tune with her audience. She hoped the millions of television viewers were with her as well.

"We must provide the leadership that not only America, but the rest of the world also needs. We will do this. And, I'll tell you right now, the policy of our government toward our allies will have to be modified. I do not believe we can or should be top cop to the world. Germany and Japan and the other countries will have to pay for the cost of their own defense. This must happen if we are to compete in the world marketplace.

"It is essential, too, that we develop fair trade policies—truly fair—worldwide. No longer should other countries have the advantage. No longer should the oil cartel be a continuous threat to us."

These words struck another nerve.

"In this campaign," Katy declared, "we will be open with all Americans. We will dare to think out loud with them. We will dare to insist on freedom and opportunity—not just for the 'haves,' but for the 'have-nots' too. A lot of lip service has been given to the have-nots; little has been done to help them help themselves. Our program of renewal will change that."

As a wave of applause welled up from the assembly, Katy was given the signal—one minute to go.

"As of tonight I am running for president of the United States. The only greater honor I can think of is to be elected to that office. And this is what I am going to ask the people of America to do—elect me for your president. There will be those who will denigrate the idea of electing a woman to the presidency. But there will be more who will think it an idea whose time has come.

"We believe our country needs new leadership and this is what the American Coalition party is offering. We believe in the fundamental freedoms that have made America great. We invite all free-thinking Americans to join us. The change will be so vast, so profound and so far reaching that it will leave the world breathless. Thank you!"

Katy stepped back from the lectern, and the Convention exploded. Applause shook the hall. The drummer was booming like thunder on the big drum. The pent-up worries about Margaret that beset the Convention at its beginning were gone. The party had their candidates. Relief showed in their applause. Balloons rose in a mass of color. Delegates stomped around the convention floor. They stood on chairs. They clapped in unison, all with new words on their lips. "Katy J.—Katy J."

"Katy J.!—Katy J.!"

11

Reverend Thomas Atwood's influence went far beyond the control of his own Christian empire. Not that his empire wasn't impressive in itself. The congregation in his own church in Birmingham, Alabama, numbered in the thousands; his Christian Television Station WCTV reached over a million viewers, the majority of them contributors; and he boasted his own Christian College. Prideful achievements, all of them.

The sting of his "Christian Majority" organization made itself felt all the way to the halls of the U.S. Senate and House of Representatives. His greatest personal satisfaction, though, was that for some years now his influence had extended right into the White House. He was even consulted by the president on Supreme Court appointments!

The Reverend's usual cheerful countenance changed to a questioning frown as Katy Jenkins came on the Network newscast he was watching. She was accepting the nomination for president! *What happened?* He scowled to himself. *How come I didn't know about this?*

That Jenkins woman, of all people! That feminist-touting liberal who made a mockery of God-fearing principles—and himself for that matter. She was nuisance enough in the Congress, with her outcries against cooperation of church and state. Preposterous that she would be running for president.

And where did Andy Barker from Pennsylvania fit in? The upstarts from the American Coalition party did themselves proud getting him, but why would he do it? Some unanswered questions here, he thought.

As Jenkins' speech proceeded, Atwood's mood grew darker. His now somber features were invaded by an ugly frown; by the speech's end his whole being was immersed in a smoldering fury.

Sacrilege! This was the very same woman who supported murder in the womb. Intolerable. What did misguided people like her know about steering the nation to the ways of righteousness? And now the likes of Andy Barker, a former governor, was being carried away by her evil influence.

Always before it had been best to avoid her. Now the time for confrontation had arrived. Katy Jenkins could not prevail over this Christian nation.

He would have to undermine her. He knew that knowledge and the ability to organize and persuade provided the key to power. Unknown to the general public, his latest power play involved consolidating the Organization of Southern Christian Ministers to control thousands of individual churches. No more would the churches be allowed to go their own way. A new policy would replace the old policies of self-determination. Church doctrine would be established by the governing body—as it should be.

The church and state together could do so much more to establish the perfect God-fearing Christian nation than either could accomplish alone. The Jenkins woman's philosophy of keeping church and state completely separate would defeat his purpose.

As the Convention went wild after Katy's acceptance speech; drums beating, balloons floating, and people cheering and stomping around like mad, Reverend Thomas Atwood made his resolve. He would fight her openly. He wouldn't allow her to make a dent in the southern states. He also knew that almost any of his parishioners had a skeleton in the closet somewhere. All people were sinners. A headstrong woman like Jenkins, who always defied convention and never stayed in her place as a woman should, must have strayed. President Katy Jenkins? Over his dead body! He would see to it that her sins would catch up with her.

* * *

Katy slept soundly as the door to her room creaked open. The light from the hall was sealed away again as the door was slowly closed. At the first small noise of the latch, Katy's eyes snapped open. At the second, her hand went to the lamp and pushed the switch on.

A man with a camera stood at the foot of her bed looking as startled as a cockroach in the kitchen. The flash unit erupted in a burst of light just as Katy leaped from the bed and enveloped the intruder in a snare of bed clothes. His camera bounced across the carpet. With both feet to his chest, she shoved the struggling man to the floor, stepped over him, picked up his camera, and went for the door. At the balcony rail she peered down into the lobby six stories below and seeing no one there, pitched the camera. When it crashed on the hard surface below, she turned and caught a glimpse of the interloper as he fled down the wide stairs.

Bursting with adrenalin, heart pumping hard against her throat, Katy staggered to the bedside table.

"Intruder in Room 608," she said into the phone. She heard the operator call for security. A man's voice came on the line.

"Are you all right?"

"I'm fine. Never mind that. A sandy haired man, maybe five foot eight, slender build, was in my room. Pass key maybe. He tried to get a picture. Went down the stairs."

"We'll head 'im off."

Katy dialed Room 404.

"Ms. Arnold, I've had a visitor. Some guy got into my room and tried to play Candid Camera."

"Katy! I'll be right up." Then she asked a quick question. "Were you alone?"

"Alone and dressed for beddy-bye."

What a question. It dawned on Katy that someone had seen Andy leave the Ship's Tavern and board the elevator with her on his arm. Andy had escorted her to the door, and said good night with a light kiss. He left via the stairs for his fourth floor room.

One political career and a whole political party could have been scuttled tonight, Katy mused. "Who would do that?"

* * *

Katy awakened the next morning with one thought so pervasive it crowded even the intruder incident out of her mind. What could she do about Ellen Steele? She didn't want an insider like Ellen for an enemy during the entire campaign. She liked Ellen's courage; nothing devious about her; she had convictions and she would fight for them.

She dialed Ellen's room direct. When Ellen came on the line, she said, "Katy here. We have to talk." Ellen hesitated and Katy quickly asked Ellen if she could come up to her room. "It's the only private place around here," she said.

Ellen's response was painfully slow. "I'll come on up...might as well."

"I'll order up some coffee."

"I could use some. Okay, I'll be up shortly."

They sat opposite each other in the two overstuffed arm chairs in Katy's bedroom. Ellen's attitude bordered on the belligerent as she started the serious conversation. "Women are a divided lot, Katy; they're hard to get organized. We've had such a frustrating time so far. We've made progress, of course, but we have so far to go. It seems like we take a big step forward, then two backwards. I had new hope when Margaret Kincaid came up with the American Coalition party. But when she put you up for president, I felt women's issues going by the wayside again."

Katy didn't interrupt. She wanted to hear Ellen out.

"But even if you weren't such a milquetoast about women's causes, I doubt if they'd back you in big numbers. You have about as much chance to win the presidency as you would have to win the New York lottery—without a ticket."

Katy winced, but Ellen didn't seem to notice. "I admit, though, I went overboard talking about withdrawing support by the Movement. We might as well get in what money we can, and get all the mileage possible out of this thing."

Now Katy responded. "Thank you, Ellen. I'm glad for that. But you must remember I'm not running for president of Women's Lib, or Black Lib, or Mens' Lib, or Teenagers' Lib. I'm running for president of the most liberated nation on earth. We're at a turning point all right. We can go for freedom and equality for all, including women and everybody—or we can opt for a government-run society with less and less personal freedom."

Ellen didn't look convinced. "Liberty and justice for all, huh?"

Katy chuckled. "I'm afraid our worst enemy is peoples' indifference. Or, even more sinister, people thinking the government can do everything for them. The government may well be our own worst enemy."

"Maybe so, but if you are going to do anything about it, you gotta' get elected first."

Katy relaxed. "My chances aren't quite as bad as you paint them."

Ellen responded with a grin. "Still not exaggerated. No chance is no chance. And you'll find out that being a woman doesn't help any. But I wish there was a way." Ellen became reflective. "My speaking out was more in frustration than anything else. Women either give politics so little thought they ignore what goes on—or they're so idealistic they can't see what goes on."

"I know some sharp ones."

"Oh, there are some. Arnold is one. And, in her own way, Kincaid. Landsdale is an idealist, but she has political savvy too. I wish they were the rule rather than exceptions. All I'm trying to say is that you can't count on women's political loyalty as a bloc."

"I think I know what you mean." Katy was deliberately non-committal.

"Katy, I was born on the wrong side of the tracks, as they used to say. I had to fight every inch of the way just to survive. I can work with you in this campaign, and God knows I'd like to see a woman become president. That would be a victory!"

Katy felt that her next question to Ellen was critical. "Can you still work with women's organizations as you and I and Harriett discussed?"

"That's the best place for me. Out in the field."

"Okay, then we're back on track. Can you be around most of the day?"

"Sure, I planned on it."

"Okay. Organizational meeting in the Prospector's Room starts at 10:00 after most of the delegates leave. Be about a dozen people altogether."

"Thanks, Katy, for having me up here. You're going to be surprised at what I can do in this campaign."

* * *

The coffee shop and lobby of the hotel replaced the mezzanine as the center of activity on Sunday morning after the Convention. Delegates felt a sense of achievement. They had come together and launched a new political party, and thereby made themselves a part of history.

As the delegates thinned out, the dozen who would now implement the campaign gravitated toward the Prospector's Room upstairs. By ten o'clock they were assembled.

Now Katy was in the leadership role that came so naturally to her. When everyone was seated at the large circular conference table, she started the meeting.

"I've been doing arithmetic," she said. "The fourteen people here today will be making a $480,000 contribution in time and property to the American Coalition party during the next four months. It's as if each of us made out a $35,000 check to the Party. And even if we did that, and had the cash, it would be impossible to buy the talent we have here today. This is a remarkable group.

"Like the warmth from the sunshine, this vast energy will cost the party nothing. Margaret will be the power in New York state, working with Jay Sperling the State Chair. Harriett will coordinate all the state organizations from the office complex she is furnishing in Santa Fe. She will be writing a weekly newsletter, a vital connecting link to every state.

"Ruth assures me that the overriding project of the Women's Movement for the next four months will be to elect a woman president. Think of the grass-roots organization we will have! Ellen will be out in the field working with some forty-two women's groups.

"Madge will be devoting her full time in Texas. The same goes for Lila in California.

"And now I have an especially happy announcement to make. Ms. Arnold has volunteered her services, full-time, to work in our National Headquarters. For lack of a better title, she will be called 'chief-of-staff,' but actually she will be in charge of national PR, publicity, advertising, and finance as well; she will have a full-time accountant helping with campaign finances, recruited from her PR office.

Katy hurried on. "And that isn't all. Andy has hired his former campaign manager in Pennsylvania to run the campaign in his home state—no charge to the party.

"Now, I have a proposal. My Georgetown home would be surprisingly suitable for our National Headquarters. I would like to donate it for the campaign. Some of you have been there. It isn't typical 'Georgetown.' I designed it myself—with a ballroom-size living area, a two-car garage downstairs, and a storeroom same size above it. We can convert it all to office space."

"Terrific!" exclaimed Margaret. "What a boon that will be. How many staff will it accommodate, do you guess?"

"Ms. Arnold and I went over the floor plan, drawn on a paper napkin, and we estimate up to thirty."

"Are you all in favor of the proposal?" Margaret asked. The group chorused an affirmative.

"We're getting organized," Katy said. "Now, let's hear from everyone here, and get ready to upset this election. Andy first. Will you tell us..."

* * *

Sunday morning after Katy Jenkins' nomination, Joe Domino was having a little meeting with the Union heads of Local 861 in Jersey City. There would be a bigger meeting Monday evening when the general membership met at the Union Hall. The subject under discussion was the Women's Movement's million dollar presentation to Katy Jenkins and Andy Barker on the Capitol steps next Friday morning.

"I thought that damned Andy Barker was our friend," growled one of the participants.

"He's a traitor," said another, "from the time he joined up with that crazy woman."

"Well, we know how to deal with traitors," the third participant said. "And it seems like we gotta straighten our Senator out some too. Did you see he wasn't even there to vote for 763 last week. Damn careless of him."

"He'll be here tomorrow evening. Why not bump him around

a little?" asked Joe.

"Good idea," said the first speaker. "I'll set it up."

"Just a little," ordered Joe. "We want to concentrate on what we're going to do on Friday."

"Okay, okay, I don't mean no rough stuff on the Senator. Just a little reminder which side his bread is buttered on. Sure, the woman and the traitor are the first priority."

"What's the plan here, boss?"

12

"What's eatin' Pop?" asked Peter Barnes, the handyman at Big J Feedmills in Caprock City.

Betty Crawford answered from behind her desk that now boasted a computer terminal along with her old adding machine and typewriter. "It's that Baptist preacher from Hereford, Texas. He's been snooping around town all morning. He was up at the courthouse, then he came down here trying to pump me for information."

"Oh him," Peter said. "I don't like him. He was askin' me questions about Johnny, but I didn't tell him nothin'. Didn't know he was a preacher."

"Well, it's hard to tell since he was totin' a briefcase instead of a Bible. When Pop caught him in here trying to butter me up he got mad enough to chew nails and spit them out." Betty looked around. No one was in earshot. "He told him to get the hell out and never come back. The guy slunk out of here like a rooster-bit hound-dog running for cover."

* * *

Jack and Jimmy were at the private plane hangar at Stapleton Field having coffee when Katy arrived. She flew into her brothers' arms. The years hadn't dulled her joy when she saw them; the two men returned her hugs, looking a little embarrassed.

"How's Dad taking it?" asked Katy.

"He thinks you're off your rocker," Jack said.

Katy was startled when someone came up behind her and slapped his hands over her eyes.

"Guess who," a low, vibrant voice asked.

"Johnny!" Katy turned and threw her arms around him. "You jokers," she yelled. "Oh, I'm so glad to see you. You all came for me. Say, who's running the store? Is Big J Enterprises just drying up on the vine?"

"Pop's on the job," said Jimmy.

"So Pop thinks I've gone off the deep end?" Katy asked.

Jimmy grinned. "He'll get over it. Remember when you ran for Governor? He couldn't believe you'd do such a crazy thing, but he backed you all the way. He'll come around."

Johnny piped up. "Sis, we're all so proud of you we're busting our buttons."

"Let's get going," Jack said. "We've got a thermos of coffee in the plane. Mrs. Bayze is waiting for us in Caprock with a 'welcome home rally' for you."

As the Cessna approached Caprock County, in Eastern New Mexico, Katy spotted the hundred mile long limestone escarpment called the caprock. It rose two or three hundred feet above the wastelands below. On top of the geologic formation began the largest plains area in America. The Cessna was closing in on it fast. In the old days the unpaved road at the caprock was steep. There was an element of danger in driving a car down the incline and it was a challenge to drive up. Most cars had to shift to low gear to make it. Nowadays, with the new highway and modern cars, many people drive up or down the three hundred foot rise and never know they have traversed a landmark. The Cessna acknowledged it when the down draught from the southwest winds pouring over the rim bounced it around.

"We just went over the caprock," announced Jack.

"I know. I've been watching it for some time," said Katy, "trying to figure out where New Mexico ends and Texas begins."

"You can't tell from here," Johnny advised, "a fence line is all that marks the boundary. The first cows you see will be ours, sis. I moved them over to the rim yesterday. The grass is a bit better. The caprock place runs clear into Texas; some of our calves will be born in Texas next spring."

When Katy was ten, Pop gave her a heifer calf, of her own choosing, from the white-face Herefords. This was the beginning of her own herd. When Johnny was ten, Katy gave him a half-interest in the herd; the partnership was a success from the beginning; the herd grew over the years to some two hundred head.

"There they are, right down below," exclaimed Johnny.

The vast miles of plains of eastern New Mexico and west Texas were divided into one mile square sections of 640 acres each. Wheat fields and cattle ranches, like a giant checkerboard, stretched as far as the eye could see.

Big country, Katy thought.

Jack piloted the plane around the west side of Caprock City, followed the path of the railroad tracks and flew over the Big J Feed Mills—the signal of their return. He followed the tracks for a couple of miles and then banked off to the left to the airport.

* * *

Pop was relieved to hear the sound of the Cessna's engines, but it surprised him when Alice called shortly after. She asked if he could come by for her when he went out to the airport to pick up the kids, to which he readily agreed. As he pulled the car into the drive, he felt surprise again when he saw she was wearing one of her fanciest summer dresses.

"Gosh, you're all dressed up. You'd think you were goin' out to meet the president of the United States." Realizing that Alice was making this a big occasion, he got out of the car and went around to open her door. As she slid past him, he gave her a quick kiss on the lips.

Pop drove the bronze Cadillac. His pick-up, as much a part of him as his Levi's, stayed parked in the barn this morning. Empty blue sky stretched to the horizon. He absently drummed his fingers on the car's steering wheel.

As the car moved out of the long driveway onto Caprock Road, Alice mentioned that Katy had called from the airport; the boys were servicing the plane at the hangar.

"Good," Pop grunted. "Durn fool kids of mine," Pop swore mildly under his breath. He glanced sidelong at Alice. "I don't ever want more than two Jenkinses flying in that plane together again."

Pop Jenkins controlled just about everything in his world. He had parlayed his parents' homestead into a small empire on the plains of Eastern New Mexico: the Big J Feed Mills and all the related enterprises that bore his brand; cattle, wheat fields, range land, and grain elevators.

After mentioning the phone call, Alice sat back in her seat.

"Roy," she said, "I'd support Katy even if she were running on the dog-catchers' ticket and her platform was equal rights with humans for all dogs."

Pop knew Mom was serious when she called him Roy, but he tried to make light of her comment. "What dog in his right mind would want equal rights with humans?" he asked.

"Roy, Katy is going to ask you for a thirty thousand dollar advance."

"Advance on what? Her chances to be president? This is a hell of a time for her to turn her back on a $135,000 a year job with more benefits than the King of Siam."

"I know, Roy. I don't think she even knows how tough things are in your business right now."

"Hell, not only our business—the damn farm banks are broke. Even the bank I deal with in Dallas is insolvent. If the government wasn't pouring in the money they're borrowing from the Japanese and Germans, they'd all go down the drain."

"I know, Roy, but don't lecture Katy and don't turn her down. Just tell her it may take a little time to work out."

"It damn sure may," growled Pop. Then he brightened, patting Alice on the leg. "All right Mom, I'll take it easy."

"Thanks, Roy."

"One thing about it, Mom, we've never had a dull moment since Katy came along. She'll be so damn glad to see us, and we will her, nothing else matters."

Years ago, when the two oldest brothers first saw their baby sister, the scene wasn't much different. Their dog had been plagued by an infestation of fleas. When Jimmy examined the tiny pink baby in his mother's arms, he gave his approval exclaiming, "...and not a flea on her!" And that, as far as the Jenkins boys were concerned, still held true today. When another baby brother arrived, a sort of postscript, twenty-one years later, the family opened their arms to the endearing child immediately. Although Katy was "off to school" at the University, she visited home often, including weekends and every holiday, after Johnny's arrival.

* * *

When she was eleven, Katy took a hand in Caprock City community affairs. It started on the school grounds at the afternoon recess. Peter Barnes, who must have been fourteen at the time, was a slow learner. He made it to the fourth grade mainly because his teachers passed him to get rid of him. Several of the boys were taunting Petie.

"You can't even read," one of them said.

"I can too read," Peter blurted out, trying unsuccessfully to hold back the tears.

"How much is eight plus nine?" another boy asked.

Petie groped for an answer that didn't come.

"How come you've been in fourth grade for two years?" one jeered.

Katy watched as Petie tried to get away from them. Sympathy for Petie welled up inside her. The guys blocked Petie's escape every way he turned. Katy looked in vain for a teacher. Then one of the bullies dropped to his hands and knees behind Petie; another guy shoved Petie and sent him sprawling into the dirt while the others laughed uproariously.

"You bastards!" Katy spat out the words as she lunged toward Peter, strong-arming a big boy to one side. She helped Petie up. "Out of my way," she said so fiercely that the boys quickly made way for her. She pulled Petie along with her. "You're coming with me."

"I want to go home," Petie choked through his tears.

Katy paused, considering the request. She had seen him have to leave school before—and go home. *What's the use? If I let him go home he'll just be back here tomorrow in the same pickle.*

"I reckon we better talk to my Pop about this," she said as much to herself as to Petie. Instead of walking him home, Katy marched straight for the Big J Feedmill with Petie in tow. Her gentle words made the going easier for him.

Katy saw the surprised look on Pop's face as she led the still reluctant boy into the feed sacking area where Pop was working.

Petie stood a foot taller than Katy.

"Pop," she said, "Peter can't go to school anymore. The boys tease him too much." She squared her shoulders. "We've got to fix him up with something here."

Everybody knew Petie wasn't "quite right." Town folks looked after him. His dad worked long hours at the hardware store; his mother, weighed down with three other children, did the best she could with the boy.

Katy's words rang in Pop's ears. "We've got to fix him up with something here." He turned off the feed grinder and tried to think. He put an arm around Katy, the other around Petie and led them into the office.

"You kids sit down," he said, indicating the two caned back chairs that were hand-me-downs from the house. He picked up the single line phone and dialed Mom.

"I've got a couple of truants here. Katy and Peter...Yes, Peter Barnes." He looked at his self-assured child and then at the nervous Petie. "Katy says Petie can't go to school anymore—boys are ornery to him. She says we've got to fix him up with something here...Good...We'll be waiting for you to get here. I'll give some thought to it in the meanwhile."

Jimmy came in from school and began his sweeping. Katy, restless with waiting, leaped to his side.

"Can we help you?"

Jimmy stared at the pair. Sweeping out the mill after school wasn't exactly his idea of the best way to spend his time.

"Sure. Come on."

Katy jumped up from the chair still clasping Petie's hand and followed Jimmy to the broom closet; they grabbed heavy push-brooms and began sweeping. Jimmy gave Petie the once over, looked at Katy and said, "I won't ask." When Mom Jenkins arrived they were busy sweeping and cleaning.

Mom went directly to the office where Pop was shuffling papers on the only desk at the Big J. After a quick consultation and a phone call to the school principal, they hurried out to the car. Mom called over her shoulder to Jimmy to keep the kids there until they got back.

Peter's mother, and the teacher, met them at the principal's office and discussion began. The consensus: school could do nothing more for Petie. Pop, who had been quiet throughout the discussion spoke up.

"Mrs. Barnes, if it's all right with you and Carl, maybe I could find a place at the feed mill for Peter, perhaps doing clean-up and odd jobs. He wouldn't make much to start, but it would keep him out of mischief."

"You'll do that?" Mrs. Barnes spoke with a tear-choked voice. "God bless you!"

It was quitting time at the mill, and as two or three of the men filed by the office on their way out, they noticed Katy and Petie sweeping.

"What's goin' on here?" one of them asked.

"Petie's my friend," snapped Katy.

Pop overheard the conversation as he came in the door. "Yeah," he drawled, "we're fixing Peter up with a job here. And I'll appreciate everybody's help on this."

*   *   *

Miss Bayze figured the contemporary airport setting was the perfect place for a rally. A modern low-slung building with landscaping outside, an efficient looking ticket counter inside, a lobby with floor level windows facing onto the runway, seats for two dozen people with room for more, self-serve coffee station, and tiled restrooms. Eight, twelve, and sixteen passenger planes serviced such points as Hobbs, Carlsbad and Albuquerque; two commuter flights came in daily—most of the time.

When she took on the County Chair of the American Coalition party two years ago, Miss Bayze never imagined Katy Jenkins, whom she taught to read in the first grade, would be their candidate for president of the United States.

Nothing less than a miracle, she thought. *To think that we're having the very first rally in the nation right here in Caprock!*

*   *   *

"What in tarnation is going on here?" exclaimed Pop as he saw cars parked along both sides of the road for a quarter of a mile before the airport.

"It just may be that your daughter is running for president," said Mom.

"Well, I'll be damned."

Pop was still marveling at the number of cars when he pulled into the loading zone in front of the terminal.

"Park your car right here," said an authoritative young woman who Pop recognized as the head teller at the Sunwest Bank. "We've been holding the space for the candidate's family."

"Thank you," said Mom. Pop murmured another "Well, I'll be damned" as he maneuvered the car to the curb.

The five piece band in front of the terminal struck up "Stars and Stripes Forever."

The lobby was jammed with excited people, mostly women. Katy was circulating through the crowd, shaking hands, calling names. Her excitement and pleasure showed in her every movement. When she saw Mom and Pop, she yelled happily to them; the people nearest her shifted to help her make her way through the crowd. Katy hugged them both at once and escorted them through the mass of people to two seats being held by Jack and Jimmy. Johnny was helping Mrs. Bayze get a small platform into position in front of the panel of red, white, and blue star-studded bunting.

Mrs. Bayze didn't look her seventy-two years. She might have been the dedicated school teacher addressing her first grade class, except now she was white-headed. She was as vibrant as ever; Katy stood to one side and slightly in back of her on the small platform as Mrs. Bayze opened the program. She started it with a question.

"How many of you were at Katy's high school graduation twenty-eight years ago?" Quite a few hands went up throughout the room. Mrs. Bayze continued. "I was there—and as proud as I have ever been of one of my students. You remember? Katy was co-valedictorian of her class. She and Robert White shared the honors. I'm glad to see Robert here today.

"I wrote down the last part of Katy's speech." Mrs. Bayze paused for emphasis. "What she said that night may have been a sort of prelude to the American Coalition party. Let me read what seventeen-year-old Katy said:

" 'It's a man's world out there, but from now on men are going to have to share that world with the other half of the people—the women. Men must share the opportunities, the freedom, the power, the glory, and the honor. Oh, I know women must share the responsibilities, too. I hope we are ready, and that men are ready as well, because humanity is about to take a giant step forward.' "

Mrs. Bayze looked around the room triumphantly. "That same Katy Jenkins is here this morning. Some of you call her Governor. She was. Some of you call her Congresswoman. She is. Do you know what we'll be calling her next? President!

"And now she has a few words for us. Katy Jenkins, American Coalition party candidate for president!"

Katy helped Mrs. Bayze get comfortably seated in the one chair on the platform, looked around the group and spoke in a confidential tone.

"Mrs. Bayze had me worried there for a minute when she asked what you'd be calling me next. I wasn't sure what she was going to say."

The crowd tittered.

"You might be surprised at what all I've been called; some of it I couldn't repeat here."

Katy became serious. "I'm not going to make a speech. It's impossible for me to impress you, knowing me as well as you do. I'm going to pose some questions and I hope you'll give me some answers.

"The first ones are simple. Have women won equality? Do we have equal standing in the marketplace? Are the responsibilities of marriage and homemaking shared equally? I ask you for an answer."

The audience howled, "No to all three!" "No! No! No!"

A look of total perplexity crossed Pop's face as he heard the reaction, but he sat impassive. Mom smiled.

A male voice pierced the room. What he said was intended only for the few men near him, but the discordant note in Robert White's voice was unmistakable and carried throughout the room. "What the hell," he muttered. "Women have the best of both worlds."

Katy's mind whirred with the speed of a computer. She

remembered the graduation night celebrations. The dance in the school gym and the glorious time she had dancing with the fellows. She could hear the music still.

She saved the last dance for Bobby White, of course. She wished it could go on forever, dancing across the gym floor, floating on a cloud with Bobby.

She put his varsity sweater on over her party dress when they arrived at his car. She wore it at school regularly, a bold announcement that they were going steady.

It was after two in the morning when Katy got home, the latest she ever stayed out on a date. Mom waited up. They sat at the kitchen table and talked about the graduation speech, the dance, and what happened after the dance.

"We drove clear out to the caprock and parked," Katy said. Then she added, "Mom, I almost let Bobby go all the way tonight."

"Almost?" Alice Jenkins' breath caught in her throat, but she made the query as casual as she could.

"Don't worry, Mom; I didn't go through with it. All of a sudden I couldn't. Bobby said something about me being all his and I realized that I would be making a commitment I didn't want to make." Katy brightened. "I don't want to live in a white house on a hill just outside Caprock all my life and spend my years having kids and keeping house. I want to be somebody, somebody in my own right."

As Robert's remark penetrated the room, a hush fell on the crowd. They expected a snappy comeback from Katy. She had handled hecklers before.

Only one other person in the room could have known what went through Katy's mind in the seconds that followed his outburst. Mom looked at Katy with loving understanding.

Katy looked pensive, deep in thought. Then she spoke.

"There are men, and even some women, who feel exactly what Robert White just expressed so clearly. And they are as right as rain—according to their own lights." She paused. "And this is what makes the problem so difficult. There is no meanness here. Many men have no greater satisfaction than providing for their wives and families. What these 'best men in the world' don't realize is that their good intentions impose a sort of tyranny on women.

"It's hard to explain." Katy seemed to be at a loss for words.

Robert knew he had transgressed against his first love and reacted with remorse. He rose and cleared his throat. "Katy, I apologize for the disturbance." He paused and said, "Katy, I have to say that I've voted for you every chance I had—and I'll probably be voting for you for president too."

"Thanks, Bob."

No hurrahs. No clapping. The people there seemed to understand that this was personal, between Katy and Bob. Robert sat down and Katy resumed.

"This is only one of many issues we will be exploring in the campaign..."

13

"That was a helluva turnout," commented Pop as the Jenkins family packed into the Cadillac after the rally.

"Sure was," said Jack, "and Katy had them eating out of her hand. Reminds me of when she was running for governor."

"Where to?" asked Pop.

"Our cars are at the feed mill," Jack advised.

"Good," said Katy. "I'd like to go by and say 'hello' to Peter Barnes."

"He'd be mighty disappointed if you didn't."

As they pulled up to the feed mill, Katy's eyes took in the panorama before her. The grain elevators, a dozen high-rise cylinders looking like giant silos, dominated the scene. The highest structures in the county, they towered over the plains like sentinels. The buildings in front, with their loading docks and tentacles reaching out to granaries around them, hummed with activity. The heart of the complex was the business office in the center of the compound. A prominent sign on it said BIG J FEEDMILLS. Smaller signs offered Feed, Seed, Veterinary Supplies, Tanks and Trailers. Trucks, semitrailers, and pick-ups were scattered around the yard in front of the buildings in various stages of loading or unloading. Men wearing levis and wide brimmed hats gathered in small groups to talk about the weather, and wheat, and cows. A Santa Fe switch engine industriously spotted boxcars on the tracks that ran through the complex.

Before they disembarked, Mom made the dinner plans. She counted sixteen people altogether, including six grandchildren. "Seven o'clock," she announced.

"Gloria's coming in, too," Johnny spoke up.

"Wonderful," said Katy, "I'd love to see her again."

"She'll be in on the bus this afternoon. Can she stay up in the guest room with you, sis?"

"Sure, Johnny."

"That will work fine," said Mom enthusiastically. Katy knew Mom was aware that Johnny and Gloria lived together in Albuquerque, but she wouldn't approve of them sharing a room in her home—not until they were married.

* * *

Katy sat in the front seat with Pop, and Johnny and Mom sat in the back seat as they headed out to the home place after the visit to the feed mill. They stopped at the supermarket to pick up a few last minute things. Johnny went into the store with Mom. Katy thought: This is the best chance I'll have to talk to Pop.

She hesitated, "Pop, I need thirty thousand dollars to handle all of my own expenses during the next four months while I'll be campaigning." She paused, but when there was no immediate response, continued. "I could borrow, of course, on the Georgetown house or something, but I'm going to be hard-pressed for time to handle all the details on something like that."

"Do you have to quit your Congress job? Can't you sit on it?" asked Pop.

"I probably could, but I don't want to do that. I'm going to go all-out on this campaign."

"It looks to me like you're burning your bridges behind you."

"Maybe I'll be hitting you up for a job."

"Well, I hope this all works out for you."

"I'll probably sell the Georgetown house after the election. You can't believe how much I can get for it."

Pop had a funny thought: "You won't need it after you move into the White House, huh?" He grinned at the ludicrous idea.

Katy chuckled. "That isn't exactly what I was thinking." Then brightly, "In either event, win or lose, I won't need a house in Georgetown."

Pop sobered, "This isn't the best time in the world for me to come up with thirty thousand dollars; I'm borrowed up to the hilt at the Caprock bank—and my bank in Dallas is being 'consolidated,' so I'm sitting tight with them. This drought is hurting. I don't know for sure where that much cash will come from right now."

Mom and Jimmy came out of the store, Jimmy pushing a grocery cart. Pop wound up the conversation, "Give me a little time, and I'll see what I can work out."

The wheat fields on the three mile drive out to the home place looked fairly good to Katy. Maybe forty bushels to the acre, she thought. The fields were irrigated from deep wells drilled into the giant underground aquifer.

Beyond the irrigated farms, Katy noticed that the dry land farms and range land reflected the severity of the drought. The grass was as brown and devoid of life as a paper sack. The amazing thing was that it still had enough food content to support livestock. *The cows don't look too bad yet*, she thought.

The Jenkins' ranch house sat back from Caprock Road about a quarter mile. The trees surrounding it loomed up like an oasis on the plains. They hid the house from passersby on the road, but the windmill, sheds, corrals and barn extended outside the perimeter of the trees.

The house faced toward Caprock Road, but only strangers used the front entrance. All traffic gravitated to the side entrance where screened doors led into the big kitchen/living area. This room was the true headquarters of the Jenkins family. Mom's spacious kitchen ran across one end. At the other end stood an old fashioned oak roll-top desk that came from the old feed mill office. The telephone had a wall extension in the kitchen area. The living area nestled in between, with deep, comfortable leather chairs and couches facing the fireplace. The expandable dining table fitted comfortably against the wall near the kitchen. The more formally furnished living room was readibly accessible through a door alongside the old roll-top desk. The door was open, adding to the overall air of spaciousness.

As Pop headed for the desk to make a phone call, and Mom and Johnny put away groceries in the kitchen, Katy once again stood in awe as she viewed the George Phippen western paintings on the wall. In oils and watercolors, her cowboy artist friend from Taos, NM and Skull Valley, AZ, had captured the true spirit of the old west. As she studied the roping and round-up scenes, and the saddling of a wild bronc, she marveled at the intensity of the action—the genius of the artist.

Her reverie was broken by Johnny's appearance with her bag from the car. "I'll take it upstairs for you," he said.

"Oh, thank you, Johnny, I'll go up with you." As they topped the stairs, Katy mentioned that they should get their heads together about the herd, what with the drought and all.

"We'll do that," Johnny answered, "but I don't think we have much to worry about. The grass is better over on the caprock place than anywhere." He put the luggage by the second double bed, closest to the full bath. The sloping ceiling of the room was broken by the alcove with bay windows. White chintz curtains rustled in a breeze slipping in from the partially open window. Katy's desk from high school days fitted comfortably in the alcove.

Johnny gave his sister a quick hug as he took off. He bounded down the steps two at a time. "Be right back with Gloria," he yelled from the bottom of the stairs.

Realizing she had some campaign organizing to do, she went downstairs and settled in the swivel chair at the roll-top desk to make some phone calls.

The most urgent call was to Andy Barker. She got him at his family's home in Philadelphia, and gave him a quick report on her welcome at the Caprock airport, and the plans for Albuquerque.

"I'll fly to Philadelphia tomorrow afternoon after the Albuquerque press conference."

"Katy, my parents offered to have you stay here with us. They accepted this whole thing quite gracefully. Nothing planned for Tuesday evening, just your arrival. My brother, Harrison, and his wife want to drop by if you get in early enough."

Katy gave him the flight details. Then she said, "I'm looking forward to meeting your folks and seeing Harrison again."

"You'll like my parents, Katy. And Harrison has been helping out here like you wouldn't believe. Incidentally, you and I are booked up solid for Wednesday and Thursday: a luncheon here on Wednesday, V.I.P.'s, and Harrison has arranged meetings with some of our newspaper and magazine editors in the afternoon; Thursday, all day workshop with the party leaders here. I'll fill you in on details after you get here, I'm still working on it. We have some good talent here."

"Good, good. And remember we have to be in D.C. for the Women's Movement check presentation Friday."

"Right!"

* * *

Maria Romero answered the phone in Albuquerque. "Katy! Wait a minute, Harriett is here; I'll get her on the line, too."

"Hi, Katy, I'm on."

"Harriett! How are you guys doing?"

"Great. Maria is a real pro. The press conference is all set. Ten in the morning—here at the hotel—in the ballroom."

"Harriett and I are a team," chimed Maria. "We will have media from all over the state."

"Hey, your suite is a nice place to stay," said Harriett. "I'm enjoying it. And the headquarters is shaping up. Party volunteers are helping us to get things done."

"I'll try to be there by 8:30, 9:00 at the latest. Jimmy is going to fly me up in the Cessna."

Maria came back on. "Oh, Katy, H.B. was by to see us—loaded with curiosity. But he's still shaking his head."

"I'm glad he came by anyhow. It all sounds great. I'll see you in the morning." Katy liked the press conference format. More give and take than speechmaking, more feedback.

Well, H.B., she thought, *whatever happens, this is more exciting than another run for Congress.*

* * *

Katy enjoyed her call to Dick Donovan. She visualized him sitting in his high-backed captain's chair across from her office—where she had started her law career, and which Dick still kept reserved for her.

She started the conversation with an invitation to the press conference.

"Yes, yes, I know about the press conference. I'll try to get there, but I do have a conflicting appointment." Katy knew Dick wouldn't miss the press conference if he had to cancel every appointment he had for the month.

She asked the question that was uppermost in her mind. "What has H.B. done about a replacement candidate for me?"

Dick warmed to the subject. "The Central Committee has put him out to grass, it looks like. They've already tapped John Stover, but it hasn't been announced yet. They didn't even consult H.B. They have their own fundraisers. Old H.B. isn't saying much of anything, just grins that little mysterious grin of his."

"Have you talked to him today?"

"No, I haven't seen him since the press conference was announced. Don't know if he'll be there or not. But, Katy, you've got some hellaceous boosters in Maria and Harriett. You don't have to worry about your press conference. They'll pack the hall."

"Thanks, Dick. Hope you can make it."

"I will if I can, Katy."

* * *

Clifford King answered the phone in his big study in Santa Fe. "Katy!" he exclaimed, "I'm glad to hear from you. How's it going?"

"I'm off and running," she answered.

He had lots of questions for her. "The meeting last Sunday with the core group in Denver—how did it go?" He drank in the details as Katy filled him in. "Mrs. Bayze's reception at Caprock Airport—how many people were there? Who were they? A banker? What was Pop's attitude?" As soon as Katy answered one question, he had another—eagerly exploring all angles. Fifteen minutes later, he wound up the conversation. "Yes, I know about tomorrow's press conference in Albuquerque. Harriett called me, all excited. I'm driving down. Elizabeth is coming with me; she can't wait to see you."

Clifford sat in quiet meditation for a few minutes after he hung up. *Wish I could tell Katy everything*, he thought, *but it will all come out in due course.* He was glad that the years of keeping secrets from Katy were about over. Not that he hadn't enjoyed his activities. He had. But now there would be new projects, even more exciting. He pushed one button on the telephone; now it automatically placed the phone call to his New York confidant. The adrenalin stirred in his blood as he heard the receptionist put his call through immediately. He had a good report for John today.

* * *

Last, Katy called Mrs. Arnold, who was at her Georgetown home converting it into the National Headquarters.

"How's it going?" Katy asked tentatively.

"Couldn't be better," boomed Mrs. Arnold. "I'll scrounge office equipment and furniture from somewhere. There's an office furniture rental place I know. Meanwhile, the stuff in the garage and storeroom is all being moved into a storage warehouse. Katy, this is going to make a beautiful headquarters. We can have some staff in here next week.

Katy asked the question that concerned her most. "What about the temporary zoning permit?"

"We'll have it Friday night when the Georgetown Council meets. I have it oiled. And a battery of phones will be put in next week."

"Sounds like you are cookin'. We're doing all right here, too. Half the town of Caprock turned out for the 'welcome rally' at the airport. And, I just talked to Harriett and Maria in Albuquerque. They have the New Mexico State Headquarters set up in the two meeting rooms on the east end of the mezzanine at the hotel. The press conference will be at ten in the morning in the main ballroom. After that, I fly straight to Philadelphia to work with Andy and his people for a couple days. Andy and I will be in Washington Thursday night to prepare for the million dollar check presentation Friday."

"Good! I was over to the Movement headquarters this morning and they are all set to make a big affair of the check presentation."

* * *

Phone calls finished, Katy was glad to see Jimmy come in. She wanted to ask him about something that was on her mind. Jimmy plopped down on the couch nearest her. She wheeled the swivel chair around to face him.

"Jimmy, how are things, really, at the Big J?"

"Sis, there's an ill-wind a' blowin'. No question about that. But, if the county dries up and blows away, the Jenkins will still be here, scratching out a living and helping everyone in sight. The only reason we're borrowed up at the bank right now is that Pop and Jack have been selling a lot of seed and feed on credit."

"You mean they're selling all comers?"

"Oh, No! You know Pop. He likes the good operators—good farmers, good stockmen. He hates speculators with a passion. Won't advance them anything."

"I hope the Big J isn't getting in too deep."

"Don't worry, Jack and Pop know who to go with. When it rains again, and it always has, we'll be awash in cash flow. Right now it's tight as hell. Pop is sweatin' it."

Mom's voice came from the kitchen. "Jimmy, you want to drive me on an errand?"

"Sure, Mom."

As Jimmy left, Katy sat pensively. Maybe she had gotten carried away offering her Georgetown home gratis, and giving up her job in the Congress. It all seemed so right in Denver. On the flight to Caprock, she had figured out how much she would need for operating capital. That hadn't been of much concern then, but obviously Pop was hurting. She could borrow the money at her bank in Albuquerque, but that was Sunwest, too, same as Pop's bank at Caprock; they might question it now—especially since she would soon be out of a job. This was a new problem: no income. Her bank in Washington might take a dim view as well. I can cash some of my Certificates of Deposit. Lose some interest. That would solve the problem temporarily. But there aren't thirty-thousand dollars worth of CD's.

Johnny came in with Gloria, and Katy dismissed the financial problem from her mind.

* * *

Katy lost herself in the family dinner. Sixteen family members and Gloria. Five grandchildren, assorted sizes and sexes, all very important to themselves and to Katy. Political talk was subordinated to family and the drought, which hung over Eastern New Mexico like a pall.

Two-year-old Patsy Jenkins, Jack and Peggy's youngest, unknowingly brought politics into the conversation. "Patsy reminds me so much of Katy when she was that age," commented Mom. "Katy, you know what your great-grandmother said about you? You were the light of her life the last few years she lived. You walked before you were a year old. I take that back. You didn't walk, you ran, with your rear bobbing up and down like a jumping jack. Your great-grandmother was a pioneer woman. Women couldn't vote then. But your great-grandmother Nicholas picked you up and said to me, "Alice, some day this little one is going to be president."

Gloria responded. "And, sure enough, she is. Elected in November. Inaugurated in January. And, I want to hear the State of the Union address. Everyone will be there listening to Katy lay it out; the House, the Senate, the Supreme Court, everybody that runs the country. Katy will be the president and Andy Barker the vice president. I want to sit on the front row of the Gallery, and see it all.

"I'll reserve your seat right away," laughed Katy.

Johnny put his arm around Gloria, and pulled her close. "And me right next to her," he said.

* * *

At six o'clock the next morning, Pop was driving Katy and Jimmy to the airport.

"Katy, I don't want to make more out of this than it is," Pop said, "but something happened here yesterday that I didn't like."

"What was that?" Katy asked, wondering what would cause Pop concern.

"Well, that new preacher over at the First Baptist Church in Hereford was snooping around in Caprock. May not mean a thing; it's only an hour's drive from Hereford to Caprock. But, it seemed like more than idle curiosity the way he was poking around in the County Courthouse and asking questions. Even had the brass to stick his big nose in the feedmill."

"What did he want at the courthouse?" Katy asked.

"He was trying to find Johnny's birth certificate. Of course, it wasn't there. Johnny wasn't born in this county."

Katy caught her breath. Why would a Baptist preacher from Hereford be so interested?

"Who is he?" asked Katy.

"I don't know that much about him. I heard him preach over here once: hell fire and damnation, and pass the hat. He's been over there about a year. Has a southern drawl. He came from Birmingham, Alabama."

Katy filed that last bit of information away for future reference.

* * *

It was a beautiful morning for flying. The Cessna 414 took off with ease and power to spare. Jimmy took it up to 9,000 feet, headed due west, and leveled off.

"This is for you," he handed Katy an envelope.

Filled with curiosity, Katy opened it. Out fell a cashier's check issued by the Caprock County Savings and Loan Association. It was for $30,000.

"Jimmy! What in the world?"

"I took Mom over to the Savings and Loan yesterday afternoon. Remember, right after you and I talked?"

"Yes, I remember. I wondered where she was going; she didn't say a thing."

"Well, I have a message for you from Mom." Jimmy paused for emphasis. "She says this isn't a loan. It's a gift to you. It was her private stash. When Grandma Nicholas's homestead was sold after her death, it didn't bring that much, but Mom put it in the Savings and Loan and it has been compounding ever since."

"And Mom drew it out for me." Katy said in a hushed voice.

"And never was any happier about anything in her life."

14

The hum of the Cessna as it slipped through the air above New Mexico's landscape put Katy in an easy mood. She took over piloting the plane about an hour out of Caprock City, flying without effort, immersed in her own thoughts. Jimmy watched the landscape below.

"Want me to take over now?" he asked. "That's the Manzanos straight ahead."

"Jimmy," she said, suddenly aware of him. "Yes, please do." As he took control she added, "Gosh, the time flew by. I'm afraid I haven't been very good company."

"I could see you were thinking, sis."

Jimmy scanned the instrument panel and the rapidly changing landscape below. The plains gave way to mountain ranges running north and south.

Katy watched Jimmy's long, slender fingers skillfully handling the controls. *He is the gentle one of my brothers, takes after Mom.*

Albuquerque spread out for miles along the Rio Grande and across the valley from the mountains on the east to the mesas on the west. Its beauty never failed to thrill her.

As they crossed the Manzano Mountains, however, she studied the land, and saw something other than beauty. The most destructive bombs on earth rested in the bowels of the mountain below her. Security fences and roads leading to a tunnel into the mountain marked the spot of their residence. A shudder ran through her at the thought of the danger to all humanity.

She gripped the armrests as terrifying thoughts washed through her brain. Less than 30 minutes away, although thousands of miles distant, are enough of the same type bombs, aimed at

Albuquerque and hundreds of other U.S. targets, to decimate America. A hundred million people could be killed, maimed, or poisoned by radiation. At any time! Our country would be in its death throes, in agony, within the time it will take us to get to the hotel today. And we have no defense, none at all. We must remember that the bombs are still there—no less threatening than before the breakup of the Soviet Union.

Her usual good humor began to assert itself. *There's nothing between us and the Russian bombs but a barbed wire fence—and it's down.*

"What's the matter, Katy? We're okay. The mountain turbulence is always worse in the summertime. We have clearance to land straight away."

"Oh, I'm sorry. I wasn't thinking about the plane. My mind was half-way around the world."

He looked at her, wondering, then set about the business of landing.

I've got to convince the American people that we must be able to defend ourselves against missiles, thought Katy. *If I don't do anything else, this campaign is going to make that possible.*

"Good landing, Jimmy," she said as the plane settled down gently on the runway.

* * *

Manuel Garcia stood a discreet distance in back of Harriett Landsdale as she welcomed Katy. He was proud to be there and to have Katy's Cadillac sparkling clean, ready for her arrival.

He observed the welcome, and Katy's introduction of Jimmy to Harriett. Then they turned toward him.

"Manuel!" Katy exclaimed. "Como estás?"

Manuel advanced to take Katy's hand. "Muy bien, gracias, and how is my candidate?"

"Good, Manuel, muy bueno. You know Jimmy don't you?"

"Si—yes, we are acquainted from an earlier trip." He extended his hand and it was accepted warmly in Jimmy's.

"Vamos?" Manuel asked.

"Vamanos!" said Katy. "Let's go."

The women began a high energy conversation. Jimmy got into the front seat beside Manuel.

"I understand you've had plenty of rain in Albuquerque," commented Jimmy.

"Albuquerque has been like a mountain village—showers everyday, sometimes twice. I've lived here all my life and have never seen anything like it."

"Wish you'd send some down our way."

The backseat conversation ran non-stop while Manuel and Jimmy continued chatting.

Manuel observed, "These are important times when our congresslady runs for president." He paused. "The candidate today; next I'll be driving the president."

* * *

Katy exchanged her usual happy greetings as she made her way through the lobby of La Posada. She was filled with anticipation as she and Harriett went up to the mezzanine to see the New Mexico campaign headquarters for the first time. Maria Romero showed her around, jubilantly pointing out the changes. The meeting rooms at the east end of the mezzanine were converted to working units with desks. A technician was busy installing the telephones. At the north end was a private room that held a big conference table. From these quarters the campaign to carry New Mexico would be waged. Maria introduced Katy to several volunteers who had helped with the preparations for the press conference.

As soon as she could, Katy broke away to her own suite. She locked the door behind her, switched on a floor lamp and pulled open the curtain to the patio. It was good to be home. Was it possible that Margaret's call came only ten days ago? It seemed as though ages had passed, so much had happened.

Katy kicked off her clothes with abandon, searched through the wardrobe and found a creamy white linen suit that would look perfect with her turquoise batik silk scarf. She laid it out on the bed and headed for the shower.

A knock came at the door. Still dressing, Katy glanced at the clock. Thirty minutes until press conference time. She opened the door a crack, enough to identify her cousin, Elizabeth, then opened it wide enough to let her in.

"Oh, Katy, you can't believe how excited we all are," exclaimed Elizabeth. "Anybody else would be scared to death, but you look great. And Dad says that Jack, Jimmy, and Johnny all flew up to Denver to get you. Funny thing about Dad, in all the years he's been in politics, I've never seen him as excited about anything."

Elizabeth's non-stop conversation slowed down just long enough for Katy to slip in a word. "Honey, it's good to see you. And I can't wait to see Uncle Cliff. Hope we have time to talk before I take off. I'm flying to Philadelphia this afternoon to join Andy."

"Oh. Dad is getting a table set up in the dining room downstairs for a dozen or so of us for lunch."

"Good!"

"Katy, what is Andy Barker like? From what I see on TV he looks like a dreamboat."

"He's a nice guy."

"Is that all?"

"Elizabeth, don't be getting any romantic notions about us."

"Wouldn't that be something? A woman president and her husband vice president." She paused. "Dad thinks you may be able to pull it off. The election, I mean."

"It's super to have him so upbeat, but that would be a miracle and Uncle Cliff knows it." She finished her make-up with a bit of blush, added a touch more lipstick and finally brushed her hair in place. "I'm ready to face the nation."

* * *

The press conference was set up in the ballroom off the mezzanine opposite Katy's suite. Parquet floors glistened in the cheerful morning sunlight that fell through curtained windows on the east wall. Hammered tin chandeliers furnished additional light, enhancing the overall southwestern ambiance. An area was roped off for the press corps at one end of the room. A couple hundred stack chairs, set up for spectators, were mostly filled when Katy arrived. Other people were standing in small groups around the perimeter.

Katy proceeded directly to the press section, greeting friends and shaking hands with television crews.

Katy greeted the group, "Welcome! It's good to be in Albuquerque! And it's especially nice to see so many of my old friends here."

Tom Clarke of the Santa Fe New Mexican posed the first question. Tom was an old friend; he and Steve had worked on the New Mexican together. "My question has two parts," he said. "First...your chances to have been re-elected to the Congress were reported about ninety-eight percent positive. Your chance to be elected president seem about ninety-eight percent negative. Why are you willing to go against such odds?"

Katy needed little time to think about this one.

"Any gambler would say that I should have my head examined." The audience laughed. "Some of the biggest decisions we make in life, however, come not from the head but from the heart. I feel very strongly about the issues confronting this nation, and I feel that I can get a broader hearing, and be more effective, running for president than sitting in Congress."

Clark seemed satisfied. "Now the balance of my question is this: do you feel that you are doing right by your party and the state of New Mexico?"

This question was a bit more loaded, but Katy decided on a light answer. "Oh, I think the party, and the state, and the Congress, too, will survive. I'd like to think they'd miss me some though." Again the audience responded warmly.

Katy recognized Sam Dunn, Albuquerque Journal political reporter.

"Running for the highest office in the land is quite a responsibility. Do you think the nation is ready for a woman president?"

Katy liked the question. It opened a gate for her. She took her time. "Israel was ready for Golda Meir. England was ready for Margaret Thatcher. Others come to mind: Indira Gandhi, Corazon Aquino. Yes, I think we are ready for a woman president. And this year, for the first time in memory, Americans will have the chance to elect a woman president."

Bud Reilly of the Albuquerque Tribune was on his feet. His

weekly column brimmed with the most controversial issues.

"Bud Reilly," Katy said.

"The majority of your campaign support seems to be coming from the Women's Movement. Are you taking their stand on the abortion issue?"

"I'm pro-choice." She was deliberate. "There are just too many times when a woman has no other way out. It's hard to comprehend a woman's desperation at these times. They become severely depressed, even suicidal. Everything on earth is against their having a baby. They may not be able to support or care for a baby. Or their husbands or boyfriends may refuse the responsibility of a child. There are many reasons."

"Don't you realize there are alternatives?"

"Yes. Adoption, for example, solves a few cases. But, not many. Most women who would seek an abortion would not carry a baby to term. They would get an abortion, legal or not."

"Do you think women are entitled to do that?"

"It takes two to tango," Katy said easily, "but only one gets pregnant. She bears the burden; it has to be her choice."

She continued. "An unwanted pregnancy can be horribly traumatic. Let me give you just one example. In my hometown, Caprock City, some years ago, a family moved into a little two bedroom home: man, wife, and three children aged from two to six. The father was working in the wheat harvest. The mother took good care of her kids. She kept them in clean clothes even though she used a scrub board to wash and a clothes line to dry.

"Then, the doctor told her that she was pregnant again. She couldn't take it. She went from anger to depression to hopelessness. A couple mornings later she gave her little ones breakfast, dressed them in clean clothes, and sent them outside to play. Then she locked the doors, and turned on the gas oven without lighting it. Neighbors realized something was wrong when the kids were crying to get into the house. Their mother was discovered when someone pushed in the door. This is the reality of how desperate a woman can become. Fortunately, this story has a happy ending. The mother was revived; the natural gas hadn't been lethal. Ironically the doctor had made a mistake, and she wasn't pregnant after all. But you can see what an unwanted pregnancy can drive a woman to do. More about this subject later. Keep tuned."

Reilly nodded and sat down as Katy called on Ollie Brown from the Farmington Times.

"This is a different subject. Would you as president, let OPEC control oil prices as they have done in the past?"

Katy warmed to the subject. "Not if there was anything I could do about it! That was an ugly thing—it destroyed competition, distorted the economy, and hurt consumers. I'd use strong measures to forestall another OPEC crisis. We don't need any more economic problems."

"That's what I wanted to hear," said Ollie as he sat down.

A youth, perhaps eighteen or twenty, had stood for some time. Katy recalled seeing a name on the press list from the University of New Mexico newspaper.

"You're from the Lobo?" she asked as she recognized him.

"Yes, I'm George Caplin, Lobo staff. I'm working on a profile of you for a future edition—you know...a former student running for president of the United States. We keep hearing about an affair between you and a man who now heads a multi-national corporation. Would you enlighten us on this romance."

Katy's heart raced. Her breathing became faster. She tried to look casual. "It was a 'romance' all right. Lasted one short summer. Everybody dated a lot. I'll bet you're doing the same. I hope you're not one of those fellows who kiss and tell."

Onlookers tittered, but Caplin was not abashed. "Just one more question," Caplin insisted. "Isn't your younger brother, now a UNM student, driving the same Jaguar—restored, of course—that you drove twenty-eight years ago while at the University?"

"You're right. The car sat in a shed at Caprock for many years. Our uncle, Clifford King, restored it as a high school graduation gift for Johnny. Uncle Clifford is in the audience. I'm quite certain he'd be glad to talk with you about the car."

"Thanks, and the Lobo staff sends best wishes for a winning campaign."

I'm glad that line of questioning didn't go any further; Uncle Cliff will know how to handle Caplin. The next question interrupted her thoughts.

"Who's going to take your place as Congressional candidate?"

Katy couldn't tell who asked the question, but she welcomed it. "I won't be able to submit my resignation to the Congress until next week. As you know, they're in recess for the Democratic National Convention. After my resignation is accepted the state's Republican Central Committee will announce a candidate. It's up to them to pick the nominee."

Other questions and answers followed in rapid fire, until Katy was asked about her stand on the Strategic Defense Initiative. Her answer began simply enough. "My stand is the same it has been during my eight years in the Congress. We must develop a defense against incoming missiles. You will hear much more about this from me as the campaign progresses. But, I do want to say we're doing much better than many people realize. And so much of it is happening right here in New Mexico."

There were more questions on this subject, all of which Katy fielded with more clarity than the reporters and spectators had heard before from a candidate.

When the press conference was officially over, Katy took questions from the spectators. Her enthusiasm about the American Coalition party inspired discussions. Katy concluded the session by asking everyone for their votes.

Went well, Katy thought as the conference drew to a close.

"Katy, you showed them you are presidential," enthused Harriett Landsdale. Maria Romero's face reflected adulation as she pressed Katy's hand and said, "You were great." Neither could have guessed the apprehension Katy felt as she noticed George Caplin in an animated conversation with Clifford.

* * *

Katy had seen H.B. McGee come in just as the press conference was getting under way. He stood at the back, exchanged greetings with a couple near him and watched the proceedings impassively. Now she headed straight for him.

"You did all right," was all H.B. said.

"Thank you, H.B. I'm glad you came."

An awkward silence stood between them for a moment. Katy pierced it with an invitation. "Uncle Cliff is getting a few people together for lunch here in the dining room. Care to join us?"

"Better not, Katy. I've got a one o'clock appointment in Santa
Fe. Thanks anyhow."

Uncle Cliff, with Elizabeth on his arm, stopped to shake hands
with H.B. and said in an aside to Katy, "Caplin wants to get
together with us for a minute."

Katy accepted Elizabeth's warm hug and encouraging remarks,
and asked her to come along and see the campaign headquarters.
"I want you to meet some of the party's workers." Katy moved
with the group out onto the mezzanine, but H.B. excused himself
with a lukewarm, "Be seeing you."

Katy felt a twinge of remorse. She missed having H.B. on her
side, his support and never-ending good humor and enthusiasm.
She was aware, too, that many of her supporters of the past were
conspicuous by their absence today. And some of those who were
present appeared to have tongue in cheek. Much of the press was
second-string, too. Of course, quite a few of them were at the
Democratic National Convention. But the camaraderie of the old
times was somehow missing without H.B.

Press corps and onlookers dispersed rapidly. Katy saw Caplin
waiting in the conference room, the most private place around. I
had better see him, and get it over with, she thought. She excused
herself from Elizabeth and the others, and joined Clifford to go
talk to Caplin.

* * *

George Caplin had no official capacity at the New Mexico
University Lobo newspaper. In fact, he was only a part-time
student. He had submitted some stories and "Letters to the Editor"
which were printed because his offbeat approach appealed to the
editor; he also submitted photographs from time to time, some of
which were used because they, too, were "far out." He received
nominal payment for his submissions.

Katy noticed that he was small, wiry, aggressive, and had a
new Nikon camera. She couldn't shake the feeling that she had
seen this young man before.

"Miss Jenkins, I saved this question for you in private," he
began, "because I think you would prefer it."

"What's on you mind, son?" Clifford asked.

"My question is to Miss Jenkins," Caplin came back quickly. "No use beating around the bush about it. Isn't it true, Miss Jenkins, that Johnny Jenkins is your illegitimate son, and that you have kept it secret all these years?"

"Mr. Caplin, that would be an ugly rumor to get around," Katy snapped. "I hope you will drop it." Then she added, "Just like you dropped your camera when you broke into my hotel room in Denver."

"What?" Now Caplin was on the defensive.

"The Denver police have your fingerprints. If you ever so much as mention that crazy idea again, you will be in serious trouble."

Caplin reddened. "Well! It's a closed case as far as I'm concerned." He grabbed his camera, scooted through the door, and disappeared down the steps.

Katy watched him go with an uneasy feeling that it wasn't a 'closed case' at all.

15

No one accompanied Andy to Philadelphia International Airport where he picked up Katy. However, he had alerted two of his friends, a reporter and a cameraman from the Philadelphia Enquirer.

Andy resolved to be on his very best behavior. But when he saw Katy coming into the reception area, approaching with the fluid grace of an alerted deer, he threw caution to the wind, bounded over to meet her and planted a kiss on her cheek. The cameraman had positioned himself perfectly to record the occasion for the morning edition.

"Oh boy," said the reporter as he watched Andy. "That picture has possibilities: Warm greeting for presidential candidate—Liberal and Conservative get together to make a new chapter for history books."

Katy returned Andy's warmth with a radiant smile. He took her one small bag and introduced her to the two journalists. Then she and Andy were off to the parking structure. Andy's bright red Corvette was easy to spot. The car seemed to match his attire of slacks and flashy sport coat. Not very vice-presidential, Katy thought, but not without a cavalier appeal.

"Tell me about Pennsylvania," Katy said as they pulled out of the parking structrue. "How are the political winds blowing? Do we have a chance in Pennsylvania?"

"Katy, the AFL and CIO were birthed in Pennsylvania. This may be the peace-loving Quaker country, but it is John L. Lewis fighting country, too. Now, I'll ask you a question: do you think you can win over labor?"

"You mean win them over to our side, or win over

them—without them?"

"Take it either way, and we still have a problem."

"I'd like to talk to them. One on one. This may surprise you, Andy, but I'm not anti-labor. In fact I think AFL-CIO are quite progressive. I am against labor racketeering."

"Katy, these people don't think like you do. They think with their hearts and prejudices. Most of the time, their minds are already made up about any given subject. They react almost by instinct, you might say."

"That isn't too different from people everywhere. Sometimes you wonder why so much money is spent on political campaigns. But, the basic question is: do you think we have a chance in the state?"

"You know I got thrown out in my try for reelection as governor. But, almost half the people voted for me. We'll get some votes. That's all I can guarantee at this time."

"That makes sense."

Katy knew Andy risked as much as she. The problems in Pennsylvania might be insurmountable. Andy needs to win one in his home state, she thought.

Andy guided the Corvette beyond the urban sprawl into the rolling green hills and wooded areas of Bucks County. Suddenly he braked and veered into a long private drive to the Barker family home. Maples and oaks pushed to the edge of the road on both sides. Katy gasped as the home came in view.

Once before in her lifetime, the sheer size and grandeur of a home had overwhelmed her. That was twenty-eight years ago when she hired a car in New York and drove to Long Island. She was alone then and scared. She never saw the inside of the Van Dorn home. Such was her hurry to get out of there that she tried to turn the car around too sharply and killed the motor. A gardener solicitiously inquired if he could be of help; but she managed to get the car started, uttered a quick "thank you anyhow," and drove away as fast as she could.

The mansion looming in front of her reminded her of Monticello in Virginia, Thomas Jefferson's masterpiece of American colonial architecture. "It's beautiful!" she exclaimed.

"Third generation Barkers," Andy commented, "built in 1844, and maintained like a jewel. The west wing was added a mere forty years ago, after my parents were married. The guest rooms upstairs, where you will be staying, are part of the original structure." Changing the subject he added, "The first event for the American Coalition party in Pennsylvania will be a reception-luncheon tomorrow, on the veranda. You can't see it from here, but we can accommodate a hundred and fifty people out there, and it will be packed. I'm sure some of them are coming out of curiosity to see you; but many are really interested in our campaign. Mother and Dad will help host it. Nothing formal about it, except we will have a receiving line so everyone can meet you right away."

"Andy, it sounds wonderful!"

"Nothing scheduled for this evening, except Harrison and his wife, and their teenager, Beverly, will be coming for dinner. You're going to love Beverly. She wants to be a big political personality like you," he said teasingly.

Katy loved all the Barkers. Mrs. Barker was a gracious hostess. Mr. Barker, at seventy-one, was still a power in the publishing business. The signed editorials and features he contributed to the newspapers from time to time derived their broad readership from his hard-hitting, straightforward approach. Shortly after meeting Katy, he had her to one side, telling her the one about the Episcopalian, Catholic, and Jew who arrived at the pearly gates at the same time...

Harrison came to dinner without his wife; she had a meeting to attend; Katy would meet her at the reception. Beverly came in bubbling. Sixteen or seventeen, outgoing and personable, she had a hug and kiss for each of her grandparents, then turned to Katy. "Dad and Uncle Andy have been telling me all about you!" she exclaimed. "I'm so happy to meet you in person."

"I've heard about you, too." Katy extended her hand to Beverly. "We'll talk," she said and winked conspiratorily.

Harrison advanced and greeted Katy like an old friend. "It's nice to have you here."

Dinner was served by a primly aproned woman in a small sunroom extending off the kitchen onto the terrace, with casualness fitting the occasion. She poured chilled white California Chardonnay when her charges were seated. The menu was designed for the hot weather, cold poached salmon flanked by asparagus, and a lightly dressed salad.

The sunroom windows overlooked a clear area surrounded by woodlands; the view made Katy feel as though she was miles away from civilization. Lightning flashed in the clouds above the trees. Katy wondered aloud why there was no thunder.

"That's what we call heat lightning," Beverly advised her. "It stays right in the clouds giving them the lovely gold color, and no thunder."

"It's beautiful," said Katy, "gentler than our thunderstorms in New Mexico."

The conversation turned to Beverly and her plans. "Uncle Andy, can I work in the campaign for you and Katy?" she asked.

"Well, I don't see why not." He looked at Harrison for affirmation and continued, "We're going to have a state campaign headquarters at the Penn Plaza. We need all the help we can get."

"I can start tomorrow."

"How about the next day? We're having the reception here tomorrow, then moving the action downtown."

"Sign me on," Beverly said.

Harrison introduced the next round of conversation. "Guess who was in to see me today?" He continued without waiting for an answer. "Johnny. I hadn't seen him for months."

"You mean Johnny Van Dorn?" asked Mr. Barker.

"Who else? And he looks good."

"I haven't seen Johnny since Stephanie's funeral. Almost two years now. I'd like to see him again."

Mrs. Barker caught the startled, questioning expression on Katy's face and hastened to explain. "Goes back in time. Harrison and John were boyhood pals. This is the only household left that still refers to them as 'Harry' and 'Johnny,' I'd guess."

Katy watched as the gold-colored heat lightning flashed in the clouds with greater intensity while Mr. Barker pursued the subject of John Van Dorn.

"Johnny's done all right with LAND & SEA. He's lived up to all his grandfather's expectations. I knew the old man well in his later years. Not only a business genius, but a square shooter. Always ahead of his time. Made LAND & SEA an international company when the United States was still treated like a colony.

Katy, as you know, they used to say 'the sun never sets on the British Empire.' Britain controlled the commerce of the world. But Johnny's grandad carved a notch in it."

Harrison cut in. "John seemed interested in Katy's and Andy's present undertaking."

"You don't say!" exclaimed Mr. Barker. "Never knew Johnny took an interest in politics. But, he can afford to do anything he wants to. His grandad gave him a hundred thousand dollars when he was just fourteen. No trust or anything. Just turned it over to him: stocks, bonds, cash. That would be the equivalent of a million dollars today. Turned it over to a fourteen year old boy! His dad had to sign papers for him; but he managed it himself. No telling how much his personal funds are now, even though he's a bit of a philanthropist."

Katy felt Harrison's eyes on her. Fortunately Mr. Barker's discussion had given her time to adjust to the new development. Her annoucement was almost casual. "I went around some with John Van Dorn when he was down in Albuquerque at the University. But I didn't know he was rich. Or that he would become a worldwide business tycoon. He was just a nice guy having fun then."

Harrison shot a quick glance at Katy. Mr. Barker was startled by Katy's information. "You knew our Johnny? It is a small world! I remember now. He was in New Mexico when his father had the heart attack. He barely made it home before his dad died."

Mrs. Barker interrupted the conversation. "Why don't we move into the library for coffee?"

Katy had glimpsed the library when she was shown to her room earlier. Now she entered the spacious high-ceilinged room which served as the central living place. Massive windows high on the north wall provided subdued natural light without affecting privacy. Stacks of books reached to the ceiling on the inside walls. A moveable ladder made the higher stacks accessible. The flowered-fabric sofas on each side of the stone fireplace were set off nicely by the warm paneled walls of the room.

As they grouped themselves around the heavy glass-topped coffee table, Katy noticed the conference table with its dozen overstuffed arm chairs at the far end of the room. It was flanked by a massive dull-lighted world globe in one corner, and an unabridged dictionary on a pedestal opposite. Katy relaxed as she sat chatting and drinking coffee. A stained glass and cherrywood hutch caught her attention. Noticing her interest, Andy explained that it was brought by his grandmother from Oxford after his grandfather finished his Rhodes Scholarship.

An overwhelming sense of wonder enveloped Katy as she thought of John Van Dorn being a part of this new world she was discovering.

* * *

"We've been sabotaged," Ms. Arnold said as she slammed her fist on the desk. Katy listened quietly on the telephone in the Barker library as Ms. Arnold explained what happened.

"The District of Columbia Authority canceled the permit for our million dollar check presentation. Something about its 'strictly political nature' disturbs them. Hell, they've permitted plenty of political gatherings on the Capitol steps."

"What do you suppose happened?" Katy questioned.

"I don't know for sure. I can't get a handle on this. Anyhow, the ceremony is moved to the park across from the White House and it can't be on Friday. It has to be Saturday morning. Tour buses are the only action in D.C. on a summertime Saturday morning. And who is going to be home watching T.V.?"

"Must we still have a public ceremony?" Katy asked. "I don't like being maneuvered into a corner."

"I don't think it's that serious. The Women's Movement needs the coverage for their internal campaign. Ruth wants to go through with it. They have people coming from all over."

"I'll sleep better when we have the money in the bank," Katy said. "Go ahead."

"Yes, and maybe it's just as well the media coverage will be skimpy. We don't want to get the image of being just a 'womens' party. But I have some arrangements to rework.

"Good luck. We'll see you Friday."

* * *

The Penn Plaza complex, built in downtown Philadelphia under the code requiring no buildings to be higher than William Penn's giant statue on the square, provided a major hotel, shopping, restaurants, offices, and served as a central meeting place for Philadelphians and their visitors.

After the highly successful reception-luncheon, followed by enlightening conferences with editors and publishers of various Barker publications, Katy and Andy looked forward to the task of mobilizing the Pennsylvania campaign.

They arrived with Beverly at the Penn Plaza Hotel lobby at 10:00 A.M. Thursday. Katy would see the state headquarters, have lunch with key people, followed by an organizational meeting in the afternoon. And, in the evening, a public rally at the Civic Center. Good advance publicity assured a crowd. A contingent of University students would be there. Andy's arrangements have been outstanding, thought Katy.

"What's goin' on here?" The question burst from Beverly as the trio entered the lobby.

"I don't know," answered Katy. "But it must be something special. Lots of media here, three T.V. cameras that I can see."

"Nothing like this scheduled for us," Andy said.

"I'll find out," Beverly said. She wormed her way through the crowd and questioned a couple of official looking people in the area of the microphones. She reappeared shortly and advised Katy and Andy that the president of the Pennsylvania Right-to-Life Foundation was going to make a statement on the decision handed down yesterday by the State Supreme Court that further weakened Roe vs. Wade. "He's a creep," Beverly added.

"Let's see what he has to say," Katy suggested. An officious looking woman, whom Andy knew well as an activist in the fight against strip-mining coal and other causes that would put her in the limelight, introduced the president of the Foundation.

The bespectacled, gaunt man, who appeared at the microphone didn't match the description in his introduction—until he began to speak. He spoke with intensity and conviction. Must be a preacher, thought Katy. His message was stern. He heralded the Court decision briefly, then declared that the people of Pennsylvania must act. His moral indignation was aimed at the moderates and the ambivalents who wouldn't stand up and be counted for God. "There can be no compromise with God's word," he said with finality.

Katy nudged Andy. "Let's get out of here."

"Wait a minute. Isn't that the Reverend Thomas Atwood making his way toward the microphones?" Andy asked. Smiling congenially, shaking hands with everyone he could reach, Reverend Atwood pushed toward the podium.

What a pompous ass, thought Katy. I wouldn't trust him any more than I'd trust a pickpocket in a crowded subway. She chuckled to herself. The near collisions she had with Atwood never resulted in any great harm to her.

Suddenly, there was an arm under her elbow guiding her toward the bank of microphones. "They want to hear from you," said the voice connected to the body pushing her forward. Katy was startled, but when she recognized Michael Richards, NBC's Philadelphia correspondent, she went along. Richards maneuvered to block Atwood's approach and gently shoved Katy in front of the mikes. The "emcee" quickly introduced her. "Katy Jenkins, Congresswoman from New Mexico, now running for president on the American Coalition party ticket."

Katy took the situation in hand. Sharp shadows sprang up around her as the camera lights flicked on. Questions came at her from all corners. Video cameras whirred. Katy motioned for silence. "I'm so happy to be here in your beautiful state with Governor Andy Barker." Beverly started the applause and it spread uneasily across the room. Andy waved cordially as many eyes turned his way. Then everyone's attention turned to Katy.

"And, I'm happy to have this unexpected opportunity to say a few words about the subject so much on your minds, and mine. It isn't quite as simple and clear-cut for me, and many other Americans, as it is to the president of the Foundation. I have a question for you: shouldn't these issues be individual choices rather than imposed by the church and state, by law? History proves over and over that this problem cannot be legislated away."

Katy could see her audience was restive. She knew that most of the people present would be anti-choice. She chose her next words carefully. "The search for religious freedom, freedom from the tyranny of government in religious matters, brought many Europeans to Pennsylvania. The Quakers, Amish, Mennonites,

Brethren, and others. Here in a new land they had freedom of choice for their own cherished religious beliefs. Do we now want to sacrifice this freedom for the dangerous philosophy of government control?" Her voice filled the room. "To what new land can we escape to regain religious freedom?"

Katy decided to end her remarks on a low key. "We as a people need to seriously think about how much control our government should have over our personal lives. Do we really want a combination of church and state imposing laws upon all of us? Thank you for hearing me out." As she stepped down from the platform, Katy glimpsed the malevolent scowl on Reverend Atwood's face. *He probably helped create this media opportunity.*

His victory tarnished, he brushed with Katy as he stepped up onto the platform. Unaware that the television cameras were already focusing on him, and that the sensitive microphones picked up his voice, he glared at Congresswoman Jenkins and muttered condescendingly, "Well, girlie, you had your say, didn't you?"

Reporters tittered as the remark bounced from satellites into millions of homes. Katy stiffened. She struggled to control her temper. Then she leaned toward the microphones and intoned in a low distinct voice that she was well aware would be heard over the networks, "Well, sonny boy, now it's your turn."

The Reverend, sensing that something had gone awry, moved directly in front of the microphones, and raised his arms to get attention. All eyes, however, were on Katy as she left the microphones. There was brief, scattered applause as people made way for her to get through the crowd back to where Andy and Beverly waited. The three of them boarded the elevator, the easiest way to get upstairs to the headquarters.

"What a comeback!" Beverly burst out as soon as the elevator started up, "You fixed him good."

"Good going," Andy said. "Those people were dangerous; they're possessed by the killer instinct; Daniel in the lion's den had nothing on you today."

The arrogance of the "Foundation" president-preacher who anointed himself with God-given wisdom appalled Katy. She saw hatred in the faces of his followers, hatred for her when she dared question the only truth. Religious intolerance is scary, she thought, even here in America.

Katy shuddered, haunted by the menacing look on the face of the ever-popular and increasingly powerful Reverend Thomas Atwood.

* * *

Katy's fame as a match for Reverend Atwood preceded her to the Coalition party organizational meetings. Her run-in with the prominent "Bible belt" personality gave verve to the meetings. Participants rallied to the cause. Pat Reilly, the fighting Scotch-Irishman who had managed Andy's campaigns for governor, warmed to his new job as Katy and Andy's state campaign manager. Florence Knight, a highly visible personality in the Daughters of the American Revolution, became State Party Secretary and full-time office manager. She was delighted when Beverly volunteered to be her assistant.

An estimated seven hundred people attended the evening rally at the Civic Center, twice as many as expected. Katy's television appearance spurred attendance. At the rally, Katy's speech came through as an inspiring pep talk. She was feeling her way and making friends with Andy's friends.

* * *

Katy and Andy took an early flight to Washington, D.C. Friday morning. They took a cab to Katy's Georgetown home where a burst of activity greeted them.

A dozen vehicles were parked around or below the house, on both sides of the street. Katy's Cadillac, very much resembling the one she drove in New Mexico, was parked alongside the curb. A telephone company service truck, side doors swung open, sat in the garage driveway. Plumbers, carpenters, and electricians poked around the trucks that carried the tools of their trades.

Inside the house Ms. Arnold was scurrying to give everything a semblance of order as Katy and Andy came in the front door.

"Come on in!" she greeted them from across the room. "And make yourself at home, if you can recognize it as your home."

Katy gasped. The twenty-four by forty-six foot living room,

which was her personal masterpiece of design, had been transformed into one grand office. Only the bookshelves along the wall and the built-in kitchen remained intact. All of her beautiful furnishings were replaced by an array of desks and chairs, typewriters, computers, and assorted office furniture. The floor length windows facing onto the patio were largely blocked out by rows of filing cabinets.

At the far end of the room, Katy noticed a screen giving the entrance to her bedroom area some privacy. "We haven't touched your bedroom and bath. We're installing some toilets above the garage where the laundry room was," Ms. Arnold advised. Katy hadn't thought about losing her laundry room. She realized the practicality of this, however, as she moved toward the area above the garage which had been her storage area and laundry. Workmen were everywhere. Telephones, tools, and materials were scattered across the floor. Katy went downstairs to the garage that had housed her car and found a similar scene.

"It's a good thing you built this house on the side of this hill, with no houses across from it and abutting that convenience store below. We're legal here for the duration of the campaign," Ms. Arnold said. "Your being a Congresswoman and candidate for president helped with the Georgetown city council. By the way," she added, "your private unlisted phone is still in place in the bedroom, with an extension on your desk. Your desk is the first one this side of the bedroom. Mine is this side of yours, separated by the files. And Andy's desk is there beyond the conference table. We covered your dining table to protect it; it will serve as a coffee-break table as well as a conference table."

"You're a miracle worker!" Katy exclaimed. "The whole thing is so comfortable and efficient-looking, I can hardly believe it. We can put on a hell of a campaign from here."

Ms. Arnold beamed as Katy excused herself and headed toward her bedroom for a shower and a change.

"You guys did all right in Pennsylvania." Mrs. Arnold's comment to Andy expressed genuine appreciation.

Andy grinned. "That Katy is one heck of a campaigner. My family and friends fell in love with her."

Ms. Arnold looked searchingly at Andy. "She has a penchant for getting publicity, too. The media attention you two got was uncanny. You would have thought the Democrats having their National Convention would have knocked us off the airwaves and out of the newspapers. But, they had to share space. The reception at your parents home, with all the celebrities, got coverage all over the country including pix in the New York Times. Katy got a lot of mileage out of her comeback at the Bible-thumping Atwood, too."

"She's fast on the trigger," Andy said. "Altogether, quite a remarkable and lovely woman."

* * *

Matt Tilden, senior Senator from New Jersey, squared his shoulders, which were broad even for a man of his build. Short, stocky, and heavy jowled, he came by his nickname, Bulldog, because of his physical stature, and earned it by the stubborn tenacity which was his nature.

He felt no trepidation as he entered the Union Hall in Jersey City. He greeted friends and acquaintances cordially as he moved among the men. The first man in the hall who bumped him was quick to say, "Excuse me." The second said nothing. When a third man deliberately bumped into him, the Senator hunched down and lunged sideways against the offender, almost knocking him down.

"What in the hell is the matter with you guys?" Now, he was the bulldog; hunched, threatening, ready to take on one or all of them. No one took up the challenge. "All right, now what's eatin' on you guys? If you got a beef, let's have it."

"You been kinda' neglecting your constituents lately," one of them spoke up. "Where was you when the vote on that bill against public unions came up in the Senate?"

"Is that what's eatin' you? Lemme tell you, I was doin' somethin' a damn sight more important for you. The bill passed, didn't it? I had the votes counted. We had plenty—and then some."

Joe Domino heard the exchange as he came in accompanied by Big Jake from the bus company. Joe's voice rang out, getting the immediate attention of the eighty or so men there. "Come on. Sit down. We got a meeting scheduled here, and the Senator will have something to say."

Folding chairs scraped on the old wooden floor as the men took their seats. The large framed picture of Franklin D. Roosevelt, flanked by a picture of John L. Lewis, went unnoticed.

The president called the meeting to order. The Senator, now completely composed, sat at the table up front with the president and Joe Domino. Big Jake sat on the front row at the left end.

The president spoke. "This special meeting was called to talk about Katy Jenkins. If you don't know who she is, you soon will. She's running for president of the United States on a woman's ticket. You've heard about it—the American Coalition party. Well, she's about as likely to help labor as the Arabs are to help the Israelis in Jerusalem. She'll kill off the American Labor Movement if she can, as Joe can tell you." He nodded toward Joe, who took his time getting up to speak.

"This Jenkins woman has some queer notions," Joe began. "She thinks management and labor ought to sleep together in the same bed. And you know who's gonna get fucked in that deal. She comes from New Mexico where the Indians and Mexicans elected her Governor. We whipped her ass there when she tried to get "Right to Work" through the Legislature. But, they still elected her to the Congress five times in a row. How she got to be a candidate for president, I don't know, but she's got connections. She's bad news.

"Now, the Women's Movement is making a million dollar campaign contribution to her. A big ceremony was set to take place on the steps of the Capitol Friday morning, but somebody threw a monkey wrench into that."

The Senator grinned. "Their 'grand affair' won't be held on the Capitol steps, and it'll be Saturday—not Friday like they thought. The little old ladies will be moved up to the park on Pennsylvania Avenue where they'll be sitting ducks."

"Don't tell anybody, but the Senator took care of that," said Domino. "Now, we're here to organize some fun and games for the occasion."

The Union meeting suddenly became a buzzing affair. An hour later Joe Domino summed it up. "We're all set."

16

Mourning dove grey skies hung sullenly over the city Saturday morning, oblivious to the group assembling in the park on Pennsylvania Avenue. The flowers blooming in the carefully maintained flower beds seemed washed-out and dismal.

Ms. Arnold, unruffled and in control, saw to the last minute preparations herself. She chatted with the campaign volunteers as she gave direction to the set-up crew.

She checked her watch. Almost 9:30. The candidates and the officials from the Women's Movement should arrive momentarily.

The crowd was larger than she expected, hundreds of women from the Movement, and a respectable showing of men. Margaret Kincaid had helped to get the turnout.

Margaret stood ready to greet the dignitaries for the occasion. Katy and Andy arrived first, in a Gray Line limousine. The driver bounced out and opened the door for them. Margaret escorted them toward the speaker's platform. Andy detoured to move among the assemblage, and stole a great deal of the attention. He greeted the nearby women with handshakes, hugs, and a few light kisses on the cheek. Cameras clicked and television cameras whirred as the media recorded the event.

Andy then turned his attention to Katy, placing his arm under her elbow and guiding her to the platform. The limousine carrying Ruth Silverton and Ellen Steele swept up to the curb; Margaret greeted them and all three fell in behind Andy and Katy, moving toward the platform.

Ms. Arnold watched as Katy reached the last step up to the platform. A newsman asked for a picture. Katy and Andy turned, Katy on the top step, Andy just below her on the next step, Ruth with Ellen below him, and Margaret still on ground level.

"Everyone face the camera," she shouted. As they did, cameras flashed and TV cameras rolled for the best pictures of the day.

As others who had been invited to sit on the platform made their way up the steps and exchanged greetings, Ms. Arnold surveyed the weather and the crowd. Her media triumph euphoria soon dissolved.

The brooding sky deigned to permit the park assemblage, but made no guarantee of continued tolerance. The low slung clouds threatened to settle upon them any minute. Activity at the park's edge caught her eye. A dozen men, blue collar types, emerged from a Intercity Transport bus, mingled briefly and dispersed into the crowd. Had the clouds suddenly become more menacing? Another cluster of men wearing leather jackets and windbreakers bore down on the assembly from the north. They, too, split up and merged into the crowd.

She tried to pin-point some of the men working their way toward the platform when a marching band of teen-agers, boys and girls, carrying placards and banners, came into view on Pennsylvania Avenue. Ms. Arnold strained to see the legends on the banners that reporters rushed to photograph. Light bursts fired off from upraised cameras, lenses trained on the advancing group whose slogans were now quite clear to everyone. "Babies have a right to life, too." "Abortion -- Just say NO." "We petition the evil Coalition." "Christ is Lord." The signs bobbed up and down in time to rhythmic chanting.

Ms. Arnold gasped as Katy descended the platform steps and headed straight for the demonstrators. Upon reaching them, Katy extended her hand in a gesture too innocent to decline. A young dark-haired girl holding a pole of the lead banner accepted Katy's outstretched hand. A hush went through the group.

Katy spoke in her clearest voice to the young people. "Listen to me, I hope none of you ladies ever need an abortion." A soft flurry of comments skimmed through the crowd of picketers, but Katy easily continued above the murmur. "With all my heart, I hope none of you will ever have an abortion. The thought is as abhorrent to me as it is to you. But, by the law of averages, statistically at least one of you here will be caught up in a dilemma you can't even imagine today. I hope that you and your physician will continue to have the right to make a reasonable decision and neither of you will be criminalized because of that decision."

"She speaks for Satan! Don't listen to her blasphemy," yelled a tall youth at the back of the crowd.

Katy locked her gaze on him and asked, "What's your name?"

"Jim Beam," came the startled response from the tall smart-alec.

"Sounds like Satan may have had a hand in that answer," Katy said to the group. Head cocked to the side she continued directing her comments to the group. "Ladies, take my advice—steer clear of the Jim Beams of this world or you may become one of the statistics I mentioned."

For some reason, known only to the fates and what makes the male ego, the young men erupted into laughter. The tension dissipated.

"I want to be able to talk with you all. Why don't you stick around for the program and we can learn more about each other right after. What do you say? Give me a break and I'll give you a listen?"

The young woman who had accepted Katy's hand in peace now spoke up. "Let's wait, and have a talk."

Agreement spread through the young demonstrators. The chanting was silenced. Katy hugged the young woman, saying a word of thanks in her ear and returned to the podium.

Ms. Arnold, relieved that Katy was safely back on the platform and not wanting to give form to the phantom fears she felt, turned her attention to the program which was getting under way. Margaret introduced dozens of dignitaries from the Women's Movement, then presented Ellen Steele, the first speaker. Although dazzling in its delivery and content, Ms. Arnold felt a growing sense of unrest as Ellen went on and on. From where she sat in front of the platform, she signaled, without success, for a quicker pace.

Ellen's speech droned in her ears. "...women couldn't vote. Women's rights to own or inherit property were severely limited. Women were chattels! The law on the books in some New England states 'protected' women: no man could legally beat his wife with a switch larger around than his thumb."

Ms. Arnold nervously eyed the men swelling the crowd near the speaker's stand. Their coat pockets bulged. They weren't listening to the speaker. *They seem to be waiting for something, a signal perhaps*, thought Ms. Arnold. A big drop of rain splattered on her cheek.

Ellen continued: "...razor straps were kept handy for punishing miscreant wives. Now the old straps are museum pieces, but the practice of battering wives, unfortunately did not disappear with the straps. We must..."

Ms. Arnold moved close to the uniformed officer near the platform and spoke to him as if passing state secrets. Thoroughly convinced that trouble was at hand, she caught Katy's attention and motioned to her. Katy moved to a vacant chair on the platform and leaned down so she could hear Ms. Arnold's whispered warning, "There's trouble brewing. Ask Ruth to cut her remarks short and present the check quick. You take the check, pass it to Andy, and we'll get out of here as fast as possible. No speech. Just say 'thank you' and go before all hell breaks loose. I've signaled the limo to be ready."

Katy nodded. She, too, had noticed the peculiar assembly of men surrounding the platform and the bulges in their coat pockets.

The raindrops fell faster now.

Four patrolmen unobtrusively moved closer to the dais, each with a threatening nightstick. Katy consulted with Ruth, then Andy. Ellen ended her speech, and Ruth took over during the applause. She called Andy and Katy forward. With a flourish she presented the million dollar cashier's check to Katy. Katy quickly accepted the check, waved it in the air and slipped it to Andy.

"Keep it safe," Ms. Arnold heard her whisper.

Ruth was about to say something more, but Katy moved in front of the microphones saying, "Thank you! Thank you! This generous contribution will help elect the first woman president."

The sky opened up. Ms. Arnold raised an umbrella for Katy. The audience ran for cover. Partially protected by Ms. Arnold's second umbrella, Andy helped others down the dais steps. Limousines rushed to the curb to pick up the soaked passengers.

"Some speech I made today," commented Katy as she and Andy headed to their limousine.

Katy caught a glimpse of three or four of the parading young people, who hadn't dashed for cover, huddled under their banner. They stared in her direction. Seemingly on impulse, Katy darted out from under the umbrella and across to the girls huddled in the rain. Now what? thought Ms. Arnold. She saw the group raise part of the banner as a cover when Katy reached them. Katy conferred briefly with the dark-haired girl who had spoken up for her, and hurried back toward the limousine. Ms. Arnold met her halfway with the umbrella.

"What did you say to her?" she asked.

"I asked her to call me collect sometime. Her name's Barbara Lee. She's from Birmingham, Alabama."

"Thomas Atwood's town," commented Ms. Arnold as they got into the car.

The rain abated a little, but the driver still hunched forward concentrating on seeing through the heavy drizzle. Ms. Arnold noticed the same mysterious Intercity Transport bus she had seen at the park; it was crawling through the traffic on Pennsylvania Avenue. Not wanting to alarm Katy she commented, "We really lucked out back there."

"I know," said Katy.

* * *

The limousine driver took Ms. Arnold home after dropping Andy at his hotel. Then he took Katy to her Georgetown house. As they turned off the thoroughfare onto Katy's uphill street, Katy noticed a bus parked in front of the convenience store on the corner.

She knew the limousine was complimented by the local Gray Line; two businesswomen owned the company and participated in the Women's Movement as well as the Coalition party. She thanked the driver, tipped him liberally, then dashed up the stairs, let herself in, and made for the shower. In a matter of minutes, she washed and dressed. With the wet clothes picked up and tossed over the towel racks, she collected her things to leave for the luncheon some of the women were having out in Alexandria.

There was a noise outside. What the heck is that? she asked herself. It sounded like someone slipping in the gravel.

As she opened the front door she made a cursory inspection of what could be seen from there. No one alongside the house. A few men stood on the street up beyond the house. Why would they be standing and talking out in this drizzle? But, they seemed to be minding their own business so she walked to the car.

Once inside the car she pushed the button to lock all doors and pushed the other switches to make sure the windows were closed tightly. She inserted the key and turned it to start the car. No response. She turned it again, harder. A chill rushed up the back of her neck; the small hairs bristled when again there was no response.

Panic claimed her flesh as she spotted several men rounding the corner of the garage. The driver's side window crashed from a heavy blow. Pellets of safety glass rained in on her as the window caved in from repeated blows. More glass was being shattered. Men surrounded the car. At first she thought she was imagining the rocking sensation, but realized it was real as she saw the men shoving the car one way, then the other.

A piece of glass stuck on one cheek and when she wiped it off in the bouncing car, blood streamed down her face. Chips of safety glass covered her lap and the seats. With a mighty effort, she shifted her body toward the middle of the car where the motion was less. The windshield was shattered, too, but it hadn't caved in. She gasped for breath and tried to get her bearings. The car still rocked but seemed to be settling down some. She could hear men laughing and yelling.

"That's enough," an authoritative voice said. The car quit rocking. Fury surged up in Katy as she saw the right door opening.

"Hey Jake, let's give this girl a lesson she won't forget," growled the man opening the door. Katy saw the lower part of his body in the open doorway. She leaned back across the seat and drove her right foot into the man's groin. Her shoe fell to the driveway as he let out a yowl of pain and staggered back with both hands grasping his crotch. Katy didn't hesitate. She slipped off her remaining high-heeled shoe and out of the car door she went, shoving the wounded man hard into one of his pals. Before they realized what was happening, she lunged toward the thugs at the back of the car, catching them by surprise. She struck the nearest one on the left side of his head with the spiked heel of her shoe. An instantaneous look of disbelief flashed on his face as he lurched sideways holding his injured jaw in both hands. Katy went through the opening he left, darted across the street and scrambled up the hill toward the house at the top of the block.

"Well, I'll be damned!" the man called Jake said. "That broad has guts." Two of the men started to pursue her. "Let her go, you damn fools." They stopped short as a car approached. The driver slowed when he saw the men, then quickly shifted gears and headed up the hill toward Katy. The driver pulled up beside her and asked, "Need some help?"

"Let's get the hell outta' here," yelled one of the men. Straggling down the hill as the rain intensified, the men looked like a football team leaving the field after defeat.

The woman at the convenience store counter watched them clamber on to the bus. As the bus maneuvered out of the parking lot she noticed it had several license plates including New York, New Jersey and Pennsylvania. She wrote down the numbers and noted the time. For forty-five minutes they had blocked her parking. She could tell the police quite a lot about what she had seen.

Katy called the Georgetown police from her neighbor's house at the top of the hill, and then called Ms. Arnold. Both arrived about the same time. Later they called Andy and he came out, too. Katy responded to investigator's questions and filled out reports, barely able to control her outrage.

As they left the scene in Ms. Arnold's town car to go to the Alexandria luncheon, Katy watched her Cadillac being hoisted up by the tow truck. "Somebody's going to pay for this!" she vowed.

* * *

When Jake saw the angry woman at the convenience store writing down their license plate numbers, he realized he'd made a colossal blunder in letting the guys give the Jenkins broad a scare. He should have known better, but he went along with the idea. After all, they had come all that way and didn't get to have any fun at the downtown ceremony. Now he was going to have to explain it. As their bus pulled out of the convenience store, Jake yelled instructions to the driver: "Detour around the block, reverse directions and head for the bus terminal at the far end of K Street." He had friends there.

At the bus terminal Jake found a phone that afforded some privacy and called the boss.

At times like this, Joe Domino never lost his cool. Too much at stake. His Intercity Transport bus company operated two hundred motorcoaches. In addition to airport shuttle buses, he ran scheduled passenger service round-trip from Jersey City to New York and from both points to Atlantic City several times a day. A bigger share of the business was his fleet of charter buses which plied the east coast and sometimes roamed nationwide.

His teamster drivers got the top pay on the road and they were loyal, but not just because of the pay. They knew better than to double-cross Joe Domino. He transported lots of people, but that was only part of the business. His outfit moved more white powder around than any other single operation in the country. Intercity Transport was the best front in the business.

Joe's was a careful operation. He sensed danger the minute he realized what happenned in Washington. "You say the weather's soupy down there? That's good. Now listen to me," he said over the phone. "Charter a late-model bus with tinted windows from the outfit where you are, and get it on the road back here with the men as soon as possible.

"Now get this: take all the plates off the old bus you're driving. Borrow some kind of plate there even if you have to charter a whole damn bus to get the plate. Fuel the old bus, and I want you and Pete to drive it non-stop to Memphis. Got it?"

"Got it," said Jake. "I saw an old coach in the yard with a Tennessee plate."

"That's it! See how quick you can get going. Drive straight out to the Beltway. I-66 takes you to 81. That'll get you into Tennessee by the shortest route. Drive the limit, but don't go over. Don't attract any attention. Just get the damned bus to Memphis."

"What do I do with it when I get there?"

"Take it to Dock 13 and deliver it to Wolfgang Mueller. I'll call him."

"Got it," said Jake.

By the time the police reports were out to all points, complete with bus and occupants' description, and plate numbers, the old bus was well on its way to Memphis. Monday morning, Joe talked to Wolfgang and the bus was on a river barge headed for Mexico.

* * *

An 80,000 pound bus disappearing into thin air! Houdini himself couldn't have done that. But Joe Domino did. He grinned to himself.

Now he was having a belly laugh with Jake. "You mean they had to pack his balls in ice to get him home?"

"Sure as hell did. He's still walking carefully, three days later. Pete's head is still swelled up pretty good, too."

"Hell," Joe laughed, "if those goons had fooled around with her a little while longer, she would have beat the hell outta' all of 'em."

Joe was still chuckling when Jake departed. Then he sobered. *Handling that woman isn't a job for Union goons. This one has to be handled like when I knocked Kincaid out of the running. This one'll be tougher though—take some planning.*

An idea was beginning to take shape. *Just might work*, he thought, *and it sure would fix her good.*

17

This would be Katy's last speech in the House of Representatives.

The surge of excitement she felt when she first took her place in Congress had been repeated a thousand times—in the Committees on which she served, on the foreign missions, over the hard fought bills—all of it. Of late, however, the excitement had too often been replaced by a recurring sense of anxiety: raising money, being re-elected, looking good on television, living the good life; these things had become the goals of the members of the Congress. The fact that the well-being of the nation depended on their actions drowned in the sea of self interest; patriotism and duty to country smothered in the process. Now she understood clearly why she moved on to a new battleground and what her mission was all about.

She wouldn't come back to this seat again. After her final speech to the Congress, she would go directly to the foyer where Andy and Ms. Arnold waited with friends and reporters.

"The Chair recognizes Katy Jenkins."

She rose from her seat and strode to the microphone. A lightning survey of the assembly revealed a reassuring array of friendly faces.

"I asked for a few minutes to speak to you today as I turn in my resignation from the Congress. I thank you for granting me the time. You may regret this, as today is perhaps the first time since I joined your ranks ten years ago that I can speak words untainted by political expediency. Always before I have had to weigh my words carefully so as not to offend Allen Marchbanks...."

A ripple of laughter spread through her audience. Of all her

Congressional colleagues, Allen Marchbanks was the one she had tangled with the most often. He laughed, too.

Katy sobered. "Leaving the Congress is a painful experience for me. The most difficult political decision I've ever made was to accept the nomination of the American Coalition party to be its candidate for president. I accepted the challenge, however, and I have been happily encouraged by the Party's viability and serious agenda. It is a significant political development." Already, the members moved restlessly in their seats.

Katy's manner became contemplative and deliberate. "There is another reason why I'm changing my party registration from the Democratic party to the American Coalition party. I love Democrats and I love Republicans as individuals, but I believe the two-party system has evolved into something the authors of the Constitution never foresaw. The country was intended to be run by citizen-legislators, not professional politicians such as we have become. The system, as we make it function, is tilted toward re-election of incumbents. It has become a one-party system in the Congress; all committees, all committee Chairs, and all agendas have been controlled by one party for most of the last fifty years.

"Now, I want to speak to you as a colleague in the Congress about a matter in which we all have a very personal interest, so personal that we ordinarily cannot be objective about it. But, one more time: let's eliminate Political Action Committees—PACs, and corporate campaign contributions altogether. No more Savings and Loan contributions, or dairy industry, or car maker contributions. Instead, accept contributions only from individuals, and enforce the limits set by present law; then furnish additional campaign funds from public monies on a per-capita basis for all qualified candidates. *No Loopholes!*" She paused. "I see some heads shaking out there, but I think members of Congress should do their jobs instead of running perpetual fund-raising campaigns.

"This simple, straightforward change will do more to renew faith in the Congress with the American people than anything else we could do. Have we become so greedy and self-serving that we're willing to continue to corrupt our entire government rather than make these changes in campaign financing laws?

"You have it in your power to set things straight. The

responsibility rests here. If Congress passes the bill to rid the system of PACs, and all other than individual contributions, the president will sign it."

She paused. "As president that would be my policy."

Katy watched the reactions to her last statement. Surprise registered on some members' faces; obviously it hadn't occurred to them that she might become president.

Allen Marchbank's countenance changed as she spoke. Outright hostility replaced his earlier good humor; she would face some mean opposition in the campaign from him and others like him who didn't want the status-quo upset.

Katy smiled. She handed a single-page document to the sergeant-at-arms. "This is my resignation," she said simply. Her voice faltered for the first time as she turned back to the Congress.

"Thank you for everything."

* * *

Ms. Arnold handed out copies of Katy's resignation speech to reporters and other interested parties in the foyer of the Congressional Chambers. It contained good headline material. A voluntary resignation from the Congress made news.

"That was strong stuff," Andy said as Katy approached.

"We're all set up in the House Press Room," Ms. Arnold advised. You'll be on display in that 'press box' they put newsmakers in. I guess it simplifies the media's job."

Katy felt confined in the press box but welcomed the media interest. The questions were what she anticipated after resigning from the Congress—all but the last one. A reporter from the Washington Post asked Katy point-blank if she really expected to be elected president of the United States.

"Don't underestimate me—or the American people," said Katy. "Next year I could very well be answering your questions at White House press conferences."

18

At six a.m., the first morning after her resignation from Congress, Katy made coffee for herself. She strolled out into her garden, cup in hand. The air was refreshing, although not as crisp and clean as in New Mexico. She pulled the weeds that poked up through the earth in the flower beds and enjoyed the beauty of the trumpet vines. She had started the vines from cuttings gathered near the well-house at Caprock. For Katy they meant continuity.

Ms. Arnold arrived early, as usual, and let herself in without ringing. The aroma of fresh-brewed coffee greeted her; she poured herself a cup and joined Katy in the garden.

"We can catch our breath a little for a couple or three days," she told Katy, "and get organized here in the office, work on staff. There's a bunch of phone calls for you to return."

"Sounds good to me," said Katy. They drifted back into the house; Katy surveyed the expansive living room of her Georgetown home, now the nerve center of the American Coalition party. The desks, in order now, looked comfortable and workable. Secretaries' desks and computer stations were fitted in efficiently.

The job of assembling a staff had already begun. Two people were available from Katy's Washington office, a secretary and a "whiz-kid" computer operator. Ms. Arnold "loaned" an accountant from her office who was qualified to work with her as Party Treasurer. Volunteers for the mail room and phone room would be recruited from the D.C. memberships of the Coalition party. This group now boasted over 400 members. They would have their first rally to "meet the candidate" this coming weekend.

"I can't believe how well this office is coming together," Katy commented.

"Everything is, Katy. The Women's Movement offices are humming with activity; they're out to elect their first president. And, I talked to Harriett Landsdale yesterday. The Santa Fe office is in high gear; Harriett put out her first newsletter. She has three full-time employees and a crew of volunteers. And, Albuquerque is in full operation under Maria's management. La Posada cooperates every way they can: furniture, work tables, phones, and all. They're even throwing in the housekeeping.

"We're getting it together. I tell you, Katy, our impact will jar this nation off its duff." Katy laughed. "And you're going to be pleased with the coverage on your resignation speech. I have a clipping service working and they'll be getting stuff in from all over. But the Washington Post started the ball rolling. Front page this morning! I have it with me."

"Let's look at it over breakfast," said Katy. "Will you settle for cereal, fruit, and coffee?"

"Sure. I also want to show you the newsletter Landsdale got out about the Convention. Pure inspiration. Printed 25,000 copies, and is sending hundreds to every state. I've had some good writers, but Harriett is one of the best I've seen. And Margaret sent out a personal letter to the Party founders. She suggested that some of them may want to get together and sponsor hundred-dollar-a-plate dinners, in Texas, California, Pennsylvania, and New York. She has a little New York office set up and wants you to visit as soon as you can."

Katy whistled. "Things *are* moving." She hugged Ms. Arnold, then backed away and looked at her. "Remember, I want you to keep me informed on anything that goes wrong, too."

A slight frown crossed Ms. Arnold's face. "Two things," she said. "That busload of men that went after you still bothers me. I can't accept them disappearing into thin air like that. Which in turn makes this other problem that much more thorny."

"And the other is...?" Katy asked.

"Well, I applied to the Secret Service for security for you. They want us to put up $100,000 cash bond from campaign donations of $250 or less, made especially for that purpose—to prove that we are a 'serious' party."

Katy, obviously relieved, let a small sigh pass her lips, "Let's not take that on; let it ride for now."

* * *

"Katy, do you know a Barbara Lee?" Even as she asked the question, the answer came to Ms. Arnold. "Oh, isn't she that dark-haired girl who was with the picketers at the check presentation? She's on the phone, collect."

Katy accepted the call, greeting Barbara cordially.

"You said for me to call you," Barbara said. She rushed on, "I'm sorry about the picketing; most of us went along for the bus ride to Washington. The trip was a lot of fun, but I've been thinking about what you said, and I'll never be in another demonstration just for the fun of it. You talked to us like you thought we were important."

"You are, Barbara, and I appreciated the way you accepted me." Katy hesitated a minute, then decided to go ahead. "I don't know whether you would be interested or not, but we're hiring some staff for the Coalition party here at the Georgetown headquarters. Would you maybe like to come up and talk to us?"

"Work for you?" Barbara gasped. "I'd love that! But...I don't know if my mother would let me. Work in your campaign office? It would all depend on Mother; she would be living all alone without me."

"Are you out of high school?"

"I graduated in June. I'd love a job like that. In Washington!" Barbara's enthusiasm mounted as she continued. "I didn't dream that maybe I could actually work for you. I'll call tomorrow. I do have an aunt in Alexandria, and maybe Mother will let me live with her." Her voice faltered, "I would like to work for you."

"I'd like to have you, too, Barbara. If I'm not here when you call, talk with Ms. Arnold."

"Yes. Oh yes, I'll call tomorrow."

The morning was a marathon of telephone calls. Katy saw Andy come in while she spoke with Margaret and motioned him to get on the line. He picked up the phone on the desk next to the conference table and it became his permanent spot.

Margaret repeated the news to Andy about the fund-raising

dinners confirmed in Texas by Sam Pickens and in California by Lila Stanford. Only the dates of Katy's availability were needed. Andy finished up the call with Margaret while Katy fielded a call from Harriett; Andy got in on that conversation, too.

"It looks like we're in business," boomed Ms. Arnold. She advised Katy she had a staff meeting set up right after lunch. "I have a couple good applicants," she confided. "They've worked in campaigns; one of them is already a Party member and the other is enthusiastic about joining,"

"Sounds good," said Katy.

* * *

The call came mid-afternoon. Sensing its importance, the receptionist immediately transferred it to Ms. Arnold.

Ms. Arnold slapped her hand over the mouthpiece and turned to Katy. "I think this is Van Dorn—John Van Dorn in New York. He wants to talk to you."

Katy stiffened. *Can it really be him? Why is he calling me now? Handle it for me Ms. Arnold. No, that makes no sense. Okay, I'll have to do this.* She grasped the receiver. *Oh, please let my voice be steady.* "Katy Jenkins here."

"Katy, this is John."

It was he; no doubt about that voice.

"Are you there, Katy?"

"Yes, I'm here," she said evenly. "It's been a long time since we talked."

He hesitated briefly, then said quietly, "Katy, I want to help with your campaign."

"You do?" Her voice registered her amazement.

"Yes. I *can* help—maybe more than you realize." He spoke with the same sincerity and cautious enthusiasm he had years ago.

"Well, I need all the help I can get," she said simply.

"Katy, I've followed your career; it's been brilliant."

How much does he know about me? she wondered. Then a thought thrust itself into her mind. *He knows about Johnny. No—that's impossible.* She wasn't quite prepared for his next statement.

"I think you are the outstanding political personality of the day."

"That sounds good anyhow."

"I mean it. And now that you're in the big time, you need big league backing."

"I know," said Katy, "and I'm not sure the American Coalition party can achieve the necessary financial status. We're a grass roots outfit: the Women's Movement, Margaret Kincaid's group of backers, and Harriett Landsdale's little state organizations. And a country girl candidate."

"I know the candidate," he said with emotion, "and I like her."

Katy's breath audibly caught in her throat.

Van Dorn continued. "What I really called to say is: we want to set up a national organization to support you, with headquarters here in New York. We won't conflict with Margaret Kincaid's local organization. We can put on quite a campaign for you. We'll have substantial funding. And it'll certainly give your campaign a new dimension."

Wonder and disbelief in Katy's voice came through in her next question. "John, this sounds almost too good to be true. What's the catch?"

John laughed easily. That same deep-throated laugh she heard so many times when he was amused at her innocence—so long ago. Well, she wasn't naive now, and she wouldn't be taken in by that laugh now either. Her thoughts were interrupted by his voice.

"There is no catch, Katy. No strings attached. If you can come to New York, to LAND & SEA headquarters, I can show you better than I can tell you. Then you can decide."

I've got to go, she thought. "All right." She glanced at the big appointment calendar on the wall and checked with Ms. Arnold. "I can make it Tuesday, ten A.M."

"Good. I'll look forward to seeing you."

Katy hung up the phone and stared numbly at the instrument. Ms. Arnold, bursting with curiosity, had overheard Katy's half of the call. "He wants to help us," Katy told her.

"My God, do you know the Van Dorns could buy and sell the Rockefellers."

"I know," said Katy.

Ms. Arnold paid no attention to Katy's pensive mood. Her exuberance could not be dampened. "Katy, I don't know how you happen to call Mr. Van Dorn 'John' just as if you were old friends, but whatever the deal is, he's going to help make 1600 Pennsylvania Avenue your personal address."

19

With her car still in the repair shop, Katy took a cab to the Mayflower Hotel on Saturday morning to meet with H.B. McGee. Must be important, she thought, for him to fly all the way up here to see me.

He waited in the lobby for her. She went to him eagerly anticipating his usual comforting bear hug; she wasn't disappointed; he hugged her with all the warmth that was so much a part of his nature.

He had called her yesterday from Albuquerque. Told her that he had to see her, would she be free for breakfast Saturday morning? She quickly assured him she would be.

She had missed H.B. more than she realized. But, the question remained, why was he here to see her?"

H.B. was already on a first name basis with the waitress, Peggy. She seated them promptly, in an area set off from the rest, at a table for four, now set up for two. As she poured hot coffee, she stole glances at Katy, aware that she was the woman running for president.

After small talk about the sunny weather in New Mexico, H.B. extended greetings to Katy from a few New Mexicans he had seen after calling her the day before, including Uncle Clifford.

Leaning forward and speaking in a confidential tone, Katy opened the serious conversation, "I'm dying to know why you came to see me; I hope it's good news."

He didn't answer her directly. "Katy, you know you don't have a chance in hell to win this election." He ignored the setting of her jaw and her beginning protest. "But you know what some of us in New Mexico are thinking? We're thinking how nice it would be for you to carry your home state." He paused only briefly for this to sink in. "Clifford has already started the 'Republicans for Katy for President.' Not surprising, of course. What's interesting is that a bunch of Democrats want to come out for you, too."

"Rather than for Owen Mallory?"

"Yeah, I guess so. We could have had a better candidate; I'm afraid we flubbed this one. I've backed every Democrat they've ever nominated, and I guess I would've backed Mallory too, except for one thing."

"What is that?" Katy asked, voice low.

H.B. looked surprisingly uncomfortable, but held her gaze.

"They want me to head up the 'Democrats for Katy for President' in New Mexico."

"That would be wonderful!" She knew the answer, but had to ask: "Are you going to do it?"

Ruefully he replied, "Yes, I guess I am," and took a gulp of coffee.

"H.B., I appreciate what you're doing very much."

"Hell, they by-passed me on the important thing anyhow, so I didn't have any commitments." He was himself again. "They're already coming to me with campaign money for you. We'll be printing up some things next week, and we've already talked to the agency about some media stuff. Maria's working on it so we'll get our money's worth."

"H.B., I really do appreciate this very much." She looked at him with genuine fondness. "Everything seems to be coming together." She leaned toward him like a conspirator now, and ticked off developments. She told him about the heart-warming reception at Caprock—and Mom's $30,000—the two exciting days in Philadelphia with Andy, the million dollar check from the Women's Movement, and confided in him about the incident in her driveway.

"The dirty bastards!" He exclaimed.

Then she thought about John's call. It came back into her mind with overwhelming force, all other thoughts crowded out. *Why would he offer help to my campaign? Can I trust him?* I did once, trusted him with all of my being. He really left me in the lurch—without so much as a word of explanation. And now he proposes to prance back into my life—just like that! Resentment welled up inside her. Her fist clenched. Her heart pounded. Forcibly, she pulled herself back into the present. *Should I tell H.B. about the call from John?* Sure, I have to. He may even know about it already. She plunged in. "You know who John Van Dorn is? Oh, of course you do. You two had dinner together here in Washington a few months ago."

"Yes, I remember it well. I couldn't figure out why you ran away. Acted like you saw a ghost or something, and just disappeared. First time I ever saw you do anything like that. I really liked the guy."

She didn't bother to respond to this. Instead she came right to the subject. "Van Dorn's offering to back my candidacy. Says he can help me a lot. Can you believe it?"

H.B. looked at her for a long moment, making no effort to conceal his admiration. Finally, he said, "Well, that figures."

"What do you mean? Doesn't it suprise you?"

"No, it doesn't. Now, I might as well tell you, Katy. I couldn't have told you before, but now I can." He looked concerned, "Don't ever tell him I told you."   .

"Told me what?"

"I couldn't figure it out. From the time of your very first campaign for the State Legislature and every campaign since then, including your runs for Congress, your Uncle Clifford always had the first money up front. He never failed. I couldn't figure out where the hell it came from. When you needed it the most, he came through with the most."

H.B. leaned forward, now the conspirator. "Well, two years ago when I had dinner with Van Dorn, I knew where the money had come from all those years."

Katy sat silent for a while, her thoughts whirling. "I didn't know. H.B., I swear to God, I didn't even suspect it."

"I know you didn't."

"How much did he tell you?"

"Only that he knew you at UNM in the sixties. He didn't tell me, but I figure you must have shacked up. Isn't that what you called it then? We talked a lot, but didn't really say much; I just let him talk. Most of all he wanted to talk about you. He told me how you took him to Santa Fe in your little Volkswagen bug, going on the Turquoise Trail, up to the Crest—all over. He said it took you guys all day to get to Santa Fe to the Kings for dinner, and about meeting Elizabeth there. He told me about going to Indian feast days in the pueblos with you, about going down to Caprock and staying all night and meeting Pop, Alice, and your brothers, and about your riding the range together, and touring the Big J Feed Mills. We talked a long time, Katy, and drank more Cutty Sark on the rocks than probably either of us had in a long time...it must have been a hell of a romance."

"It was." Her mind filled with memories, but she still wanted to hear more.

"He said one thing that has stuck in my mind ever since."

"What was that?" her voice was insistent.

"Hell, Katy, by that time our conversation had degenerated into pure male talk. I couldn't tell you exactly what he said. Anyhow, it was probably just the Cutty Sark."

"What did he say?" Katy had to know.

Once again, he looked at her, glanced around the room to make sure no one overheard. "I will tell you this much. The man still carries the torch for you."

H.B. sat back in his chair and waited. He knew Katy needed time to absorb all this.

Katy felt emotion tugging at her from two directions. The resentment she felt was still there. Then why did her pulse leap at the sound of his name? *And he still professes a live interest in me. Why?*

Changing the subject, H.B. said, "They've picked Jay Stover to run for Congress; I guess you know. I wasn't even consulted. In a way I'm glad I wasn't. The young Turks may have to learn the hard way."

"I'm sorry, H.B."

"Oh, hell, he may win. I hope so. We don't need to lose a Congressional seat that we already owned."

Once again H.B. waited. He knew Katy would talk to him about Van Dorn.

"I've missed you, H.B., and I appreciate what you are doing more than you will ever know. With you and Uncle Cliff, the money, and all the rest, I think Katy Jenkins just may be elected president by New Mexico."

She looked at H.B. "I'm going to New York to see Van Dorn Tuesday. I don't know what to think about his sending money all these years."

"I guess you know his wife died—couple years ago."

"I know, it was in the papers; when a Van Dorn dies, it's news. They said she never enjoyed good health. Finally developed diabetes which became debilitating. That might be why they never had children."

H.B. suddenly felt a surge of sympathy for Katy. It all came home to him now. The lonely years she had spent—Johnny raised by her family. He had suspected Johnny was her son, but it took the birth certificate to verify it. He felt a twinge of conscience about taking it from the Santa Fe County Courthouse. Never did anything like that before in his life. Now he had better tell Katy about it. It would take a load off her mind anyhow.

"Katy, I brought you something I filched from the records file in Santa Fe some time ago." He handed her the record of Johnny's birth certificate.

Katy sat numbly, looking at the proof of Johnny's birth. "Father: unknown." She remembered the agony she felt when she filled out the form. The old doctor who delivered Johnny insisted on it. Mom was there; she had come from Caprock to stay with her sister in Santa Fe weeks earlier; she would take the baby home.

"H.B., you've known all this time. And you've kept my secret?" Then she asked, "Was this the only record in the Court House? How in the world did you get it?"

"Yes, the only record. I stole it when you ran for governor. I was doing some research for a closing, the Jaramillo estate. They gave me the run of the place. I searched the Jaramillo file, and on impulse looked at Jenkins, too. I cut the whole page out of the record book with my pocket knife, and put it in my pocket. Then I went back to the Jaramillo file."

"Oh, H.B.!"

"Guess it was a good thing, too. That Lobo reporter, Caplin, was snooping around in Santa Fe last week; he was looking for it, for sure."

Katy's relief was evident. "Thank God he didn't find it. And you did that for me? I don't know what to say."

"Don't say anything—ever. Just tuck that paper away some place where it's safe. And don't ever remember how you got it."

H.B. signalled Peggy for a warm-up on the coffee. He seemed relieved to change the subject. "Katy," he said, "I'm just talking politics now. Personal stuff aside, if you want to make a splash in this campaign of yours for president, I can't think of anything better that could happen to you than John Van Dorn."

"Thanks, H.B. Now I have to take his offer seriously."

20

Once, out of curiosity, Katy had gone to the LAND & SEA offices. Not actually into Van Dorn's office, but into the building on Fifty-third Street, a block from Rockefeller Center. It was a red brick building, with windows trimmed in white, looking very much like Independence Hall in Philadelphia, and just as well-kept, the main difference being that it was four stories high. Dwarfed by the skyscrapers around it, it maintained a certain dignity sitting sixteen feet back from the sidewalk, partially shielded from view by hunkering old maple trees. A narrow drive ran along one side. On the entry-way was a street number, a modest black metal sign with silver letters: 47 - LAND & SEA ENTERPRISES.

As she was assisted out of the airport limousine she had engaged, Katy glanced at her watch—9:40—she had arrived twenty minutes early. Time to get a cup of coffee first. She headed for the Manhattan Grill down the street.

Catching her reflection in a store window, Katy admired the beautifully detailed skirt which moved about her, setting off her trim waist and shapely hips. *Hardly recognize myself.* She smiled and relaxed, confidence renewed.

A few people still breakfasted at the long counter. The row of small tables along the wall now sat empty.

She took the third table, and ordered coffee and a bagel.

Strange, she thought, that this little grill with its big-sounding name would be so very much the same after all these years. It was here, at this same table, same time of day, twenty-eight years ago, that she had made her most far-reaching decision.

She had come to New York alone. Only Elizabeth knew

where she was. An angry young woman, in town for a showdown, she came to find out why she couldn't get a phone call through to John Van Dorn, and to confront him with the news that she was pregnant.

She took the Santa Fe Chief from Albuquerque, changed trains in Chicago, and arrived at the Pennsylvania Station in the middle of New York. She retrieved her bag, and lugged it across the street to the Penn Station Hilton. New York was a bewildering place. Fortunately, she had Sunday to reconnoiter. She rode a subway for the first time and disembarked at Rockefeller Center, gawked at the tall buildings, marveled that NBC was a real place, and saw Van Dorn Square for the first time. All the buildings were skyscrapers, except the LAND & SEA corporate headquarters. Glad everything was closed, she found the subway entrance, got on the wrong car to get back to the hotel, and found herself riding to the end of the line, winding up at the South Ferry in Battery Park. She was amazed that the fare for the tour of New York harbor on the Staten Island Ferry was only a nickel.

Thrilled at the sight of it, she singled out the Statue of Liberty for a visit and climbed the spiral steps to the observation deck near the top for her first breathtaking view of the New York skyline.

She managed to negotiate her way back to Penn Square and her hotel on buses.

She built up nerve enough to rent a car at the hotel and, fortified with a map and instructions, she drove across the Triborough Bridge, through Queens, and into the exclusive residential area along the north shore in Nassau County where the Van Dorns lived. She wasn't sure what she planned to do. Knock on the door and see if he was home? Should she have phoned first? She boiled at the thought.

With the help of a friendly equestrian, she found the Van Dorn driveway. She pulled in and gasped at what she saw. An English country mansion loomed before her. Surrounded by elegant gardens and carefully trimmed hedges, the home outshone even those in the fairytale books of her childhood. She couldn't just walk up and knock. Suddenly overcome, she wheeled the car around, killing the motor. When she got the car started, she sped away.

That evening in the lobby at the Penn Station Hilton she picked up the Sunday New York Times. Startled by the sheer bulk of it, she read the front page first, then browsed through the many sections. Something caught her eye in the Society section. She whipped it open, not believing what she saw. "ENGAGEMENT ANNOUNCED." A three-column picture showed John Van Dorn IV and his bride-to-be, Stephanie Hancock. The newspaper fell from her hands. Realization burned in her brain. She felt like a summer garden the day after a hard freeze: wilted, drooping, life gone. She sunk down in the chair, gasping, wishing she could just disappear. She couldn't stand this. It couldn't be.

She retrieved the paper, looked again, read the announcement, and knew it was true. Devastation settled on her as she looked at John's picture. No passion there. She couldn't see what he saw in Stephanie; she didn't look like a match for John. She felt no resentment as she studied the aristocratic but somehow pathetic face of Stephanie. Surprisingly she felt no anger as she looked at John's picture either. She was beyond that; this whole unreal thing was beyond her comprehension.

Somehow, she walked casually to the elevator, as if nothing had happened. She went to her room, threw off her clothes and dropped into bed, dead tired from the long train trip and her first day in New York. Pulling up the covers to close out the world, she fell into exhausted sleep.

The next morning she walked all the way to Rockefeller Center, and the block beyond, to Van Dorn Plaza. Her gaze travelled up the height of the Tower Building. How small the grain silos towering over Eastern New Mexico at the Big J Feedmills seemed by comparison. She spotted the Manhattan Grill down the street, went in and sat at the third table along the wall. It was there she decided to go home. This wasn't her world. John wasn't of her world. She wouldn't mess up his. She'd go home to New Mexico where she belonged. She felt a lump in her throat when she thought of the baby John would never know.

* * *

Katy was glad for a chance to collect her thoughts before facing John. Her heart and mind sent up ambivalent responses. John Van Dorn? He was just a guy on the make when I knew him at UNM. What is he really like? And why has he taken such a personal interest in my political career over the years? Sending contributions all those years through Uncle Clifford! Does he know about Johnny?

Keep it strictly business, Miss Jenkins, or rather strictly politics. I won't ever be as vulnerable as I was all those years ago. I can handle myself now. I need all the good breaks I can get. And I'll make the most of this one!

"Good morning, Katy." The voice came from over her shoulder. "May I join you?"

Katy's heart pounded in her throat, but she struggled to be casual as she turned to see John. "Please do," she said.

"I saw you get out of the car and followed you here," he said as casually as if this were a routine meeting.

Katy hoped the inner turmoil she felt didn't show. She did feel a sense of relief; his sudden appearance here made it easier, whether that was his purpose or not. "Thank you," she said. "Your office building looked rather formidable."

"I had everyone alerted," he said. "You would have been welcomed."

John sat down across from her. She had forgotten just how tall he was. A little grey at the temples, she noted, but as handsome as ever, in a more mature way. She was glad to see that he looked a little nervous too.

"John," she said uncertainly, "I have to know something before we talk about anything else."

He looked her in the eye. His voice was steady, gentle. "All right, Katy, you were never one to beat around the bush. Let's have it!"

"When you left Albuquerque twenty-eight years ago, you left a note that you would get in touch with me—but you never did."

"God knows I tried, Katy. My father died a few hours after I returned here. I called you before his body was even cold. I called you at your 'little house' a half dozen times that first night, and for days afterward. What happened to you?"

The memory of that night rushed into Katy's mind with crushing force. She had come home, reeling from John's sudden departure, and found Elizabeth in a state of shock, in the shower with the bathroom door locked, trying to scrub off the degradation of rape. She remembered trying to comfort Elizabeth, and how she had packed their things, got in the Jaguar John had left her, and driven all the way to Arizona.

"John," she said numbly, "Elizabeth and I did take off that night, and we never lived in that little house again. Something terrible happened. I can't even tell you about it now. But, I tried to call you."

"You tried to call me?"

"Yes, maybe I overdid it. I talked to your mother at the hospital. I couldn't leave a phone number because we weren't settled down yet. I called the next day, from the Saguaro Lodge in Tucson, and learned your father had died. I left my phone number at your Long Island home and at LAND & SEA. I lived by the telephone. If I wasn't there, Elizabeth was. When you didn't call me, I tried to call you again and again."

John spoke softly. "Katy, I was trying just as frantically to get you. I called Elizabeth in Santa Fe, but Aunt May said she was in Albuquerque. I even called your Mom at Caprock. She thought you were in Albuquerque, too. My mother was frantic at the time, what with funeral arrangements and everything. I even slipped away from her and tried to call you from the funeral home. I remembered I had left the hotel with a few days paid up and called you at the room there, hoping to find you, but you seemed to have disappeared from the face of the earth."

"Oh John, I'm sorry." She struggled to collect her thoughts—remembered she hadn't acknowledged his help on her campaigns. "I want to thank you for the campaign contributions. I didn't know. Uncle Clifford never told me. I didn't really know about it until last week."

The tension went out of John. "Katy," he said, "there is only so much a person can spend on himself. The most enjoyable expenditures of a personal nature that I have made in years is the money I sent to Clifford for your campaigns. I wrote each check myself—for the sheer enjoyment of it."

Now Katy was at ease, too. She chuckled. "Well, thank you anyhow, even if your motives were purely selfish."

A mischievous grin tugged at the corners of John's mouth. "Well, then," he said, "I presume you will let me indulge my selfish pleasures and help you in your campaign for President."

"Why not," she countered. "Let yourself go." Then she sobered. "John, why were you calling me so urgently?"

His tone was casual. "Oh, that. I just wanted to ask you to marry me. Nothing more. I was young and didn't know any better. I completely forgot that I was engaged to Stephanie, and I didn't know that LAND & SEA was in deep trouble if I didn't keep the engagement, or that there was no way I could go traipsing off to New Mexico again. But Mother knew. I see what happened. She undoubtedly had your calls intercepted. She had to, I guess. Had to give the engagement picture to the Times, too, a week after Dad's service." Now it was John's turn to ask a question. "Why were you calling me so frantically?"

Katy's mind flashed back to how much she ached all those days and months to tell him that she was having his baby. She remembered her trip to New York where she decided it wasn't meant to be. "Oh that," she said airily. "Seems like there was something, but I guess I was just a silly young girl wanting to tell you how much I loved you."

The very flippancy of their remarks established a rapport. Their hands touched across the table, and both knew the electricity was still there.

John became very businesslike. "Katy, I have an appointment for us today that could really help your campaign."

His voice and mannerisms reminded her so much of Johnny that butterflies flooded her stomach. Again she wondered if he knew.

John continued, "We're to see Tom Snelling, President of Bankcity, 11:30, his office. He's having us for lunch with none other than the publisher of TODAY, Henry Shaw."

Katy's mind snapped to attention. *The biggest banker in New York! The most important news magazine in the nation!* Ms. Arnold herself couldn't have set up a meeting like this.

"That takes my breath away," she said.

"It was just good luck that I could get them together. It's an informal luncheon in the President's private dining room at the bank. I set it up for myself and a friend that I want them to meet. Tom Snelling and I graduated in the same class at Harvard.

We've always been close friends. Tom is a comrade of Henry Shaw—they did duty together in 'Nam."

"They were in the service? They fought in Vietnam?"

"Not exactly. They were both on special assignments for the government, but they got into some pretty tight places together. That's where you make lifelong friends."

Katy thought about the scenario for a minute. Three old friends, all rich and powerful males, getting together for lunch. That's why John could get them together.

She had to ask the question: "Do they know who you are bringing to lunch?"

He looked sheepish. "No, they don't." Then he chuckled and added reassuringly, "No, they don't know who is coming to lunch. But this will be a refreshing experience for both of them."

Katy considered this. He is really putting me on the spot. They could easily resent me, figure I'm an opportunist. No, be reasonable. John is putting himself on the spot even more. He must be pretty sure I can carry it off, she concluded.

John suggested they should go on over to his office. "I'd like to show you around before we go to Bankcity." As they left the Grill, he asked, "How are Pop and Alice, and all the family in Caprock City?"

"Truly great" she answered. "Jack and Jim both have families—it's quite a clan now. Pop is still up at five every morning, and keeps an eye on everything. Mom is the one who gets tired."

"And the caprock place? Are you still running cows?"

"Oh yes. As a matter of fact the herd has grown. We have quite a few head now." She realized she had said "we" and wondered if he had picked up on it. Without waiting to find out she continued, "I've a partner now, my kid brother—you never met him. He was born late in Mom and Pop's life." She sensed no special reaction on John's part. Silent, they continued up Fifty-third Street.

After a moment he said, "That's really nice."

It occured to her that she would like to see his face now, to see if there was any emotion there, but she didn't look up at him.

His voice was perfectly casual. "You have quite a family. I liked all of them." Then his voice showed concern, "Your mother is okay, isn't she?"

So he was hearing everything she said. "Oh yes, she isn't sick or anything like that. She just works too much. She has extra help now, but she never quits."

"Alice is one of the good people. I liked her from the first moment I met her."

"Thank you. I didn't realize you had gotten to know her that well." Then she remembered going into the kitchen that morning long ago and finding John there, dish towel in hand, drying dishes as Mom washed. They had talked and laughed together.

"Mom has a dishwasher now."

John took a quick, sideways glance at Katy. He was surprised at what she had said. He, too, had thought about that morning in the kitchen drying dishes and talking to Alice.

They were nearing the building now. John took her elbow to guide her up the steps and into the headquarters of LAND & SEA.

He doesn't know about Johnny, she thought. She was sure of that now.

They entered a high-ceilinged room that looked more like the foyer of a grand home than an office entrance. The hardwood floors, covered with an exquisite, Colonial-era rug, spread before them. Farther back was a simple desk. The elderly gentleman behind it sprang to attention and awaited John's approach. To the left, French doors dressed with white curtains partially blocked the view of a substantial, somewhat conventional-looking office area. On the right, a wide curving stairway wound up to the second floor. The elevator was tucked neatly under the middle landing of the stairway.

John acted as a tour guide. "This building was built in 1793, the same time construction on the Capitol was begun in the new District of Columbia," he advised. He walked over to the only picture on the wall. "This is the original John Van Dorn," he said. "That was six generations ago. America fascinated him and he was one of the first to realize that Manhattan Island would become the great port city of the New World. That is when he bought land here. Originally, it was considered far inland, and included all of what is now Rockefeller Center. Pieces were sold off at what were considered huge profits in those days, but this square block has always stayed in the family. All of the buildings in the square are family-owned. Although the others are built of glass and steel, each one has an entry, or a wall, or lobby, or something built with the same red brick as this building."

Katy moved in close to look at the portrait of great, great-grandfather Van Dorn. He looks so stern, she thought, yet there is a certain gentleness in his eyes. She looked up at John and said, "I can see the family resemblance."

John smiled. "Come on upstairs." Immediately the elderly man, who was standing by, stepped over and pressed the elevator call button.

"Thanks, Bert. By the way, this is Katy whom I mentioned to you."

Bert's face lit up. "I'm pleased to meet you," he said. As the elevator doors opened, Katy said, "I'm glad to know you, too."

As the elevator delivered them upstairs, the doors opened and Katy stepped out directly into the main offices. The desks were spaced far apart on this floor, with planters and comfortable small-group seating areas. Across the far end of the room ranged three private offices, looking homey with their French doors and side window panels. John took his time, introducing Katy to most everyone. The women were especially enthusiastic; they gathered around her asking questions and wishing her success.

They exited the general office area through the Conference Room from which a private entrance led into John's spacious corner office.

Katy noticed that John's desk had several stacks of official looking documents. Several memos, laid out in an orderly fashion, awaited him.

As if reading her thoughts, he commented, "We've just put two new tankers into service. We kept building tankers when everyone else quit. We were lucky to have sold off some of the old stuff before the bust in oil prices. We scrapped some more and now we have the best tonnage on the seas. I doubt if you're interested in shipping right now, but there are a couple of things in the building I do want you to see. We will catch them on the way down to the car."

"I'm interested in everything here," she said. "It's all exciting."

"Sometime, I'll tell you more, but for now we'd better slip down to the next floor. If it's all right with you, we will take the stairs. Not so many roadblocks that way.

"Down here we keep track of the current exchange rates on all the world's major currencies and we pay bills in like currency all over the world."

Katy wanted to see more, but John kept going. Halfway down the hall, he stopped short, opened a paneled door, and advised that this was the Communications Room. He introduced her to Carrie Brooks who, with a couple assistants, ran the operation. Katy was astonished to learn that here the names, private addresses, direct phone numbers, and telex and FAX numbers were kept up to date on computer printouts for the most important people all over the world: heads of state, bankers, oil magnates, shipping tycoons, large land owners, important families. There were hundreds of names on the printout. Various symbols were used to indicate who were customers, who were associates, and who were personal friends. The VIP list, as it was called, was up-dated and printed out daily.

"We are working on a little project for you here," John explained.

Katy broke in, "What in the world kind of project are you talking about?" She was thumbing through the printout for Israel. Then she saw the one for New Mexico, a rather small one. "This is amazing," said Katy.

"Your name is in there," he said.

She found her name along with the dates she had been in the Congress, and up-dated to the fact that she had been nominated to run for President of the United States on the National Coalition party ticket. Her Washington address and Albuquerque address were right, and her phone numbers, too.

"Carrie can explain what we are working on," John said.

Katy looked at Carrie.

"Well, the project, as John has outlined it, is to let everyone on the list know we think you are a viable candidate for President and to be taken seriously. Our goal will be to let most of the VIPs in the world know that you are a significant candidate." She paused, "It's a big job because there are so many angles."

"Katy, we're still in the planning stages on this," John said.

"I have approval of the executive committee here, so there will be full cooperation. First, of course, I want your approval."

"You have that," murmured Katy. "I just want Ms. Arnold to see this."

"I know Ms. Arnold," said Carrie. "We could sure use her help for a day or two to get this going—if you can spare her."

"We can do that," said Katy.

"Soon?" Carrie asked.

"How about tomorrow?"

"That would be great."

"Then it's all settled." John said. "We will have a desk and private telephone for her so she can stay in touch." He was obviously pleased with Katy's reaction.

"Lady Candidate," he said, "we have an appointment at Bankcity. We had better be on our way."

21

New York City had always been the symbol of grandness and power to Katy, and now as they rode she felt the awesomeness of it all. World commerce originated here. Decisions made in Rockefeller Center and up and down the Avenues today, would be felt in every nook and cranny of the world tomorrow. Somehow she never felt the same about Washington, D.C. Certainly, the power of the government superseded that of the industrialists and the bankers, but it didn't seem as real. Here, the power was real.

The top floor of Bankcity, where Tom Snelling reigned over one of the largest accumulations of money and credit in the world, was spacious. That was Katy's first impression. Her second impression was that Mr. Snelling embodied the power that was New York. She sensed in him a certain arrogance peculiar to the very rich and powerful, and it sent a little shiver through her body.

Henry Shaw was different; he had been a reporter, and she could detect his keen interest in the great human drama in which he played a lead. Any fears Katy had about this meeting were quickly allayed. John Van Dorn obviously "belonged to the Club." He assured Katy's acceptance by his own enthusiasm as he introduced her. Katy fell easily into the light talk. Since she had grown up in the company of her brothers, she could relate to men simply as people; she could become friends with them, speak their language.

Lunch was served in a small private dining room on the same floor, with a tinted glass view window overlooking the city. The fresh broiled Ahi Tuna prepared in the adjoining kitchen and served by an efficient, but diffident, uniformed waiter, was all that it might be.

After some small talk with his colleagues, John brought Katy into the mainstream of the conversation when he mentioned that her dad didn't think much of bankers.

Henry Shaw asked, "Why not?"

Katy knew she was on the spot, but her answer was quick and straight: "Pop thinks in terms of the banks in Eastern New Mexico and West Texas, the ones he knows. He thinks they run with the tide, making as many loans and as much money as they can when things are good, and then they retreat like scared rabbits when they are needed the most, adding to the cyclical problems instead of acting as stabilizers."

Tom Snelling was watching Katy closely, but she felt compelled to make another statement. "Not unlike the big city banks, who couldn't resist getting on the bandwagon to make gigantic loans to third world countries. The only difference is the small banks just mess up the economy in limited spheres, but the big banks could be jeopardizing the national economy—or that of the entire world."

She thought maybe she had said too much, but when Tom Snelling said, "I agree," she breathed easier.

John seemed to enjoy the exchange, but it was Henry Shaw again who posed a question. "What do you and Pop think of the farm subsidy program?"

Once again Katy didn't hedge. "We agree that it is a disaster not only for the taxpayers, but for the farmers as well."

John couldn't resist posing the next question: "If you are elected president, do you think you can get us out of these two problems?"

"John," she chided, "you are supposed to say 'when' you are elected."

He grinned, "Okay—when you are elected."

Now, Katy became more reflective. "These problems, and the federal budget deficit, must be resolved or we're in deep trouble. The Congress should take the initiative, but I've been in the House for ten years and progress has been so slow that it is scary. Surprisingly, about sixty percent of our farmers are making money now and would prosper with no program of any kind." Then almost as an afterthought, "The banks are going to have to take responsibility for their own actions. They have to help themselves." She looked at Snelling. "I'm glad some of you already are working on this seriously, setting up meaningful reserves for losses." She hesitated. "If the banks do their part, hopefully, the responsible governments of the world, including our own, will see to it that there is no collapse."

Snelling didn't respond but, from his attitude, Katy had a feeling she hadn't struck out with him.

"May I ask Katy one more question?" Henry Shaw directed his query toward the two men.

"Sure," said John, and Snelling nodded affirmatively.

"Katy, who is going to make it to the World Series?"

Katy liked this question. She knew that men are more comfortable talking about sports than almost any subject, and knew just how to field the question by asking one. "Do you think 'Gordi' will give the Dodgers enough power to win a pennant?" Farm supports and bank loans gave way to good humored agreement and disagreements on who would do what to whom during the rest of the season.

As is so often the case, the most important occurrence at the luncheon took place at its end, when Henry took Katy aside.

"TODAY will run a feature story on you. We'll take the dark horse candidate approach and it will be in an early issue. I'll personally select the reporter for the story."

Katy grasped his hand. "Thanks, Mr. Shaw. Thank you."

* * *

They said nothing as the elevator started its descent. Except for the illuminated floor indicators on the control panel and the faintest sense of vibration, Katy felt no movement at all. Certainly John could hear her pounding heart. A whiff of his cologne sent color into her cheeks.

John broke the silence.

"Katy, I think we did some good."

"More than I could have imagined, and I really appreciate it."

What must he be thinking about? Probably some deal or other now that the meeting's over. She wanted to have a hand holding hers, but surely that was just for teenagers. With surprising suddenness the doors opened.

Forty-eight floors already?

Katy wasn't surprised when John's car pulled up as they stepped out. He opened the door, putting her in the front seat with the driver. The man set the brake as he got out and John slid into the driver's seat.

What is this? Katy wondered. The chauffeur had driven, while she and John sat in the back seat, enroute to Bankcity. Now she watched John deftly guide the limo into traffic on Sixth Avenue, the street New Yorkers proudly dub the "Avenue of the Americas." He drove north.

Rockefeller Center and the LAND & SEA complex slid by. Outside Radio City Music Hall, a crowd waited for the matinee doors to open. A silhouetted line of shapely Rockettes, frozen in a high kick, danced on the marquee. World-class hotels and office buildings lined the Avenue. The New York Sheraton Centre would be ahead on the left and then, in the very heart of the city, Central Park, the green oasis of plants and trees with its bicycle routes and jogging paths and the ever-romantic horse drawn Hansom cabs.

"Katy, I want you to see my place."

"I'd like to," she said on impulse, forgetting Margaret and the New York Headquarters. Guilt intruded on the moment, but soon dissipated as the next adventure began to unfold.

John turned the car onto Central Park South. Only a small brass plaque identified the high-rise brick building as the Park Plaza. John swung the car into the short driveway. Doors opened when he touched a switch on the seat. He drove onto the elevator and folding metal doors closed behind them. Almost immediately they were whisked to the top floor. By the time Katy recovered from her astonishment, the doors of the elevator opened and John backed the limousine into his private parking area. Helping her out of the car, he took her hand as they went the few steps to the entryway of his apartment.

Katy entered ahead of John. She absorbed the grandeur of the room and skirted around the furnishings to stand at the window overlooking the park. "John...if it weren't for the flat tops of the yellow cabs darting around down there like so many minnows, you'd think we were in the countryside. Who fixed the place up so beautifully? Doesn't look at all like a bachelor's pad." She grinned at him, suppressing the urgent need to know whose hand directed the decorating.

"It was all done when I bought it. I just moved in. Makes a nice getaway, don't you think?"

"Lovely," Katy responded, privately wondering why she felt such a sense of relief at his answer.

"Make yourself at home and I'll get us something to drink."

Katy could see John plug in an appliance and busy himself with something in the refrigerator. Whatever he took out was below her line of vision. She looked around the room again.

John returned. "Be ready in a couple minutes. I've been too busy to shop or move in my own mementos." With an easy shrug, he stooped and kissed her lightly on the cheek; he did it so naturally, and it felt so comforting, Katy began to swim in a sea of giddy desire. The whole day welled up within her; seeing him for the first time in twenty-eight years, his poise and self-assurance; what he was doing for her at LAND & SEA, what he accomplished for her at Bankcity, the yearning for his touch. No place in her for resistance. He gathered her into his arms and held her tight. She wanted this. All of her being responded to his hungry kiss.

What am I doing? I can't go on like this. The thought crowded out the other emotions that threatened to engulf her. *I've got to tell him.*

As if sensing her changing mood, John released her, went to the kitchen and busied himself preparing the drinks.

"I hope you still like coffee royals." He set the tray with the two steaming cups topped with whipped cream on the coffee table. He sat opposite her on the sofa.

He remembers, too, that first intimate embrace in the "little house" by the campus. She had served the coffee royals then. *He remembers!* Somehow his remembering made everything better.

Centering herself, Katy took a deep breath, and steeled herself to make the announcement that had waited for twenty-eight years. She picked up the cup.

"John, may we drink to our son?"

John picked up his cup, too, but it never reached his lips. His hands shook as he sat it back on the table. His face went blank, making no immediate acknowledgement of what he heard. "What did you say, Katy?"

"You heard right, John. You and I have a son. You left me pregnant when you left Albuquerque."

He looked at her in disbelief. Tension stilled her.

"My God, Katy. I don't know what to say. A son? Our son?" He struggled for words, his mind groping with the enormity of this announcement. His voice was barely audible when he spoke again. "—that would make him twenty-six or twenty-seven. You didn't tell me?"

His questioning tone rang in Katy's ears. *How can I explain?* "John, it's a long story; how desperately I wanted to tell you; I even came to New York to tell you. Elizabeth and I were in Arizona for only a few days. I couldn't get you on the phone so I came to New York the next week-end. But I couldn't tell you, not after I saw your engagement announcement in the paper the same Sunday I arrived here."

"You were here then?" John's voice was incredulous.

"I went back home for an abortion; but I couldn't go through with it." Katy's hands were steady as she picked up the cup in front of her and tasted the hot drink.

John took a sip, too, lost in the sea of emotion he felt. "I'm sorry, Katy." He rose and walked to the window, careful not to face Katy until he steadied. "This is no real excuse, but you should know. I was caught in an avalanche of crises. From childhood I was groomed to head LAND & SEA by my father, and my grandfather, too. But I wasn't remotely prepared for those first few days and weeks after my father died." He paced up and down in front of the window, still not facing Katy. "There was nothing in business school about the kind of upheaval we faced. Mother was better prepared. She knew what we were up against. She knew her duty well. I had to learn mine the hard way. It became apparent to me soon enough that I was to marry Stephanie. Mother pushed it through. I didn't know the announcement was going to be in the paper. Mother acted on this with determination born of desperation."

Now he faced Katy. "I don't know what I would have done

if I had known you were pregnant." He paused as he considered this. "I tried to write you, but didn't know what to say. Finally, I threw all I had into LAND & SEA. It engulfed me. The burden of family control of a giant business is awesome. I took on that burden—but you were lost in the shuffle. Somehow I should have done better."

"What the heck," said Katy. "We both made it. Let's drink to that." She raised her cup. John covered the distance to the coffee table in three long steps, picked up his cup, and clicked it against hers.

"What the heck," he said. As he drank he felt a burst of admiration for the woman across from him. *What a gutsy one!* His voice became low, questioning. "How did you manage it? To raise a son, and do all you've done?"

It was Katy's turn to explain. "I didn't, John. I almost lost him to the world. I even went as far as the back-street doctor's office in El Paso. But, by the grace of God, there was another way." Her voice faltered. "I gave him up, John. Mom and Pop raised him as their own at Caprock, as my brother. He and I are partners in the herd of cows down there. His name is Johnny Jenkins. He calls me 'sis.'" She looked at John. "He graduates from UNM next year."

John swallowed deeply, but didn't say anything.

"John."

"Yes?"

"Johnny doesn't know."

John considered this. His voice was hushed as he responded. "A well-kept secret. Clifford mentioned your kid brother over the years, but never so much as hinted at this. Maybe he doesn't know either."

"Over the years?" Katy's question hovered in the air.

"Yes, Clifford called me 'out of the blue' nineteen years ago when he happened to be in New York. He told me you were a promising lawyer in Albuquerque and mentioned that you were running for the legislature. I was surprised at how happy I was to hear about you. We lunched at my club. I asked him if he would accept an anonymous contribution for your campaign. 'Well, I don't see why not,' he said, and that sealed it. Clifford stays at the Club and we lunch together when he's in the city. He has a wry sense of humor, and such refreshing observations on national and international affairs! I've enjoyed Clifford a great deal, and the big bonus for me was his updates on your activities."

Katy's surprise was obvious. "And you two have been in cahoots all these years?"

John chuckled. "I suppose that's as good a way to put it as any. One thing I'll say about Clifford, he's on your team every inch of the way."

"I don't know what I would have done without him."

"Katy, do you have any recent pictures from New Mexico?"

She fumbled in her purse and found the right compartment. She produced a recent picture, taken in Caprock, of Johnny and Gloria alongside the Jaguar. The blooming trumpet vine climbed the windmill in the background.

"The Jaguar!" he exclaimed. "Looks like new! How in the world?" He studied the picture. His voice was gentle, inquiring. "Katy, this might as well be you and me at Caprock. Same fellow, but the girl looks a little different."

"Even his actions and voice are like you. The girl is Gloria. She's from Santa Fe. Goes to UNM, too. Johnny moved in with her this summer."

"Sounds serious."

"It is!" Katy leaned closer to John and studied the photograph. "Clifford restored the Jaguar for Johnny when he graduated from Caprock High School. It was stored in a barn at the home place. Must have cost him a fortune."

John laughed. "Well, that sneaking, conniving, old devil! So that's what his 'special project' was! He had a chunk of my campaign contribution left over from your first Congressional race that he said he wanted to use for a special project. He never told me what it was; but I had a hunch that I would have approved."

Katy laughed, too. "I wondered how he came up with that much money."

"Katy, let's borrow the car from Johnny and take a drive."

"I have a campaign ahead of me, John."

He averted his eyes from the photograph. "That you do!" His voice was low. "May I keep this?" He held up the picture.

"Sure."

"Thank you." He seemed hesitant about his next question. "When you tell Johnny—and Katy, you must, sometime—will you tell him I'm his father?"

"Do you want me to?"

"Yes, Katy, I do. Somehow you and I stumbled, but Johnny must know that we're glad he's our son."

Some of the years of hurt dissolved as Katy heard John's words. *He's going to acknowledge his son. Acknowledge us.* She hesitated, then picked her words carefully. "I thought God had forgotten my prayers: it always seemed so remote, so unlikely that we could acknowledge our son..."

John didn't respond. Couldn't. He had to get his bearings first. He fumbled with the cup on the coffee table. When he finally found his voice, he tried to keep it steady. "Looks like our drinks got cold."

Katy sensed the emotion John felt, and guessed rightly that it was for her. She drifted to the window overlooking Central Park. She wished she could raise herself above her own inner turbulence like John's apartment rose above the tumultuous city. John came to stand beside her, putting his arm gently around her waist. Trying to sound light-hearted, he asked if he should make new drinks.

"Please don't, John. I don't dare have another one right now. I have to go to Margaret's."

"All right, Katy." There was no rancor in his voice.

"John, I feel an overwhelming responsibility at this time to a great many people; this must compare somewhat to what happened to you after your father's death. Everyone in the Coalition party is depending on me. So many commitments to so many people. Margaret and all her people, Andy and his people, Ms. Arnold and the staff, the entire Women's Movement...in New Mexico H.B. McGee is going all-out for me with his 'Democrats for Katy' and Uncle Clifford is doing the same with his 'Republicans for Katy.' They're all depending on me! My mom even gave me $30,000 to help out, all the private funds that she ever had."

John's answer was slow, deliberate, "As you often say, Katy, 'I know.'"

"I'm glad, John. All of my life, it seems, has been

preparation for this. I've been groomed for it just as you were for LAND & SEA. Now that it's here, I'm engulfed—even as you were." John was listening; Katy hurried on. "You were right for LAND & SEA, and you know what? I had to run for president. I'm afraid the American political system is out of control, draining the life blood from free enterprise, and threatening Democracy itself. I think I can do something, just by running."

"I think you can, too."

"Thank you, John, for understanding." Her eyes glanced quickly at her wrist watch. "I must call Margaret. I'll get a taxi to her place."

"No way! I'll take you; she isn't far from here, just around on the other side of the park. I'm expected at Mother's on Long Island. Can you get back to Washington okay?"

"I'm flying back this evening. Margaret's taking me to the airport."

"Speaking of flying, Katy. The 'Friends for Katy and Andy' here in New York, which I'm heading up, wants to furnish one of our company jets for the campaign. If you accept, it will be ready, with crew on hand, in the morning. Have Ms. Arnold call me tomorrow when she's ready to come up, and I'll have the plane pick her up. Sort of a trial run."

"A jet? I can't believe I'm hearing right."

"You heard right. You'll like the plane and the crew."

"Like it? It will be like manna from heaven. I can't think of anything that would help me more in this campaign."

"That's the idea. We recently took delivery on a new GULFSTREAM IV. We kept our GULFSTREAM II and converted it at the factory to the II-B model, new wings, engine overhauls, updated cabin; and we have an excellent crew for it, too. But we haven't put it in service yet, so we're making it available to you for the duration of the campaign."

Katy groped for words. "John, how can I ever thank you?"

"You don't have to. It's all settled."

Katy made the call to Margaret. As she hung up the phone, remorse flooded through her that she wasn't having a new coffee royal with John.

John came to her, and held her. They relaxed, arms around each other, for several minutes before they left for Margaret's.

22

J. Ross Temple picked up the phone, hesitated, and put it back in the cradle. Sam Pickens and I have only one thing in common, he thought: Katy Jenkins. He had never liked Pickens' style. Or his politics.

Once more he reviewed the series of events that were now creating his dilemma. With her reporter husband missing in Vietnam back in 1974, Katy had arrived at his Dallas home with the rest of the MIA/POW wives hoping to gain a strategy for getting the POW'S out. Her keen mind and matter-of-fact dedication to the project set her apart from the rest. She made a good consultant and slipped into their friendship as easily as he shrugged on his favorite coat, staying as constant as the tides, no matter how long the space between their visits. It still pained him that no trace of Steve was ever found.

As he watched the news that evening, settled comfortably in the high-backed leather chair, sipping a cold drink, faintly aware of the ceiling fan's motor hum, he tensed with suprise when Katy stepped up behind the American Coalition party podium and accepted the nomination for President.

Until then, he had never given the new party any thought. After hearing her acceptance of the nomination, he called at the Brown Palace Hotel and wished her success; he asked her to let him know if he could be of any help.

He hadn't heard from Katy directly since then, but the phone call from John Van Dorn, a few days after he talked to her, firmed his resolve to somehow help Katy in her campaign. Van Dorn, with his working knowledge of the most remote regions of the world, had discreetly been of great help to him on several projects. They had become friends. And John had gone out of his way to let him know that he was backing Katy Jenkins for President.

He wondered how John had become personally interested in Katy's bid for the presidency, but didn't ask. It was enough for him to know that John was interested.

He picked up the phone and personally punched in the numbers for Texas Electronics.

"May I tell Mr. Pickens who is calling?"

"Tell him, J. Ross." He almost added Temple but decided this had to be a friendly call from its inception. Most of his associates called him J. Ross.

Pickens came on the line right away. J. Ross disregarded the somewhat less than cordial, "Good morning, Sam here."

"Sam, this call is about Katy Jenkins. It seems we have a mutual interest in her campaign."

"What do you mean?" asked Pickens warily.

"I understand you're organizing a fundraiser for her."

"Yeah, I guess I am. The response so far hasn't been overwhelming. It isn't like raising money for Democrats."

"I can help you."

"The hell," grunted Pickens warming up a little.

"It won't be easy to get Republicans on a band wagon either. They couldn't care less about a new party. We would have to make it a personal thing."

"What you got in mind?" Some enthusiasm crept into Pickens' voice. He knew he had a problem. He'd welcome a way out even if he had to crawl in bed with the damnedest Republican in town.

"What we have to do is talk about Katy Jenkins—not your new party."

Pickens started to rebut the remark, but thought better about it. "I'll buy that. Let's get together and talk."

* * *

Katy felt a rush of exhilaration when she saw the plane streaking along the runway at Washington National, and then, with head held high as if alert and curious about it's new role, come to a casual stop within a few yards of where she and Ms. Arnold waited.

The trip to Texas would be Katy's first in the sleek

GULFSTREAM furnished for the campaign by Van Dorn's "Friends for Katy and Andy." The two-engine jet seated twelve in maximum comfort and had a three man crew: a pilot, a copilot, and a security man to protect the plane. On each side of the plane, below the American Flag insignias, new "Katy for President" decals covered the LAND & SEA emblems.

Ms. Arnold's previous descriptions of the plane's crew intrigued Katy. She could see Captain Bill Burke sitting tall in the pilot's seat as the plane came to a stop.

Burke was checking her out with an appraising eye. Not beautiful, he thought, but a striking woman. He couldn't tell her age; mature, but still good looking. She must have a lot on the ball, he thought, for John Van Dorn to be backing her for President. Even in a bright yellow tailored summer blouse and a navy blue pleated skirt she looks the part, he thought.

He disappeared from the cockpit and appeared shortly at the plane's door. Katy watched him come down the steps. She noticed his lean angular build and prominent features. His confident manner and enthusiasm confirmed Ms. Arnold's observation that he loved the plane and his job.

Coming down the steps with Burke was Glen Copeland, the plane's security man. An older man, Copeland flew helicopters in Vietman, survived, and started his long career in the FBI. When he retired from FBI Van Dorn offered him the security job. His agility and trim figure belied his gray hair and slight stoop.

Burke strode forward and acknowledged Ms. Arnold, who introduced him to Katy. He took Katy's hand in a firm, reassuring way. He, in turn, introduced Copeland. Katy's immediate reaction was one of trust and confidence in both men. She looked for evidence of the "tough streak" that, according to Ms. Arnold, Copeland was reputed to have, but saw no particular evidence of it. She did notice the gun he wore underneath his unbuttoned sports coat; the grip stuck out of an inconspicuous shoulder holster.

Bill picked up both ladies' bags. He led the way up the steps, followed closely by Katy, Ms. Arnold, and Copeland.

Katy caught her breath when she saw the comfortable elegance of the plane's cabin and furnishings. *This is the way to go*, she thought.

She could see the other crew member in the cockpit poring over a navigation map. He had already filed their flight plan to Dallas and now was memorizing the landmarks on the route.

"You must be Gordon Gates," she said when he looked around. As he folded up the map, she worked her way forward and extended her hand. He took it gingerly. "So you're the Katy Jenkins that John and Ms. Arnold have been telling us about. Welcome aboard!" Then he added, "Excuse my not meeting you out there, but one of us has to be in the cockpit."

"Makes sense," said Katy. "I'm glad to know you."

Katy saw that he was a small man. Ms. Arnold had told her that he was a former airline pilot and that he had four kids. There wasn't time for Katy to learn any more about him, because Bill was moving forward. She selected a seat on one side of the built-in conference table, and Ms. Arnold sat opposite her. Copeland sat beyond the sofa across from them.

The plane taxied to the runway, waited for clearance from the tower to take off, and soon was in the air.

Ms. Arnold had kept tabs on the ticket sales for the two fund-raising events in Dallas. Sam Pickens kept her informed on a daily basis. At first, it didn't look too good, but when Sam joined forces with J. Ross Temple, things picked up. Now, there would be two banquets: the first one this evening at the Country Club—at $1,000 per plate with Temple introducing Katy; the second, tomorrow evening at the Convention Center at $100 a plate, with Pickens handling the introduction.

Ms. Arnold wrote on a pad she had taken from her purse, and handed it across to Katy. In her bold scrawl was written: Tonight, 122 people at $1,000 per. Tomorrow night, 970 people at $100 per...$219,000!

Katy's face lit up when she saw the figures. Her mind whirled with the significance of this development. This was more than double what she had expected. Oblivious to the plane crew, she leaped up out of her seat, into the aisle, and gave her hand to Ms. Arnold. "Put 'er there, partner!" she exclaimed. "We're in business in Texas!"

As the women clasped hands in a sort of Texas handshake victory celebration, Glen Copeland watched with mild amusement.

But as Katy resumed her seat, the smile playing at the corner of his lips was replaced by a grimace of concern. He was watching a small capsule about the size of a Contac cold capsule roll across the floor. Probably nothing to worry about, he thought, but I'll check it out. He remembered the thorough briefing Van Dorn gave the three man crew the day before. "Don't underestimate the hazards of an American political campaign," he told them. "There are a lot of 'kooks' out there. And they're dangerous. They're less predictable than professionals, and the police are generally less well prepared to cope with them. Let's keep this operation safe."

Casually, Copeland went up the aisle, stooped and picked up the capsule. A quick glance convinced him it wasn't Contac. The contents inside looked like white powder.

"Either of you ladies know what this is?" he inquired casually.

Neither did.

"Are either of you taking any kind of medication in capsules?" Both assured him they were not.

"May I borrow your writing pad?" Katy tore off the sheet with Ms. Arnold's notes, and handed the pad to him. He sat down on the sofa across from Katy and Ms. Arnold, took a pen knife from his pocket and cut the capsule open. He tapped some of the white powder from the capsule onto the top sheet of the pad. He spread some of it out with his knife, looked at it closely and decided to test it. Ms. Arnold and Katy watched as he took an ampule tester, slightly larger than a household thermometer, from his briefcase, poured a tiny bit of the white powder into one end and pressed the vial firmly. The contents turned a pale beige color.

"This seems to be very high grade cocaine," he announced solemnly. "Do either of you know how it got here? It must have fallen out of Katy's clothes, or something, when she bounced out into the aisle awhile ago."

Katy and Ms. Arnold were both alarmed, but neither had any explanation for where the capsule came from, or how it got there. Copeland watched their reactions closely and was satisfied that they were telling the truth.

His next question elevated the incident into a major problem.

"Would anyone have any reason to *plant* drugs on you?"

Katy's mind flashed to the camera incident at the Brown Palace Hotel and the unpleasant events following the million dollar check presentation.

"It's very possible," she said.

Copeland had no more questions. His manner changed into that of a friend with a mutual problem. "All right," he said, "we've got to see if there's any more." He looked around. "Take everything out of your purse; let me check it out. We had better check out the clothes you are wearing, too. And, your traveling bag. Without any more prompting, Katy dumped the contents of her purse onto the table in front of her. She handed the emptied purse to Copeland and began a methodical search of the purse's contents. Inspecting each item, she handed it to Ms. Arnold for further investigation.

Neither of them found anything unusual in the purse, but Copeland let out a sharp whistle. He had found something suspicious in the lining of the purse. He used the razor sharp blade of his pen knife to slit the lining, and found a small flat white thick-plastic package about the size of a sugar or sweetener packet. A close inspection left no question in his mind. The packet contained cocaine.

He advised the women of his find, then made his way to the cockpit. Burke and Gates sensed that something out of the ordinary was going on in the cabin, but didn't know what.

Katy talked in a hushed tone to Ms. Arnold. "I don't like the looks of this. Who would be out to get me? It just about had to be someone inside our own headquarters."

Ms. Arnold ticked off everyone in the office in her mind. "The Lee girl from Birmingham is the only one I haven't known for years. Even the volunteers in the phone room, I know from way back." Her brow wrinkled, "except for two new volunteers."

They were flying at 40,000 feet, above the commercial airliners and turbulence, on the beam, weather clear, and ahead of schedule. Burke turned the controls over to Gates and joined Katy, Ms. Arnold, and Copeland in the cabin.

"Is there any chance you have any of this stuff on you?" Copeland asked Ms. Arnold.

"I don't think so," she said thoughtfully. "We didn't pick up my things until we left for the airport. The 'plants' must have been made at Katy's house, which also serves as Party headquarters. There are a lot of people around there, day and night. Party employees, and volunteers, and drop-ins. Katy lives there. All her things were there."

"That would make it easy," commented Copeland. He picked up Katy's suitcase. "Okay if I look in here?"

"Sure."

"And while I'm checking this out, you better get off everything you're wearing."

Katy looked around the cabin. The restroom and galley at the back didn't give her much room to do a strip-tease, but there was no question in her mind now. They would have to go through the clothes she had on and those in the suitcase.

Ms. Arnold moved back in the plane and helped Katy with the undressing. First off was the pleated skirt. Ms. Arnold took it up to Copeland. He temporarily lost interest in the bag. His fingers deftly searched the pleats of the skirt. In less then a minute he had found another capsule. It was fastened under a pleat with a small strip of sticky cloth that just about matched the skirt. He yanked the strip loose, and out fell the capsule.

Hell, he thought, no telling how many of these might be around. He looked at the suitcase again, and methodically began to unpack it. Even before he finished the unpacking, he detected the hairline slit at the top of the lining. He stacked the rest of the contents on the sofa and studied the bag.

Ms. Arnold brought up more of Katy's clothes. "Put them on a separate seat," he said. "I found another capsule in the skirt. And this suitcase looks suspicious." Ms. Arnold watched as he ran his hands over the suitcase's lining. "There's something there all right," he said aloud. Now his hand was shaking. He cut the lining. As it came open, he realized he had cut a plastic bag inside also. White powder was falling out into the suitcase. He didn't like that. He worked the plastic bag out of the lining, but was careful not to remove it from the suitcase. Don't want to scatter this around, he thought.

He sat up straight, and drew in a deep breath. Katy came up the aisle draped in a blanket Ms. Arnold had found in an overhead rack. She saw the plastic bag and white powder.

"Ladies, we have enough cocaine here to start a dealership." Katy could feel the tension in Copeland's voice. "Don't touch anything. I don't know how in hell we're going to get rid of this stuff. My guess is there'll be a reception committee at the airport when we land in Dallas."

The scene flashed through Katy's mind. Police, with badges and guns and handcuffs. Reporters and cameramen recording every detail. Front page stuff, all of it. And her campaign as dead as a three-day-old corpse.

Her eyes fastened on Burke. "Where's the best place we can land this craft between here and Dallas, where we can get rid of some cargo and I can do some fast shopping?"

Copeland looked appreciatively at Katy. Without hesitation he said to Burke, "That's what we gotta do, Bill."

"Let me talk to Gordon." Burke was already making his way up to the cockpit. Katy followed closely, oblivious of her unorthodox attire. Gates had heard enough that he was already aware of the problem.

"I think we better go for Memphis," he said. "You can damn near see it from here. Just over the horizon to the west." He grinned. "I think we need to make a fuel stop."

Burke slipped back into the pilot's seat. John was right. This flying candidate Jenkins around wasn't going to be dull. As Copeland got on the radio, Burke changed course for Memphis.

* * *

This would be a night to celebrate. He'd need a girl. Joe Domino picked up the phone, and dialed Stella.

"Stella, you got anything special up there exclusive for the evenin'?"

"Sure, I do, anytime for you, Joe. This is Tuesday; dead as a door nail; none of 'em out. Just lazin' around here. You can take your pick and keep her as long as you want."

"Any new ones in?"

"Got two girls from Wisconsin last week."

"I like those milk-fed dairy girls. How old?"

"Nineteen."

"Hell, they're all nineteen."

"I'm not kidding you, Joe, this is the first time these girls have been out of Wisconsin."

"I don't want one that'd be squeamish about going down, or that'd yell her head off at a little spankin' on her ass-cheeks."

One of these girls is a 'looker', Joe. It'd be good for her to get a little paddlin'. All my girls go down, you know that. They spend more time on their knees than on their backs nowadays."

"Oh, hell, I know. I used to own the girls. They worked their asses off in those days. When I bought the old Savoy, they didn't know it, but they paid for it in two years." Stella wasn't surprised at this. She paid Joe plenty of rent for the Savoy, and more for protection. No one knew just what their deal was. Joe didn't believe in telling anyone anything they didn't need to know.

"You want the 'looker' or the plain one?"

"Hell, send 'em both over if they're not doin' anything anyhow. I'll buy 'em some drinks and corned beef sandwiches at Pete's. Then take 'em out to my place."

"You want them over to Pete's?"

"Yeah, in the bar."

"What time?"

"About an hour."

"I'll get 'em ready for you, Joe. The beauty's Carmen, the other one's Joanne. They'll be out there waiting for you. Have fun."

It was understood that there was no charge to Joe. He usually tipped the girls a fifty or a hundred dollar bill, depending on how well they behaved. Stella got her half of this.

Even before he left for Pete's, Joe felt apprehensive. Why in hell didn't they call from Dallas? Should be all over by now. No way anything could go wrong. The plants were perfect. Clothes, purse, suitcase. The smartest thing he ever did was get a volunteer worker right inside her house from day one. That Arnold woman never suspected a thing. By the time they figure out what happened, the plant will have disappeared into thin air, he thought happily. Everything was set up right in Dallas, too, Court order for the search—everything! Why in hell don't they call?

Carmen and Joanne lounged in a booth when Joe arrived at

Pete's. He ordered bourbon and tonic for them, and a double scotch and soda for himself. The girls seemed anxious to please. Plenty good looking. Young. Just the kind he liked. He put his hand on Joanne's leg. She caught her breath, but made no move. She was going to be all right, he thought. He anticipated seeing the 'looker' stripped.

"Phone call for you, Joe." It was the bartender. "You can take it over here."

He went around to the end of the bar and took the telephone. "Yeah."

It was the call from Dallas. Joe clutched the phone in his hand and listened to the caller. "She was clean, boss, and so was her luggage—and her purse—and the plane. Nothing. Not a trace. They couldn't hold her. Security man came off the plane with her. Tough as hell. No way they could hold her."

"Not a trace?" Joe was leaning hard on the bar, his face contorted in agonized disbelief. "Not a trace?" he repeated, more to himself than to the caller. "Did anyone from the plane see you?"

"No, we were mixed in with the press."

"Mixed in with the press," Joe groaned; "they'd a crucified her...okay, get your asses out of there and lay low a day or two."

"We're already at the airport, going to Atlanta."

"All right." Joe hung the phone up heavily, still shaking his head in disbelief. He walked back over to his table in a daze. Seeing the girls there brought him back to reality. He ordered a repeat on the drinks and corned beef sandwiches. "Make them to go," he said, "and then call me a taxi." He wanted to get out of there. "I've been royally fucked," he muttered half aloud.

"What did you say?" Carmen asked.

"We're going out to my place," he said. As upset as he was about the phone call, he still relished the idea of taking the girls out there. He liked to see their eyes pop at his 27 x 47 foot den, with its own bath and showers, and the king size chaise lounge, and the adjoining enclosed swimming pool where swim suits were not part of the standard equipment. He looked straight at Carmen. "And I'm going to give you a royal fucking."

"Oh. I thought that's what you said."

The air was warm outside and Joe was feeling the warmth of

the drinks, too. Even so, he shivered as he thought of the phone call he was sure to get from New York in the morning. He had assured them the damn woman would be derailed in Dallas. His people didn't like excuses.

He put the girls into the back of the cab, and got in front with the driver so he could direct him out to his place.

His body shook again. He knew that every operation he had was in some way dependent on the syndicate. What-in-hell went wrong? The damn woman was messing him up.

* * *

J. Ross will be here in two hours to pick me up for the dinner, Katy thought anxiously. At $1,000 a plate they'll expect me to really be something.

Resentment flooded through her for the ordeals she had suffered coping with drugs and frantic shopping during the day. The day was planned to be leisurely, to get ready for tonight. She desperately needed time to think.

Ms. Arnold, bless her, was getting the one dress she had rescued for this evening's event pressed and ready. A corsage was delivered shortly after they arrived at the hotel. From J. Ross. Luckily, it went beautifully with the dress. What she needed now was a warm bath, and time to think. For years, she had thought out her most important speeches in the warmth and privacy of the tub. She threw off her clothes.

For days a plan had been drifting into her mind, as if buried in the subconcious, tentatively welcoming every opportunity to emerge. She had intended to put it in focus, get it organized, and talk to somebody about it. But who? Ms. Arnold, brilliant tactician though she was, wouldn't understand its importance. She considered talking to John about it. On the phone? Didn't seem like the best way. He could too easily demur or express doubts. There hadn't been an opportunity to tell him personally, and if there had been, she doubted that she would have taken it. Its boldness might appeal to Andy Barker, if presented right. Andy was looking for a new campaign theme. She hadn't considered going to Ellen Steele or Ruth Silverton with it—just wasn't quite the right kind of an idea to stir up the Women's Movement.

And here she was in Texas—the very place where it would have the best chance. In a couple of hours a hundred-thousand dollars worth of contributors would have all eyes fastened on her. Tonight, and the next two days, would make or break her with Sam Pickens—and with J. Ross—and with Texas.

She had suffered for ten years in the House of Representatives because of the Congressional blind spot on energy. The shattering Iraqi crisis, and the continued uncertainty in the Middle East, now made a long-range U.S. energy policy mandatory.

A tingle of excitement rippled through her body. She knew oil flowed through the veins of the Texas economy, ignited it and gave it direction. And she knew that nothing could be more American than Texans' enthusiasm and their bigger-than-life optimism when it centered on boom times, everyone working and making money. She could speak to them tonight in their own language.

She turned on the hot water briefly, welcomed its reassuring warmth, and laid back in the tub to think it through. She would be considered an opportunist by many Americans, catering to a powerful special interest group. They would point accusing fingers at her. The plan would raise gasoline prices; people would scream about that. A hidden tax to benefit the oil barons. Restriction of trade. She could hear the uproar.

The media would grab the sensational angles, then put the important aspects of the plan way down in the story—if they included them at all.

And what would John Van Dorn think? After all, he had the biggest oil tankers on the seas. She grimaced. I do like the GULFSTREAM, she thought.

Finally she decided—*it's better this way.* Let it be an accomplished fact before she consulted with anybody. That way no one else would have any blame if it didn't work out. She knew she had to go for it.

As she put on her make-up, the details for tonight's presentation developed. She hardly heard Ms. Arnold's approving comments as she slipped into her dress. She glanced at the clock; she had made it.

23

Impressive as heck, thought Katy; I don't see even one Stetson.

As the elegant parfait arrived, Katy's mind automatically shifted to her opening remarks. Then J. Ross was introducing her. His sincere, complimentary remarks rang true.

He specifically mentioned the new party. "With her American Coalition party on the ballot in all fifty states, Katy gives Republicans, Democrats, and Independents a unique opportunity to vote for a new voice in America." He paused briefly. "It is my pleasure to present Katy Jenkins."

Katy rose, acknowledged Mr. Temple, thanked him for the introduction, addressed Mr. Pickens, and a full dozen other dignitaries "—and ladies and gentlemen:"

"I have never thought of Texans as Democrats or Republicans, or even as Independents. Texans were always the affluent neighbors to the east and south of New Mexico; larger than life neighbors, with the most wide-open spaces anywhere, jackrabbits bigger than any we see in Eastern New Mexico, and a Texas brand of politics and economics impossible to be confused with any others.

"As you know, of course, I'm a New Mexican. And we in New Mexico have a long tradition of vilifying Texans. In fact, a long time ago, a New Mexican official wrote words that have endeared him to generations of people in my home state: 'Poor New Mexico, so far from heaven and so close to Texas.'

"But I'll let you in on our little secret. It's all in fun. We really do love our Texas neighbors and welcome you to our state—to our mountains, lakes and best of all, our good green chile."

The people in the room liked Katy's homey style; they were ready to hear more. The dining room radiated coziness and made it easy for Katy to communicate. And the lectern! She had never used such a fancy one. Bullet-proof, she had been told, but the real luxury was its built-in air conditioner. *Only in Texas*, she thought.

"We Americans are surely the luckiest people in the world. But, as a result of our generosity at home and abroad, we've gotten ourselves into a position where we are constantly spending more than we are taking in. We have, in just a decade, gone from the world's greatest creditor nation to the world's largest debtor.

"A big reason for this trade imbalance is the billions of dollars Americans pay for the ten million barrels of oil we import each day. So let's talk about this tonight. About oil. About Saudi Arabia and a United States energy plan."

As Katy surveyed the faces in the room she knew she had their interest. "First, Saudi Arabia has about 70 percent of the world's known oil reserves, and it's so cheap to produce that it can be hauled halfway around the world and still be sold cheap. A real bonanza, any way you look at it!"

Katy paused dramatically, then added, "Well...almost any way you look at it. But let's take a closer look." She launched into an explanation of the OPEC cartel and its manipulation of oil prices during the last two decades. Then she advised, "In 1979 the OPEC monopoly deliberately cut production deeply, scarcities resulted—and prices for crude oil soared from $20 a barrel in 1976 to $40 a barrel in 1980. Remember, gasoline prices jumped fifty cents a gallon! And long lines formed at gas stations across the country.

"America responded in typical American fashion. We cut consumption, re-designed our gas-guzzling automobiles, developed alternative energy sources, brought in a giant new oil field in Alaska, helped England develop off-shore oil in the North Sea, helped Mexico develop its oil reserves—and began new oil exploration in our own country, finding new reserves at greater depths. The high price of 'crude' made all of this economically feasible. Texans played a big role in this development world-wide.

"The Arabs hit the panic button. They opened the spigots on their cheap oil wide enough to knock out American competition; low enough to make all other forms of energy non-competitive! By 1986 they had forced crude oil down to $15 a barrel. Our energy industries and conservation efforts stopped dead.

"Texas and Oklahoma went into depression. Great Texas banks were taken over by out-of-state institutions. Houston alone lost ten thousand jobs in a matter of weeks.

"I tried to get a bill through Congress to put a five dollar a barrel fee on imported oil, to benefit our entire energy industry. But my bill, which was co-sponsored by your Senior Senator, didn't even get out of committee. The House, the Senate, and the administration, sat on their hands, and we continued importing cheap oil in a fool's paradise."

Her pace slowed. "We moved bravely when Iraq invaded Kuwait and eyed Saudi Arabia. Now, can we move as bravely toward a national energy policy?"

She relaxed, becoming conversational on the most important point she wanted to make: "An oil import fee is the ONLY energy policy we need to start a turnaround. Not only will this revitalize our oil industry; it will also encourage development of other energy sources including natural gas, solar, wind, thermal, and more."

Katy waited for audience reaction.

Sam Pickens' voice boomed out. "We've got to wrestle this energy monopoly to the ground, and this will do it."

"Are you with me?" Katy asked the assembly.

"Damn right," a male voice was heard above the other exclamations of approval.

"Any questions?" Katy knew there would be some. A well-dressed woman, who was famous in Dallas for being the devil's advocate, was the first.

"This sounds like having your cake and eating it, too," she said. "What's the catch?"

"You're right," Katy said firmly. "There really is a catch. The Congress and the American people may not be ready for more increases in gasoline prices. But, we must become less dependent on foreign oil, and we'll put some of our people back to work on our own energy production."

"How much will it raise prices at the pump?" snapped the questioner.

Katy took her time answering the question. "Maybe a nickel a gallon, or even a dime a gallon."

"Isn't the administration against any and all tax increases?" someone else asked.

"Depends on which administration you are talking about," replied Katy evenly. "In the Jenkins-Barker administration we'll be for this one. Both the other candidates promise to strengthen the economy, and reduce the deficit without raising taxes. But they don't tell you how they are going to do either one."

"How about our allies?" asked someone at the far end of the table. "Won't exporters resent a tariff on oil they ship to us?"

Katy was quick to respond to this question. "The OPEC nations just may, at that." She looked around. "Does anyone in this room care if OPEC loses some control?"

No one did. She shifted gears. "Now, I want to hear from you." She called on a well-known banker first, then others. As they spoke, Katy felt support growing in the room. This was the kind of meeting she liked, lots of participation.

When Katy called on J. Ross, he rose to the occasion. "Katy, there is genuine enthusiasm here for your plan. This plan will catch on like wildfire in the state of Texas, and I hope all across the country."

* * *

J. Ross Temple observed Katy's handling of the group with admiration and awe. The woman has political savvy, he thought as he watched her get her audience involved and listened to her relevant and well selected comments as various persons in the room spoke. She made every one feel personally a part of it, and in this way she made each one feel important, too. All with high good humor.

He couldn't help but wonder, however, if John Van Dorn had approved the plan she was pushing. Somehow, he doubted it. The presentation had been too spontaneous, too direct, to have been beat around in discussions and committee meetings. This is Katy's idea, he decided, and it computes.

* * *

Next morning, Katy and Ms. Arnold pored over the Dallas Morning News and the Dallas Times-Herald in the hotel coffee shop. Katy saw it first, a feature story all the way across the bottom of the front page, bylined Casper. "CANDIDATE ASKS FOR OIL IMPORT FEE TO BOLSTER ENERGY INDEPENDENCE."

"I couldn't have written as good a headline myself," beamed Katy.

"Here's more front page," exulted Ms. Arnold. "'OIL IMPORT TARIFF PROPOSED BY JENKINS.' They go on about how it will help the overall energy plan," she added as she read.

"Listen to Casper," Katy said excitedly. "'I was curious when I went to hear Katy Jenkins speak at a thousand-dollar-a-plate dinner sponsored by prominent Dallasites last night at the Fairmont Hotel. I came away convinced.

"'In case you've never heard of Katy Jenkins, she's a candidate for president on the American Coalition party ticket. And, I assure you, she is a candidate to be taken seriously.'"

"Katy, you know what?" exclaimed Ms. Arnold, "we're off and running in Texas. Wait'll you get through with the Party organization meeting this afternoon, and a thousand people tonight!"

* * *

Katy was in for two surprises before the day was over. Combined, they would make her name a household word from one end of Texas to the other.

The luncheon for Party workers was at the Holiday Inn at the Market Center in Dallas. Seventy-six people were there; a few more would show up for the sessions during the afternoon. When Katy walked into the meeting room, she heard the disjointed sounds of a musical group tuning their instruments. The sounds continued as Katy was introduced to Party members.

Then delightful, joyful music floated across the room. Everyone paused to listen. *This isn't the usual political band,* thought Katy. *Here's something special.*

"Who in the world are those musicians?" she asked as Madge Bloomfield introduced her around.

"The Texans, they call themselves. Fellow playing the guitar is Tex Richards. That's his wife playing the fiddle." Then Mrs. Bloomfield proudly added, "They are charter members of the Party. They're here for the meeting. They're furnishing the music."

"Are they professionals?"

"You mean, are they making any money? They're trying to, but I'd guess they're starving."

"They shouldn't be, with music like that."

"It's nice, isn't it?"

The music was temporarily forgotten as Sam Pickens made his entrance. He made his way directly to Katy and Madge. "Oh, I see you two are organized," he said, as he greeted them. "I can't stay, but I wanted to come by."

"Can you say a few words to get the meeting started?" asked Madge quickly.

"Sure," he agreed, "if you can get me on right away."

Salads were on the table, and as soon as everyone was seated, Madge rose, welcomed the group, and immediately introduced Pickens. As he rose to his full six foot four, the musicians hit build-up chords that climaxed just as he cleared his throat.

"That is good music you play," he addressed the musicians. "Thank you!" He looked over the audience, addressed Katy and Madge, and members of the American Coalition party. He looked at Katy. "I've had the pleasure of hearing our candidate, Katy Jenkins, twice: first, the day after she was nominated in Denver. Judging by that experience, you are in for a memorable meeting this afternoon; and I heard Katy again last night at the big fund-raising dinner at the Fairmont. Incidentally, we raised a hundred-thousand dollars, and we're going to do it again tonight." Spontaneous applause greeted this announcement. The musicians struck up Happy Days Are Here Again, and played until the applause ended.

"But that isn't what I came over here to talk to you about. I want you to know that Katy was the senior statesman last night.

Her plan to put an import fee on oil coming into this country is a bold, practical proposal. I'm sure you will get the details here today, and Katy will answer any questions you'll have." He looked around appreciatively at the people. "I hope every one of you, and the Party nationwide, will go all-out to back Katy on this one."

The Texans sensed that Pickens was through speaking. As he shook hands with Katy and Madge, and a half dozen others at the head table on his way out, they noisily resumed playing Happy Days Are Here Again. The music subsided as Pickens went out the door.

This was the opportunity Katy was waiting for. "Excuse me a minute," she said. "I want to meet Tex Richards and his Texans." She scooted out of her seat and headed for the musicians. Tex saw her coming and met her part way. Madge observed that they looked more like old friends getting together than strangers meeting for the first time.

"You guys are great," Katy burst out. "What I'm wondering is—could you play for a big meeting at the Convention Center this evening? There are supposed to be a thousand people there. We'll pay your regular booking rates," she added quickly.

It didn't take a long consultation.

The meeting started during the luncheon and continued until three o'clock. Katy was delighted when Tex and his wife, Susanne, both participated in the meeting with lively comments and enthusiastic support. Both have wonderful stage personalities, she thought.

* * *

When J. Ross picked up Katy and Ms. Arnold to go to the Convention Center for the second fundraiser, he looked Katy over with an appraising eye. *So this woman was John Van Dorn's college sweetheart*, he thought. John didn't hesitate to tell him about her on the phone. "It was a short-lived affair," he said, "one summer back in the sixties. That's when Dad died. I had to high-tail it back to New York, and Katy got lost in the shuffle. She was something," he added.

She still is, thought J. Ross.

They were welcomed at the Convention Center meeting room by the vibrant music of The Texans. J. Ross looked puzzled. "Where do you suppose the music came from? Sam must have thought of that."

"They're The Texans. They played at the Party luncheon today," Katy said. "Madge Bloomfield had them at lunch. I invited them here tonight."

"They're good."

"Charter members of the Party, too. I want you to meet them."

Sam Pickens welcomed everyone in his booming voice and called on Reverend Wilson for the blessing.

Katy listened to the groan of the air conditioners trying to offset the summer's heat and the heat generated by a thousand bodies, and added her own small prayer.

Random thoughts drifted through her mind, catching only a phrase or two of the reverend's mini-sermon, until she realized Reverend Wilson had stopped and conversation had grown to the point of drowning out the hard working air conditioners. A roasted, golden-brown cornish hen, nesting on a pile of wild rice, appeared on the table in front of her and she noticed waiters delivering plates to the seated crowd.

That's when she saw them. Just an illusion, she thought. But, sure enough, there they were, sitting at an outside table half-way down the room. Mom, Pop, Johnny, and Gloria!

"Sam! J. Ross! My family's here!" she exclaimed and left her seat to greet them.

"You rascals, you! Not telling me," she said, as she threw her arms around Mom and Pop, and then Johnny and Gloria. "Oh, I'm so glad to see you!"

"Want you to meet someone here," said Pop when Katy settled down a little. "This is Mr. and Mrs. Walters—and Mr. and Mrs. Collier."

"I'm glad to know you," enthused Katy as she shook hands all around.

"Walt and Don are our friendly bankers here in Dallas," Pop said.

"You look like a banker yourself, Pop. I didn't know you had such a fancy suit. And a tie!"

"Mom made me spruce up for the occasion."

"I'm glad, glad, glad you're here." She put her arm around Gloria. "You look lovely, honey. And, Johnny, you handsome devil, I'm just glad a nice girl like Gloria has you in tow." She kissed him on the cheek.

"Hey, I want to see the GULFSTREAM," interjected Johnny.

"Okay, first thing in the morning. You'll love it. We're going to Austin and San Antonio. Can you go with us? There's plenty of room." She looked at the head table. "I had better get back up there. It's nice to know you folks," she said to the Walters and Colliers. Then to her family, "I'll see you all after the meeting. I want you to meet Ms. Arnold and everybody."

* * *

Burke had already rolled the GULFSTREAM out when Katy and her group arrived. The crew had carefully inspected the plane that morning and taken it up on a test flight, even though Copeland employed round-the-clock security from the moment the plane touched down in Dallas.

Introductions made, Katy took Mom and Pop aboard the plane. Pop had business in Dallas that day. Johnny, Gloria, Ms. Arnold, and the five musicians would accompany Katy to Austin and San Antonio. Perfect, thought Katy as she and Ms. Arnold settled down in seats nearest the galley. Johnny, Gloria, Tex, Susanne, and the rest sat as far forward as possible, entranced by the GULFSTREAM's operation.

Katy and Ms. Arnold talked in privacy. "You didn't see that mob of 'right-to-lifers' outside the Convention Center last night," commented Ms. Arnold.

"No, I didn't," said Katy. "They were pretty well dispersed by the time my meeting with Sam, J. Ross, Madge, and The Texans broke up. Incidentally, they approved my plan to engage The Texans for the entire campaign. We're booking them full-time."

"Katy, it's the best way we could ever spend the money. What good would a conventional campaign manager do us with maybe 15,000 party members in the entire state? These guys are 'good will' personified."

"That's what I think." Katy switched the subject back to the 'right-to-lifers' demonstrations. "I understand the Dallas police had their hands full."

"They did. The demonstrators got down on their hands and knees and crawled through police lines. When the police arrested them, they went limp and it took several police officers to drag each of them in. It wasn't a pretty sight."

"I'm glad my folks, and Johnny and Gloria, were inside with me. Of course, they saw the papers and undoubtedly the TV, too."

"Everyone did. Your getting J. Ross and Sam and your family out the side entrance saved us. Kept your mugs off the TV. We came out pretty good overall on the publicity. Dallasites know there was a Katy Jenkins rally in town anyhow."

"Still don't like it though."

"Me neither, and I'm afraid we're in for more."

"What do you mean?"

"When I called Mrs. Allsup in Austin this morning, where the 'coffee' is being held, she said some protesters were already out in front of her house."

"Oh, hell."

"What I don't understand is how they knew about it. There wasn't time for advance publicity. Mrs. Allsup says she just called her friends on the phone within the last two days."

"How about Georgetown?" Katy asked suddenly.

"Georgetown?" Ms. Arnold was puzzled. "Oh sure, I did call the office, and gave Amos our itinerary for the next few days. But, nothing would be put out from there about the 'coffee' in Austin."

"You had better head back to Georgetown tomorrow, right after the Petroleum Club luncheon—and see what's going on. It seems like we have someone on the inside who isn't on our side."

"You know something funny?"

"What's that?"

"Well, one of those two new volunteers in the phone room hasn't been to work since we left. When Amos tried to call her, the phone was disconnected."

"Follow up on her. It had to be someone on the inside who

planted the drugs."

"I know," said Ms. Arnold. "I'll be glad to get back. And now you'll have The Texans for traveling companions." She looked at Katy. "You going to invade Colorado and New Mexico with The Texans?"

"Yes, they'll get along fine in Colorado and New Mexico. I thought about a name change for them, but The Texans fits too well. In New Mexico we act as if we don't like Texans, but we love for them to come and see us. They keep Colorado and New Mexico green with their greenbacks. Most of the time The Texans will be in Texas anyhow. I want to work with them the next few days. They're going to be the heart and soul of the Coalition party down here."

The engines decelerated; they'd be landing in Austin in a matter of minutes.

*   *   *

"Ten o'clock, eighty degrees in the shade and humidity to match," commented Johnny as he and The Texans boarded two cabs headed for the Allsups'.

"You get used to it," said Tex cheerfully.

Katy, Ms. Arnold, Gloria, and Susanne had gone ahead with Mrs. Allsup. Loaded with musical instruments and people, the cabs raced across town by the back ways and arrived at the Allsups' ranch style home just as Mrs. Allsup's car pulled in the driveway. The cabs pressed through the crowd of young people in the street and pulled up behind her.

"They're singing hymns," called out Susanne, who was the first one out of the lead car. Katy climbed out next. She surveyed the situation. Full fledged demonstration, she thought. Press, television crew, two police cars. It's organized all right.

"Let me handle this, Miss Jenkins." It was Tex. Before Katy could say anything, he took charge. "Everyone go on inside. Quick!" He beckoned to the musicians. "Get your instruments ready to play!" He pressed a bill into Johnny's hand. "Take care of the drivers. Tell them to come back in two hours." Susanne lagged behind the others. Tex put his arm around her waist. "Honey, you and Josh join the party inside. Get your fiddle and have Josh get his bass. Make dinner music, just the two of you. Play 'background.' Tim 'n Hank 'n me are going to be busy out here for awhile."

"Gotcha." She dashed toward the house. Tex followed at a more leisurely pace.

The picketers sang Onward Christian Solders as Tex, Tim, and Hank reappeared with guitar, banjo, and mandolin.

"Hit it," said Tex. The music joined in harmony with the voices.

"What th' heck?" yipped one of the leaders.

Tex's voice rang out. "Everybody sing!"

". . . ONWARD CHRISTIAN SOLDIERS, MARCHING AS TO WAR . . ."

Johnny watched as Tex consulted with the picket leaders to select song after song. The police loafed around their cars parked in the shade of a big tree across the street. The newspeople shot all the film they wanted and left. One of the police cars took off to answer another call. The singing slowed after awhile and the picketing began to break up. No confrontations. All over in less than an hour.

"That Tex is cool," Johnny told Katy.

* * *

"Next stop, San Antonio," sang out Ms. Arnold as the group settled down in the comfort of the GULFSTREAM. "Chalk up the Austin 'coffee' as outstanding. If Katy could do a hundred of those a day, we'd carry Texas by a landslide. River Walk next."

"What's that?" asked Gloria.

"You'll see," said Josh, his voice almost as deep as his base fiddle. "You stroll along on both sides of the river. It's down below the street level, trees and flowers along the banks. Boats loaded with tourists chug up and down in a colorful procession. And, hotels, sidewalk restaurants, shops by the dozen. It's San Antonio's showplace."

"We're staying in The Menger, an historic place one block from the Alamo and only a block or two from the River Walk," said Ms. Arnold. "You kids can have a real vacation."

"I'm going to hang out in the swimming pool," said Johnny,

"until the sun goes down."

Tex spoke up, "We're going to be troubadors this evening. We'll be making the music while Katy and Ms. Arnold play political games."

"What's our schedule?" Katy asked Ms. Arnold.

"Just a little get together with some of the local people. Dinner at the new Marriott hotel with the Balcombs and Andersons. They're disenchanted Republicans. They want to meet you; that's all I know. After dinner, I thought we'd go down to the River Walk and circulate with the Texas troubadors.

"I like that," said Katy.

* * *

It was a short hop to San Antonio, but it gave Katy time to reflect.

She noticed Johnny's arm around Gloria. He gave her a light caress. Gloria looked up at him. "Love ya," he said. "I love you, too," she responded.

When am I going to tell Johnny? Katy trembled at the thought. *How will he react? What on earth will he think when he finds out about John?* She had to tell him soon.

* * *

Vacation is over, thought Katy sadly. She watched the Dallas-bound airliner take off. Johnny and Gloria were on it. So were The Texans who were looking forward to a day and night in their hometown; Saturday morning they would head for Denver with Katy.

"I wish last night could have lasted for a week," Katy said to Ms. Arnold as they boarded the GULFSTREAM. "I can't remember when I've had such a good time."

"Everyone on the River Walk had a good time last night. Johnny and Gloria were campaigning as hard as you were. I wonder how many people you made friends with. I never saw anything like it. The people down here are the friendliest people I ever saw."

"You know, I have a feeling today isn't going to be as good."

"How come?"

"Don't know. Just an uneasy feeling. You say a dozen industrialists? Lunch at the Petroleum Club—on the top floor of a bank building?"

"Supposed to be one of the showplaces of Houston. And the people we're meeting with are big fish in a big sea."

"How come they invited me?"

"I suspect they're curious to see the candidate that J. Ross and Sam Pickens are backing.

"Not suprising."

"You can handle them."

* * *

"This is the way the other half lives," commented Ms. Arnold. She and Katy got off the elevator on the top floor and entered the Petroleum Club's opulent lounge. To the left, the floor-to-ceiling view windows caught their eyes.

The receptionist greeted them.

"We're guests of Nathan Bushnell," said Ms. Arnold.

"Right this way, please. Mr. Bushnell phoned; he is on his way." She seated them in the Library Bar. Bookshelves accented the panelled walls. Deep sofas and overstuffed chairs arranged for groups of varying sizes surrounded glass-topped coffee tables.

As Katy sipped Perrier water and Ms. Arnold white wine, Katy asked a question that suprised Ms. Arnold. "Do you think people are going to understand my plan? Is an oil import fee, meant to solve our energy dependence, too wild for them? Are they more interested in national child care?"

"You want the truth?"

"Shoot."

"The American people don't trust the big oil companies; they think of corporate giants, big profits, and oil spills. They don't stop to think that we have the cheapest gasoline prices in the world, and the cleanest service stations with the best service and products at the lowest prices." Ms. Arnold paused to collect her thoughts. "As I see it, your plan won't help, or hurt, the big oil companies much either way." She paused. "It's the little energy companies who will be the gainers; exploration and drilling companies especially, and small producers."

Katy had listened carefully. "I hope the American people will think this through as well as you have, especially women."

"Oh, women are well aware that we fumbled the ball on energy; they saw their sons, and some daughters too, waging war in the Persian Gulf, and they know oil had something to do with that."

"You're so right." Katy became thoughtful. "Women can work miracles in this country if they see the big picture."

"I know. I know. And, Katy, you have no choice. You have to speak up to women with something besides platitudes."

Katy saw the hostess approaching with Mr. Bushnell. As hearty and friendly as the other Texans they met, he sported a diamond stick-pin in the center of his maroon tie. The dark suit must have been specially tailored to fit so perfectly over his expansive midriff.

"You must be Katy Jenkins—and this must be the famous Ms. Arnold. Pleased to make your acquaintance." He was no taller than Katy; his brown eyes sparkled behind wide rim glasses. He obviously enjoyed his piece of the Texas pie. "I'm glad you're here early. I want to warn you. These are a bunch of tricky bastards coming here today."

"Tricky?" asked Katy.

"They'll be testing you. Don't believe anything they say. They'll just be feeling you out. They wanta' know what kind of stuff you're made of. I told John I'd get you together with some real Houston Texans."

"John?"

"Sure. Van Dorn. With him on your side, you don't need to get buffaloed by these guys."

"You know Mr. Van Dorn personally?"

"I know him. He's a square shooter if there ever was one. My grandpa did business with his grandpa."

* * *

The meeting room looked more like a Board Room than a dining room. Dark stained oak panelled walls accented hand proofed colored etchings of the sea; the oak conference table seated twelve people comfortably.

Conversation remained light during the luncheon of select sea foods, rice, and vintage wine.

The fireworks started when coffee arrived.

"Miss Jenkins, are you serious about your proposal to put an import fee on oil?" asked a stocky red haired man.

"I believe it would work," Katy said firmly. "This is the most practical, direct way to put our energy program back on track, and raise billions of dollars of new revenue every year. Of course it will push up domestic oil prices $5 a barrel too, which will stabilize our oil industry."

"It'll do that," the man answered. "But most of us in this room are in petrochemicals. This industry is creating some new pockets of prosperity in this state. These chemicals are profitable because of the availability of cheap oil and gas."

"What chemicals do you make?"

"Benzene, ethylene, methane, to name three."

"How many of you are in oil or some part of oil production, like drilling or oil field machinery?"

"Most of us," admitted the questioner.

A Mr. Calkins spoke up. "My company makes plastic trash bags, another oil based product." Katy appraised the speaker. Not quite the typical Texan, she thought. Definitely not your "good ol' boy." Tougher. Must be an import. She decided to feel her way with him.

"Your product has revolutionized the way America lives," she began. "The garbage cans that we used before plastic have gone the way of the dinosaurs. But, plastic bags do pose some problems." Immediately she realized she had touched a raw nerve.

"We're aware of the problem," he snapped, "but raising the price of oil won't help on that."

Katy weighed her next statement carefully, knew that it might be better left unsaid, but decided to go ahead anyhow. "The ecological problem is a far greater hazard to your business than the slight increase in price that will result from an oil import fee." She pushed on. "Incidentally, are you making any progress on the development of a biodegradable product?"

"It's easier said than done, but I hope the government will help solve the problem rather than compound it as they usually do."

"I do too," Katy said easily. "Help elect me, and I'll guarantee we'll work with you, and all business, to solve the ecological problems, not aggravate them."

"Sounds good anyhow." That concluded the discourse.

"All right," Katy continued, "something about our energy program puzzles me. Since we are blessed with vast stores of natural gas, the cleanest of all fossil fuels, economical and extremely efficient, too, why don't we use more natural gas to solve our energy problems?"

"Miss Jenkins, I think I can give you some answers here." The statement was made by Nathan Bushnell. Katy nodded and he launched into his explanation.

"Problem is, we don't have the distribution facilities. We don't have the pipelines to transport the volume of gas we would need, and like everything else these days the red tape to get permits and rights-of-way to build pipelines is so aggravating, and costs are so high, that most of the time it isn't worth it." In a disgusted tone he added, "and the *Federal* regulations and red tape don't help any."

His countenance brightened a little. "Even if we could build the pipe lines we still wouldn't have the service facilities to put gas in millions of cars in the country. And the carburetors and gas tanks would have to be switched over. It would be quite a job. About the only practical use of natural gas is for fleets, where all the vehicles return to the same terminal for refueling."

Katy's attitude became thoughtful. "This is all very illuminating to me. One thing that occurs to me right away is that our public bus systems are one of the best bets for natural gas. Another thought: we now have big truck stops all over the country; wouldn't they be the most likely locations for natural gas distribution?"

She called on others for their comments. One of them countered with a question. "Going back to your proposal to impose a tariff on imported oil, does this mean you are for protective tariffs on other things, too?"

"No, not at all," Katy replied. "But how else can we overcome a deliberate monopoly set up to control oil prices?

Otherwise, they control the world market. I don't know any other way for us to achieve enough energy independence to cope with them.

From then on, the questions ranged far and wide.

The most loaded question came from a stocky, red-haired man, whom Katy had learned was a "wildcatter". "Are you for drilling on the coastal plain of the Arctic National Wildlife Refuge in Alaska?" He asked the question and settled back in his chair to see how Jenkins responded to this one.

Katy began slowly, "Naturally I have given this some thought. I can't see why we shouldn't keep this known reserve intact, and keep faith with our designation of this area as a national wildlife refuge. Ninety percent of Alaska's North Slope is already open to oil production; the portion in the Wildlife Refuge has perhaps a potential of producing about one year's U.S. oil supply—not much of an answer for our total energy needs. Our natural gas reserves dwarf this modest source.

She continued. "Let's get on with meeting our over-all energy needs by turning the American free enterprise system loose with profit incentives—combined with some assurance that the rug will not be pulled out from under them by the OPEC cartel. And we will build the gas piplines and distribution centers we need; we will be able to drill deeper oil wells for more production on the mainland; moreover, we will harness the sun and the wind. These energy sources are all inoffensive to the environment."

The questioner wasn't satisfied. "I'm sure you believe in what you're saying, but you haven't run up against the environmentalists on this; they will cheer your stand on not opening up more drilling on the North Slope, then fight you on building piplines and everything else you try to do; they're crazy."

Katy felt empathy with the speaker. "I know," she said. "In my ten years in the Congress, many times I wished I was president of the United States where I would have more clout. Elect me, and we will have an energy policy: it will start with an import fee on foreign oil, and end with alternative energy sources that will be cleaner and better. We may have to inject a strong dose of Americanism into our society, but I believe that the special interests, no matter how vocal or how rich, can be fitted into an energy policy that will benefit all Americans. I think that with leadership from the top our people will not only go along on this, but will insist on it."

Katy fielded other questions with the same clarity and forthrightness. After the meeting, Nathan Bushnell summed it up to Ms. Arnold. "These guys will back Katy to the end of the world now. They just wanted to make sure she really meant what she said. You have all kinds of support here; we Houstonians will swell your campaign coffers even more than those Dallasites did."

Ms. Arnold had a parting thought at the airport. "Katy, you want to know something? You made a whale of an impression in this state. We're rolling in Texas."

24

The gold dome of the Colorado State Capitol glistened in the Saturday morning sunshine as Katy's motorcade turned off Broadway alongside the Capitol grounds. A new coat of gold leaf, recently applied to the dome, accentuated the mellow lustre. The sight of the Capitol bouyed Katy's sagging spirits. Back in Dallas, takeoff for Denver was delayed almost an hour by the late arrivals of two rather sheepish looking band members. By the time Hank arrived with his mandolin, seemingly unaware of the panic his delay generated, Katy let him have it. "If you're ever this late again, the plane will be long gone. We should be half-way to Denver."

"Guess I'm just a night person," Hank said.

Tex Richards attempted to smooth things over. "It looks like the boys celebrated our new job a little too much last night."

Katy snapped back, "There won't be any job if this happens again." Tex's jaw clenched as he nodded at Katy and returned to the seat next to Suzanne.

Her visit with Madge Bloomfield, who accompanied her to Denver, hadn't cheered her either. "Your former colleague, the Congresswoman from Colorado, is subtly putting you down," Madge had commented. "Very clever about it, too."

"I know," responded Katy glumly. "I'd rather be attacked outright than deal with what she's doing—that condescending attitude! She thinks I'm a lost cause." Katy sat quietly for awhile. "I'm going to respond to her today on her home turf."

They made up some time on the flight, arrived in Denver, and hurriedly boarded cars to the State Capitol.

"There's a heck of a crowd up there!" exclaimed Madge as she surveyed the grassy slope leading up to the Capitol steps.

The Texans piled out of their car, assembling their instruments and tuning them even as they headed toward the congregation of people. They moved into the crowd playing and singing, "This land is your land, this land is my land..." By the second chorus they had the crowd singing with them as Katy and her entourage reached the Capitol steps where the microphones waited.

Artie Freeman, Colorado State Chair of the Coalition party, greeted Katy, clasping her hand in both of his own while he shook hands. "Look who's here," he exclaimed to the mayor of Fort Collins. "Katy Jenkins, Mayor Livingstone." The same enthusiastic introduction brought her face to face with key Coloradoans from Boulder, Greeley, Aspen, Grand Junction, Durango, and Trinidad.

When a break came in The Texans' welcoming music, Artie stepped to the microphone. "A few short weeks ago, right here in Denver at the Brown Palace Hotel, the American Coalition party nominated Katy Jenkins for president. Already the Party has raised, and has commitments for, millions of dollars for campaign funds. Katy raised a hundred-thousand dollars at one dinner in Dallas this week. The message is loud and clear, the American people are going to elect Katy Jenkins our first woman president."

As Katy moved in front of the microphone, The Texans struck up a chord in accompaniment to the welcoming applause. The old thrill rushed through her as she stepped to the microphones waving a newspaper clipping taken from her purse.

"Here's a newspaper story with a picture of Harry Truman speaking from these same Capitol steps in 1948." She unfolded the clipping, getting everyone's attention. "At that time it was common knowledge that Harry didn't have a chance to win. People felt sorry for the little guy. Well, your Congresswoman, Barb Litton, feels sorry for me now; sorry that I'm not running on the Democrat ticket, sorry that I have no chance to be elected. She said so yesterday on a national news show. Well, she would probably have been sorry for Harry Truman, too."

She surveyed the crowd and sang out: "Let her save her sympathy for the other candidates who are going to be just as surprised as Tom Dewey—anyone here remember him?—when Truman beat the socks off him."

Katy's good humor reappeared in a confident smile. "Now,

I want to tell you how and why we're going to win this election..."

Twenty minutes later Katy had her audience cheering wildly, convinced that they would personally help rejuvenate America. As she concluded her remarks on this dramatic note, The Texans struck up God Bless America and everyone joined in the singing. For the next half-hour, Katy walked about the grassy slope, circulating among the audience. She fielded questions from businessmen on proposed tax legislation and enjoyed discussions with students on educational and environmental issues. As she moved from group to group and issue to issue, she noticed Tex and Suzanne joking with a group of youngsters wearing Future Farmers of America jackets, and pilot Bill Burke engaged in an animated discussion with a couple of military people. She smiled as she observed Madge and Artie engaging in a heated discourse on women's rights. When the motorcade took off for the airport, Katy knew she had a nucleus in Colorado. New Mexico was next.

* * *

The big event in Albuquerque, set for 5:30 pm in the ballroom at La Posada, would bring together for the first time "Democrats for Katy" and "Republicans for Katy" with her new supporters, the Coalitionists. Both H.B. and Clifford expressed misgivings at this arrangement, but gave in to Katy's insistence. "You're playing with fire," H.B. warned her. Maria had sent out some 250 invitations by mail, informal, just "inviting friends to a reception for Katy." Now Katy wondered who would show. She would have to be careful. Democrats were Democrats and Republicans Republicans. The usual campaign rhetoric wouldn't do at this meeting. She had a plan and hoped it would work.

Hotels are usually dull places on Saturday afternoons, few guests, little activity. But on this Saturday afternoon, La Posada bustled with anticipation of the reception.

Katy caught her breath. She had never seen the ballroom like this. It looked more like a garden than a ballroom: large areas of floor covered with green outdoor carpet; all the tables sported yellow checkered tablecloths, a few covered by umbrellas, still others had bright-colored arrays of balloons tethered above; spigotted kegs dispensed white or red wine, and between the kegs a deep trough of ice offered cans of soft drinks and beer. The picnic table along the wall nearest the kitchen wasn't set yet, but Katy could visualize the spread.

"You can't believe what Harriett has put together." Maria flung open the double doors leading into the office off the mezzanine. Maria was right. Katy couldn't have imagined it. Placards on the wall, more on the work tables, with literally hundreds of newspaper clippings, magazine articles, photographs of Katy on the campaign trail, and stacks of the two newsletters Harriett had already mailed nationwide. All with datelines since Katy's nomination.

"How in the world did you get all this together?" yelled Katy as she circled the room.

"I didn't," said Maria. "It was Harriett and somebody else."

"Somebody else?" Katy's question shot across the room.

"Oh yes," said Maria. "She's around here somewhere."

"Around here...?" The question froze on Katy's lips as Ms. Arnold popped through the door of the one private office in the headquarters.

"We've been doing well on publicity," she said casually.

"Good!" enthused Katy as she careened around one of the worktables and enveloped Ms. Arnold and Harriett in a big hug. "It's out of this world." She stepped back. "It's good to see you!" she exclaimed to Ms. Arnold. "When did you get in?"

"Got to Santa Fe last night," she said. "To Harriett's. We finished up the display this morning."

At that point Ms. Arnold stepped out onto the mezzanine peering in both directions as if looking for somebody. "I thought I saw a camera flash a minute ago," she said, "but I don't see anybody."

"I'll see you guys in a while," Katy said. "I want to see more of this, but I must get ready for the party." She dashed across the mezzanine and opened the door to her suite just as Elizabeth, already talking a mile a minute, joined her.

Inside the bedroom, Elizabeth helped Katy pick out her picnic attire. Katy started the bath water and Elizabeth talked. "Oh say," Elizabeth interrupted the other topics of conversation, "Johnny wants a conference with you—before the thing starts in the ballroom, if possible."

Katy's gaze darted toward the clock. Forty-five minutes 'til the party. I'll *make* time!

Elizabeth continued. "He and Gloria are up in Mom and Pop's suite. Mrs. Bayze and Tex 'n Suzanne are up there, too. They're talking to Pop very seriously about something."

Katy turned off the bath water and flicked the drain. "I'll just take a quick shower," she said as she started peeling off clothes. "Will you go up in a little while and tell Johnny to come on down?"

"Sure," said Elizabeth.

* * *

The Texans were already playing their bluegrass music routine when Mom, Pop, Mrs. Bayze, Johnny, Gloria, and Katy appeared at the ballroom. Katy quickly joined Clifford and H.B. to form an informal reception line. The first guests were arriving. For almost an hour she played her favorite candidate's role, greeting old friends and making new ones as H.B. and Clifford introduced new recruits to her.

As many Republicans as Democrats, and almost as many men as women. *Good mix.* Katy grinned to herself.

Dick Donovan received a startling welcome. At a signal from Katy, Tex stopped the music and announced, "Ladies and gentlemen, I'd like to introduce Katy's first political mentor...Mr. Dick Donovan!" With that the band launched into a lively chorus of "For he's a jolly good fellow."

"What the heck is this?" grumbled a red-faced Dick Donovan.

"Oh, you know you love it," H.B. laughed.

When Katy saw that most of the guests had made their first rounds to food and drink, and there were few new arrivals, she decided it was time to take over. She made her way across the ballroom floor to the bandstand, and Tex signalled the band to sound a chord as he handed the microphone to Katy.

"I want to introduce our music makers," she began. All eyes were on The Texans; applause filled the room as she introduced each musician. "Tex and Suzanne Richards on the guitar and fiddle,—and the mouth harp and chimes. As you know they sing, too. And Tim Handley here plays the banjo; did you ever hear anyone rev up a banjo like he does? Hank Martin on the mandolin. He makes the rhythm. And, last but not least, our bass, Josh Davis. His is the big fiddle we sometimes have to hire an extra car to transport." She waited for the laughter and cheering to die down.

"And now, two announcements. Our campaign is off to a flying start. It has taken wings in Texas—literally. Where's Pop? And Johnny?" They appeared from opposite sides of the room. "Come on over here, and bring Mom and Gloria, and Mrs. Bayze, too." They all made their way through the crowd. "Many of you know my mother and father, 'Mom' and 'Pop' to everyone in Caprock County. And my brother, Johnny. He and Gloria, here, are at the University of New Mexico."

More applause.

"Well, Johnny just came to me with some good news." Katy beckoned Johnny to the mike. "Johnny, tell this grand assemblage about your new role in the campaign."

Johnny fumbled with the mike and cleared his dry throat. "I, well uh...first of all, I want to just say how proud we all are of my sister here." More applause. "With being a full-time student, I haven't felt like I've been able to make much of a contribution to Katy's campaign. So, I've decided to take this semester off. And, with a little arm-twisting, I convinced Pop to loan me the Big J Feedmills Cessna airplane to fly The Texans all over Texas and the southwest as musical ambassadors ...from now until Katy wins this election. Everywhere they make music, I'll be making a pitch for Katy Jenkins for president!"

The ballroom erupted with cheers and clapping.

"Where's Mrs. Bloomfield?" Johnny asked over the mike.

"Over here," someone shouted.

"Yes, can everyone see her? Mrs. Bloomfield is going to coordinate this thing—and listen to this—she already has over forty bookings, all over the state of Texas. No telling how many appearances we'll make before this campaign is over."

Johnny backed away from the mike still grinning as Katy replaced him.

Holding up her open palm to still the applause, Katy put her arm around Mrs. Bayze. "I want all of you to meet my first-grade teacher, Mrs. Bayze, our Campaign Chairwoman in Caprock County."

Mrs. Bayze reached for the microphone. Everyone was quiet as she spoke. "I've always hoped Katy would amount to something someday," she said. "This is my big chance to make it come true." She grinned. "I'll guarantee you, she'll carry Caprock County, even if we have to vote every sheep and cow in the county!" She looked around expectantly. "But Katy is a straight-laced one, she says she wants to win fair and square, so we can't vote any *dead* ones in this election." She handed the mike to Katy as the room reverberated with laughter.

Katy laughed, too. "How can you lose an election with a campaign manager like that? Has everyone seen the avalanche of publicity we've been getting? It's all mounted on placards in the campaign office. We have a national clipping service and Harriett and Ms. Arnold put it all together. They're in there now. Don't miss seeing it."

A disturbance at the ballroom entrance caught the attention of nearby guests. Although across the ballroom, Katy heard Clifford's firm voice. "This is a private party. No cameras or reporters invited."

Wonder what that was? Katy immediately diverted attention away from it. "There's plenty of food and drink and good company," she announced. She whispered to Tex, "Loud music—for dancing." The music started and she motioned to Johnny; he and Gloria glided onto the dance floor like professionals putting on an exhibition. Soon joined by other couples, the music, dancing, and din of conversation took over, giving Katy an opportunity to make contact with Clifford. She had to satisfy her curiosity about the individual who tried to crash the party.

* * *

After midnight, the party ended. With the last guests and hangers-on gone, Elizabeth and Katy had Katy's suite to themselves.

"The whole evening was a complete success," exulted

Elizabeth. "Even H.B. and my dad admitted it worked out great."

"Liz, sit down; I'm dying to tell you something."

Elizabeth was not only an avid talker, she was also a good listener. She sat quietly on the sofa opposite Katy.

"I told John about Johnny!"

"Oh, Katy!"

"He didn't know."

"How could he? We've all kept the secret. Tell me everything. Where did you tell him? When?"

Katy started with the phone call from John, her trip to New York, their meeting in the Manhattan Grill, LAND & SEA, the luncheon at Bankcity, the ride down the elevator, the drive with John up Sixth Avenue, John's apartment, John making the coffee royals, and how she finally just blurted it out, "John, may we drink to our son?," how the drinks got cold, and then how she longed to stay there with him—but didn't; that John wanted her to tell Johnny, how she chickened out telling Johnny at San Antonio, and how she planned to tell Johnny while in Albuquerque this time, but hadn't broached the subject yet.

"Katy, honey, don't you see? The whole world has opened up for you. Johnny's a big boy now, he can handle this; you must tell him."

"I know, Liz," Katy said dismally. "I was all set to, maybe tonight or in the morning. But I'm scared."

"You're scared?" Elizabeth was incredulous.

"Scared to death. When I tell Johnny, he'll tell Gloria, and she'll tell someone else." She hesitated. "You know about George Caplin?"

"Sure, but he's nothing but an opportunist."

"A determined one. Glen Copeland, our security man on the jet, saw him taking pictures of the plane when we landed. Glen recognized Caplin when he tried to crash the party this afternoon. Caplin's brassy, and he's absolutely determined to unearth some scandalous tidbit. If he discovers Johnny's true identity, he will throw a monkey-wrench into my whole campaign."

"Oh, Katy!"

"You saw all that publicity in there? Well, the media would just love some new angles, especially spicy ones. The Coalition party is precarious enough anyhow. They would discredit me completely."

"Let 'em, Katy. Get out of this thing before it destroys you."

"I am destroyed if I get out; I have a story the American people must hear."

Elizabeth sat quietly for awhile considering this. Then she brightened. "Okay, Katy, you've waited twenty-seven years to tell Johnny—what would a few more weeks hurt?"

* * *

In Phoenix, Katy hadn't touched ground for more than two minutes when the Arizona Campaign Co-chairs, Becky and Leonard Phillips, vented anger at Allen Marchbanks.

"Did you hear what that contemptible Congressman Marchbanks said at the San Diego Club yesterday?" Leonard asked Katy.

"I haven't heard a thing about it. What happened?"

Becky broke in, "The pompous snob confided to his big- shot friends that women don't have the background for high political office."

"Oh?" It took a minute for Katy to become fully aware of what a sensitive nerve Marchbanks had hit. She thought about her run-ins with Marchbanks in the Congress.

"He said no woman in the country has the political background to be president of the United States."

Katy's mind raced. Marchbank's remarks would infuriate women from one end of the country to the other. Incredible blunder on his part, but a Godsend for her. *I'm going to make the most of this*, she thought happily. *Thank you, Mr. Marchbanks!*

Leonard broke in. "He said women have little political awareness, get bored with politics, and don't have the vision to be political! But you should hear what he said about *you*."

"Oh?" Katy's voice was non-committal, inviting more comment.

Becky obliged. "He was reckless with his words. He said that you're a small-timer, never won a campaign outside New Mexico, and that you're out of your league."

Katy took her stance. "I'll make him eat those words."

* * *

A brunch at the airport Holiday Inn for state workers, and an early afternoon session with university students at the landmark Gammage Center, a renowned structure designed by Frank Lloyd Wright in Tempe, comprised the Arizona agenda.   At both meetings, workers and students alike knew about Allen Marchbank's comments at the San Diego Club. His denigration of women gave the meetings extra purpose. Katy capitalized on his comments. "I suppose all women here know they're political non-entities, that no woman is capable of being president—least of all Katy Jenkins." Then she paused. "Well, we're going to make these words haunt the man who uttered them. I knew the guy in Congress—all too well—his philosophy on women? Keep them barefoot and pregnant!"

As Katy's troupe boarded the two rental vans waiting in the fire zone outside the Gammage Center, Leonard Phillips pulled Katy aside.   "Why don't you ride to the airport with me 'n Becky." Katy looked over at the vehicles stuffed with briefcases and bodies, and quickly accepted the invitation.

On the drive from Tempe to the airport, Leonard handed Katy an unsealed envelope.   She peeked inside and found two five-hundred dollar bills.   "That's an anonymous campaign contribution," he said. "If you have to, you can put my name on it, but it came from one of Arizona's leading citizens with the simple comment that he likes what you're doing."

Katy put the envelope in her purse. She would never know for sure who made the contribution, and even if she did she wouldn't mention it to anyone; but the thought was exhilarating—a prominent Arizonian approved of her efforts enough to contribute a thousand dollars to her campaign. Her message was beginning to be heard.

25

Perhaps it was because news of Katy's pithy rebuttal to Marchbanks' comments reached California before she did—via the LA Times. Perhaps they just wanted a look for themselves. No matter the cause, the Monday morning 'coffee' Lila Stanford arranged out at Knott's Berry Farm was attended in overwhelming numbers.

Katy made the most of the occasion; "Does anyone here think a woman isn't capable of being president of the United States?" Resounding "No's" shook the rafters, and Katy was off like a rocket propelled into the stratosphere. The rumblings of women's anger were felt on Katy's California campaign trail from Mission Bay at San Diego to the redwood forests of northern California.

Katy was aware from the first rally at Knott's Berry Farm, and throughout the state, that a great many of those attending were associated with the Citizens for Better Government, groups who supported certain citizen initiatives known as "Propositions," on California ballots. Lila Stanford, state Coalition party chair, who would work with Katy on the entire California tour, obviously enjoyed a strong relationship with the "Citizens" groups. The notices in neighborhood newspapers, however, didn't mention these groups and only made slight mention of the American Coalition party. The messages instead invited people to a public meeting to meet Katy Jenkins, candidate for president of the United States.

Harriett Landsdale took off for Santa Fe after the first rally, from the John Wayne Airport in Orange County, carrying with her the thrill and excitement Katy generated at Knott's. "Get all the info to me on this blitz with Lila for a special newsletter featuring California," she admonished Katy. "I got some good pictures of you and Stanford in action."

A precedent was established for the next rally, held in the new Convention Center on the bay at San Diego. The evening before the rally, Katy was interviewed on San Diego television. How Lila managed it Katy didn't know, but from then on she was on radio and TV interviews everywhere they went.

By the end of the week, Knott's, San Diego, Los Angeles, Long Beach, Santa Barbara, Sacramento, and radio and TV interviews, coffees, conferences, and crowds blurred together in Katy's weary mind. But every one of the rallies brought out more supporters then she'd hoped for. The Thursday night rally down on the Berkeley shipping docks was no exception. The massive tankers symbolized both America's strength in commerce and her lop-sided dependence on foreign goods. And it was a place where labor felt at home, where Katy could get in touch with the down-to-earth types she'd grown up with at the railroad yards down by the Big J Feedmills in Caprock.

The phone's loud ring in the Berkeley Holiday Inn, coming so early the next morning, startled Katy nearly out of her skin. Until then she hadn't realized how deep her exhaustion ran.

The S.O.S. was from Ms. Arnold.

"Katy, we've got to get you to Pennsylvania ASAP. Andy's in trouble. He's getting clobbered; can't get anything to work; he needs you."

Katy moaned inwardly. Lila Stanford had insisted that Katy extend her California stay through Saturday. "For a very important meeting in Beverly Hills at the Beverly Hilton." She had said, "A 'retreat' with a group of key workers and policy-makers whom I've worked with on three big California 'Propositions'—we've got to have them on our side in this campaign." Though this meager information was all Katy had to go on, she had agreed to stay over because of Lila's insistance. So Saturday was taken.

Now Ms. Arnold's call forced her to fly directly to Philadelphia on Sunday. This made two baffling situations for the upcoming weekend. *God*, she thought, *how I was looking forward to a day or two at home.*

* * *

The wake-up call came all too early Saturday morning. Katy groped for orientation, remembered she was in San Francisco. Today would be the "retreat" at Beverly Hills.

Bill Burke and the crew liked flying in the early morning; they departed San Francisco just as the sun peeked over the Middle Range; and although the Gulfstream was packed full of people, the plane rode easily on the quiet air currents. Their course was to Burbank Airport, the best landing field for Beverly Hills.

A deluxe motorcoach with giant GRAY LINE letters painted on each side, met the group at the Burbank Airport to transport them to the Beverly Hilton Hotel on famous Wilshire Boulevard. Hollywood adjoined on the north and Santa Monica extended to the Pacific Coast on the west. Eastward the megalopolis of Los Angeles sprawled for miles, packing millions of people in an area not much larger than the Big J spread in Caprock County.

As the motorcoach pulled into the hotel entry, Katy wondered again what this day would bring. A secret "retreat" of several hundred people, admission by invitation only, held in the heart of the largest population center in the country, seemed a strange climax to the week-long campaign she had waged in California. But Lila Stanford had insisted, so here she was. Some of Lila's guests on the plane she had met during the past few days; others she met for the first time this morning. This same allocation seemed to prevail with the crowd here, which she quickly estimated at three hundred people; some familiar, others not.

First to greet Katy as she arrived at the slightly elevated speaker's platform were Tom and Carol Bullard, the retired couple with whom she had famous boysenberry pie at Knott's Berry Farm; they looked chipper and charming in their informal attire. "It's so nice to see you again," enthused Carol as she embraced Katy. Tom was equally gracious as he extended his hand.

"Here are the stars of today's show," advised Tom, indicating two young people busily checking projection and sound equipment on the platform. "Meet Eddie Young and Monica Swift; they run Beverly Hills Productions; they've been helping Lila a lot."

The two young entrepreneurs exuded enthusiasm as they

greeted Katy. She learned later that although their post office box was Beverly Hills, their place of operation was a second-floor conglomeration of rooms in a modest office complex on Santa Monica Boulevard beyond Beverly Hills.

A large movie screen sat off to one side of the platform; obviously a presentation of some sort was being readied. Monica made a final adjustment on the sound control, and turned to Katy. "So you're the one who took Margaret Kincaid's place. I wondered who could ever replace her."

This caught Katy by surprise. "Oh? You know Margaret?"

"We got more signatures to put the Coalition party on the California ballot than all of Margaret's volunteers put together. We helped Margaret pull it all together."

Lila Stanford's call to order interrupted the conversation, and Katy grabbed the nearest chair, waiting to see what would happen next. She didn't wait long.

"We're here to talk about Proposition X," Lila stated. "So-called until it is assigned a number. Two of the proponents of this very new proposal, but who have worked hard for other Propositions we supported, are here to discuss Proposition X. Before I call on Tom and Carol Bullard, however, I want to introduce our very special guest today, whom many of you already know, Katy Jenkins, candidate for president of the United States on the American Coalition party ticket."

Katy arose amid enthusiastic applause, and said simply, "I'm very glad to be here with you today."

"And we're delighted to have you, Katy," rejoined Lila Stanford. "And now for Katy's benefit and others of you who are with us today for the first time, I want to explain why this is a very private meeting, admittance by invitation only, no press. This is because Propositions, by their very nature, are presumed to be spontaneous initiatives by citizens. They are not sponsored by political organizations, but by people."

She paused. "But, as we all know, to get the thousands of signatures on petitions to get a proposition on the ballot, and to create public interest and get out the vote for a Proposition, requires organization. Furthermore, professional help is required on advertising and publicity. We have the owners of one of the best professional public relations firms for promoting a proposition in the state of California here today, and Eddie Young and Monica Swift of Beverly Hills Productions will make a proposal on handling the promotion of Proposition X for us a little later on.

"But the first order of business is the presentation, for our consideration, of Proposition X. To kick this off, I call on Judge Tom Bullard. Judge Bullard spent many years in our criminal justice system, and is the first to admit its limitations and inequities. He will tell us about the most original plan to make our Penal Code more effective that I have ever heard. May I present Judge Tom Bullard."

From his bearing when he rose to speak, Tom Bullard might have been wearing his black robe instead of the pull-over sweater and sports jacket he wore. "Thank you, Lila," he said graciously, "and Ladies and Gentlemen of this retreat."

Despite his amicable, self-assured manner, Katy detected a trace of nervousness as the old Judge began to speak.

"This initiative measure will be submitted to the people in accordance with the Constitution of the State of California, and will amend the Penal Code to provide for alternate and/or additional punishment for the crimes of First Degree Rape and for alternate and/or additional punishment for Habitual Criminals who have been convicted of three or more felonies, one or more of which included bodily harm to another person.

"Simply and directly stated, the Judge or Jury as the case may be, may order that a person convicted of First Degree Rape, or convicted of Habitual Criminality, as defined in the statutes, be punished by castration."

Katy hoped she'd covered her nearly unguarded reaction, as gasps of surprise and outright shock went through the audience. She noticed some of the men grimace as the thought registered. She thought Judge Bullard showed a trace of embarrassment himself, but he continued after only a short pause. "I submit to you that the possibility of this punishment would be the best deterrent for the perpetrators of these horrible crimes we could ever devise."

Katy wondered if Lila Stanford was aware of the controversy she'd landed her in. The Judge seemed to be at a loss for words at that point. His wife came to his rescue, "May I please add my two cents worth?" she asked. Her husband happily yielded.

"Most of you remember the Manson murders. Manson engineered the degradation of young girls, and boys, to the extent that they willingly and mercilessly killed and mutilated an entire family. Remember the court scenes where he flaunted his actions, blaming everyone in society for his heinous crimes, except himself. Under California law, we could not put him to death, and rid society of him forever. No, we put him in prison, where he not only costs us as much tax money every year as it costs to keep thirty children in school, but where he can continue to exude evil, and may someday be out on the streets again." She nearly screamed the last phrase. "Do you remember the last thing he said to his attorney in the court room after his conviction? He said, 'Oh, it won't be so bad; I can get plenty of sex in prison.'"

Then Mrs. Bullard asked shrilly, "Can anyone in this room think of a more suitable punishment for Manson than castration?" Her voice quavered. "And there are so many other cases. Horrible rapes and murders. If we can start something that will deter these crimes, and deter one or two-time offenders from becoming habitual criminals, I think we would be doing a great service to the people of California."

Lila Stanford took over quickly. "Wow, do we have a Proposition to consider today! To inform us on the status of Proposition X, I'd like to call on Art Balcomb and Frank Goodrich; Art is a script writer and Frank is a film editor at Universal Studios. They have been the frontrunners for this proposition."

Two Hollywood types whom Katy had noticed before, both bearded, but young, handsome, and ambitious looking, rose and moved to the platform.

"I'm Art, and this is Frank," said the spokesman. "Frank and I have worked for over a year getting this proposition on the ballot; we had to get almost half a million signatures on petitions; of course we had a lot of help, and some financial backing, but it was quite an undertaking. You can't believe all the deadlines we had to meet. We've had tremendous support on it, outstanding help from two women's organizations, and the idea caught on like wildfire with students at the Rape Crisis Center at U.C.L.A. and other Universities and Colleges in the state. We have it on the ballot for the next general election, and now we need help."

Frank broke in. "You see, we visualized a quiet campaign, mostly by direct mail and phone. But, now with the National Civil Rights Foundation, the NCRF, entering the picture, we need broader support."

Lila interrupted. "What are they doing?"

"They're moving a campaign fund into California. I can't tell you for sure why. You know they like publicity, and they thrive on being the Devil's Advocate."

"The entire proposition is quite interesting," observed Lila. "What kind of a campaign are you thinking about now?"

"We would like to have the backing of the Citizens for Better Government to help put on a comprehensive campaign: billboards, radio, TV, the works."

"How much do you figure all this to cost?" a big man on the front row asked.

Frank didn't seem to be quite ready for the question. "Whatever we can raise," he answered. "We will tailor the campaign to fit, but we should buy all the air time we can get, and California is a big state to cover with billboards."

"That's going to cost a lot of money," the big man grunted.

Art jumped into the conversation. "We can do quite a bit with carefully selected radio spots and even a limited number of well placed 'boards,'" he assured the group. "Our pitch would be low key—reduce crime, and lower costs of the entire criminal justice system."

As the presentation proceeded, doubt clouded Katy's mind. When she first met Lila Stanford at the Brown Palace Hotel in Denver, she felt Stanford's background in organizing propositions benefitted the party's objective. Now, it began to look as if Lila had a double agenda, working with the same people on Proposition X with whom she would be working for Katy's candidacy on the American Coalition ticket. If this didn't become an outright conflict of interest, it would dilute their efforts by working on two major projects at the same time. And Proposition X, as being presented, would be controversial, and probably distasteful to a great many voters. Katy felt tightness crawl up her neck as tension mounted. What was going on in front of her eyes could spell disaster.

She heard Lila introducing Dwight Sloane, the "Citizens"

legal counsel. "We have with us here today a legal expert on 'Propositions,' our own Dwight Sloane whom I would like to call on at this time."

A short, bald man wearing thick-lensed glasses came to the speaker's stand. He proceeded slowly, matter-of-factly. "I agree with Mr. Balcomb and Mr. Goodrich that the entry of the National Civil Rights Foundation presents a problem; they will harass you every inch of the way. But they don't spend much money on publicity; that isn't their method of operation. They go for free publicity, and lawsuits. I can see that Proposition X gives them an opportunity for both. The more noise you make about it, the more free publicity they will get in opposing you."

He peered over his horn-rimmed glasses. "And, if you win the Proposition, and it becomes law, they will select a case, say, where a man has been convicted of rape and his sentence includes castration. They will pay all of his legal expenses, claim that this is cruel and unusual punishment, and therefore unconstitutional. If they were to win, the law would be thrown out."

As Mr. Sloane left the stand, Lila Stanford moved into the next act of the drama. "Now it is my pleasure to present Eddie Young and Monica Swift who have a presentation for us on how to sell a Proposition to the voters."

Monica opened the discussion. She talked about direct mail proposals, publicity releases, a get-out-the-vote phone campaign, and billboards. Eddie showed illustrations of billboards, advising they were the most effective medium for getting voters to go for propositions. He pointed out the boards deliberately appeared as if they were made by amateurs, but were actually state-of-the-art: eye-catching, just the right touches of color, with brief, strong messages. By the time the presentation was finished, he had built a good image for Beverly Hills Productions. Katy couldn't help but think how nice it would be to have them working for her campaign instead of Proposition X.

Lila Stanford rose. "This seems like a good time for a coffee break. Refreshments are all set up in the hallway out the side door." She turned to Eddie and Monica, "Thanks for a beautiful and informative presentation. Can you please stick around awhile for questions?"

As the crowd moved toward the exit, Katy fell in alongside the man who had asked the questions about costs. "Have you figured up the costs of this whole thing?" she asked directly. Without even looking at her, he answered, "They're talking about a million dollars, for starters, and they're going to have a hell of a time raising it for a cause like this. This ought to go to the Legislature."

"That would be a better place for it," said Katy softly.

"You think so?" Now he looked at her. "I thought you were probably in on it."

"No way," she said quickly as Mr. and Mrs. Bullard approached. She greeted them cordially. "This is quite an idea," she said easily. "Have you worked on propositions before?"

"Oh yes." Mr. Bullard beamed. "We worked on an Orange County Proposition that kept a freeway from belting right through our community."

Mrs. Bullard spoke up. "And we led the movement to get the Orange County Airport name changed to John Wayne Airport."

"Very nice," enthused Katy, "and appropriate."

"Since Tom retired we have had so much more time to do things together."

"Isn't that wonderful?" Katy liked the Bullards. Good people, she thought, I don't want to hurt their feelings. Her question to them was casual. "I wonder, though, if this Proposition X is a good one for us?"

"We will have to think about it," said Tom Bullard as if this hadn't occured to him before.

"Let's give it *careful* consideration," was all Katy had time to say before Lila Stanford joined them.

"That coffee smells good," said Katy. "I wonder if I dare to have a Danish with it. The most difficult thing about campaigning is trying to eat sensibly."

"It must be, Katy," said Mrs. Bullard; it was the first time she had addressed her as Katy. "Tom and I are going to split one."

"You want to split one with me, Lila?" Katy asked.

"Good solution to the problem," said Lila, moving toward the sweet rolls. "I'll cut, and you choose."

"Its a deal." Katy drew two cups of coffee and deftly maneuvered Lila to one side where she could have a word with her. "Lila, I'm not sure about Proposition X." She had to say it.

"You aren't?" Lila acted genuinely surprised, then relaxed and said, "Okay, let's see how it works out."

Katy relaxed. Eddie Young and Monica Swift, along with several other people, moved towards them. Katy got into a conversation with Eddie and Monica. "You guys made a tremendous presentation. I just wish we could work it out so you could put on just such a campaign for Katy Jenkins for president." She had telegraphed the message; now she listened.

Monica quickly responded, "We would love to do that!" Then she added, "I can't think of a campaign we would rather do. Right, Eddie?"

"Right on! Put us on your case, and we will put Katy Jenkins on the map in this state."

"I believe you," Katy said sincerely. She hoped Lila Stanford had heard the entire exchange, but she wasn't sure. Lila had started back toward the meeting room. Others followed, and the meeting was soon under way.

Lila Stanford took over. "I see a hand up in the back of the room. Is that you, Gertrude? You have the floor."

Gertrude liked to hear herself talk. She analyzed the subject, mentioned some pros and cons, and wound up making a motion to approve Proposition X. "Just to get the discussion going," she said.

"We have a motion; do I hear a second?"

Balcomb seconded the motion, and spoke for it. Lively discussion followed. The Chair called on everyone who wanted to speak.

Katy watched the people closest to her to catch their reactions. The proposition seemed to be catching on.

"Before we jump into something like this, I think we had better look at the cost," stated the big man who had spoken earlier. "I kept a running total during the presentation: billboards all over the state, direct-mail, phone campaigns. I came up with a minimum of a million dollars. I know that more than this has been raised to promote Propositions in this state, but they were popular subjects affecting people's pocketbooks. I don't think any change in the Penal Code would attract much support."

Katy's pulse quickened. Her inclination was to jump up and

shout "amen," but she restrained the impulse.

As the speaker sat down, spots of conversation broke out all over the hall. The Chair pounded her gavel for order, and called on one of the conversationalists to tell everyone what was on his mind. He obliged, and others followed.

Katy became impatient, but realized these people came from all over California, and wanted to be heard. So she busied herself analyzing speakers' attitudes and calculating how a vote on the matter would come out. Uneasiness flooded her again as she realized that a slight shift could swing the vote either way.

Dwight Sloane addressed the Chair. "May I make a personal observation?" the counselor asked.

"Go right ahead," said Lila, "this meeting is off the record, as you know."

"I think the proponents of Proposition X will be better off to pursue their original course of letters and phone calls, and forget the advertising campaign." He paused for this to register. "I abhor special interests coming in from outside our state, and with their tens of millions of dollars, affecting the decisions on initiatives that we should be allowed to resolve ourselves. When the Gun Control Initiative was advanced, the Gun Owners of California at Sacramento put up $55,000 to oppose it, while the National Rifle Association in Washington, D.C. contributed $172,000 and 'loaned' another $2,302,000—whatever that means. This war chest helped defeat the Proposition. These importations of great sums of money may very well help the economy of our state, but they may also lead to the loss of our right to direct legislation such as we are considering here today. In any event, I think Citizens for Better Government would be better off to take no stand on this one."

The momentum of the discussion slowed. "Any more discussion?" asked Stanford.

"May I speak?" Katy asked the question.

Lila addressed Katy. "Everyone who received an invitation to this retreat is a full-fledged voting participant. The Chair is pleased to recognize Katy Jenkins."

Katy caught her breath, rose and addressed the Chair, and the group. Now the adrenalin flowed. "I have a counter-proposal for your consideration." She smiled broadly. "I would like to see this group, and your associates all over the State, support Katy Jenkins for president of the United States. Lila Stanford is State Chair of the American Coaliton Party for this candidate. Jenkins is a woman candidate who holds so many of your views; an activist on the environment, for equality of men and women, and for just plain better government." Then she added, "And my name is already on the California ballot, too."

Katy cocked her head slightly and came on strong with her next statement. "I like Eddie Young and Monica Swift, and their entire campaign. I think it could be adjusted to be one of the most sensational presidential campaigns ever devised.

"Would it work?" Katy directed the question to Eddie and Monica.

"Would it work?" exclaimed Monica. "Would it work? I ask all of you, and Eddie."

Eddie jumped up and yelled, "Will it work? Certainly! We could do wonders for the Jenkins presidential campaign."

Someone sang out: "Damn sight better idea than Proposition X."

"That answers my question," said Katy. "Now, there has been a lot of talk about money and propositions here today, so the American Coalition party, running Katy Jenkins for president, has a proposition for you. The Party will put up $500,000—yes, you heard right, half a million dollars—to launch this presidential campaign. When the California organization matches this amount the National organization will come up with another bundle."

"What a proposition!" exclaimed Lila. "But, before we can vote on accepting or rejecting this proposal, we must dispose of the motion on the floor regarding Proposition X."

"I move it be tabled indefinitely." The speaker was the big man who had questioned the costs earlier.

"It has been moved that we table the motion to back Proposition X indefinitely."

"Question!" came from several voices.

"All in favor of the motion to table."

The vote was overwhelming for tabling. In the back of the room , Gertrude popped up. "Madame Chair."

"The Chair recognizes Gertrude Rawlings."

"I move that we accept Katy Jenkins' offer, and combine our

efforts with the American Coalition party to elect the first woman president of the United States."

Several "seconds" for the motion came from around the room. Katy watched as Lila Stanford acknowledged the motion and seconds. Lila stood tall on the platform obviously pleased with the course of events; Katy felt a surge of appreciation for her as Lila began to speak.

"This group, and our friends and associates throughout the state, have fought some great campaigns together. We broke the ice when we supported Propositon 13, the famous property tax referendum, which held down the crazy escalation of property taxes and assessments—and saved many families, especially older people, from being moved out of their homes.

"I admit we lost a big one when the Proposition we supported for No Fault Insurance failed. The California Bar Association, and I suspect some of the Insurance companies, overwhelmed us with their overflowing campaign chests and their mountains of misleading propaganda. The people of California lost that one, and liability insurance rates continue to go through the ceiling.

"Then we won one. We got the Insurance Initiative through, which forced lower rates on the Insurance companies. They weren't good sports about it. They threatened to leave the state if they couldn't charge whatever their hearts desired, but instead they went to the Courts. The law to lower rates languished in one Court after another. But rates didn't go up as fast as they had been, anyhow."

"Now we have the greatest opportunity we've ever had. I know Katy Jenkins well; I know what she stands for—and it's good, not only for California, but for the entire nation."

"We're open for discussion on Gertrude's motion, then we will have lunch."

Several people made remarks supporting the motion; not a single dissenter among the speakers.

"I'm getting hungry." The big man on the front row said, as he stood up to face the group for the first time. "I move that we end the discussion, and accept Gertrude's motion by acclamation."

"All in favor of ending the discussion and passing the motion to combine forces and support Katy Jenkins for president by acclamation, say AYE."

Ayes resounded throughout the room.

"Motion carried," exclaimed Lila.

Lunch was served to an amiable crowd in the adjoining room. Tensions dissipated. The two Hollywood fellows assured Katy she would have their full support. Mr. and Mrs. Bullard seemed happiest of all; only Eddie Young and Monica Swift of Beverly Hills Productions showed as much pleasure at the way things had gone. Lila Stanford assured everyone at the luncheon that the afternoon session would be kept down to two hours; everyone would be on their way home by 3:00 p.m.

Stanford opened the meeting with a grand announcement that the California Coalition party had almost a hundred-thousand dollars in cash and pledges. Mr. Bullard immediately announced he and his wife would like to contribute $1000; he asked how the check should be made out, and presented the check to Stanford with a flourish. Others followed; the room sounded like an auction; $250—$100—$50—$500. Monica and Eddie and the two Hollywood fellows circulated through the room collecting checks, announcing every one as received. Their "thank you's" rang out across the room.

Eddie and Monica brought a handful of checks to Lila who had recruited an assistant to make out receipts. They sat again at the head table and asked Katy to join them for a quick consultation, after which Eddie announced to the assembly that they would be getting out mailings right away to the thousands on the mailing list of the Citizens for Better Government announcing the new partnership to work for the election of Katy Jenkins. Of course, each recipient would be given an opportunity to contribute to the cause, and to volunteer to work on various projects, host 'coffees,' and other fund-raising events. "We will get as many people involved as we can," Eddie assured the group.

Stanford had to push right along to accomplish everything on her agenda which she made up as she went along.

Katy made the final "thank you" speech, to great applause, and the "retreat" ended exactly at 3:02 p.m.

A whirlwind of activities followed for Lila, Katy, Monica, and Eddie. First was the visit to Beverly Hills Productions on Santa Monica Boulevard. Upon arrival, they climbed the flight of stairs to find a pleasant reception area behind which a long hallway ran full length with offices on both sides. Midway, a couple of office spaces had been combined to make a conference room.

Another wing of three or four offices lay vacant. "Here's where you can set up your regional headquarters," advised Eddie. "The rent is cheaper here than anywhere, and parking is more accessible than in most places."

"We'll take it," Lila said without hesitation. "I will plan to spend a couple days a week down here." Then came consultations on over-all programs. Katy found a phone she could use, and called Ms. Arnold advising her of everything that had happened. She also assured Ms. Arnold that she would be taking off for Philadelphia early the next morning.

"Andy is expecting you," Ms. Arnold advised. "It sounds like your set-up in California is better than you could have imagined."

"It is," Katy agreed.

Eddie dropped Katy off at the Beverly Hilton, where she would stay overnight, and took Lila to L.A. International Airport to board a flight home to Palo Alto. Katy invited Monica and Eddie to have dinner with her at the hotel later in the evening to discuss strategy, and they eagerly accepted.

As Katy relaxed in a hot tub at the hotel, she reviewed the events of the week, and particularly the day. She was sure of it now. What had happened was as carefully orchestrated as a symphony. Lila never intended to cope with a double agenda—she had faced a dilemma with her Citizens for Better Government groups: how could she get them off "propositions" and transfer their support to Katy Jenkins for president during this election? When Proposition X came along, she saw an opportunity. She organized the secret "retreat" and just let things happen. Katy had first suspected what was going on when Lila said to her, "Okay, let's see how it comes out." Then she knew she had to help pull it off. *She knew she was living dangerously*, Katy thought, *and she had to have me there to see that it came out right!*

The circulating water in the hot tub felt good. *Was Dwight Sloane a plant?* she wondered. *No, I don't think so.*

Katy sat up in the tub. *Lila Stanford has a streak of political genius*, she thought triumphantly, *and the Democrats and Republicans are never going to know what hit them in California.*

26

Well, where am I? The question Katy put to herself wasn't a literal one. Cruising at 45,000 feet across America's midsection, she'd be landing at Philadelphia in a couple of hours. Now, she reflected on the Republicans' renomination of the President, visibly aged by his four years in office—not quite as exciting as the Democrats at their National Convention—was it just three weeks ago? —when Owen Mallory, liberal governor from Illinois, gained the nomination for the top spot.

So it would be newcomer Owen Mallory challenging the incumbent president on the big tickets. Mallory versus the President. *Versus Katy Jenkins*, she thought. It suddenly occurred to her that Democrats and Republicans had bashed each other, but neither had so much as mentioned her or the Coalition party. Reporters and news commentators had attempted to inject the subject into interviews, but any official recognition or acceptance of her candidacy, or the Coalition party, was peculiarly missing at both conventions.

She had been too busy to think about it, but now something Ms. Arnold said to her at Albuquerque loomed large: "The barracudas in this campaign aren't the candidates themselves, but their campaign managers. They're both ruthless, Katy. They know every trick in the book, and they'll bury you if they can."

By the time Andy picked Katy up at the Philadelphia airport, her usual exuberance had returned. She was jubilant about her Texas to California campaign. "Andy, we're off and running in the Southwest and California!" she exclaimed.

"So I've been hearing," Andy said heavily. "We're not doing so good up here."

Andy's response sent a chill through to her heart.

"Tell me about it."

"There's a ghost on my trail."

"A ghost?"

"The record of one Katy Jenkins in the Congress and in New Mexico when she was governor."

"My record isn't so bad," snapped Katy. "I've fought for every women's issue in the book."

"Oh, it isn't that, so much."

"Then what is it?"

"Now Katy, don't get uptight. It's your stand on labor. They don't exactly consider you their friend."

"Maybe I am, and they just don't know it."

"They keep a scorecard."

"Compiled by the workers, or their Union bosses?"

"Anyhow, I was glad you didn't make any issue of this the last two weeks. I was praying you wouldn't."

He became a bit more cheerful. "You seemed to be making up your own platform as you went along in Texas and California."

Katy could still feel the anxiety in Andy's voice. Better to take it slow, she thought. "You're right, of course, Andy. I came up with things that appealed to Texans and New Mexicans—and a California constituency, too."

Andy mellowed. "Original, for sure. But we've got to do the same thing up here or I'm cooked."

"I guess you know I'll have some rebuttal time after the debate between the President and Mallory next week."

"I know. Ms. Arnold was moving mountains to get it done. Do you know how much the seven minutes would have cost at regular advertising rates?"

"Unbelievable, Andy. A million dollars a minute! But by using some of her connections to put the pressure on the networks, Ms. Arnold got it on as a public service—all except the thirty-second introduction which they say promotes the Coalition party. The only requirement is that I respond only to issues disscussed in the debate."

"That's fair enough. But the thirty seconds must have cost a quarter million dollars if it cost a penny. Maybe twice that."

"It's bought and paid for as of last Friday, a blockbuster, all networks, four minutes and fifty-eight seconds, immediately following the debate."

"That must have made a hole in the bank account."

"It did, but we'll survive."

"Oh, I know, Katy, but I don't see how that will help me in Pennsylvania."

Dinner at the Barkers was beautiful, as usual. Beverly, vivacious as ever, listened with rapt attention as Katy and Harrison talked about the western campaign.

"Working down at the campaign headquarters is the most exciting thing I've ever done," enthused Beverly. Then she asked, "Where does the vice president live?" The question was directed to Andy.

"I don't know." His answer was so short that Beverly recoiled.

"I'm sorry I asked."

"Oh, I'm sorry, Bev." Andy sounded more like himself, but not for long. "At the rate we're going, I probably won't need to find out."

"That bad?" asked Mr. Barker.

"That bad." said Andy.

Katy thought, I've never seen him like this. She shook herself in an effort to throw off a growing sense of foreboding.

As the dinner party ended, Katy suggested to Andy that they should talk.

"Excuse us, please," Andy said. "We'll be in the library."

Katy surveyed the magnificent Barker library. The room always impressed her. Must be ten thousand volumes here, she thought, and they look as if they are used all the time. Katy sat on one of the flowered sofas.

Andy sat on the opposite sofa.

"Katy, even my old friends and backers won't support me. They think I've abandoned their causes."

Katy's voice showed the genuine concern she was feeling. "Andy, I don't understand. Why?"

"You'd have to know my background. I've always been for the working people and the less fortunate. Running with you doesn't jibe with that. In New York state, especially, they're crucifying me. I'm pictured as a deserter. They're accusing me of selling out. At one Union meeting where I had support, they called me a "scab."

Katy had a fleeting thought about the goons who roughed her up. Andy kept talking. "They've dug up everything. Your fight for right-to-work laws in New Mexico. Even though it was years ago, and nothing came of it, they still hold it against you. And, you're on record in the Congress: against the Teamsters; against the International Laborers' Union. They're putting you on the rack, and me along with you."

Anger surged through Katy. "Are they telling the rest of the story; that I've had the highest praise for AFL-CIO and their enlightened policies of recent years?" Andy didn't answer her question, so she continued. "I'm not against the Teamsters—just the corruption that goes on there. Robert Kennedy was pro-union and Mr. Democrat, but his crusade as attorney-general was to rid the Teamsters of their organized crime-based leadership. The battle goes on. And I'm part of the fight." She looked at Andy. "Don't you agree?"

"Yes, sure," said Andy. "But that's just the Teamsters."

"Andy, I'm against any business having a monopoly—or any union. The Postal Union, controlled by International Laborers, is a monopoly which by its very nature is dangerous; I suspect we're headed for trouble somewhere down the line."

"Maybe so, Katy, but why borrow trouble?"

Katy disregarded the question. "I was against the closed shop in New Mexico because I didn't want the mobsters controlling labor in our state. I was against legalizing horse racing because I didn't want the Mafia moving in. Unfortunately I didn't prevail and organized crime is running gambling and dealing drugs in our state today."

"It isn't just the unions, Katy. It's everything. I know you have your reasons; I just wish I was out of the whole thing."

"Out? Oh, Andy!"

"We have a hopeless situation up here, Katy. I want out."

Katy moved numbly throughout the rest of the evening's socializing. The only concession she had been able to get from Andy was that he wouldn't say anything about his decision that evening.

Katy, relieved finally to be alone in the spacious guest bedroom, undressed and showered like an automaton. She slid between luxurious sheets, but sleep escaped her.

What to do now? What to tell TODAY magazine? And what to say on the nationwide TV hookup Tuesday evening after the debate? The questions flashed through her mind in endless procession. Questions, but no answers.

She talked aloud to the down pillow under her cheek. *What really happened to Andy?*

Is it a basic difference of viewpoint? The liberal versus the conservative? Could be, she thought, but I was in the Congress for ten years and Andy was governor of Pennsylvania. We both know the art of politics is compromise. I wouldn't have had to compromise my basic beliefs, nor he his.

"I want out." The words rang in her ears.

Now what am I going to do? Who could I get to run for vice president with me? It would have to be one of the thirty-six original organizers, she thought. Otherwise the Coalition party will fall apart.

"Andy Barker, maybe you can quit, but I can't." She made the statement with such force that she found herself sitting up in the bed. She put the pillow behind her head, and pulled the covers up around her waist. "I've got to figure this thing out."

Names ran through her mind. Harriett Landsdale? She could do it, but she'd be happier right where she is—coordinating the state organizations from her beloved Santa Fe. Sam Pickens? No way. Madge Bloomfield in Dallas? Wasn't one of the original thirty-six. Margaret Kincaid? Not a chance. Ruth Silverton or Ellen Steele? Either one would probably still be available, but a famous feminist on the ticket? Unh-uh.

Lila Stanford. Plenty of political savvy. One of the originals. And California's important. Any other man? Not one she could think of.

"Andy Barker!" She spat the words out feeling a strange mix of anger and sorrow. "He's so right for the job. Whatever can I do to get him back on the team?" But, any quick or easy solutions escaped her.

* * *

The bad dream dissipated as Katy awakened early Monday morning. It always did when she came fully awake. The doctor was ugly, his office hidden away on a dirty little El Paso side street. The curtains, grayed with years of airborne grime, hung limp and threadbare on the rod. The sofa chairs seemed diseased and dying with their unpatched, worn-through places allowing matted stuffing to spill out. Down the dark hall with one naked bulb hanging crookedly from the ceiling...through a door on the left...past an ante-way leading to the abortion room, a dismal place without windows.

She had gone with Elizabeth. And now it was her turn. She had paid in advance. "All money up front," the ugly little doctor had said. It would be over in a few minutes: into the windowless room, lower garments off, up onto the ancient obstetrics table, feet into the stirrups...

Katy awakened, her mind groping for orientation and relief. She was out of the ugly, dark hallway, past the evil little man, and out through the doorway—into the El Paso sunshine. Relief swept over her once again as the dream ended. The early morning sunshine was shining through the open curtains in her bedroom. She thought of Johnny, and thanked God.

Now, something else was prying its way into her mind. Andy! She sat up in the bed. What was she going to do about Andy? She reached for the telephone. The first button was lit up; she pushed the button for the second line. Ms. Arnold, or Margaret, or who?

Then it became crystal clear; Margaret was the only one who could help in this situation.

Margaret answered on the second ring. Katy recounted the events of last night.

"Katy, we can't lose Andy," Margaret said.

"Unless we already have."

"I don't know. I just talked to Andy. He called me."

"Oh?"

"He's really upset. I'm coming down there on the train as soon as I can get away. Stay put 'til I get there." She paused. "Katy, it's only fair to warn you, I'll have to get John Van Dorn in on this, and Ms. Arnold, and Ruth and Ellen, too."

"You think John can help?"

"Sure do. I've been at LAND & SEA a lot lately. Working with Carrie Brooks. You can't believe how much they're doing. I think John has to know."

* * *

Mr. Barker welcomed each guest personally and escorted them to the library where Mrs. Barker and Katy took over. Mrs. Barker served cheese sticks, cookies, and tea from a silver set. Iced lemonade waited in crystal pitchers on the coffee table.

Ms. Arnold, Ruth, and Ellen arrived first. Harrison Barker came in as John Van Dorn and Margaret arrived.

John approached Katy and she greeted him casually. "I can't thank you enough for all you're doing for me," she said.

Harrison observed John as he responded to Katy. "You're an exciting candidate to work for, Katy. There hasn't been a dull moment." Ms. Arnold approached them, and John added, "Of course, I don't see as much of you as I do of Ms. Arnold. She and Carrie are the politicos. I just try to keep up with them."

"Don't let him fool you, Katy. John comes up with angles that none of us could think of."

Margaret greeted Ellen and Ruth with big hugs, and called to John.   "I want you to meet the powers at the Women's Movement." John approached them quickly. "Ruth Silverton. Ellen Steele."

"I'm glad to get to meet you personally. Your work is legendary. Margaret says she could never have gotten the ball rolling without you."

"Please everybody. Get refreshments and bring them with you.   Let's gather around."   Margaret's voice rang out enthusiastically.

Andy poured tea and talked amiably with Katy as they seated themselves at the oval conference table.

Everyone looked expectantly at Margaret. "Andy wants to pull out of the race," she said matter-of-factly. "And I don't want him to. I don't think anyone else does either. This meeting is to see what can be done to keep him on the team."

"What's wrong, Andy?" Ellen blurted out.

Andy looked around nervously. The suddenness and directness of Margaret's statement suprised him. "I don't think I fit into this organization the way it's going," he said. All eyes were on him.

"What do you mean?" Ellen pressed him.

"Okay, I'll tell you. The candidate and I don't see things the same way. I like Katy very much as a person, but her attitude toward labor is reactionary. Her philosophy on nuclear warfare is dangerous. She's almost psychotic on cutting spending—except on 'Missile Defense.' She questions the integrity of our young people on Social Security. On foreign affairs she's so prejudiced against the Germans and Japanese she seems to want to fight World War II all over again."

Katy sat impassive, listening. The group was quiet.

Andy decided to hit harder. "I don't see how she could really be for a giant tax increase, call it oil import fee or whatever, as she advocated in Texas. Her plan would raise the price of gasoline five or ten cents a gallon. I visualized the party as champions of the poor and under-priviledged, not as their enemies. Our Party is about rights for women, rights for people, and for peace—not war."

Andy's frustrations poured out in his next statement. "We have become a party of the rich. Maybe that's the way it was all the time. Maybe it started out that way; and I was just suckered into it by my big brother, and his best friend, who just happens to be even richer than he is. What do they want? More riches? More power?"

Katy froze. *What had Andy said?* 'Suckered into it by my big brother and his best friend.' Was it possible that Harrison wasn't in Room 824 at the Brown Palace in Denver quite by accident—as it had seemed? Was it possible that John was in on it with him? That not only Andy was suckered into it? *That she was, too?* Van Dorn was capable of anything; she knew that for a fact. Was she just a pawn in his hand? A plaything for him just as she had been twenty-eight years ago?

She sat down heavily.

If Margaret was suprised at Katy's sudden withdrawal, she didn't show it. She resumed control of the meeting, intent on getting John Van Dorn on.

"John took it on himself," Margaret began, "to find out who masterminded the conspiracy that knocked me out of the race. He suspected the same forces might be responsible for the dirty tricks on Katy, the harrassment and intimidation the day of the Women's Movement check presentation, and the planting of cocaine on Katy when she flew to Texas."

Margaret's voice had a note of triumph. "John, tell us what you found."

John leaned forward. "Margaret got herself into trouble with a very powerful group in the 1960's," he began. "She never knew who they were, or what lasting enemies she made. All because she was a crusader. She came out of Berkeley with stars in her eyes and took a job in the Welfare Department in New York City. She was appalled to find marijuana and sometimes other drugs being sold to school children. Law officials seemed helpless to do anything about it, so Margaret organized MAD—Mothers Against Drugs. Black women, Puerto Ricans, who spoke little English, and other mothers and teachers joined. 'Just report to us,' Margaret pleaded. The meetings were primarily 'report' sessions. Notes were taken. Kids were given small cameras to take pictures. Sometimes she got enough information to prosecute. Though convictions were few, Margaret's crusade was effective. Drug sales to kids declined dramatically."

John looked around at the group, and continued. "But Margaret wasn't satisfied. She wanted to know where the drugs came from. That's what got her into trouble with a Mafia family that later would become quite powerful. As luck would have it, she was successful in getting a young member of this family to trial. He wasn't sent to jail, but the publicity was abhorrent to the mobsters. They like to stay behind the scenes. Margaret exposed the very one who would later take over the 'family.' She was unaware of the extent of the organization."

"Twenty-some years later, he struck back. But not up front. That's Margaret's style, but not his. She was openly running for president; they went underground to knock her out.

"It was difficult to get the facts, but my people unearthed the vicious and damning evidence somebody had put together against Margaret's son, Eric. It had gone to the Grand Jury. How it got there was the mystery.

"The break came when it was discovered that the Senator from Jersey City, New Jersey, had submitted some of the evidence from his office, and that affidavits and depositions in the file were sworn to by members of the International Laborers' Union."

"Meanwhile, the investigators had run down the license plate numbers on the bus which transported the group who attacked Katy. Somehow the bus vanished. But the plates were issued to a coach out of Jersey City.

Ms. Arnold had a question. "You mean the bus that hauled the guys to Washington and up to Katy's house to rough her up was from New Jersey?"

"No question about that. The question was, 'why?' And was there any connection between the bus incident and the Grand Jury in New York? This had us baffled."

"This is like Perry Mason," commented Ruth.

"Only this is real," added Ellen. "You say, '*had* us baffled?'"

"The profile on one Joe Domino gave us the clues we needed."

"Part of the Mafia?"

"Not the big time, but he's tied in. He owns Intercity Transport! A hoodlum who grew up on the streets in Jersey City, Domino started out with a pool hall his father left him. As a kid, he ran numbers for the local syndicate, later got into prostitution.

"All this information was easy to come by. Domino is a prominent fellow." John paused a minute. "But guess what? He has a stranglehold on the local unions. And he practically railroaded the good Senator from Jersey City into office."

"Well, I'll be damned," said Harrison. "Now it adds up. He's tied in with New York. He engineered Margaret's ouster through his union connections."

John leaned closer to his listeners. "Now, listen to this. The FBI suspects he transports drugs for the syndicate, too. Quite likely he supplied the cocaine, and set Katy up."

Katy spoke for the first time since John started. "This Joe Domino seems to have us singled out for his worst pitches."

John's voice was sympathethic. "We're sure of that now. Your proposals to clean up the unions is an anathema to them. We know that Joe's henchmen openly bragged at a Union meeting in

Jersey City that they were knocking you out into left field—just before the drug plant."

"My God," said Katy.

"Jersey City isn't the only place. The information we have is that they're poisoning New York state and Pennsylvania against you and Andy."

"Andy has fought for the labor unions."

"Katy, this isn't being orchestrated by the rank and file union members. The word went out from New York to all the Joe Domino's in New Jersey, New York, and Pennsylvania. Nothing ever in writing. They have their own communications, but they're getting blanket coverage. They're infiltrating every union local, and all the media, with the deadliest propaganda you can imagine."

John looked at Andy. "That's why your supporters have melted into the woodwork."

Andy apppeared uncomfortable, defensive. "If Ms. Arnold hadn't been so high-handed in turning down the Unions' Political Action Committee offer of a substantial campaign donation, none of this would be happening."

Katy recalled Ms. Arnold's frantic early morning phone call to her the day she and the Texans left Dallas for Colorado. The offer from the Union PAC was tempting. But she turned it down, because she couldn't be beholden to them. Now she realized she should have delayed the refusal until she had a chance to consult with Andy. Maybe she could have kept him on the team.

Katy felt the entire campaign slipping away from her. Was it all based on a false premise from the beginning?

She had to know. "John," she said, her voice on edge, "I've got to have a couple straight answers from you."

"All right, Katy." John fidgeted with the tea cup in front of him."

"Did you have anything to do with Andy and me being nominated in Denver? In collusion with Harrison, or Margaret, or anyone else?"

Andy jerked to attention. As John hesitated, tension heightened around the table.

"I want to give you a straight answer, Katy. Certainly there was no collusion on my part to get you or Andy nominated. I had no contact with Harrison at all on the matter."

The tension eased. Ms. Arnold was the only one who still sat up on the edge of her chair. She was nodding almost imperceptably, but affirmatively, to John.

He caught the signal and continued. "I did call Ms. Arnold, and suggested that she attend. She was our Washington information specialist, and on a retainer with LAND & SEA. She did, however, catch me completely by suprise when she joined up with the campaign."

"I did that on my own," interjected Ms. Arnold. "It's an inspiration I haven't regretted. I'll be working for Katy night and day through the campaign. And for Andy, too, I hope."

"John, what is your interest in this campaign?" asked Ellen. "Don't get me wrong, we appreciate your help. But, we don't know why you want to get Katy elected, or just what you're expecting from it."

"We are getting some questions from members," added Ruth, from the other side of the table. "They're asking questions about your views on women's rights—abortion especially."

John laughed easily.

"To answer your first question, Ellen, I'm not at all sure I'd want Katy, or anyone else I like, to be elected president of this country. It must be an awful job. But, she's running, and I'm backing her as much as I can—for better or worse, as they say. I don't really have any other goal than to support Katy. I'm a kindred soul with Ms. Arnold apparently."

He turned to Ruth. "But since I am so involved, the least I can do is tell you where I'm coming from. I met Katy one summer twenty-eight years ago at the University of New Mexico. We met in the only Political Science seminar I ever attended. Her political ideas were as refreshing and down to earth then as they are today. It was a great experience. I learned a lot in that seminar."

Katy listened quietly.

"About the issues," John continued, "put me down for 'freedom-of-choice' and for all the women's issues that I know of. Anything else—just ask Katy. I'll go along with her."

Ellen wasn't satisfied. "How about the oil import tax Katy proposed in Texas? Can you swallow that, being in the oil tanker business?"

John laughed again. The low, happy chuckle Katy had heard so many times.

"Texans are going for it," he said. "And it will be a tremendous boost to our own energy independence."

"All right!" Ellen eased off. "I'm all for it, too."

Harrison spoke slowly, picking his words. "John could honestly disclaim any responsibility for Katy and Andy's nominations. I don't get off so easily. I was there when it happened, and I was an accessory."

He looked at Andy. "I plead guilty as charged—but it wasn't premeditated. I was there to try to lure you back into the family business. And you were listening. But when Katy asked you to run with her, I could see where your heart was. Here was a chance for you to run for vice president of the United States with the party you helped to found."

Andy cleared his throat, but said nothing. Harrison continued. "Neither John nor I ever had such an opportunity. We were sent to big schools with one purpose—preparation to take over the family business. We had few choices. There were times, Andy, when I would have given my chance at heaven to have the freedom you had. You could go to California, to Berkeley, and take any course you chose, engage in any activities you wanted. John and I had no such choices. You came home, and became Governor. I never had that option.

"You had fun and excitement. I lived some of that fun and excitement vicariously, through you. Now you are up against some terrible odds. Your political career is jeopardized forever if you don't carry Pennsylvania in this election. And you are being discredited by some powerful interests. I have been aware of this for some time, but didn't know who was back of it until today."

He looked at Andy. "Andy, I don't think Katy's political philosophies are the problem. She seems to be politically astute, and 'straight' at the same time. No, what you are up against is outside forces. They are discrediting Katy with you. Seems to be an effective strategy, but not one you have to buy. You're not in favor of Mafia controlled unions or an insolvent Social Security system. And you see eye-to-eye with Katy on human rights. Katy calls it human 'freedom' instead of 'rights.'"

Harrison looked around the table suddenly feeling

self-conscious. "I'm sorry; guess I got carried away."

Ruth was sitting next to Harrison. She touched his arm as she spoke quietly. "I'm glad to be here today. I've wondered where this campaign is going, too, and if I'm in the right place—whether it's worth all the effort. I feel better now that I know the people here in this room."

Katy had a question. "John, do we have any legal evidence? Proof of criminal activity, on the part of this Joe Domino or any member of his organization?"

"Not enough," said John, "we wouldn't have a chance trying to prosecute anyone now."

"All right," Katy said, "then we'll have to fight them on their own terms. They're after us; we'll go after them. They're ruthless; they live by the code of the jungle; so will we."

"I'm beginning to understand what we're up against," said Andy. "I don't know how we could go up against them in New York state and have any chance of winning."

Andy's coming around, thought Katy. Her response was quick. "I think you're right, Andy. They have too much going for them up there. New Jersey's the same." Katy was very deliberate. "Andy, we might have a chance here in Pennsylvania—with you—but it would be the toughest part of the whole campaign."

"All right. In view of the revelations here today, I have to stay in. But you must know: I'm scheduled to be the speaker at a big union meeting in Uniontown next Thursday. I know they're planning to nail me to the cross."

"We can clobber that one," snapped Katy. "Tell them you are inviting me, too. Let them plan a blockbuster." Katy knew she didn't have the slightest idea just how they were going to "clobber" this one, but the adrenalin was flowing.

Andy looked surprised. "You'd do that? They're going to be mean." He considered. "No, you had better let me handle this one."

Approval registered on the faces around the table. Ms. Arnold put it into words. "Andy, I should have checked with you as well as Katy on the proposed PAC contribution. I can see that you were put in a bad spot. I'm sorry."

"So am I." Katy's words were sincere.

Harrison Barker cleared his throat. "Andy, the Unions let you down in your last run for governor. They gave you money, but not support. As governor you hadn't bent to their every demand."

"Maybe I'll just fight 'em. Tell the members the truth."

"You will win some votes that way, Andy. Not only with members but with the rest of the electorate, too." Harrison sat back.

Katy spoke up. "Go ahead, Andy, and tell 'em you're inviting me for Thursday. We may just surprise them."

"Okay, Katy, but don't expect to reason with those guys. What they expect is absolute loyalty."

"I know," said Katy.

"Oh, there is one more thing, Katy," Ms. Arnold broke in. "Now that we know what kind of people we're dealing with, I've arranged for security."

"I really don't think that's necessary."

"It's too dangerous for you," Ms. Arnold shot back. "I think it's necessary and so does the Secret Service. They've finally decided that you are a bona fide candidate; operations are set up at the Georgetown Headquarters. You're going to have two 'round-the-clock' agents wherever you go. This may save your life before this campaign is over."

* * *

The damn woman is dumber than I thought she was, mused Joe Domino, to invite herself right into my mousetrap. The trap will snap shut on her. He clapped his big hands together. The snapping sound reverberated through the room.

She'll squeal a couple times, try her damndest to wriggle out of it, and wish to hell she hadn't stuck her big nose into Pennsylvania. He picked up the telephone to call Big Jake.

27

"No dining car on this train, advised Ms. Arnold, "but there is a good snack bar with hot food and cocktails." She had the porter turn the seats around so the four faced each other after they boarded the train from Philadelphia to return to Washington.

A perfect set-up for a 'visit' with Ruth and Ellen, mused Katy. As they munched snacks and sipped cocktails, everyone loosened up.

"You'd think women anywhere and everywhere would jump aboard the Katy bandwagon," Ellen said wistfully, "but they're holding back. A lot of our people got mad when Allen Marchbanks spouted off while you were in California, and contributions picked up, but most of them will soon forget.

"The women's political groups are the worst of all," she continued. "They pride themselves on being objective. I hate it when they're so damned objective they don't seem to realize that here is an opportunity to elect a woman to the highest office in the land. Why wouldn't they jump at the chance?"

"I've been through this before," Ms. Arnold said. "Voter apathy has always been a heartbreak for politicians. But, when Katy gets on national TV after the debate next week and on the cover of TODAY, there will be a new awareness of the Katy Jenkins candidacy."

"I have an overwhelming job ahead of me," said Katy. "I'm going to attend a Party rally, or rallies, in every state during the next six or seven weeks. Coordinating this effort is going to tax the abilities of all of us. We're starting in the boondocks, in the states with the fewest electoral votes and working up to the big states."

"Good plan," said Ruth, "but it sounds like a marathon."

"That's the way I campaigned for Governor in New Mexico. It worked. Ms. Arnold will do all the scheduling with the state chairpeople, working with Harriett Landsdale. I'm planning to be on the road five or six days a week. I'll try to be in the Washington headquarters on Mondays most of the time, getting there on Sundays, taking off again by Tuesday. Harriett will coordinate with Ms. Arnold. She will keep you two advised every day of every arrangement so you can get as many of your people to the rallies as possible. Ellen will be on the road talking to women's groups. We will each be kept advised of the others' schedules on a daily basis."

Then Katy directed a question to Ruth. "How is the 'Second Million Club' doing?"

"We'll get it, but like Ellen says, even our own members and supporters aren't scrambling to get their checks in, although contributions did pick up the week Marchbanks blasted women. We're getting a stack of checks every day, but it may take longer and require more mailings than we thought. So far, we're getting in only about double our costs."

Ms. Arnold spoke up: "The second mailing will be better than the first, and the third even better; and we're getting money in from different places; a lot of fund-raising 'coffees' and breakfasts are set up on Katy's tours, half the money to stay with the local organization and half to us at National." A frown crossed her face. "Even so, we may be hurting for money in the short pull. We're committed to a half-million dollars in California when they raise that much; Lila Stanford called yesterday and advised they are approaching $250,000, and asked if we could go ahead and match this right away. I stalled her for the time being."

"Somehow, we've got to do that," Katy said. "Let's have a meeting on finances Wednesday, after the debate."

The conversation veered from one aspect of the campaign to another. Katy felt the enthusiasm mounting as they talked; playing for high stakes in the power game stirs the adrenalin.

Commotion in the aisles caught the group's attention. "What's going on?" asked Ellen.

The conductor answered her question. "D.C.", he said, "check to see that you have all personal belongings."

* * *

Ms. Arnold waited to see Katy's reaction to the security guards, as they entered Katy's townhouse headquarters. Katy was aware that the house was now under twenty-four hour security, but she wasn't quite prepared for the two young women who welcomed her into her own home.

Even as she was introduced to Bert Kelly and Jean Shaw, she had a sinking feeling as she realized any semblance of privacy was now gone. Every move she made would be under watchful eyes. The two women assured her that they had checked the house and garden carefully. All clear. The house would be under surveillance from the garage across the street. Another station was in the telephone room, above the garage, from which the garden and back of the house would be monitored.

When Ms. Arnold arrived at the Georgetown Headquarters early Tuesday morning, several of the staff people were already there drinking coffee and organizing for a new week. Katy was working out ideas for her TV speech. So Ms. Arnold went straight to her desk leaving Katy to her thoughts.

This may be the largest audience I'll ever have; I don't want to blow it, Katy contemplated. In front of her was the editorial from the New York Times, "THIS IS THE TIME TO PUT ON AN OIL TAX." Good, my Texas plan—it's catching on; "a solid energy plan will help renew America." She liked that: RENEW AMERICA!

She began to outline current issues. This is my big chance, she kept thinking.

She would speak from notes she would make as she listened to the President and Mallory; this would not only conform to the network requirements, it would also give her an organized format. The debate between the "big party" candidates would furnish her plenty of material.

She evolved a plan. She made a list of the subjects most likely to be discussed. They would almost certainly mention the subjects she had explored in California: that would give her a chance to expose the Social Security fraud, the rip-off of Capitol gains tax breaks, and certainly she would goad Congress on cleaning up the banking laws. For each subject she formulated her response, but not in writing; she simply thought each one through. *Actually, I will have the last word.* The thought calmed the butterflies in her stomach. She began to look forward to her role in the big event. Then she heard a noise. Sounds like someone sobbing, she thought. Then Ms. Arnold heard it. "What's that?" she asked aloud.

The answer wasn't long in coming. Barbara Lee, in tears, came toward Katy. "I'm sorry, Miss Jenkins," she stammered, "I didn't know what I was doing. I'm terribly sorry. I'd rather work for you and Ms. Arnold than anyone in the world. And I think the world would be a better place with 'freedom of choice'...and if the church wasn't so mean," she said miserably.

All thoughts of the debate vanished from Katy's mind as she vaulted out of her chair, and put her arm around the distressed girl. "Tell me", she coaxed, "what's wrong?"

Barbara let out a sharp cry and pulled away. "I'm sorry," she said again. "I'm going now. You'll never trust me again." She darted to her desk, took the small picture of her mother off it and put it in her purse. She grabbed her coat and dashed out the door.

Security guard Bert Kelly braced herself for the collision as Barbara Lee lunged through the front door. Barbara saw Bert seconds too late, as she slammed into her.

"Hey, slow down." Bert withstood the impact and managed to keep them both on their feet. "Did you see a ghost or something?"

Katy appeared at the doorway. "Barbara! What's happened to you?" To Bert, "Don't let her get away." Then an afterthought, "she may be a security risk."

Barbara's eyes flashed. "I'm not the kind of risk that your security guard has to hold me."

Bert released her grasp on Barbara's arm, but still blocked her way.

"I didn't mean that, Barbara." Katy's tone was conciliatory now, a smile playing at her lips. "I don't really think you're a security risk, but we do need to talk. Let me drive you wherever you're going and we can talk."

"You'll drive me?" Barbara's question emphasized the "me."

Katy saw a look of distress cross Bert's face. "I'll need to ride along," she said, "or get Jean and another car so we can follow."

Katy felt rebellious but decided to accept the inevitable. "Barbara, is it all right if Bert rides along with us? You can depend on her confidentiality."

"Oh, well sure, yes." Barbara wiped her eyes.

The three went down the steps to the car.

"Don't you need to get your keys?" asked Bert.

"They're on the visor," said Katy easily.

Bert watched in disbelief as Katy retrieved the keys.

"This is where we always keep them in Caprock. I guess it's just habit."

This woman may be smart enought to be president, thought Bert, but she's about as security-wise as an unlocked bank vault.

Already Katy was talking to Barbara. "Is there a connection between you and the 'right-to-life' demonstrations?"

"You don't know?"

"Not really. I'm just trying to figure it out."

"I didn't know, Miss Jenkins."

"Didn't know what?"

"My mother is awfully lonesome; she's living all alone now that I'm gone. I call her every night, and we talk about everything; everything I do. We've always talked."

"Your mother must be nice."

"She is, Miss Jenkins. But she's wrapped up in the church. She's always helping out at First Baptist."

"First Baptist?"

"It's the biggest church in Birmingham. Reverend Atwood's church." Barbara spat out the words. "I hate him."

Reverend Atwood, thought Katy. Her last confrontation with him flashed through her mind. His pious face turning so angry; his threat.

"You hate Reverend Atwood?"

"I was going to Birmingham Baptist University, but I'll never go there now, no matter how many scholarships he offers me."

"Barbara, I've had run-ins with Reverend Atwood myself. Our philosophies on some things clash. But—hate him?"

"For what he did. Can't you see, Miss Jenkins. He 'used' my mother."

Katy suspected she knew the answer to her next question. "He used your mother? How?"

"Don't you see? I told mother everything. I should have known better. I didn't think about her passing everything on to him. He has her working in his office."

So that's how he knew my every move in Texas and everywhere I went, thought Katy.

"I think I understand what happened," Katy said. "That was an unscrupulous thing for Atwood to do." Katy dreaded to ask the next question. "Was your mother deliberately pumping you to get information from you to give Reverend Atwood?"

"I'm sure she wasn't at first. My mother may be a church bug, but she's a good person. I didn't know about the demonstrations in Texas, at private homes and everywhere, until Ms. Arnold came back. I still didn't connect it all. Mother didn't either until I told her about the strange demonstrations, and how you were being picked on. She went to Atwood and asked him point blank. He tried to evade the subject, but you can't fool my mother. When she called me last week, she was in tears. She didn't intend to hurt me, or you, or anyone."

"I'm sure of it, Barb, and you didn't intend to hurt me either." Katy became quite cheerful. "Actually not much harm was done. It's all part of politics. That's one reason church and state shouldn't be mixed up. Either one can be dangerous by themselves, but when combined they can be disastrous."

"You're not mad?"

"Oh, I'm mad all right. But not at you or your mother."

"Can I go back and help Ms. Arnold? We have so much to do."

"You sure can."

* * *

Katy settled at her desk, again thinking about the upcoming debate, but was distracted by something Ms. Arnold was saying.

"This picture isn't exactly glamorous, but you do look like you could run the country."

"What are you talking about?" Katy looked questioningly at Ms. Arnold.

"TODAY magazine," exclaimed Ms. Arnold. "You're on everything but the back cover."

"You tease! Let me see it! Where did you get it?"

"This is an advance copy, sent to us by express mail. It was delivered a few minutes ago." She continued to study the cover picture, keeping it tilted so Katy couldn't see. "Not bad," she said, "pretty good, in fact."

"Let me see it!" Katy screeched, as she lunged toward Ms. Arnold's desk.

Katy grabbed the magazine, and sure enough...there she was, big as life, right on the front cover. The caption grabbed her: "First Woman President?" The question mark was oversized, giving it emphasis. Eagerly Katy flipped through the magazine.

"Page eighteen. The Nation. Feature story."

"Here it is! Oh, Ms. Arnold, double page spread, and pictures—someone has been down to Caprock with a camera—and it continues on."

"There's stuff about you I didn't even know," Ms. Arnold said. "I couldn't have written a better story myself. I love the caption under the picture of you and Johnny riding herd on your cows: "Country girl candidate riding herd with her 'kid brother' partner at Caprock City. Now, she proposes to ride herd on the nation."

Katy laughed. "That's a good picture of Johnny. Looks like he was born in the saddle."

"You're riding tall in the saddle yourself. Looks like you were having fun."

Katy looked wistfully at the picture. "You'll never know how much." She began eagerly reading the article. "This is great!"

* * *

David Wells, Democratic campaign manager, studied the article in TODAY. Fear gripped him. He felt he had a good shot at electing Owen Mallory president. Then he would be on the gravy train. Could this upstart woman from Caprock City upset the apple cart? How in hell did she get such a write-up in TODAY? And that damn Ms. Arnold, and those Women's Movement feminists, were already making a public clamor to get Jenkins included in the next debate.

He felt panicked. What if the crazy Republicans invited her to participate? He had to head that off. He couldn't call the President; he was the incumbent and wouldn't admit that any women had a chance to beat him. Wells would have to deal with his counterpart, Gene Boggs, the President's campaign manager. He had a friend at Boggs' headquarters. He'd start with him. By God, he'd keep that damn woman in her place. And the next time that nuisance Arnold woman called, he would put her in her place. Politics is a man's world—no woman should be running for president anyhow. *What's the damn country coming to?*

He picked up the phone, got the Republican Headquarters right away and spoke to his friend confidentially about the problem. Gene Boggs came on the phone almost immediately.

"Have you seen the new TODAY?"

"Just looking at it."

"It looks to me like we gotta put out a brush fire."

"Sure as hell does."

"Maybe we better get together. Somewhere we can talk."

"Okay."

"How about the little fish house?"

"Sure, the Fish Net. Lunch? 11:30?"

"I'll see you there."

28

Katy's breathing came in short gasps and her mouth went dry as she took her place behind the lectern at NTB for her rebuttal to the presidential Candidates' nationally televised debate. She had watched the long debate on a monitor; now she would have seven minutes to respond. She heard her own introduction; the floodlights came on—and she was on the air with the biggest television audience of her career.

Confidence replaced her initial nervousness as a tantalizing smile tugged at the corners of her mouth and she started with a disarming question. "Well, who won the great debate?

"Mr. Mallory is a spellbinder; his voice rings with goodwill and patriotism. But what did he really say? He said he would spend your money—on everything from pre-natal care to environmental utopia. That was his message. You name it and whatever your special interest is, he offers everything you ask for. What he fails to tell you is, that as he caters to each special interest group with its noble sounding 'causes,' he will take away your cash and freedom on the installment plan."

Some of the severity left Katy's manner. She began to relax and smiled at her viewers. "The President's rhetoric sounds pretty convincing too, at first. He knows all about world affairs, has traveled all over the globe helping everybody in sight with your money; he is 'Uncle Sugar' to the overseas crowd.

"Oh, and he's not raising taxes, just borrowing money from Social Security trust funds, big banks, insurance companies, local banks—anywhere he can get it. Repayment? Let your kids and grandchildren worry about that."

Katy was speaking to the millions of viewers she knew were out there behind the glare of the spotlights.

"So," she continued, "who won the debate? Certainly not the American people." There was scorn in her voice. "Tonight you heard the same old empty promises, the same old non-answers to the serious problems facing this country.

"The Republicans and Democrats are living in the past. They don't realize that we're going into the 21st century, not winding up the 19th century. If we choose to follow their lead, we will sink deeper and deeper into a quagmire of runaway debt, a continuing exodus of jobs outside our borders, and a failure to create jobs and prosperity in our own country.

"During the ten years I've been in the Congress, our government has dawdled over one urgent matter after another, leaving little time for the really important matters.

"Health care is a case in point. We have squandered our time, day after day, year after year, while health care costs have become so prohibitive that no working person in America can pay today's doctor's charges, medical costs and hospital bills. A heart by-pass operation, which is routine now, may cost $49,000. This is for a few hours of a surgeon's time and use of some modern equipment, and ten day's care in the hospital. What working family has this kind of money?

"The answer is, of course, practically none. So we have evolved a patched-up system where some Americans are covered for part of the costs, part of the time, by various insurance plans and government programs, often leaving our most vulnerable people with no coverage at all.

"The giant insurance companies have too little interest in their clients. Their answer is not to cut costs, but simply to raise rates.

"Meanwhile, the lawyers have developed a lucrative business suing doctors. The doctors, who already charge as much per hour as most of their patients make in a week or a month, now are forced to add more to their charges to pay for exhorbitant malpractice insurance. What do lawyers have to do with health care in the first place? Considering how much they add to health care cost, isn't it about time to get them out of the business?

"Why not make the doctors pay for their own errors? And make this possible by limiting the amount that can be collected by a patient, from ten times up to a hundred times the doctor's charges. Then maybe the American Medical Association will accept some responsibility for the members they accept and approve; as it stands now they just look the other way when patients are being mangled by members.

"The cost of health care has been a great concern of the American people for years, and it becomes an urgent matter when workers lose their jobs, and lose their health coverage along with the job. But don't expect Congress and your elected president to work together to solve the problem. They are too busy playing politics. Under the present system it would take Congress a month to make instant coffee.

"Wouldn't it be better to elect a new president with a plan, who will work with both parties in the Congress?"

Katy took a sip of water before plunging ahead.

"Both candidates tell us they will keep Social Security safe and sound. But this isn't urgent, so they just plan to keep on spending the money intended for your retirement on current expenses."

Katy lowered her voice. "Social Security deductions, FICA, take a nasty bite out of every paycheck—and the same size, and just as painful, bite out of business income on every paycheck issued. Combined, more than fifteen percent of all wages goes into this huge fund.

"We show a multi-billion dollar surplus in the Social Security fund. But the money isn't there."

Katy looked straight into the camera. A confident, calm sensation enveloped her; she felt like a runner getting a second wind.

"To create real social security now and in the future, I propose that we invest the billions of dollars surplus we are collecting for the Social Security program in low-cost housing loans.

"Using Social Security funds in this way will not only create thousands of new jobs in construction, it will also give working people new homes and new hope. And the payback from long-term, low-interest mortgages will assure Social Security funds for future generations."

Her demeanor changed, becoming more accusatory as she switched subjects.

"The President," she said, "wants to lower or eliminate taxes on profits from capital gains. Who benefits? The rich, that's who. Not the bulk of hard-working Americans. It's ludicrous, when you think of it, to tax at the full rate every dollar of income earned by work and giving a tax break to unearned income, money that people don't work for."

Katy paused for a moment to let this sink in. "Proponents of capital gains tax cuts say investment creates new jobs, but most of the money made in capital gains accrues from speculation—in real estate and in the stock market. Does buying vacant land or stocks and holding them for a higher price create jobs and increase production?

"Now if a tax break could be given to investors in new business enterprises only, I would favor that. We need to encourage long term investment, not short term speculation. If capital gains were spread out over a ten year period, allowing ten percent a year as capital gains, that would make some sense. Again, encourage investment—not speculation."

Katy paused again to shift gears.

"Mr. Mallory and the Democrats have a bushel basket full of social programs to offer you. Certainly, we must provide for people who cannot help themselves. But I don't believe the government is obliged to reward alcoholism, drug abuse, criminality or indolence.

"I would favor, however, many of the proposals you have heard this evening—including, especially, child care for working parents. But I would add this caveat: we must pay as we go! What better way to test new programs than to ask whether we are able and willing to pay for them as we go?"

Drawing on her experience as Governor of New Mexico, Katy explained that most states are constitutionally forbidden to spend more money that they take in, but that the federal government is not under such constraint.

Moving on to another subject, her manner changed and anger came through in her words. "I am especially outraged at the abysmal rip-off of the American people by the Savings and Loan debacle. The greed of bankers and developers, linked with the 'wink and nod' school of politics has come closer to wrecking our national economy than anything else we've ever done.

"And Congress's band-aid approach will improve nothing! Why not do something? I have two suggestions: that we tie every insured account to the depositor's social security number, thus eliminating insuring giant sums for money-launderers and other crooked depositors. And insure bank accounts and savings accounts for eighty percent, instead of a hundred percent—so depositors share twenty percent of any losses incurred—like the co-insurance on home owners' policies. *Then we won't let crooks run our banks.* If Congress commits taxpayers' money to guarantee deposits, they must have stringent enough requirements to protect them. They have the leverage here; if the institutions don't meet safety requirements, stop insuring their deposits!"

This led Katy to one of her major themes. "Campaign financing reform and renewal of the American ideal of public service will go a long way to help avoid a recurrence of such a debacle. Take away all business and PAC contributions to election campaigns and limit individual contributions to $1000 per person with no loopholes, put a reasonable cap on spending, and apportion public funds to qualified candidates. Let lawmakers be lawmakers, not perpetual fund-raisers."

Katy's demeanor changed. "We inherited a land of plenty, and a country with a future, but we are loading ourselves with the burdens of debt and doubt. With a three trillion dollar debt, the Savings and Loan debacle, plus unfunded billions of dollars of military and civil service pensions, and more billions of unfunded liabilities for Social Security, the combination of which dwarfs even the federal debt, we are going to find ourselves in an unsustainable society. We need to put our house in order."

Katy got the 'wind-down' signal from the director. "I have only about a minute left," she said. "I wish I had more time to talk about the American Coalition party's program for the renewal of America. But I will get that information to you in detail as the campaign progresses."

Katy smiled broadly. "I'm often asked: 'Aren't you the women's party candidate?'

"Well, I should hope so. I am for fairness and opportunity for all citizens, and that includes women. I stand firmly against any form of discrimination against women, and I do feel strongly that women should be allowed freedom of choice in personal decisions; society must have tolerance on this very individual matter.

"My time is up. Thank you and I will appreciate your vote

and support for the American Coalition party's Crusade for Renewing America. Good night."

* * *

Both the Democrat and Republican camps were uneasy after the debate. What concerned the two major candidates most was the prime time and news space given to Jenkins. This, following on the heels of the TODAY magazine story, struck terror into both camps. The Jenkins woman had scored on television, the awesome political medium.

David Wells confided his fears to Owen Mallory the morning after the debate. He assured his candidate that he came off better on the debate than the President. "But we're lucky he fumbled on abortion and capital gains."

Then they talked about the Jenkins threat. Wells presented a bold plan to Mallory: "Why don't we jump the gun on the Republicans and invite the Jenkins woman to participate in the next debate?"

Mallory considered this. He realized the President had a big edge on him as the incumbent. Maybe Jenkins would be a distraction; and it would be a noble gesture on his part. That same afternoon Mallory issued the invitation for Katy Jenkins to participate in the next debate.

"The dirty S.O.B." Gene Boggs vented his fury as he talked with the President. The President was just as angry.

"We've been double-crossed; that's for damn sure. I thought you had an understanding with Wells and Mallory."

"I did. What makes it so confounded bad is that you defended keeping Jenkins off the debates this morning, and four hours later they hit the press with this." He threw the Post down in disgust. "By God, I'll never trust them again. And before this election is over, I'll get even!"

29

Apprehension assailed Katy as she headed for Uniontown to confront the "Laborers." She shuddered, recalling the shattered glass from her car window as it crashed in on her. The same ruthless men could very well be hell-bent on giving them a rough time tonight.

Having Bert and Jean along provided some comfort; and knowing Andy requested extra police protection was reassuring; still her stomach churned uneasily as the GULFSTREAM rose into the air and headed for Philadelphia to pick up Andy. She wondered about the airport at Uniontown and even more about the hotel and the union hall where the meeting would take place.

She pulled a Philadelphia Inquirer from the stack of daily newspapers. Maybe flipping through it would distract her for the moment. Then a short piece, upper right, across from the editorial page caught her attention: "Laborers Union To Confront American Coalition Party Candidates." A premonition of disaster invaded her spirit. Another story on the same page mentioned an AFL-CIO meeting the same evening in Pittsburgh; the National President of AFL-CIO would personally address the group. Public invited. *I would much rather be at that meeting*, Katy thought.

Katy dashed to the cockpit as soon as the idea jelled in her mind. "Bill, how about putting down in Pittsburgh? Got enough fuel?"

"Sure, Katy. Philly's right below us. We just cleared the outer marker and...Pittsburgh?"

"I'll explain later. We'll put down for Andy and then we're off for Steeltown, right?"

"Right!" He smiled at her. "You don't want to mix it up with thugs, huh?"

"Something like that," Katy said.

When Andy met her at the airport, Katy took him aside. "Let's go to the Pittsburgh AFL-CIO meeting tonight instead of Uniontown." She offered the newspaper clippings.

Andy groped with the ramifications of the idea. "Hell of an idea!" he exclaimed. "I've been worried about this meeting tonight. But, what will we do about Uniontown?"

"Stand them up," Katy snapped.

Andy grinned, "I'll send them a nice telegram expressing our regrets; then I'd better phone Harrison."

Andy hurried to a bank of pay phones. Harrison informed him that he already had a reporter and photographer assigned to the Uniontown meeting. "Might as well leave them there," he told Andy. Andy chuckled to himself as to what kind of story they'd come up with at Uniontown.

Shortly after the Coalition party group checked into the downtown Vista International Pittsburg Hotel, news leaked out that Katy and Andy stopped in town. A reporter from the Post-Gazette called Katy asking for an interview. She invited him to have dinner with them in the hotel's main dining room. The invitation was so casual and sincere, he accepted before he realized he might be making news instead of reporting it, a practice frowned upon by the paper.

His awe at finding himself dining with candidates for president and vice president of the United States was soon dispelled by Katy's quick wit and cordiality, and by former Governor Andy Barker's knowledge of Pennsylvannia's labor history. He listened in rapt attention as Andy talked about Ben Medina who had announced his reform candidacy for a top job in the Laborers' International Union, LIU Local 332, in Philadelphia, several years ago. Shortly afterward, five armed men wearing Halloween masks entered his home, bound and gagged his wife and beat Medina to death.

"The alarming part of the story," Andy continued, "is no one was ever prosecuted, although there was little mystery about the murder. This is just one of many such incidents."

"I want to get more on this," stated the reporter.

"There are legislative transcripts and court proceedings that disclose a scandalous record of exploitation, intimidation, and terror. Besides drawing huge salaries, union officials plunder the members' welfare funds and shake down their employers. Rank-and-filers who protest have been blacklisted, beaten, and murdered."

"But the AFL-CIO leadership is a different world. They're an honest organization," Katy interjected. "You'll see that tonight."

"I hope your article will define my stand on labor unions and organized crime," Andy continued.

"Oh, it will!" replied the reporter. "It looks like I have a whole series of articles here."

Katy and Andy stepped out into the muggy Pittsburgh evening.

"Thank goodness it's only two blocks," Katy remarked.

"No ordinary union meeting tonight," said Andy as they entered the David Lawrence Convention Center. Once inside the vast room he pointed out the President of AFL-CIO, top people from the Mellon organization, and other business people from the area.

"That accounts for all the media present," replied Katy.

As Katy and Andy took seats on the aisle near the front, talking and making themselves acquainted with the people nearby, Katy wondered whether she or Andy would be introduced, and if they would have an opportunity to say anything. Andy, seeming to read her thoughts, headed for a group gathered near the stage. Without being obvious about it, Katy watched as he greeted some of the group by name and was himself cordially addressed as "Governor." Andy conferred briefly with one of the men who seemed to be in charge and nodded appreciatively as they talked.

As Andy made his way back toward Katy, he shook hands with several people in the aisle. Katy heard one man exclaim, "You mean Katy Jenkins is here, and not over in Uniontown?" Katy stepped into the aisle as they approached. Andy introduced her. The new acquaintance leaned toward Katy and Andy and in a low, confidential tone said, "I didn't know if I should a' come down here or go over to Uniontown tonight. I don't know how you got out of that one; but it's a good thing you did. What did you do? Just cancel 'em?"

"You might say that," Andy answered.

"Well, you'd of had some friends over there, Andy, but they'd of been outnumbered. My guess is there'd been a riot if they tried any of that rough stuff. Those goons from New Jersey don't run our business in Pennsylvania. I been tellin' our people we oughta' stand up for you."

"Thank you, Mike. I appreciate it."

The Master of Ceremonies introduced the dignitaries on the stage with fanfare. He then turned toward Katy and Andy: "We're also honored to have with us this evening former Governor Andy Barker, now candidate for vice president, and the candidate for president of the United States on the new American Coalition party ticket, Katy Jenkins...please stand up!" Andy bounced out into the aisle and extended his hand to Katy as she moved up alongside him. The scattered applause and curious looks from all over the auditorium made Katy slightly uncomfortable. TV cameras whirred and photographers flashed their cameras.

Solid applause welcomed the President of AFL-CIO. His incentives for unions and industry working together in order to increase America's competitive ability appealed to Katy.

At the end of the meeting, she got the opportunity she hoped for. The contingent of reporters and television people swarmed around her. Katy spoke eloquently. "We have seen some great new history made tonight in this state so famous for making history! The world will be changed by the working partnership forged here by AFL-CIO and industry. This far-sighted, revolutionary get-together tonight augurs well for the future of America."

Katy's style changed suddenly. Her voice hardened. "This meeting is in sharp contrast to another meeting held in Uniontown tonight. The union which sponsored that meeting is in bondage to organized crime, which is unfortunate for America. Andy Barker and I, and the American Coalition party, pledge support for every proposal made here tonight—and we vow to fight, with every resource at our disposal, the exploitation, intimidation, and terror of the mob, not only as it relates to labor, but also to drug trafficking and other criminal activities."

Her style changed again. A smile lit her face. "It's been a pleasure to be here tonight, to meet people with fresh ideas for our times, and to hear the heartbeat of America pounding with vigor."

After the TV cameras were packed up and the reporters on

their way, Mike sidled up to Andy. "Miss Jenkins told them straight, Andy. That's what you gotta' do now."

* * *

Katy and Andy lounged opposite each other at the little conference table in the luxury of the GULFSTREAM as it made the short hop from Pittsburgh to New York. Katy relaxed, and noticed that Andy, too, seemed to share her satisfaction at the way the Pittsburgh detour worked out. After the AFL-CIO meeting, they met with people from the Mellon organization, who assured them of support, and they breakfasted with a group of women who wanted to meet Katy. Now, a big rally awaited them at the new Madison Square Garden.

Andy quietly observed Katy as she sat opposite him, noticing the person beyond the surface, sensing her gentle strength of character.

"I'm sorry about giving you a rough time—quitting the campaign."

Katy's reaction was quick. "You did give me a bad time. Why in the world did you do it?"

Andy considered this. A frown crossed his face. "I didn't have the convictions you have. Nor the convictions Margaret had when we set up the American Coalition party at Berkeley. I finally read her book, Women Shakers and Movers, just recently." Then, as if an afterthought, "I read some of your Congressional speeches, too, about campaign finances, and Social Security, and energy, and Missile Defense."

"I hope you found some of the better ones."

"Must have. Pretty convincing." Andy's tone became confidential. "The last two days I re-organized my whole campaign." he said slowly. "I was lucky to be able to get rid of my campaign manager; Pat Reilly is going to manage Mallory's campaign in Pennsylvania. They propositioned him last week and Tuesday I told him to take it. We parted friends. And, his going to work for Mallory has its bright side. I think this will eliminate the heckling; the word is out that Mallory doesn't want any of his people to admit Katy Jenkins or I exist."

"Andy, this isn't a total surprise to me. Ms. Arnold asked me yesterday who was going to be your new campaign manager. I just told her I didn't know yet."

This Katy's a cool one, he thought again. "Well, I didn't know what I was going to do until I woke up yesterday morning; then it all fell into place."

Katy waited.

"I got to the office ahead of Florence Knight and Beverly; I had just finished making coffee when they came in. I poured three cups of coffee, and popped the question: Flo, how would you like to be State Campaign Manager, and Beverly move up to office manager?"

"Good move," Katy said with conviction.

"They were delighted. They never liked to work with Reilly too well anyhow. Then I discussed with them how we'd run a whole new campaign, no longer running Andy Barker for Governor, as Pat did, but running Katy Jenkins for president. And, I told Flo the first thing I want to do is talk to as many women's groups as possible. You know she's big in the Daughters of the American Revolution; she helped raise the $500,000 the National DAR contributed to refurbish the Statue of Liberty.

"And, I told her we wouldn't solicit Union PACS any more; we were losing out there."

Andy caught his breath. "Well, Florence went to work like a woman possessed. She lined up all the groups where she's been wanting me to speak. Senior Citizen's meetings; I'll talk up your Social Security plans. The oil industry people; they will like your import fee. But Beverly Barker surprised me even more."

"Beverly?"

"Katy, you won't believe this, but that kid called a meeting of the Barker clan yesterday, and shook them all down for campaign contributions. She got me for $10,000 which is the biggest political contribution I ever made in my life. But she got her dad and her granddad to pull it up to $50,000, the legal 'family' limit, then she nicked her aunts and uncles, some for $1000 each, and her cousins, too, for $100 apiece."

Katy sat back. "Andy, I like everything you're doing; you tell Beverly 'National Headquarters' is sending a check to match all she raised."

"She'll love that," Andy said. "Katy, the Barkers are going

to be with you all the way now. Harrison liked you from the first time he saw you at the Brown Palace, but he really enjoyed you at the meeting Monday."

"I didn't have that much to do with it.   Margaret was the shaker and mover behind that one."

"What Harrison noticed was your standing up to John Van Dorn.   You know, they're lifelong friends, and about as close as two men get, but even so, Harrison is a little awed by John's success.   When you demanded to know if John had set you up for the nomination, Harrison was impressed."

"I didn't intend to be 'demanding,' but maybe I was."

"Anyhow, Harrison thought you were gutsy even questioning John Van Dorn."

30

For twenty-eight years Katy Jenkins had hovered like a ghost in Mrs. Van Dorn's life, ever drifting somewhere in the perimeter of her son's life. Lately, the ghost had taken on form and shape, and dreadful reality, through newspaper articles, personal appearances on television, and the real-life cover picture on TODAY. The woman had even invaded the sanctuary of the LAND & SEA headquarters. Her suspicions that John was "carrying-on" openly with her were confirmed at every turn. When John brazenly headed up the "Friends for Katy and Andy," she thought the whole affair had gone too far, only to discover that he had loaned her the company's GULFSTREAM II-B, complete with crew, for the duration of the campaign.

Now, Katy and her retinue were coming to Madison Square Garden to put on a campaign rally. Mrs. Van Dorn decided to go see the woman herself. She went early to get a good seat up front, accompanied only by her driver.

Amazing number of people here, she thought. The crowd of enthusiastic boosters and others who were curious about the woman candidate, filled practically all the seating set up for the rally.

She recognized Ms. Arnold, as the big woman greeted Party leaders and workers and arranged the seating of a dozen or so people on the stage, placing Katy Jenkins at the center. As Katy visited animatedly with those near her, Mrs. Van Dorn made her first appraisal. Startled at Katy's wholesome physical beauty and poise, she began to understand John's infatuation, and the feeling made her uncomfortable.

A wild ovation broke out as Margaret Kincaid opened the meeting. Margaret welcomed the group, thanked everyone for coming, injecting some traditional political rhetoric into her introduction of Andy Barker—"governor of the great state of Pennsylvania, and the next vice president of the United States!"

He doesn't look much like the young boy who accompanied Harrison Barker to our house, Mrs. Van Dorn thought. She watched Andy as he spoke out with great force, buoyed by the recent success at the AFL-CIO meeting. His enthusiasm for America with the leadership of the Coalition party was so intense that the audience reacted with resounding cheers.

Margaret took over after Andy's "remarks" and with deference and dignity, presented Jane Ellsworth, former U.S. delegate to the United Nations, who would introduce the candidate. Ellsworth had her own political style. The sincerity with which she spoke about electing the first woman president and her obvious affection for Katy gave Mrs. Van Dorn an uneasy feeling again. Was Jenkins a threat not only to John, but to the entire American political system as well?

Then Katy rose amid an outburst of applause. As the spotlights focused on her and she began to speak, Mrs. Van Dorn peered closely. *Is her skin and complexion really that good, or is it make-up?*

As Katy spoke out about renewing America, Mrs. Van Dorn realized that her curiosity about Katy was giving way to grudging admiration. This was quickly squelched by the thought of John marrying this upstart when he could take his choice of New York's or London's social elite. Beautiful women with beautiful backgrounds underpinned with "old money," culture, and grace. Why, John is the most eligible bachelor in the city! The loveliest women in the city fall over him at every party. That's it! A triumphant smile spread across her face. I'll throw a party! And the women at this party would dwarf the Jenkins woman with their charm and amenities; open John's eyes.

She had seen enough of this political farce. Abruptly she rose and made her way to the nearest exit.

* * *

Mrs. Van Dorn wasn't the only one who went to Madison

Square Garden to spy on Katy that evening. Deep in the audience, disguised in working man's clothes, sat David Wells. When he got the job managing Owen Mallory's campaign, he felt it was going to be smooth sailing. The economy was scary—against the incumbent; the Democrats ached for control of the White House again; and he had the candidate with the television personality.

Katy Jenkins and Andy Barker and their Coalition party, with all the damned women's groups kicking in, and the filthy rich Republican Van Dorn furnishing her a fancy GULFSTREAM jet and shaking down the big boys, threatened him.

Disregarding Jenkins hadn't worked; keeping her out of the debate hadn't worked either—actually backfired. She gained momentum every week. Looking for a hole in her armor, he watched people, and listened, and became more concerned than ever. *She's a political animal, a predator.* He made a decision. No more handling the woman with kid gloves. She chose to be in politics, she asked for it—he'd let her have it! He liked a good, dirty campaign.

* * *

The other spy at Madison Square Garden wasn't in the audience. He belonged to one of the seventeen unions which, between them, controlled the physical plant at the facility. He stood in the wings twenty feet from Katy as she spoke. Joe Domino asked him for a full report on the meeting.

"She wowed them," was his report. That said it all.

Ever since Katy and Andy stood up his boys at Uniontown three days ago, Domino seethed with anger. She had made a fool of him; and he couldn't stand that. No one could do that to Joe Domino and get away with it.

* * *

Dick Donovan read the AP news item in the Albuquerque Journal about Katy's New York rally at Madison Square Garden and felt a pang of regret at not having been there. He had considered going, but it all happened so fast he never got around to making the arrangements. Besides, he consoled himself, another aspect of Katy's campaign interests me more right now.

What is Ellen Steele up to? The question tantalized him. He followed her string of appearances in the Midwest where she managed to stir up the wrath of women's groups everywhere she went. She seemed to especially enjoy bashing the Caucus for Women Voters groups to whom she spoke.

Dick drove to Santa Fe and dropped in on Harriett Landsdale. He sat impatiently in her office as she answered one phone call after another, interspersed with interruptions by staff who were working on the current newsletter.

"Looks like you've found work," he commented to Harriett when she finally had a moment's breather.

"You can say that again. We're going crazy around here."

Quickly, before another interruption, Dick popped the question. "Has Ellen Steele gone crazy, too?"

Immediately, Dick had Harriett's attention. She considered her reply carefully. "I can't figure out what's going on with her. Our Illinois organization's up in arms about Ellen's tactics; Ms. Arnold says the phone is ringing off the wall up there."

"What does Katy think?"

"She's aware of the problem, but she's been so busy in Pennsylvania and New York that Ms. Arnold is soft-pedaling it with her for the time being." Harriett looked concerned. "Ellen will be in Colorado Springs this weekend, at the Broadmoor, for the Colorado State Convention of the Caucus for Women Voters."

"Th' hell," Dick muttered. It didn't bother him that the phone routine began again with Harriett, and that someone waited expectantly at her office door, proofs of the latest newsletter in hand. Dick had an inspiration: he would go to Colorado Springs to see Ellen Steele in action.

Sunday was the one day of the week Dick Donovan might catch Katy at Georgetown, and with time enough to talk. He had coffee, returned to his room and called Katy collect.

"I think this little call will be worth the price of the long-distance rate," he said. "I'm in old Trinidad."

"I hope we're not back into sheep."

"No, I've been up to Colorado Springs...heard Ellen Steele

address the State Convention of the Caucus for Women Voters."

"What in the world is Ellen doing?" Katy asked quickly.

"Just telling them the truth," Dick replied.

"The truth?" Katy questioned.

"Sure. She's telling them they're a bunch of losers, because they're not fighters. She says that here they are with a chance to elect a woman to the presidency, but they are sitting on their hands, analyzing candidates and fretting over petty details when they should be united in working for Katy.

"She tells them the women's vote will be so splintered that it won't do any candidate any good, or women any good either."

Dick let this sink in, then continued. "It's all the plain truth, Katy. Ellen does give them a challenge. She tells them that the women of this nation could elect their first woman president—but probably won't."

Dick let it go at that. He never forced his opinion on Katy— he knew his comments would mean a lot to her. They always had.

The next morning, Katy got Dorothy Hastings, Ruth Silverton, and Andy Barker together to discuss the matter. Ms. Arnold sat in on the meeting and so did H.B. McGee, who happened to be in Washington. At first they were indignant, but H.B. pointed out that this kind of strategy had worked before, and that it was a fact that women weren't at all solid in their support.

Dorothy Hastings' comments surprised Katy. "I don't think Ellen will harm the Caucus any. She provides some excitement, and her final goal always is to get support for Katy."

Ruth Silverton said she didn't think Ellen could be stopped anyhow. "She's having fun," Ruth commented dryly.

Katy remembered Dick's statement, She's just telling the truth. Katy asked Ms. Arnold if they could handle the 'heat' on the phone calls. "Sure we can," Ms. Arnold assured her, "and I'll talk to Harriett."

It was settled; they would let Ellen continue to "stir 'em up." Which she did.

* * *

Ms. Arnold had saved the bad news until after the New York

rally, but shortly after takeoff on a commercial airline for Washington on Sunday morning, she felt she had to broach the subject of finances.

"Katy, we're out of money."

"Out?"

"Oh, we have enough to keep the office going, and maybe enough to send Andy the $50,000 you committed there after Beverly's fund drive, but there is no way we can come up with $250,000 for Lila Stanford right now."

"Is she pushing for the money?"

"She certainly is; she says her direct mail campaign is bogging down for lack of postage; her printer is pushing her, too. She wants to bombard the mails right now while the iron is hot after the TODAY article and the big debate response."

"Is there any place we can raise some money?"

"I put the pressure on some of the women's organizations for money for the TV debate; we had to pay the half-million dollars up front. The Caucus came up with $50,000, the Political Fund group the same amount, and Ruth managed $100,000 on their second million. Carrie sent about fifty $1000 checks that came in from Houston contributors. The balance of $250,000 we paid out of our own bank account."

"You did well."

"I know, and we're going to be getting in a lot more money, but we're hurting right now. I hate to call on John, since his group is paying the expenses on the Gulfstream."

"I agree. You have any idea what it costs to fly the Gulfstream?"

"Plenty."

"About $6 a mile, including fuel which we're buying with credit cards John furnishes, crew, insurance, and amortization; and we flew over 7,000 miles in the last two weeks."

"I thought as much."

The airline hostess brought coffee and danish.

"This coffee is good," Ms. Arnold said. Then she had another thought on finance. "We could go to Harriett; she has that kind of money. Maybe a loan?"

"I'd hate to have to do that now; she's like John, already doing so much! She's handling everything at the Santa Fe office."

"Yes, and fortunately Madge is okay in Texas. She has the money from your big fundraisers in Dallas to keep Johnny and the Texans rolling. Actually the only place we're hurting is in California, and they have more electoral votes than any state in the Union."

"Let me see what I can figure out."

* * *

Sunday afternoon Katy had her Georgetown home to herself. Basking in the rare opportunity of having some time alone, she read personal mail, called Elizabeth in Santa Fe just to visit, and took a long soak in the bathtub.

The inspiration came to her in the bath. Senator Watson had mentioned to her that he would like first chance if she ever wanted to sell her Georgetown home. She called his home in a Washington suburb, and was pleasantly surprised when he answered personally. She liked the Senator.

"Katy Jenkins," he exclaimed, "how nice to hear from you. By the way, I liked the suggestions you made after the debate the other night—the two regarding the banks."

"Thank you, Bill. In a way, that's what I want to talk to you about. You have mentioned to me a time or two that you might be interested in my Georgetown home if I should ever want to sell."

"I still am, Katy. The kids are all gone, and Anna and I don't need this big place. I'd like something smaller, without the long commute. But I heard that you've converted your place into a campaign headquarters for your new party."

"That's just temporary, until after the election. I couldn't deliver it until then, but I need the money now; and I'll make you a good deal for cash in advance."

"You sure you want to do that, Katy?"

"Yes, I am."

"How much are you thinking about?"

"Bill, I need the money tomorrow for this campaign I'm in."

"Tomorrow?"

"That's right; I'll sell it to you for $250,000, and deliver it by Thanksgiving if I lose the election, or by the end of January if I win. It's worth more than that."

"Say, you're taking this election seriously. But, Katy, I'm not sure $250,000 would help you that much."

"It's for a commitment I made."

"Commitment, huh?"

"Yes, and the property is free and clear, no encumbrances. All you have to do, if you want it, is to write me a Letter of Intent to purchase the property for $250,000, and pay for it tomorrow, with delivery by Thanksgiving or the end of January, Title Policy guaranteed."

"Katy, you're not in trouble, are you? You can probably borrow that much money on it."

"Sure, I'm in trouble; I'm running for president aren't I? Nothing more, Bill, I assure you. But, I can't borrow money by noon tomorrow, and this brings us back to banks. I want to have the money in my bank before it closes tomorrow."

"Katy, you sleep on this tonight. If you are still of the same mind in the morning, I'll write the Letter of Intent to purchase, you sign it, and I'll get you a cashier's check by noon tomorrow. I'll come by there about 9:00 in the morning to get legal description, and all, and you can back out then, or we've got a deal. That is, if you'll let an old dyed-in-the-wool Democrat inside the headquarters of the American Coalition party."

"We will. Thank you, Bill, and I'll see you in the morning."

At 2:00 o'clock Monday afternoon Katy was on the phone to Lila Stanford who was at Beverly Hills Productions in Santa Monica. "We made a bank transfer from here to the Coalition party bank account in Palo Alto for the quarter-million dollars you need now," she advised.

"Katy! Thank you for calling; that's going to put us in business." Katy heard Lila call to Monica Swift, "We've got the money; it's full speed ahead now; Katy's on the line."

Monica's voice came on the line. "Oh, Katy, we're geared up to put out 100,000 mailings a week—starting tomorrow! You should see the mailing lists we have, and individualized mailings for every category. We're going to increase that $250,000 tenfold."

Lila's final comment at the end of the conversation: "We're going to elect you president in California."

* * *

"We did the right thing," Katy said to Ms. Arnold.

"You did the splendid thing." Ms. Arnold beamed. "Here's the I.O.U. from the Party to you, acknowledging the debt, and signed Phil Hansen, Chairman Finance Committee, American Coalition party."

Ms. Arnold had already thought it through: she would leak the news that Katy had sold her Georgetown home to help finance the campaign to all the leaders in the Women's Movement, all the state chairs, and to Margaret and her thirty-six founders. She was sure that this would put their finance drive into high gear, and when Federal matching funds come through we'll be repaying Katy, she thought smugly.

Doesn't matter, Katy thought, after the election I'll be starting my life over regardless of how the election comes out. Her home in Georgetown had been a landmark in her career. The parties she gave there were the envy of Washington; invitations to these parties were coveted by the elite of the city. At the mini-conferences she held there, policies and decisions were made that affected the course of events in the nation's capitol. And, it had been her refuge, her sanctuary in the turmoil of a hectic political career.

But now it was gone. Whether the Party could ever repay was a moot question. Now serving as her campaign headquarters, its sale furnishing the big boost her campaign needed, her Georgetown house was showering its last blessings.

Another milestone. Now she would get on with the campaign; six weeks to cover as many states as she could before Presidential Debate number two, in which she would be a full participant!

31

"Keep tuned to these stations during the presidential debate," urged the NTB anchor. "We will interrupt the debate every fifteen minutes or so, to bring you an update on the situation in the Middle East. Our first questions to the two challengers this evening will be on the new Libya-Israeli crisis. For those of you who just tuned in, the President will not participate in the debate this evening; but we will have a statement from him at the White House where the President, his security adviser, and aides, are monitoring the events in the Middle East minute-by-minute.

"Now, it is my pleasure to introduce Sanford Clemens, chairman of the Washington Correspondents Group, who will be our moderator for the debate this evening."

Earlier, when Katy first arrived at the studios, Dorothy Hastings of the Caucus for Women Voters had greeted Katy with a warm, reassuring hug. In her capacity as president of the Caucus, she was there to monitor the "debate." The Caucus had ceased sponsoring the debates when they became party-controlled media events instead of debates between candidates.

"Welcome to the final national debate by our presidential candidates," Sanford Clemens intoned. "Here on the stage we have Katy Jenkins, candidate for president on the American Coalition party ticket, and Owen Mallory, candidate for president on the National Democratic party ticket."

Katy smiled into the camera as it came in for a close-up at her introduction. Both candidates stood behind lecterns, squared off with each other, five or six steps apart. Clemens quickly introduced the panel of questioners and explained procedures. Candidates and listeners were advised that the debate this evening would concentrate on foreign affairs. "Very appropriate at this time," he added.

Mallory suffered through the introductions and instructions. He had asked the President to cancel the debate in view of the Middle East crisis, but the President wouldn't cooperate. "The President'll take this opportunity to grandstand," Mallory growled to his campaign manager, David Wells, "making himself the statesman while I am subjected to debating with the petticoat politician of the minor party."

"Our first question, to Owen Mallory, is from Valerie Dole of the Washington Post," advised Clemens.

"Mr. Mallory," Dole began, "approximately seven hours ago, we heard the first report that a missile loaded with deadly nerve gas penetrated Israel in the area of the Ben Gurion International Airport at Tel Aviv, killing hundreds of Israelis, tourists, and military personnel. Acting on their own intelligence, Israel retaliated with the launch of a missile with multi-nuclear warheads which wiped out the heavily-guarded 'chemical factory' at Rabta in Libya, also killing hundreds of military and civilian personnel in the area.

"My question is: as president of the United States, how would you handle the tense situation that now prevails in the entire Middle East?"

Mallory was quick to respond. "I have two general observations: first, the American people are horrified at the thought that the Libyan dictator, apparently in a fit of rage and frustration, would launch such an atrocious attack on an unsuspecting people using a weapon outlawed by all civilized societies. The scenes we are seeing from Israel of dead bodies on the streets, in shops, in crashed cars; with no visible signs of the sinister killer that snuffed out life in one breath, shock us. Now I understand the invisible cloud is moving southeast across the Sinai, a less populated direction for it to take, but still leaving death and desolation in its wake. Just before coming here, I saw a Bedouin tent community on the desert, all life wiped out—men, women, children, and animals—the most eerie sight I ever saw on television."

Mallory's body shook as if trying to shake off the memory. "I will say that the Israelis were quick to retaliate. They picked the 'chemical factory' near Rabta, sixty miles south of Tripoli, as their target and obliterated it and the military complex around it, with a multi-headed nuclear bomb—the most powerful explosion ever released on earth. And, there is one similarity to the nerve-gas bomb; a cloud of deadly radio-activity moves across Libya, even as we speak; but this one leaves slow, lingering, painful death in its wake; I can't think of a more terrible fate for the people in its path."

Suddenly Mallory realized his time was running out. He made a quick answer to the question. "I think the President is handling the situation as well as he can. If I were president, I would act to eliminate chemical warfare from the face of the earth and to further reduce the possibility of nuclear warfare by negotiating with the Soviets to ultimately reduce nuclear weapons to zero on both sides."

"Thank you, Mr. Mallory," Sanford Clemens responded. "Now we will hear from Katy Jenkins on the same question. Miss Jenkins, if you were president of the United States, how would you handle the situation in the Middle East?"

"I agree with Mr. Mallory. The President is coping with these tragic events the best he can. Without pointing any fingers, he asked for a complete cessation of hostilities. The President volunteered help from us to alleviate suffering in both countries and anywhere else the deadly clouds of gas and radiation may hit. That's the finest role we can play. Let's seek no more death and destruction. Let's strive for peace. That would be my objective if I were president today."

Katy cocked her head to one side, a hard expression on her face, as she continued. "This use of nerve gas and nuclear warheads delivered by missiles is fair warning to us, and to the world, that war is not extinct and that chemical and nuclear bombs are the weapons of the present. These weapons bypass armies, ships, and tanks as if there were not there. Artillery and footsoldiers won't protect any country from nuclear attack; a tiny fraction of the world's arsenal of long-range missiles, ICBM's, could devastate America at anytime."

A questioning tone came into her voice. "Why do we leave ourselves exposed to disaster? Can we really believe no country in the world will ever attack us?

"Our next 'Pearl Harbor' may well be a nuclear attack on our mainland, and could be delivered by missiles from anywhere in the world. *Will we be ready this time?"*

At a prompting from the timekeeper, Katy changed pace. Now, she would ask Owen Mallory a question. "I'd like to ask my opponent this evening if he really believes we can just negotiate away poison gas and nuclear bombs?"

Mallory's confidence came through in his style and the words he chose. "The human race must rid itself of these scourges if the world is to survive. We have no choice except that of negotiation. When I am president of the United States these negotiations will have the highest priority and will be an ongoing process until at last the world is relieved of this threat to its very existence. Do I make myself clear?"

"Is this your question to me?" Katy asked.

Mallory was quick to respond. "My question to you, Miss Jenkins: 'Just what is your alternative to negotiation?'"

"All right," Katy said. "You make yourself quite clear; you will negotiate away the new weapons of warfare. That would be nice, but it sounds like wishful thinking to me. Some twenty-three or twenty-four countries have nuclear armaments now, or will have them before this decade is over. They are proliferating, not disappearing. We don't know for sure how many nations have nerve gas or other kinds of chemical or bacterial weapons; we do know, however, that poison gas was used in the war between Iraq and Iran, and even after the war to quell the Kurds in Iraq; five thousand Kurds' last breath on earth was poison gas. The worldwide outrage didn't stop it! It was used again this morning on Israel—and Israel retaliated with atomic weapons. Israel used only one percent of their nuclear capability this morning. Does anyone really think we will negotiate them out of their weapons, surrounded as they are by potential enemies? Nor will we negotiate Russia or China out of their stockpiles of atomic weapons. Our only hope is to build a defense against intercontinental, bomb-laden missiles. By the grace of God, we can do it, if we give it the priority it should have."

"Thank you, Katy Jenkins and Owen Mallory." An urgency rang in Sanford Clemen's voice. "Now we will interrupt this debate and return to NTB in Washington for a direct report from the President of the United States on the Middle East crisis."

"My report to you tonight is one of guarded optimism," the President began. "Our decisions to issue no statements of protest or condemnation to Libya or Israel for their displays of force are working well in the face of the possible disaster in the Middle East." The President spent some time reviewing the incidents of the day and his participation in working toward an early end to hostilities. Mallory watched impassively as the President exploited his advantage.

The President wound up his report on an optimistic note. "Even as I speak to you tonight, negotiations are under way with both powers. We will do everything within our means to keep this outbreak of violence from going any farther. May God bless our efforts."

As the debate resumed, Sanford Clemens made no further mention of the Middle East. He was running a nationally televised debate between two presidential candidates. "Now, we're going to talk about foreign trade and our trade deficit" he announced dramatically. "And the first question goes to Miss Jenkins who will have three minutes to answer. Then Mr. Mallory will have three minutes to respond. Are you ready?"

Katy nodded affirmatively.

"Jack Everitt of the Baltimore Sun has a question for Jenkins."

"Miss Jenkins, you profess to advocate free world trade as the best method of promoting world prosperity—and yet you have come out for an import fee on oil and stern measures with Japan on reciprocal trade. How do you justify this apparent inconsistency?"

Katy smiled, then spoke firmly into the microphone. "The antithesis of free world trade is an organized, price-fixing monopoly such as OPEC. This association of mostly Arab oil countries has at times succeeded in forcing its monopolistic oil prices on the world. They worked a real hardship on the world in the late 1970's when they cut oil production and created shortages which enabled them to "fix" world oil prices. And developing nations and countries without any oil production of their own were hurt even worse than we were in the financial upheaval that followed.

"We overcame the severe oil shortage with new oil production, conservation, and development of alternative energy sources.

"OPEC's response was to increase their oil production enough to push prices down so we could no longer compete.

"Now the OPEC countries are edging up oil prices as our percentage of imported oil goes up again. This leaves us vulnerable to another crisis, which OPEC won't hesitate to inflict when they can."

Katy caught the timer's signal. Time for one final statement: "So, do you think I should be allowed an 'inconsistency' here on 'free trade?' I would put a five-dollar-a-barrel tax on all imported oil, giving our oil industry a pad against unstable OPEC and Persian Gulf oil price fluctuations, thus stabilizing the price of crude oil enough to enable us to go for new exploration and production, and also encourage development of alternative energy sources. Another bonus of bringing our energy industry home is the thousands of jobs it would create in America."

Katy hurried to answer the last half of the question. She remembered the frustration she felt when she tried to sell New Mexico beef in Japan. "We've got to get Japan's attention," she asserted, then added, "We're going to have to use as much ingenuity to crash their markets as they use to keep us out. We do have some leverage; let's use it..."

The timer called time. Sanford Clemens took over, bringing Owen Mallory back into the debate with a flourish. "Mr. Mallory, would you respond to Jack Everitt's question regarding Miss Jenkins' proposal to put an import fee on oil and impose stern measures against Japan on reciprocal trade?"

Mallory came on with a condescending tone. "Miss Jenkins would tax oil imports. She fails to mention that gasoline would go up as much as ten cents a gallon at the pumps. The workers of America would carry the burden of this tax. But, obviously Miss Jenkins is more interested in building big profits for her oil-producing friends in Texas and California, and in her running-mate's state, Pennsylvania. Remember? It was reported in the press that the oil interests in Dallas, Texas, organized one fund-raising dinner that put a hundred-thousand dollars in the Jenkins campaign coffers.

"The Republicans have already sold out our off-shore oil

reserves to the big oil companies. What more do the oil companies want? Other, of course, than their 'right' to continue polluting the oceans, rivers, and sandy beaches with their devastating oil spills?"

He's a master orator, thought Katy, *makes people wonder, whether he gives specifics or not.*

Mallory changed the subject. "I don't know how Jenkins is going to get Japan's attention—she doesn't say—but I do know what the present administration in Washington is doing." Mallory paused for emphasis, then in his best oratorical style proclaimed, "They are letting Japan buy up America." Another pause. "Fifty billion dollars a year trade deficit! American automobile workers out of work by the thousands while a whole generation of Americans drive Japanese imports. And our president wrings his hands, and nods knowingly, as the Japanese buy up our prime real estate, and corporate America *with our own money.*"

The timer gave the warning signal. Mallory rushed to complete his plea. "It's time for America to put Americans first, cut back our wasteful, bloated military machine, and with the money saved, correct some of the social injustices in America. It's time to elect a Democrat president."

An alert cameraman caught the incredulous, exasperated expression on Katy's face when Mallory suggested "spending" savings from military cuts with no thought of cutting the deficit, and relayed it to the television audience. Mallory caught it, too.

At that moment the NTB anchor cut in. "We have an update on the Middle East crisis. We go now to NTB's correspondent in Jerusalem for this report."

A fuzzy picture came on the screen, but soon focused.

"I am at the Knesset in Jerusalem. This is the counterpart of our Congress in the United States. The Knesset has been in continuous session for the last ten hours. It is our understanding the military command of Israel has been given full authority to respond to any further attacks from Libya with an all-out nuclear strike. First target would be Tripoli, the nation's capital and military headquarters.

"Tripoli is a city paralyzed by fear. The explosion that made rubble of Rabta and its infamous chemical plant felt like an earthquake in Tripoli as early morning skies flashed brighter than the sun, followed by the deafening roar of winds blowing out windows and uprooting trees. It is reported that the government headquarters is besieged by thousands of people crying out for an end to the nightmare. Others are streaming out into the desert in an attempt to escape almost certain annihilation.

"Israeli planes, equipped with radar and heat-seeking missiles, are patrolling the skyways over the Mediterranean between Israel and Libya. Land-based radar is probing the skies from Israel's shoreline. Military authorities advise it is unlikely that another missile will get through to Israel. Meanwhile, hands are on the triggers of Israel's nuclear arsenal ready to respond to any threat.

"There is no official word from Libya, but unconfirmed reports are that the government is pleading for help from the United States to stop the crisis."

The NTB anchor replaced the correspondent on the screen. "Keep tuned to these stations for the latest reports from the Middle East. Now we return to the presidential debate."

Sanford Clemens came back on. "We left Owen Mallory answering Jack Everitt's query about oil import fees and trade sanctions against Japan."

Mallory had enjoyed Jenkins' discomfort when he said that he would take the money from the military savings and spend it on social programs. He still had the floor. "We cannot be oblivious to the poor and underprivileged in this country regardless of where we get the money. How can we justify paying out billions for Savings and Loan defaults and then look the other way when our needy cry out for help?"

Sanford Clemens broke in. "Time is up for Mr. Mallory."

The NTB anchor broke in at that point. "We have been advised that the President will have a special report on the Middle East situation in about ten minutes. Mr. Clemens, can you and the candidates conform to this schedule?"

Clemens conferred quickly with the candidates. They agreed that each would respond to one more question and follow up with a short summary.

"Our next question for discussion by both candidates will come from Dale Seymour of the Tampa Tribune. The question will go to Owen Mallory."

"The world is obviously unsafe for the human race with the new weapons we have today. My question is: how are we going to contain these new weapons, especially in the Middle East which seems to be the powder keg of the world right now?"

Mallory paused for a moment to collect his thoughts. "Israel will always be a bone of contention in the Middle East," he stated, "but Iraq brought on the biggest wars in the region. Their invasion of Iran resulted in eight years of full-scale war; this was followed shortly by their invasion of Kuwait, and we all know our involvement there. In Lebanon it's Arabs against Christians, Arabs against Arabs, and Christians against Christians. When we put a peace force in Beirut, neighboring Syrians sent in a bomb-laden truck, blowing up our headquarters and killing three hundred U.S. Marines.

"To compound the problems there, the Arab countries surrounding Israel are giant oil producers, which provides an abundance of cash to purchase modern weaponry."

Mallory readied for his main pitch. "What we must do is negotiate with the handful of nations who have the know-how to manufacture atomic, chemical, and biological weapons, to eliminate the sale of information and equipment to any country which doesn't have the capacity. Stop proliferation at its source."

Clemens interjected quickly to Mallory, "Can you give us a quick summary of your stand, now?"

"Yes, I can." Mallory seemed glad the debate was about over. "Miss Jenkins here," he purred, "thinks all wars of the future are going to be nuclear holocausts. We didn't use nuclear weapons in Vietnam, or Panama, or the Persian Gulf. Would she quell disturbances all over the world with nuclear bombs? This would be a sure path to the world's destruction. Is this the role she would have America play in the world?" He peered into the nearest camera. "It wouldn't be mine.

"We must negotiate down the number of nuclear bombs threatening the world, maintain a prudent defense, and make agreements with all nations who have nuclear capacity to stop proliferation. The present administration seems to have no goal or plan to eliminate this threat to mankind. The answer is to elect a Democrat in November."

"Katy Jenkins of the Coalition party will answer the same question and give her summation," announced Clemens.

Katy began in a conversational tone. "The world, including the Middle East, looks to the United States for leadership. Our military strength gives us this role whether we invite it or not. But our leadership requires more than talk. It's unlikely that we can talk the world into peace.

"The new weapons of warfare have one common denominator; whether launched by land, sea, or by air, their payloads are propelled to their targets by rockets. But rockets are vulnerable.

"Russia and the United States have both demonstrated that rockets in the atmosphere, or in space, can be brought down. And this simple fact may provide mankind deliverance from the terrifying threat of nuclear or chemical weapons delivered by missiles.

"Inter-continental ballistic missiles, in the boost phase, are gigantic targets. Their fiery plume can be spotted thousands of miles away. A small unarmed projectile colliding with a missile going faster than the speed of sound will disable it; or a laser beam reflected half-way around the world will do the same.

"I recently saw a new CRAY computer at the Air Force Weapons Laboratory in Albuquerque that does almost two billion operations per second. It can count to one million, sequentially, in one two-hundredth of a second. The new 'massively parallel' supercomputers currently being designed will be much faster even than that. This is the brainpower of a missile defense system. We have the other components, too, or the know-how to make them; *we already have the technology.*

"I participated in some fifty briefings on the Strategic Defense Initiative while on the Armed Services Committee of the House of Representatives. I saw what can be done. I say to you that we do not have to throw up our hands in despair and say we cannot build a defense against missiles with nuclear warheads."

Clemens signalled to Katy to summarize.

Katy spoke deliberately. "We created the nuclear bomb in the first place. We developed it and used it. As horrible as those first two bombs were, each one wiping out a city, they were like firecrackers compared to the bombs we and other powers now have...a present-day hydrogen bomb blast is over 1400 times greater than the Hiroshima atomic blast.

"The only hope the world has to be freed from impending nuclear disaster is America. We're the only country on earth with the resources to rid the world from this threat of extinction. We can do it. This will be the new thrust of our military preparedness during my presidency." Clemens signalled Katy to cut it short. "I'll appreciate your vote," she said easily.

"I'm sorry, we must end the debate at this time." The NTB anchor made the announcement. "Thank you very much for your participation, Katy Jenkins and Owen Mallory. We have had an enlightening evening. Now, we switch to NTB in Washington, D.C. where we will hear from the President of the United States."

Katy watched the President's image appear on one of the TV monitors. "The situation in Libya became so perilous today that Libya asked the United States to intervene with Israel, agreeing to make significant concessions in exchange for our help at the negotiating table. Our best information is that a hundred and forty poison gas bombs have been manufactured at the Rabta chemical plant. Israel insisted on an accounting for every one. Libya claims that most of them were blown up in the nuclear attack on Rabta and the nearby military installations, but Intelligence reports suggest that some were sold to other nations, including Syria which has launchers capable of delivering missiles to pinpointed targets in Israel. Our peace negotiations with Israel nearly stalled on this issue, but Israel accepted our proposal for a Middle East Summit to re-evaluate the non-proliferation treaty. In this summit, we will work with all nations to outlaw chemical weapons and demand vigorous inspections to ensure that there will never again be another incident like the catastrophe that happened today in the Middle East. Both sides have agreed to this.

"Chemical weapons are referred to as the poor nations's atomic weapon, because they are cheaper and easier to produce. Libya is only one of possibly two dozen nations considered capable of producing poison gas bombs. The events of today alert us and the world to this frightening situation, and I assure the American people tonight we will take a leadership role to eliminate this threat."

The President concluded by grandly announcing that through

his team of American negotiators, Libya had agreed to cease all hostilities and to dispose of any poison gas left in their inventory. Israel agreed with the negotiators from the United States to cease any further hostilities. The President proclaimed that the war was over—and the world relaxed.

Owen Mallory and David Wells listened to the President's victorious announcement on the TV monitor, then exited immediately, licking their wounds. So angered were they with the President that they largely ignored the impact that Katy Jenkins made. More Americans were aware of her candidacy tonight than ever before.

* * *

Gene Boggs watched the debate from the wings, from where Ms. Arnold also watched. He and Ms. Arnold fell into casual conversation after the President's announcement. "I like Jenkins," Boggs came right out, "...liked what she said tonight."

Ms. Arnold didn't show the reaction she felt at Boggs' statement. She knew his background was military. She knew he was in the hierarchy at the Pentagon until he took leave to direct the President's campaign. She had also heard he was out of favor with a large faction at the Pentagon because of his longterm opposition to the ABM treaty with Russia, not permitting anti-ballistic missiles.

So Ms. Arnold could see why Gene Boggs liked what Katy said. What puzzled her was why Boggs took on the political job of campaign manager for the President. It dawned on her, even as she responded to Boggs, that he must be bucking for the Secretary of Defense job after the President's re-election.

"You and Katy should be friends," she said.

Boggs thought about this briefly before responding. "Miss Jenkins and I do have a mutual friend in Albuquerque," he said.

Katy came bounding off the stage just in time to hear Boggs' statement. Without any formalities she asked, "Who could that be?"

"James Jackson out at Sandia Labs."

"He's a brilliant man," rejoined Katy.

"He says the same about you." Boggs watched Katy for her

reaction to this.

In turn she studied him. She saw a man of medium height, square build, with a determined jaw. He fits the military image well, she thought. A man you would like to have on your side if the chips were down. Casually she changed the subject. "Did you engineer the events here tonight? Because if you did, it was ingenious. No question but that the President won the debate tonight. You got their goat."

Boggs laughed. He relished the way she put it. "They had it coming!" Then he became serious. "But I'm not so sure but that you were the big winner tonight. Anyhow, good luck to you!"

"The same to you," Katy said, and as she said it, she had a feeling that both of them meant it.

32

"You'll make mincemeat out of that bible thumper," Ms. Arnold assured Katy.

Back at Georgetown headquarters, Katy was exhausted after weeks of wild rallies—sometimes as many as six or seven events in a single day, often covering an entire state, and on some days appearing in two or three states. Her theme of "Renewing America" had caught on with the American people. Finally, she had covered all fifty states. Yesterday the crew took the GULFSTREAM to New York for servicing, and got some needed time off for themselves. Katy was catching her breath, taking stock, and making plans with Ms. Arnold for the remaining days of the campaign.

The showdown with Reverend Atwood on TOWN HALL was coming up fast—next Tuesday—one week away. Katy sat at her Georgetown desk in deep thought. What revelations and accusations will Atwood make? He'll try to discredit me any way he can. What happened to the golden rule in his brand of Christianity? I'd trust any politician in the land more. I'll have to prepare for every sort of attack.

"I hope you're right," she finally responded aloud. If we win with Atwood, we're home free. After TOWN HALL, do you realize it's only twenty-one days until election day?"

"Yes, and we've got to make that three weeks count. You must take some more time with Andy in Pennsylvania; things are looking up there. But California is even more important. You and Andy have to blitz California together. We're going to surprise the hell out of 'em there. And you've got to barnstorm Texas. We have more goodwill there than any state in the Union."

"Let's get it all set up this week—just like you've outlined it."

"We're working on it. It's shaping up. Monday night before election you'll make your last campaign speech at the big barbecue in Texas; Sam Pickens and Madge Bloomfield are going all-out on it." Ms. Arnold chortled, "And the 'Victory Celebration' is at La Posada ballroom election night; Maria and H.B. are working on it. Let's get some coffee."

The phone jarred Katy's attention away from coffee. Ms. Arnold answered it.

"It's Elizabeth, for you."

"Elizabeth?" Katy's thoughts spun through her own questions. Why a mid-morning call when their custom was to chat the day's tensions away late at night?

Silence marred by soft sobbing was all she could hear. Katy's mind raced through the possibilities. Uncle Clifford? Pop? Mom? Her heart leapt in her chest and the pit of her stomach suddenly felt hot with the acid of fear.

"Elizabeth? What is it, honey? Please calm yourself and tell me what's wrong."

"Katy..." Elizabeth tried but her voice failed her.

"Take a deep breath, Lizzy, and try again." Katy hadn't used that nickname in years. She heard her cousin attempt composure. "That's it. Now, tell me slowly."

"Johnny was in an accident this morning on Caprock Road. A trailer broke loose from a car in front of him. He couldn't dodge it." She choked again, then sobbed, "Johnny didn't make it, Katy. He died instantly."

Katy sagged in her chair, barely able to hold the phone. "Oh, my God, Elizabeth." She gasped for air, her body shaking in spasms, and then sinking into an inert mass. Her mind groped for reality, unable to cope with the enormity of it. *My God! Johnny, with his whole wonderful life ahead of him. He couldn't be gone—just like that.* "NO, NO, NO," she wailed. "Let it be me! No, not Johnny!"

She couldn't tolerate the pain. Her mind shut down.

Ms. Arnold moved quickly across the room and, in a rare gesture, put her arm around Katy to comfort her.

"What is it, Katy?"

"Johnny's dead." Katy wept.

Ms. Arnold took the phone, got the details, then returned the phone to Katy. By then, Elizabeth was more articulate.

"What was Johnny doing in Caprock?" Katy asked, unable to control the sobs of grief.

"The Texans were scheduled in the Dallas area this week and didn't need the Cessna; so Johnny flew up to Caprock early this morning to meet Gloria. They were planning a three-day 'break.' He had the Jaguar parked at the hangar. It happened right after he turned off Airport Road, by the Johnston place. Dad and Mother are leaving in a few minutes to drive to Caprock. Your folks are devastated, but Dad will help them with everything." Elizabeth paused to regain her composure. "Katy, I want to be with you. Could you fly to Albuquerque—and you and I drive on down to Caprock?"

"Yes. Yes, I'll be there as soon as I can. Oh God, Elizabeth. Are you at home?"

"Yes, I'll be here. Dad is servicing the car; they're leaving shortly. You don't have to do anything but get to Albuquerque. I wish I was there with you. I'll be waiting for you."

Ms. Arnold already had Barbara phoning for reservations. They consulted briefly and she announced, "We can get you out of here in an hour -- from Washington National. I'll help you pack."

"Can I go alone?" The plaintive question was to Ms. Arnold. She thought for a moment. Katy had been accompanied everywhere by at least two security people.

"I don't see why not," she said. "This is an unscheduled trip. No one knows about it. We won't announce anything here until tomorrow morning. I'll take you to the airport, and see you safely on your way." Then she added, "Don't worry about a thing here; we will have everything under control."

* * *

"Katy, I have something I want you to see. It's in the trunk." Elizabeth pulled the car over to the side of the road. They were driving the lonely stretch of two-lane highway between Vaughn and Santa Rosa, halfway to Caprock City. Not another car in sight.

Elizabeth opened the trunk and took out the large portrait of Johnny.

Katy caught her breath.

"I painted on it for weeks. Johnny posed so patiently and so many times! It was to be your Christmas present."

"It's beautiful! Just beautiful." That's all Katy could say. Tears clouded her eyes. Her throat threatened to close completely.

Elizabeth started to put the painting back into the trunk of the car, but Katy held onto it. She clutched it as Elizabeth helped her into the car.

"I have to tell you something." Elizabeth returned the wave of a passing motorist, then spoke deliberately, "When I told Johnny I was painting it for you, he suprised the heck out of me." He said, "My mother will like that."

Katy gasped. "He said that?"

"Katy, he knew you were his mother ever since he graduated from high school. When he came up to Albuquerque to go to UNM, Dad told him." She paused, "You know how Johnny reacted? He told Dad he guessed he was luckier than anybody he knew to have a mom and pop like he had, and a sister and mother like Katy."

"My God, Elizabeth! Why didn't you tell me?"

"Well, Johnny wanted it that way."

They drove awhile before Katy asked, "Did he know who his father was?"

"Yes, Dad told him that, too. And how John Van Dorn had backed every one of your campaigns."

"There's one more question, Elizabeth."

"I know, as you would say. Yes, he did see his father. But John never knew it. Dad arranged the whole thing. When John was testifying before the Maritime Commission two years ago, Dad got Johnny a balcony seat. The boy was thrilled. He told Dad that John knew more than anyone there including the Commissioners.

"Katy, I have one more thing to tell you. Johnny told me about it when I was painting the portrait."

Katy waited quietly. "He knew when John's wife died, too. Dad said he became more inquisitive than ever after that. They must have talked a lot. Anyhow, he was going to ask you to invite

John to his graduation. He was just waiting until the campaign was over to talk to you."

* * *

"Where is Katy?" John was in his office at LAND & SEA when Ms. Arnold called him about Johnny's death. It took him a minute to absorb the news. Then his first concern was Katy.

"I just put her on TWA to Albuquerue. Elizabeth will pick her up, and they'll drive to Caprock." Then she added, "Katy got away without security. Bert and Jean are frantic."

"Tell them I can pick them up in the morning."

"You're going to Caprock?"

"I have to go. As soon as I get a flight crew together, I'll call you back to make arrangements."

"Bless you."

"I appreciate your calling."

John hung up. His son. Dead. *And he had never seen him.* Didn't even know he existed until Katy told him. Now the boy was gone. And I'll never have a chance to do any of the things I've been thinking about. As far as the world knows, I have everything. What they don't know is the price paid.

* * *

John piloted the jet himself with Gates as co-pilot and navigator. Bill Burke, away visiting family in upper New York, couldn't get back in time to make the flight. After John picked up his passengers at National Airport, he took the plane up to the requested 45,000 feet and headed southwest on a straight course to eastern New Mexico. Andy, Ms. Arnold, and Bert and Jean sat quietly in the cabin. Flying high above the clouds and other traffic, John felt detached from the world below; he relaxed at the plane's controls. Now he had time to think.

He was sure of it...from the day he went with Katy in the little Volkswagen to Santa Fe, he loved her.

Katy is the only phase of my life that wasn't preordained. His thoughts drifted back to his childhood.

He was destined to run LAND & SEA from birth. The first twenty-four years of his life were spent in preparation for this. The shadow of LAND & SEA accompanied him as he grew up in the family mansion on Long Island and followed him to the schools he attended.

The shadow of LAND & SEA hovered over him on his world travels with his grandfather. From his eleventh birthday, at every school break, they were off to somewhere, via train or plane, luxury cruise liner or freighter, to the four corners of the earth. They traveled Europe, the mid-east, the far-east, South Africa, the Suez Canal, the Panama Canal. They visited every port that hosted LAND & SEA vessels. More important, John picked up a philosophy of life that stood him well during the years.

"Never play poker to win," his grandfather said. "Play to *not lose*. Then when the breaks come your way, the winning is easy." John sat in on many a poker game with his grandad. In London, or with the deck hands aboard an oil tanker, the system worked. "Always limit your losses to no more than twenty percent of your stake," he instructed.

Grandad loved competition, any kind, in cards, in sports, and especially in business. But he had no use for speculators. He taught John the difference between investment and speculation. "You invest in business," he said, "take the calculated risks, but you don't gamble or cheat. There are no free lunches."

His grandfather's philosophy about government was simple, "There's nothing worth trading your freedom for."

Finally, the shadow of LAND & SEA accompanied John to Harvard. The spring following his grandfather's death, when he was twenty-four, he felt his time running out. One more year at Harvard Business School and he would be starting his apprenticeship at LAND & SEA and marrying Stephanie whose family owned the second largest block of company stock.

Going to Albuquerque that summer and meeting Katy may have been preordained too, he thought. No, it wasn't. This was just an accident that changed his life.

His decision to spend that summer in Albuquerque was unlikely to begin with. He had met Frank Hibben in India two years before. Famous anthropologist at the University of New

Mexico, Hibben fascinated John with true-life stories of his hunts for man-eating tigers.

Knowing that it might be the last free summer he would ever have, John decided to go to UNM and take a course with Hibben, play tennis, and get away from LAND & SEA. Then he heard about Mary Scott Radcliffe's political science seminar and signed up. He was attracted to Katy the first time he saw her there. Things happened so fast after that he could hardly keep up: the first time he felt the warmth of her lips as she eagerly responded to his kiss at Sandia Crest; Santa Fe, the Clifford Kings and Elizabeth; the little house by the campus where Katy introduced him to "coffee royals", and where the sparks of their affection ignited spontaneously into full-blown love and passion as she gave herself to him on the pillow-strewn studio couch that evening without question or reservation.

They repeated the lovemaking experience so many times that summer; in his room at the hotel, in the little house, under the stars on the sand dunes west of Albuquerque, up two miles high on the trail at Sandia Crest where they first kissed.

One weekend at Caprock City, they went horseback riding all the way to the caprock and, tucked under an overhang of limestone, they made love on a saddle blanket while the horses grazed a few yards above.

The 4th of July weekend, they drove the Jaguar to Denver and checked in at the Brown Palace Hotel. Here they spent precious days loafing and loving, aware only of each other, treasuring every moment.

Then came the day when he was summoned out of Hibben's anthropology lab for an emergency phone call. His mother was distraught. "It's Father," she said. "Coronary at the office this morning." Then she said, "John, hurry. I think he's holding on just to see you."

Katy had the Jaguar, so Hibben drove him to the hotel. He asked the hotel clerk to phone the airport—there was barely time to make the last flight east. At the hotel desk, he pulled the title to the Jaguar from his wallet, signed it, and left it with a note to Katy that said, "Emergency at home...will be in touch." At the airport, they had already closed the door to the 707, but opened it when they saw him dashing across the runway.

His mother and Stephanie were at his dad's bedside in the Intensive Care unit when he arrived at the hospital. With terrific effort, his dad said, "By God, Son, you made it. Now, listen to me...take over my office before anyone else gets there. Don't let Bud Watson get near the place. Marry Stephanie and consolidate that stock. Don't let Bud get control. He couldn't keep a rowboat afloat." His strength ebbed. "Sorry about this." He fell into a coma and died two hours later despite the maze of life-supports surrounding him.

The significance of his dad's last words were lost to John in his grief. An hour after his father's death, he was calling Katy at the little house in Albuquerque, needing to hear her voice, but getting no answer. He tried again in thirty minutes. Still no answer. He phoned Elizabeth in Santa Fe and was told that Elizabeth and Katy were both in Albuquerque. He called the little house every hour. The next morning, he called "Mom" Jenkins in Caprock City; as far as she knew, Katy was in Albuquerque. He called the University Inn; they hadn't seen her again.

"Maybe she's just not answering," he thought. He told his mother that he had to fly to Albuquerque. His mother was appalled. "I don't know what could be so important in Albuquerque," she said. "You have to be here."

It was then he realized his destiny had caught him. Within hours he was in the throes of battle for control of LAND & SEA, and Katy was out of his life.

A bold decision early in his career complied with his father's wishes; he got Bud Watson out of the corporate empire at LAND & SEA by trading the Tower Office Building for Bud's stock. The idea of parting with the fifty-two story building, the crown jewel of LAND & SEA, shocked his mother. But she soon recognized the wisdom of it. The deal pushed through the Board of Directors and John was in control.

LAND & SEA prospered beyond all expectations. LAND & SEA tankers hauled Saudia Arabian oil to the world. Real estate holdings and Corporate stock ownerships skyrocketed in value and income soared. The multi-million dollar company became a multi-billion dollar company, just as his grandfather had predicted.

For several years after that summer in Albuquerque, vivid memories of Katy haunted him always and left a dull ache inside him. Gradually, the memories receded and became almost unreal. Then Clifford King called. The big news was that Katy was doing well with her own law practice in Albuquerque, very successful, lost her husband in Vietnam...and she was running for the New Mexico State Legislature.

"Could I put something in the kitty for Katy's campaign—anonymously?" he asked tentatively, surprised by his eagerness to somehow have her in his life again.

"Well, why not!" Cliff exclaimed.

That was the beginning of the series of contributions for Katy's campaigns, the amounts limited only by Cliff's assessment of need.

When Clifford phoned him from Santa Fe with the startling news that Katy had been asked to run for president of the United States on the new Coalition party ticket, he reacted quickly, "If she runs, we will back her every way we can."

"That's all I needed to know," said Clifford.

Clifford called a couple days later advising that Katy was going to the convention in Denver. With that, John made a call to Ms. Arnold, his information specialist in Washington. "Could you drop in on the Coalition party Convention in Denver?" he asked her. "We're interested in Katy Jenkins; she's a possibility for their nomination for president."

"I sure can," Ms. Arnold said. This was the kind of assignment she loved. There were no instructions; she would know what to do.

"Katy is it," Ms. Arnold enthused on her first report. What took him by surprise was that Andy Barker, of the Pennsylvania Barkers, was nominated for V.P. *It's a small world*, he thought. When Ms. Arnold advised him that she was joining Katy's campaign, he volunteered to increase her retainer. But Ms. Arnold refused, saying, "This is something I want to do on my own."

* * *

Apprehension assailed John as the GULFSTREAM cruised five hundred miles per hour toward New Mexico. What if my presence makes things worse for Katy?

Gates took control of the plane. As the great, sweeping plains of eastern New Mexico came into view, John knew they would soon be landing at Caprock City.

I have to be honest with myself now. Katy isn't in Caprock City with her kid brother. She's with her son—*our son.* A lump came into his throat. Gates said something to him, but he couldn't respond. The pain he felt was for Katy and, yes, for himself too, and for the son he would never get to know.

33

Everyone in Caprock County, it seemed, converged at the yellow brick Baptist Church, with its high-pitched roof and white steeple, on Main Street in Caprock City. Latecomers stood in the foyer. Inside the church, pews creaked under the weight of all who crowded in to pay their last respects to Johnny Jenkins. Every spare space along the aisles and into the vestibule held silent townfolk. Small children, in their mother's tow, subdued by the somber atmosphere, watched as the mourners sat quietly.

Music from the stringed instruments of The Texans, who were barely discernable behind the sheer curtains, included Johnny's favorite "old tyme" hymns, "I Come to the Garden Alone," "Little Brown Church in the Valley by the Wildwood," and crested with "Amazing Grace."

The group from Washington, D.C. and New York sat in the second row, behind the family.

A pyramid of flowers surrounded the closed casket. A spray of red roses lay atop the mahogany. In front, on the easel on which it originally was painted, stood Elizabeth's portrait of Johnny.

Only a handful of the congregation knew the full extent of Katy's loss. They knew the Jenkins boy as the tow-headed boy who had grown up with their kids, who had lived astride a horse as a kid. He even rode his horse to Sunday School at this church; Pop had put an end to that when the horse made a barnyard of the church yard.

They knew him as the bright kid on the 4-H stock judging team, the captain of the High School basketball team. They knew him as Katy's kid brother and her partner in the herd of Herefords which the whole community held proud.

Everybody knew almost everyone else at the church that day (except the reporters and TV cameramen outside). And they wondered about John Van Dorn and why they felt they should know him. He seemed so familiar.

Seven of Johnny's peers spoke about Johnny as tears rolled from their eyes and lumps rose in their throats. They recalled memories of a young man they proudly called "friend." Tex Richards spoke, too. "I didn't have the privilege of knowing Johnny as long as most of you here. But, the past few months working with Johnny on the campaign trail gave me and the band the opportunity to get real close to him. We worked long, hard hours together. We kept impossible schedules. Johnny worked his head off for something he believed in. Yet he had the ability to not let life get too serious, the ability to seize the laughter and beauty in every day. Johnny reminds all of us that, everyday, we need to stop and watch the sunset, or tell someone we love them, or give thanks for our moment of life; because now is our only time. We will miss him." Tex's voice cracked as he finished.

The minister gave the final prayer, concluding the service.

Ushers started the procession with the people from the back of the church, those in the foyer first. They came down the middle aisle, and poured out their love to the family with hugs and quietly spoken condolences. Row by row, they came. Last came the row in back of the family. Katy was aware of John's presence in the line. He talked briefly to Mom and Pop, then took Katy's hand in his. "I'm sorry, Katy." She felt a tiny tug in her heart that was distinct and different from the grief that enveloped her.

"It's okay, John." He moved down the line.

* * *

Outside the church Katy talked briefly with Ms. Arnold and Andy Barker. She would be at the home place Friday, go to Albuquerque Saturday, and be back in Georgetown Sunday or Monday.

"I will have to be in New York Tuesday evening to face Atwood on TOWN HALL. That is the main event next week."

Andy Barker spoke up. "Katy, do you want me to take over for you with Atwood?"

Katy's brow wrinkled. Could he? The decision came quickly. "We can't do it, Andy, thanks. That interview has been too well publicized. The campaign will lose its momentum if I don't show up."

Katy went to John and extended her hand. "Thank you for coming, and for bringing everybody."

John said simply, "I had to be here." He pressed her hand in his; the unspoken words hovering between them would have to wait.

Elizabeth put her arm around Katy guiding her to one of the designated "family" limousines. Bert and Jean rode in the next car. Katy mouthed a silent prayer as the limousine moved into the procession. "God above, our heavenly Father, all the natural powers around us and all the people who touch my life, thank you for the many blessings and forgive me for my shortcomings. Thank you for the years with Johnny," she breathed, "and for Elizabeth, Mom and Pop, and for all the friends around us. Bless them all."

"What did you say?" asked Elizabeth.

"I said, 'bless us all.'"

* * *

Friday morning, Elizabeth's son, Harry, drove Gloria back to Santa Fe. Elizabeth and her husband, Hank, were the last to leave. Elizabeth gave Katy a warm hug, tears welling up in her eyes—and was gone.

As the car pulled out of the driveway, Katy asked Pop, "Is old Baldy in?"

"He was out by the water tanks awhile ago. Want me to get him in the corral for you?"

"Thanks Pop. I want to take a ride, a long ride. Maybe clear out to the caprock."

* * *

Katy let Baldy have his head. He galloped across the prairie heading northward toward the caprock. As he settled down to an easy jogging gait, she began sobbing.

Sorrowful moans from deep inside broke through her control and convulsed through the very fiber of her soul. She let herself go, in anguish, pouring out the heartbreak of a lifetime.

Her tears left muddy trails through the dust on her face. She cried for the young life cut short. She cried for Gloria. She cried for herself, for the girl who loved life so much she had to give life to her own child. She cried for the lonely university nights when she lived just to see him on weekends. She cried for the girl who, in order to dull the pain, studied and worked every day to exhaustion. She cried for the young lawyer and the young legislator. She cried for the young woman who became governor of her state.

She cried for the happy times. For the sad times. She cried for the times she and Elizabeth talked and talked about Johnny, and how wonderful it was that she had brought him into this world. She cried for the wonderful times she and Johnny had together, for the cows that were theirs, and the horseback rides together across this same pasture. She cried for Johnny's love for Gloria, and the Jaguar, and for being alive.

"God, why Johnny?" she gasped accusingly. "Haven't I suffered enough? Why this final overwhelming pain? Why? Why? Oh God, why?"

With no handkerchief to wipe her face, she rubbed her eyes and cheeks with the back of her hands. Regaining some sense of time and place, she reined the obedient horse down and dismounted; pulled out the tail of her shirt, and wiped her face. Leading Baldy along, she walked, only dimly aware she still headed in the direction of the caprock. She remounted, pushed him into a gallop for awhile, then a walk, and gallop again. At the caprock she dismounted and walked to the edge, leading Baldy as she went.

Life went on as usual in the wastelands below. A pickup kicked up a cloud of dust as it wound its way across the valley. A windmill turned lazily on a breeze out of the southwest. Johnny's cows were trailing to the windmill.

They don't know Johnny is dead, thought Katy. The world doesn't know, and it goes on.

As she rode back, she sang. First the songs she and Johnny sang when he was a little boy. "Sweet Jennie Lee from sunny

Tennessee", "My Billy Goat was feeling fine, he ate three shirts off my clothesline", "A Hula Maiden, from the Tamai Isles", "Little Sweetheart of the Rockies, of the Rockies far away." Then the Christmas carols they had sung together. "Jingle bells, jingle all the way", "Oh little town of Bethlehem, how still I see thee lie".

She said the Pledge of Allegiance, just as he had said it, and the Boy Scout Law which he had repeated to her so proudly.

She sang some more, tunes of the range they had sung together as they rode. "Well, he always sings jazzy music to the cattle as he swings, back and forth in his saddle, on a horse", "See them tumbling down, pledging their love to the ground", "With someone like you, a pal good and true".

Several times the songs and recitations submerged in her tears. There were no restraints or inhibitions now. She sang loud and cried long. By the time she arrived at the home corral, she was humming a little tune. She unsaddled Baldy, let him drink, curried him briefly, put out feed and turned him loose.

The smell of pinto beans cooking assailed her senses as she tramped into the house. As she looked into her mother's reddened eyes, tears flooded down her cheeks. They cried together, holding each other close, reaffirming their own lives. Katy hugged Mom one more time.

"Mom, I'm hungry."

* * *

Family and friends came and went during the evening. The big dining table was loaded with casseroles, salads, cakes, and pies that friends from all over the county brought in. And there were the usual phone calls. Finally, with everyone gone, Katy and Mom were alone.

"Mom," Katy asked, "what are they saying about John Van Dorn being here?"

"Their reactions were suprising. You know Caprock City is a gossipy place. John's appearance here today should have been grist for the mill. Johnny resembled him so very much. I heard one of the those reporters pumping Angie Barnes. He asked Angie point blank why she thought John Van Dorn was here. You know what she said? 'He's a friend of Katy's.' That's all she would say. And that was all they could get out of her—or anyone else. Everyone in Caprock City knows now, but it doesn't make any difference. They stonewalled the reporters."

"I love them for that," said Katy.

"John Van Dorn is an impressive man; he was gracious to Pop and me, all the family. Remembered Jack and Jim, too. He made a point of meeting and talking with their families. Put everyone at ease. I have the feeling that he is a strong man. He's like Pop; he runs things, but he is a gentle man, too. Tears ran down his cheeks at the church. I saw him wipe them off several times."

"Mom, I've never told you just what happened twenty-eight years ago. I didn't know the whole story myself until I talked to John in New York shortly after the campaign started."

"I've always wondered, Katy."

"Well, you know what happened to Elizabeth and me. We were a couple of lost souls. And Mom, I've always thanked God for what you did." Mom sat quietly as Katy regained her composure before she continued. "But what I didn't know was why John disappeared so completely." Katy retold the ironic story. "...and John's mother cut all communication lines. John called everywhere, but couldn't get me. It seems we just weren't destined to get together. I called and called, too. They never let me talk to him. He never even knew."

Mom sighed. "From what you have told me, things must have been moving pretty fast back there in New York. Can you imagine how I would react if Pop's dying wish was for Jack and me to keep the 'Big J Enterprises' out of some opportunist's hands, maybe an in-law who Pop was sure couldn't tell a bale of hay from a cow? What do you think Jack would have done?"

"He would have busted a gut to keep the 'Big J' together."

"Well," said Mom, "I expect that's what John did."

34

Tony Scarcini had never killed a woman; that was part of the fascination of this assignment. No holding up now. Nor would he wait for any more phone calls. He had worked for Domino before—that guy trying to muscle in on Joe's territory—smooth as silk.

This job paid even more, and he wanted to get it over with. He was tired of driving the beat-up farm truck, wearing dirty levis and the worn cowboy leather jacket; the damn cowboy hat got knocked off every time he got into the pick-up. In Jersey he looked and lived like a gentleman. After this hit maybe he would retire for awhile.

He let up on the gas. Be crazy to get picked up for speeding. Getting close to Caprock City. Stinking dull place, even worse than Amarillo where he had holed up.

He knew she was there. It had been front page news in Amarillo. She'd be off her guard with the funeral and everything. His mouth, which was small and usually tightly closed, briefly stretched into a thin grin. Then wrinkles knit his brow. What in hell had gotten into Domino? You don't postpone an operation like this one. He had planned it too carefully, even risked his neck figuring out how to break into the tripper room atop the row of grain elevators at Big J Feedmills. The last time the phone rang in his stinking room in Amarillo, he let it ring. He packed the battered tool box with everything he would need—the sniper rifle, bipod, and scope, broken down for compactness, and the rope and climbing gear. He went out to the pick-up, and headed for Caprock City.

* * *

Pop had adjusted to having two extra women around keeping Katy under constant surveillance. They sat in the back of the Cadillac. He and Katy sat in the front. "Jimmy will fly you all to Albuquerque, be back here tonight and head to Dallas tomorrow to fly The Texans around."

"Jimmy's at the feed mill," Pop added. I'll take you ladies down there; he'll take his car out to the airport."

"Thanks, Pop. I'm glad Jimmy can get away."

"Don't worry about it. He loves The Texans. And he makes a good pitch for you, too. Almost as good as Johnny." The mention of Johnny came out automatically. Pop hurried on, "Jimmy and the Cessna will be there 'til the last gasp of this campaign."

Katy sat silent. Pop swallowed hard and glanced sideways at her. "Say, you've been putting on a hell of a campaign. I'm beginning to think this country could use a woman president."

"Coming from you, Pop, that's something. It's worth the whole effort!" Katy grinned, if only to put her sorrow aside for the moment.

* * *

"Looks like business is good this morning," Pop said as he parked at the mill's outer perimeter parking area.

Jean and Bert left the car first. Jean squinted at the towering grain elevators forming a sensational backdrop for the activity on the ground; big trucks and pickups backed to the loading docks and scattered around the parking lot.

"This place is a security nightmare," Jean said, half to herself, half to Bert.

Peter Barnes, oblivious to the two bodyguards, made his way directly to Katy who had just emerged from the car. "I'm sorry, Katy, about Johnny," he stammered. When Katy put her arm around the man and called him "Petie," Bert relaxed her vigil. Jean watched a rancher get out of his pickup a few yards away. Her gaze riveted on the 30-30 rifle sitting in a rack above the back seat as casually as if it rode above a fireplace mantle. The man noticed the city-woman's aggressive stare as he got out of the pickup and headed toward them.

"That's my coyote gun," he said, "a sheepman's best friend."

"Right," said Jean evenly. The man proceeded directly to Pop. "Pop, I've got to have more feed. We're hurting down in my country. I'm thinkin' about giving them some cottonseed cake."

"It'll help 'em, but you gotta' take it easy with 'cake' in this hot weather."

"Can you carry me?"

"Sure, Ollie, just get your ticket for whatever you need and bring it to me."

"Thanks." The man headed toward the office.

Peter stood back out of the way as Pop and Ollie talked, his gaze roving around the lot. Something drew his attention upward. There shouldn't be anybody up in the tripper room now, he thought. No wheat coming in now. He saw it again, a glint from the tripper room atop the elevators. He squinted upward, saw the glint again. Looks like a gun barrel. I'm telling Pop about it. Shouldn't be no one up there. His eyes focused. Now he was sure it was a gun. It steadied, and he realized it was aimed right at Katy.

Why? he wondered. *Who would point a rifle at Katy?* The rifle jerked. He lunged against Katy, knocking her sideways, and he suffered the impact of the slug in his shoulder.

Pop grabbed him. "What in hell is going on here?"

Jean plunged after Katy. "Stay down!" she ordered as Katy tried to struggle out of her grasp. "Someone's shooting."

Peter howled with pain. Blood oozed through his thin summer shirt.

"Up there!" yelled Bert pointing to the top of the grain elevator.

Pop spotted the glint of the rifle as it pulled back. He waited for it to reappear, but it didn't. "Get on the other side of the car—EVERYONE!" he yelled.

Katy struggled to her feet. "Petie!" she shrieked, "come on!" She pulled him by his uninjured arm, and opened the back door. His shoulder was a bloody mess. "Slide in, Petie. On the floor! I'm taking you to the hospital!" She pushed with all her strength to get him in the back, climbed over the front seat and started the car. Bert crawled in the open back door. The wheels spun in gravel for a moment, a fountain of small stones spewing behind them, before the tires bit into hard ground and allowed Katy to aim the Cadillac for the road.

Pop and Jean took refuge behind Ollie's pickup. They scrutinized the top of the elevator from their cover. No movement up there.

A Peterbilt truck pulled alongside them. The driver, oblivious to the peril, called out to Pop. "I'd hate to have that fellow's job...makin' like a mountain climber on the side of a grain silo."

"What do you mean? Where?" gasped Pop.

"Down on the east end. He inspecting the concrete or something?"

"Jean, get to the office and have 'em call the Sheriff," Pop yelled as he opened the door of Ollie's pickup. He guessed the key was in the ignition. It was.

Jean ignored Pop's order and dived into the back of the truck. The pickup's wheels scattered another rain of gravel as it took off.

That's him! Pop saw the man as he rounded the end of the towering granaries. The man was running toward a board fence about 150 feet away. If he gets over that fence, I've lost him, thought Pop. He reached for the rifle in back of him, realized it wouldn't be loaded—shells would be in the glove box. No time for that. He pushed the gas pedal to the floor board, and aimed it at the fleeing man. *Can't let him get over that fence.*

Pop stomped on the emergency brake as he catapulted out of the pickup. It skidded to a stop. The man was half-way over the fence. Pop lunged. With all his strength, he grabbed the man's leg, hoping his body weight was enough to pull him down. They crashed to the ground, one body sprawling on top of the other.

Jean leaped out of the pickup bed. Pop struggled to extricate himself from the mass of arms and legs atop him; he saw the man's right hand snake into his jacket pocket, reappearing with a small semi-automatic pistol. Pop twisted sideways as it fired. The bullet missed his head by less than an inch. Like a viper Jean lunged at the killer as he took aim on Pop, pinned against the ground with no escape. With a scissorlike movement of her hands she knocked the gun out of his grasp. He grabbed for it in midair. As Jean fought with him for control of the weapon the hair-trigger went off with a loud report—the bullet slammed into Scarcini's own body. He didn't resist, couldn't, as she kicked the gun out of reach and cuffed him.

Pop struggled to his feet. "Well, I'll be damned," he panted. He watched Jean's efficient operation. When she looked up, he said, "Well, lady, I guess I owe you one."

The man's eyes flew open in terror as Pop towered over him. "This town will hang you for sure. Who are you? And where are you from? —so we can ship your remains."

"Like hell you will," the man gasped just before he lost consciousness.

The investigation of the tripper room revealed a chillingly detailed assassination plan. The hit man had fired from the window nearest the parking lot, then run to the other end of the tripper room, half a block away, where the rope was set up for a rappelling escape. His truck was parked just beyond the fence. He left the rifle and the rope behind; he had never touched them. A pair of latex gloves was found in his jacket pocket.

Tony Scarcini died of his wound minutes before noon without answering one question. He died about the same time Peter Barnes came out of the operating room and Dr. Beall assured Katy that he was going to be just fine. "His shoulder will be sore as a boil for a few days," the doctor said, "but no serious damage."

Katy bent over Petie and kissed him on the cheek. His eyes fluttered open. "It's all right, Katy. Ain't nobody can keep you from being president now."

* * *

"Served him right," Joe Domino kept saying to himself. "He knew I wanted to call it off. Didn't even answer my last phone call. Just took it on himself. Served him right."

Carmen and Joanne wore their birthday suits. Wisconsin girls can't swim for sour apples, he thought, just splashing around out there like a couple kids in a wading pool.

Hell, it's a good thing Tony got it. If he hadn't died in the hospital, I might be "dead" now. The thought sent a shiver through his body. He knew better than to take on a hit like that without approval from New York. It wasn't like him. *Lost my cool—and that's something Joe Domino doesn't do. Never again—if I survive this one.*

It had been a coincidence. The very next night after the damned woman and the traitor Andy Barker stood them up at Uniontown, and made a laughing stock of him, Tony Scarcini was at Pete's Place. They sat at the bar together and had a beer. Joe told Tony he had a job for him.

But, the damned woman was flying around all over the country—never settling down in one place long enough to set it up—until her kid-brother's funeral away to hell-and-gone down in Caprock, New Mexico. The closest town, Amarillo, Texas, was ninety miles away.

Tony went down to Amarillo to set it up. Then Joe got the word from New York. "Lay low—don't get involved with Barker or the woman anymore. Too much heat."

He tried to call it off, but Tony wasn't listening. Didn't call him back. Served him right, he thought again.

"Hey, you girls, get your asses out of that swimming pool, and bring me a 'double!' I'm going to get good and drunk tonight."

35

Katy was glad to be alone in her apartment at La Posada. Jimmy had flown her to Albuquerque Sunday morning, and rather than bother Manuel, she took a cab to La Posada with Jean and Bert. She unplugged the phone in her suite, something she seldom did, took a quick shower, and put on lounging pajamas. She pulled the drapes against the brillant sun and enjoyed the privacy inside. After reading a bit from the latest edition of TODAY, she fell into the sleep of exhaustion. A couple of hours later, numbly awake, somewhat renewed by the sound sleep, Katy made lunch from the cottage cheese and pineapple she found in the refrigerator.

About four o'clock, the warmest time of the day, she wandered out into the patio. The garden basked in the Indian summer weather of mid-October, some of the leaves already yellow and crimson. But the quiet of the garden only became an extension of her melancholy. She turned and retreated inside.

She sat heavily in the nearest chair, feeling the spectre of loneliness creep into the room, as it often had in other rare moments of calm. At first she attributed it to reaction after the events in Caprock. Even as she thought about it, however, she knew something else caused the loneliness enveloping her.

She was aching—and she knew it was for John. She put the plug back into the phone-jack and called the Park Plaza in New York. Each time the phone's ring echoed back through the line, she wanted to hang up, but she waited for just one more ring.

Gently, with a vague hope of an answer still lingering, Katy replaced the receiver in its cradle. At the same time, she heard a knocking on her door. I'm not dressed. Oh, hell, I'm entitled to an occasional respite, she thought as she flung open the door.

John didn't say anything. He just took her in his arms and held her. Still holding her, he closed the door and kissed her gently.

"John, I'm glad you're here." Katy's voice was hushed as he released her.

His manner was quiet, too. "I couldn't think of anything but you." he said. "I decided I had to come here."

"I was just trying to call you. I was lonesome."

"So was I. And I was concerned for you—especially after I heard what happened at the feed mill. Ms. Arnold filled me in on the details."

"It happened so quickly I hardly knew what was going on." Her voice faltered. "I don't know why I was saved from a deliberate attempt on my life and Johnny was taken away in a pure accident."

John put an arm around her and guided her to a chair, then sat opposite her before he spoke. "Some things just don't make sense. I guess that in a universe so vast, and a world so large, that nature, or God, or whatever the guiding forces are, just can't function perfectly all the time."

"I haven't been able to think of it that objectively. But that makes some sense."

They sat absorbed in their own thoughts for a short time before Katy broke the silence. "Why don't I make some lemonade?"

"That sounds good." As Katy rose, he stood up also, and followed her to the kitchenette, noticing his surroundings for the first time. "Your place is nice!"

"Thank you. I love it. But it's not quite as impressive as the Park Plaza."

"It's homier. I like the paintings."

"I'll have to tell you about them. They were all done by friends of mine."

As Katy busied herself squeezing fresh lemons, John found glasses and put ice in them.

"It will be nice out on the patio now," she said. "We can have our drinks out there."

Katy mixed the lemonade in a pitcher, went into the living room and pulled the draperies open. John picked up the ice-filled glasses and followed her. She slid the glass panel open and they stepped outside together.

"My God, I had forgotten how beautiful New Mexico is," he said. He stared at the Sandia Mountains, which were already showing shades of pink from the late afternoon sun.

As Katy poured the lemonade, John soaked up the view. "What's that big complex over there?"

"That's our new Convention Center. Pretty impressive, huh? If you peek around the corner of the patio, you can see our new twenty-two story office tower and the Hyatt Regency Hotel."

"Albuquerque's changed in the last twenty-eight years."

They sat and sipped lemonade, and talked: John's flight down in the GULFSTREAM...the refueling delay in Kansas City...the flight crew staying at the Doubletree Inn a couple of blocks up the street...the plane being readied to take her to Washington in the morning.

Katy filled John in on the attempt on her life and how Jean had saved Pop's life.

"That had to be Domino's doing," John observed, "but how could we ever prove it?"

As the shadow from the hotel extended itself over the garden, a cool breeze sprang up and Katy and John moved inside. Now she told him about the paintings, winding up in the bedroom where Elizabeth's paintings hung in three groupings. The Santa Fe paintings were nearest the door.

"Hyde Park?" John questioned as he read the title on the first one.

"Our Hyde Park is up above Santa Fe in the Sangre de Cristo mountains. Aren't the aspens pretty?"

"They're beautiful, Katy. Elizabeth's inner beauty comes through in her paintings."

Katy felt a sudden warmth. Without thinking, she put her arms around him, tilted her face up, and kissed him gently on the lips. He clasped her to him and returned her kiss.

Katy liked his strong arms around her, and his body so close. Reluctantly she pulled away and pointed out the Taos paintings on the far wall. "Ranchos de Taos in Winter," she said, "and this one is 'Taos Pueblo Hunting Ceremony.'"

"I recognize the scenes. The hundred square miles around

Santa Fe must be the most paintable area in the world."

Katy took John's hand and led him around the queen size bed, with it's massive hand-carved headboard, to the far wall. Without releasing his hand, which felt so comforting in hers, she pointed out Elizabeth's large caprock painting, a plains landscape dominated by the windmill and water tanks in the background, and accented by white-faced cattle drifting in from the range, to drink and rest.

John caught his breath. Up on a rise, appearing to have just ridden into the scene, were a boy and a woman on their horses, together surveying the landscape and cattle before them. The boy leaned eagerly forward. John stooped to read the title. "I'll Race You To The Windmill."

John felt Katy's hand tighten in his. They moved back from the painting and sat on the edge of the bed, eyes glued to the scene before them. He felt her body quivering and heard her soft sobs. Now, John's arm encircled her. His throat tightened and he felt the beginnings of tears. He rocked her gently on the edge of the bed.

Katy wiped her eyes, and began to take off her pajamas. No words were needed. She slipped under the covers as John flung his clothes over the old rocking chair that sat just beyond the paintings. He felt the coolness of the sheets as he slid under them...then the warmth of her body.

The two of them held each other close, shutting out the world, taking comfort in each other, compensating for the suffering Johnny's death brought to them, dulling the pain. John dropped a hand carressingly on her breast, hugged her to him, and kissed her passionately. She responded with her own passion and they felt and touched and explored and caressed each other. John pressed his body to hers. When they joined in the most intimate embrace two people share, tension and grief ebbed, reaffirming their faith in the world that had fallen apart.

* * *

The few people in the hotel dining room when Katy and John arrived seemed to enjoy the quiet. As the head waiter seated them in a far corner, he offered condolences to Katy for the loss of her brother and briefly mentioned that he heard she had a "brush," too. Bert and Jean discreetly entered the restaurant and sat on the opposite side of the room, keeping a clear view in all directions.

"Would you join me in a Manhattan-on-the-rocks for old time's sake?" John asked quietly.

"I'd love one."

Katy ordered the green chile omelet, a specialty of the house, available all hours. John ordered a prime rib sandwich and dinner salad.

They made light conversation until the drinks arrived.

"To you, Katy."

"And to you, John."

They clicked glasses and sipped leisurely.

"I'm making a big change at LAND & SEA."

"Oh?"

"I'm turning the day-to-day operations over to my brother. You don't know Ted. He's ten years younger than I am. He's made in the Van Dorn tradition, though." John paused. "He will be president; I'm going to replace Mother as Chairman of the Board."

Katy sensed there was more.

"I want to make my home and main headquarters at Twin Oaks, my country place outside London. You'd love it, Katy."

Katy waited.

"What I'm trying to say is, when this campaign is over, I think we should get married and live in England."

"John!"

"Oh, we'd keep the New York apartment. We'd be over here a lot. I'll still be very much involved in LAND & SEA wherever I am."

Katy's thoughts whirred. How matter-of-fact! The course of my entire life turning around and starting over between sips of a Manhattan. At the same time she realized this was not true. The change had started with the phone call from John, then took a giant leap in her fateful trip to New York. She remembered the coffee royals with which he proposed to relaunch their romance, her revelation of Johnny, and how her heart skipped a beat when John said, "You must tell Johnny." Then John came to Caprock City to share her grief. And this afternoon—she made her final commitment. Now, John's words were making his commitment. Still...

"How about your mother? Does she know what you're thinking?"

John's answer was deliberate. "She'll come around, Katy. Ted knows. He and I have a few things to work out with mother. He's willing to go all the way. He's planning to move his family to the home on Long Island; it's a sacrifice for Ted; he loves the city. But, his wife is delighted and their kids will love it. This will please mother very much; she's scared to death of being left alone."

"John, you've thought it all out!"

"Ted is in Europe now; things are changing so fast there, it's hard to keep abreast. Some of the changes are good, some are bad. We're trying to sort them out and see where we fit in." Katy was listening carefully to John's every word. He continued. "Mother and I are flying to London on the Concorde Saturday and Ted will meet us there. At Mother's insistence we're going to a big reception of some kind Sunday afternoon. Mother knows Ted and I are planning to confer with her after that. Ted will propose that he purchase the Long Island home, reserving a life-time estate for Mother in the east wing she occupies; also, that she stay on the board of directors of LAND & SEA and act as a consultant.

"I'll be spending some time with Ted, too, on the European situation. We have some London appointments for the first part of the week. I should be back in New York Wednesday. Friday, we're having a board meeting at which time we'll present our plans to them." He paused. "I'll tell them about us, too. Meanwhile, mum's the word."

"I understand, John."

"During the conference with Mother, at the right time, I will tell her our plans." He looked expectantly at Katy, "...if you concur with my proposal."

Katy smiled. "Having given the proposal due consideration and feeling great love for the man who made it, I concur."

36

The Reverend Thomas Atwood finally got his chance to confront Katy. They would square off on NTB's prime-time TOWN HALL, for which NTB projected one of the largest viewing audiences in the history of the show. With only two weeks before the election, a barrage of publicity preceded the event. The one subject—abortion—by whatever name, right-to-life or freedom-of-choice, would stir emotions.

Reverend Atwood's keen insight into what motivates people stemmed from the days when he raised the first millions for his Christian Empire on radio. Television came along as a grand new tool for furthering his endeavors. His skill at handling the new medium enabled him to expand the power of "the word of God" into the exciting field of politics. Combining politics and religion gave him great influence with his millions of followers.

The issue of abortion inflamed the minds of his disciples and gave him ammunition to shoot down his enemies. Candidate Jenkins was one of these enemies; and she was a perfect target. Knocking her down would enhance his image and his political power.

His old associate, now minister at the First Baptist Church in Hereford, Texas, less than an hour's drive from Caprock City, researched the Jenkins boy for him. The townfolk at Caprock City confirmed his suspicions that the Jenkins' boy wasn't their son at all, that Katy Jenkins was his real mother. The problem was that all of the evidence was hearsay, no conclusive proof. The courthouse records failed to reveal a shred of evidence—no trace of a birth certificate.

The exciting new angle came from that college activist at Albuquerque, George Caplin. The thousand dollars, out of the

Ministry's expense account, for Caplin's trips to El Paso was money well spent. Caplin secured the concrete evidence that the Jenkins girl and a friend, Mary Ann Jones, registered in an El Paso hotel in 1964 and visited an abortion clinic a few blocks away. The elderly clerk at the hotel verified the whole thing.

The incriminating new evidence posed a problem for Atwood though; he was convinced the boy in Caprock was Jenkins' son, in which case she didn't get an abortion. Then, the light came on. If she denied she had an abortion, she'd have to admit Johnny was her baby. He had her in a corner. She would have to "come clean" or lie through her teeth.

He would throw her to the wolves—the press.

Thomas Atwood made a grand entry as he alighted from his limousine at the main entrance to the NTB New York studios and made his way through the crowd with handshakes and expressions of good will. That he felt he would be serving God and country this evening was obvious; his assurance and self-confidence evoked a roar of approval from segments of the crowd. Tonight he would topple that brash female politico.

Security guards guided Katy, Ms. Arnold, Bert, and Jean into the studio through a rear entrance. Outside, the police tensely managed the crowds of picketers who harangued them with rhythmic chants proclaiming their stand on issues.

Bert and Jean escorted Katy to the green room off-stage. Ms. Arnold took a seat in the guest area where she could watch the interviews.

Props for the scene were sparse, an oval table and three arm chairs. Katy sat on one side, Atwood opposite her, and Jim McClellan, the host of TOWN HALL, at the end of the table between them. The background for the set looked like a Currier & Ives painting of a town hall in a New England village.

Four cameramen rolled their machines into various positions giving them the capability to zero in on one, two, or all three participants. Banks of floodlights suspended from the cavernous ceiling flooded the area with light. Tiny monitors in front of the cameras gave participants glimpses of the scenes going into millions of homes. An eerie quiet pervaded the studio as McClellan watched the clock tick off the seconds—and TOWN

HALL was on the air!

McClellan's voice crackled with anticipation as he introduced his show. "I'm Jim McClellan...and this is TOWN HALL. This evening we have with us presidential candidate Katy Jenkins...and one of her most vocal detractors, the Reverend Thomas Atwood." After a quick background on both Atwood and Katy, McClellan flashed his ingratiating smile, first at Katy on his left, then back at Atwood. "Thank you for joining us."

"Miss Jenkins," McClellan began, "every presidential candidate in my memory has told the electorate that he would balance the budget. You are no exception. Do you really think you have a major formula to balance the budget when all others have failed?"

"Presidents don't have the power to balance budgets," Katy answered. "Only Congress can. But, it is the President's duty to present the Congress a budget proposal. I will present a balanced budget to the Congress."

Atwood jumped into the discussion. "Do you really believe you can present a budget where income matches expenditures, Miss Jenkins?" he asked, barely concealing the sarcasm in his voice.

"I know this can be done," said Katy, "and I promise the American people, here and now, that I will present a balanced budget proposal to the Congress of the United States within the prescribed time after I take office."

McClellan regained control of the discourse. "What specific spending do you propose to cut?"

Katy's answer was as direct as the question. "Across the board," she said, "in every area of Federal spending, but particularly in the military budget with new priorities and considerable savings. Our first budget will not advocate cutting out any programs or services the Federal Government is now funding, but we will change the figures and operating methods."

"It sounds like you may be daydreaming," broke in Atwood.

Katy realized Atwood had scored with a condescending undercut of her position. McClellan glanced at the monitor to make sure he wasn't in the scene, then gave Atwood a scornful look before moving on. "Miss Jenkins, you know that the president of the United States is Commander-in-Chief of the

Armed Forces. What in your background would qualify you for this job?"

The question suprised Katy somewhat, but she wasn't caught short.

"During my last four years in the United States Congress," she said, "I worked on the Armed Forces Committee. I have seen every hot spot in the world, and I wasn't just sightseeing. I got the 'feel' of the countries involved."

Atwood interrupted at that point. "What did you, as a committee of one, decide about the world?" he asked, not bothering to conceal his sneer.

"I decided that the deprivation of human rights is ugly and dehumanizing, and continues only by ruthless enforcement."

The forthright answer surprised Atwood, but he felt he had her trapped. McClellan started to ask another question. But Atwood bullied his way through. "I know from what you have said during the campaign that you are a 'hawk,' so to speak. How do you propose to pay for 'Star Wars' and maintain a strong defense posture—and balance the budget at the same time?"

Katy savored the question.

"The obvious big drain on our military funds has been furnishing the defense for Europe, and Asia as well. Forty percent," she said with emphasis, "of our military budget has gone for this. The countries involved include Germany and Japan. By subsidizing them, we gave them an unfair trade advantage and dissipated our own military budget. I would cut this expense."

She continued, "I have spent more time in the Pentagon, and out in the field, studying every aspect of our Defense Initiative and our space program than any civilian I know. We are spending money as if it gushed from a bottomless well. That isn't the answer to our problems. We must get more for our money."

Katy suspected that Atwood hardly heard the last part of her answer. He had his reply ready, "Well, good luck to you with the Pentagon," he said patronizingly.

The camera panned to Jim McClellan, who put his hand to his chin showing absorption in the argument. Two combatants like these were great for ratings.

Atwood continued. "Miss Jenkins, even if the electorate could vote for your plan to cut all Federal spending programs, while you would be spending billions on 'Star Wars,' do you really believe they will approve of your views on the taking of human life by abortion?"

Katy listened to the question, felt that it was loaded against her, and decided to parry. "Do you want to talk about Federal spending, the nation's defense, or abortion?"

Atwood's response was quick, "My question is: do you believe the voters will approve your views on the taking of human life by abortion?"

"I am glad you are taking the voters into consideration," Katy said. "My beliefs concur with the Supreme Court ruling in the 1973 Roe vs. Wade case which stated that no state may pass a law interfering with the patient-physician decision for abortion during the first three months of pregnancy."

She paused and gave Atwood a chance to respond. He hesitated only for a second, but that gave Katy the opening she needed to continue.

"Within a week after this Supreme Court decision was issued, the first Bill to overthrow or modify it was introduced in the Congress. Since then, more that 200 similar anti-abortion bills have been sponsored in the Congress. None passed! The Supreme Court decision was specific and reasonable; I'll bet my chance to be president that the vast majority of the people of this country prefer a moderate stand on this very personal matter.

Atwood insisted on pursuing the question. "One of our Southern senators," he said, "has introduced a bill on the Senate agenda stating 'the life of each human being begins at conception.' Don't you agree that this is as reasonable as setting up an arbitrary time, such as three months, for life to begin? Why would there be no life before—and suddenly at three months there's life?"

This was the question Katy had expected. She worded her response carefully. "Doctors universally agree that a tiny three month old embryo cannot survive on its own. But we must go beyond this bit of truth to examine the subject fully. In a country as diverse as the United States, there are persons whose religious beliefs reject abortion under any circumstances. There are those whose religious beliefs permit abortion under most circumstances. And there are those who stand somewhere in between. In a country undergirded by democracy, it is unseemly and lacking in tolerance for government, or a president, to select one set of religious values and attempt to impose them on all."

Atwood looked at the clock. There were only a few minutes left.

Katy sensed that he was getting ready to spring the big one.

"Now, Miss Jenkins," he said evenly, "we all know you advocate so-called 'freedom-of-choice' for abortion. I have a question for you: have you yourself ever had an abortion?"

"No, I haven't," said Katy emphatically.

Atwood looked stern. "I know you are not under oath here," he said. "But, the American people are entitled to a straight answer. Didn't you visit an abortion doctor in El Paso, Texas, in the fall of 1964? October 23, 1964, to be exact."

Katy was appalled at the line of questioning. She could feel the tension in the studio. Atwood had hit below the belt. Every viewer would know that. Still, they were waiting for her answer.

"Yes, I was there," she answered.

"Were you pregnant at the time?" he shot back at her.

"As a matter of fact, I was."

"But, you weren't married, were you?"

"No, I wasn't married."

"Then, suppose you tell us just what happened in El Paso, Texas, in October of 1964."

"Yes, I'll tell you." Katy was very deliberate. "But, it is a rather long story."

Smug in the knowledge he had stymied her and halted the forward motion of the entire Coalition party, he sat back, folded his thick arms across his belly, and said, "We'll be interested in every word."

"I was at the University of New Mexico in 1964. A brutal rape occurred two blocks from campus; a nineteen year old college girl was viciously assaulted in her own apartment. She was emotionally and physically devastated. Later, when she found out she was pregnant as a result of the rape, this young girl became suicidal.

"An abortion was illegal, but she heard of the doctor at El Paso. She considered this criminal procedure to be her only way out. Well, I went with her to El Paso. By the grace of God, there were no complications, although the doctor's facilities were crude and frightening. We heard of another girl who went there and died four days later as a result of infection."

Reverend Atwood was uncomfortable with the story Katy told, but he still had his trump card to play. He asked a preliminary question.

"But, were *you* pregnant at the time?"

"Oh, yes I was," said Katy. "When I went to El Paso, and when I returned." She didn't volunteer any more.

"The obvious question," he said, "is how was your pregnancy terminated?"

"With the birth of beautiful baby boy," she said. Again she volunteered no more information. Atwood was becoming nervous, but he couldn't quit now.

"Your baby was illegit—?"

"Don't you say it," Katy yelled, "no, he was perfectly fine. He was the baby brother of the Jenkins family at Caprock City, New Mexico. Everybody loved Johnny."

Katy's anger washed away as the grief of Johnny's death flooded her spirit. "And now he's dead. The life I treasured so much, the little boy my parents raised as their own, the vibrant young man just beginning his joyful journey on this earth, is no more. He died in an auto accident one week ago." Katy's voice faltered as she said the last words.

Atwood mumbled condolences. The trap he had set so carefully to snare Katy had snapped shut without its victim. But, he wouldn't give up now.

"The boy had a father?" The question sounded almost casual.

Resentment grated in Katy's voice. "Would you expect otherwise? Maybe a virgin birth?"

Again Atwood was caught off-balance, but he continued doggedly. "I just thought you might want to tell us about the father."

Katy's temper flared. "Well, you just thought wrong!" Now thoroughly angered, Katy struck out at her tormenter. "Just like your perversion of the Christian religion is so wrong. Jesus didn't teach intolerance and ugliness! He taught goodness, and love, and consideration for others."

Atwood could not think of a response to this, so he didn't try.

He was a shrewd man. He knew he had raised the questions that would crush the woman. The press would do the rest. "I will pray for you," he said, "and for your lost son."

Katy felt loathing for the man. She wanted to spit in his face, but knew she was in enough trouble already. "Never mind," she snapped. "Save the prayers for yourself."

Jim McClellan took over. Time was up. "Thank you, Reverend Atwood, and thank you, Katy Jenkins. This is Jim McClellan—and good night."

Mike off, McClellan sucked in a deep breath, adrenalin still surging through his body. "That deserved a 50 share."

Ms. Arnold knew that the reporters outside the studio and in the building lobby downstairs, were right now falling over themselves to get to telephones. She rushed to the set and maneuvered Katy to the stairway hoping to evade the reporters by sneaking out the side entrance of the studio. She no more than opened the door when the reporters overran them. Cameras flashed. Television cameras hummed as they recorded the scene.

Katy braced herself for the onslaught of questions. Ms. Arnold stood beside her. As the reporters started yelling questions about Johnny, and why had she deceived the people of her state all these years, Ms. Arnold took charge. "One question at a time, PLEASE!"

Katy decided to try to make a statement that would answer their questions—but she couldn't bring John Van Dorn into it!

"Quiet!" Ms. Arnold's voice rose above the tumult. "Katy will make a statement."

The crowd settled down, listening. Katy knew they were ready to eat her alive. She would have to make it good!

"Okay," she said, loud enough for everyone outside to hear. "This isn't a new story; it's as old as history, and probably went on before that. I had a 'romance' in my second year of college—and I got caught!" Reporters scribbled her exact words as cameras whirred. "Never told the father because he was long gone. This isn't a new angle either. You've heard it before." She cocked her head to one side. "So I had a tough choice to make. Get an abortion...or become an unwed mother. In those days either choice was pretty grim. Some of my detractors might say that it should have been an easy choice for me, being 'for' abortion, but that is the fallacy about the whole abortion thing. Most of us are not 'for abortion.' But we are against criminalizing women or doctors on this very personal matter.

"I didn't want to have an abortion. By the grace of God, I had another choice. My mother and father volunteered to raise the baby as their own. And that's the way we raised Johnny. He was my kid brother."

Suddenly Katy's face became solemn. Ms. Arnold saw her body quiver; she thought Katy was going to break down. Two jarring questions brought Katy back to reality.

"Who was the baby's father? Was it John Van Dorn?" a reporter shouted.

Katy knew that avoiding the answer would only prolong the agony, but John's words rang in her ears. "Meanwhile, mum's the word." She had to stall for time.

"I can't tell you right now."

A belligerent reporter's voice yelled, "Answer the question!"

Ms. Arnold's voice boomed out. "Can't you hear? She can't tell you right now. Don't you understand? Katy just lost a son. This is too much on top of the grief she is feeling. These are personal matters, not political." Then with finality: "There will be no more statements or answers to any questions now. Please make way."

Ms. Arnold glowered at reporters as she and Katy pushed their way through the crowd. Jean and Bert flanked Katy on each side. Uniformed police helped control the crowd. When they reached Katy's Cadillac, Ms. Arnold put Katy in the back seat between Jean and Bert, then got in the driver's seat, wheeled the car around, and accelerated. She had an unscheduled stop to make.

37

"I blew that one," Katy said dully.

Ms. Arnold twisted around to get a glimpse of Katy in the back seat. "The cards were stacked against us tonight, and Atwood dealt from the bottom of the deck. He knew you had just lost Johnny, and he took advantage of it."

"I shouldn't have lost my temper."

"Hell, you're human aren't you? I wish you could have scratched his eyes out!"

Katy noted the direction the car took. "Aren't we headed the wrong way? We're on the New York Thruway going upstate."

"Now listen to me, Katy. I have some friends up here. They're retired, have a beautiful place, nice and private. They're friends of your candidacy, too. I just happened to talk to them yesterday. So I know they're home."

"This is a strange time to go calling." Katy sounded puzzled, impatient.

"I'm going to drop you off for a couple days of rest and recuperation."

"Oh no! I can't do that. The press will be crucifying me. I'll have to stand up to them."

"Not for a couple days, you don't. Let me handle them. It'll throw them off-balance when they can't find you."

Katy pushed forward in the seat and leaned toward Ms. Arnold. "We can't just run away..." She stopped short. *Why not?* The question darted through her mind. If the press knew where she was, they would hound her to death about Johnny, and bombard her with questions about John.

"You will disappear completely," continued Ms. Arnold with a little laugh. "It'll frustrate the hell out of 'em."

* * *

Ms. Arnold felt she was being watched from the minute she entered Kennedy International Airport after parking Katy's car in the long-term parking structure. As she purchased her ticket on the next flight to Washington, two reporters positioned themselves by the counter exit, confirming her suspicions.

"Where's Jenkins?" one of them asked without so much as a "good morning," which would have been appropriate since it was well past midnight.

"Oh, she's still partying, I guess. They all seemed to be having a good time."

"A good time? Where?" The reporter's tone revealed his disappointment.

"Private party. Just friends. No press."

The reporter realized he wasn't going to learn anything. It was a bum assignment. "Thanks, anyhow," he said. He hung around, however, and watched as Ms. Arnold went to the newsstand and picked up the early editions. It didn't take her long to find what she was looking for. On the front page of the New York Post the headline blazed: "Jenkins Admits Deception." She read a few lines of the story and went on to the New York Times. "Atwood vs. Jenkins Disclosures Startling." A picture of her trying to shield Katy from the mob of newspeople made Katy look bad.

Another, less prominent front-page story caught Ms. Arnold's attention. "Van Dorns and Nobility at London Party." She read the story hurriedly; nothing of importance in it. The article continued on page sixteen; a prominent picture showed John escorting an English lady and looking quite enamored of her. *Hell*, thought Ms. Arnold, *I wonder what kind of message that's supposed to send?*

She tucked the newspapers under her arm and headed for the departure gate. As she approached the counter to get her boarding pass, she noticed the other reporter who had been downstairs. He watched her until she boarded the plane. The hounds were out.

* * *

Publicity for Katy and the American Coalition party had almost dried up as Katy doggedly made the rounds of every state; the local papers carried accounts of the rallies in their communities; but national recognition sank to a low ebb.

Suddenly the tide turned. During the two days following the Atwood incident on TOWN HALL, a torrent of negative publicity flooded the airwaves and print media. Issues were lost in a sea of accusation, innuendo, and speculation. Newspapers with political bias, be it Democrat or Republican, rushed their prejudiced views into print.

The National Enquirer asked in glaring headlines "Is Billionaire Van Dorn Father of Katy's Illegitimate Son?" A front page picture showed Katy boarding the LAND & SEA GULFSTREAM at Albuquerque. Another showed Katy, Ms. Arnold, and Harriett Landsdale in the La Posada campaign office. Katy appeared to be kissing Ms. Arnold on the cheek, with the caption, "Katy Gives Party Workers Loving Embrace." Both pictures were credited to George Caplin.

There were also interviews with Ruth Silverton and Ellen Steele of the Women's Movement. Silverton observed that it was "too soon to assess the damage from the Atwood interview." But Ellen Steele's retort captured more attention, "Katy had a baby—so what?"

Reverend Atwood could scarcely conceal his pleasure when he was interviewed. His pious comment was, "The boy is dead; let him rest in peace." Later he pronounced, "...and the Jenkins campaign is dead, too." Seeming to agree with him, The Washington Post asked, "Will Jenkins Withdraw?"

But Katy Jenkins was nowhere to be found. When Ms. Arnold arrived at the Washington headquarters the morning after TOWN HALL aired, reporters and television crews crowded inside awaiting Katy's arrival. When Ms. Arnold casually advised them Katy would be out of the headquarters for a couple of days, they grew frantic.

"Where is she?" echoed through the room. "Where is she?"

Charlie Jones, an aggressive reporter, asked Ms. Arnold, "Is Jenkins carrying on an affair with Van Dorn now?" This angered

Ms. Arnold, but she kept her cool.

"I hardly think so. He's in London hob-nobbing in high society. Haven't you seen this morning's New York Times?" He hadn't, so that shut him up temporarily.

"No more personal questions about Katy," Ms. Arnold shouted. "I'll try to help you if you want to know Katy's stand on any of the issues." They didn't. They wanted to know Katy's whereabouts. Ms. Arnold considered how she could cut off the stream of repetitive questioning.

"What is Jenkins doing?" Charlie persisted.

The question was a slight variation; Ms. Arnold smiled for the first time since her arrival at the headquarters. "Well," she said, "I don't know this for sure, but I'd guess she's working on her acceptance speech."

The incredible idea silenced the newspeople momentarily which gave Ms. Arnold the opportunity she needed. "Now, clear out of here, all of you. This is an office, and we have work to do."

Dissatisfied mutterings greeted her request. She quickly decided on another approach. "All right," she said, "Katy will be having a press conference later in the week. Exact time and place to be announced. You are all welcome to come."

"Where? When?" the words rang out.

"Probably in New York. Probably Friday. I'll let you know."

* * *

Unreal. No other word could describe taking two days off during the climax of the campaign. Katy's gracious hosts, the Scarboroughs, had retired from the Smithsonian, where they were old friends of Ms. Arnold. Genuinely interested in Katy's welfare, they watched the procession of ugly television reports with her. Mr. Scarborough drove into Poughkeepsie the next day for the metropolitan newspapers with their avalanche of unkind stories.

Overkill, Katy thought on the second day as the media continued with more of the same. The frustration of the media became apparent as they dwelt more and more on Katy's disappearance from the political scene and speculation grew that maybe she had abandoned the campaign. Katy began to wonder if she had any friends left in the news world.

Doubts flooded her mind as time dragged. What would John and his mother think after Atwood's public exposure?

She wondered how the Women's Movement was taking the barrage of bad publicity and her untimely disappearance. And Andy and the Barkers—and everyone down in New Mexico. She couldn't even call Mom and Pop. Ms. Arnold was firm...no phone calls!

Sadness about Johnny tugged at her heart. When this campaign was over, she wouldn't have Johnny; she wouldn't be the senior Congresswoman from New Mexico; her political career would be ended. Everything down the drain. Perhaps Ms. Arnold is laying the groundwork for a graceful withdrawal right now, she thought.

Then she caught one television reporter's editorial quip:

"Arnold says Jenkins is preparing her 'acceptance speech.' Well, Ms. Jenkins, it will have to be acceptance of defeat because *your* campaign is *over.*"

What I need right now is a miracle, Katy thought.

* * *

Ms. Arnold told the reporters the truth when she said she had work to do. John's call to her from London had come shortly after she arrived back at her apartment following the Atwood fiasco. He seemed highly pleased with her action in hiding Katy away for a couple of days. "That gives us time to take the initiative. That's all we need," he said matter-of-factly. "Katy was doing well until this thing happened. Now, you and I are the only ones who can get the campaign back on track. Here's what I'm thinking..." Ms. Arnold's adrenalin pumped vigorously as she and John worked out a plan.

"Office meeting at 10:00," Ms. Arnold announced to the staff. Then she sat down at her desk and began making phone calls.

First to Margaret Kincaid. Her booming voice carried throughout the headquarters. "Margaret, can you call all the Party founders and the New York organization, and tell them to disregard the news for the next couple days?" Margaret wanted details which Ms. Arnold couldn't divulge. She would take no chances on the plans she and John made leaking to the press. "Tell them we have a 'secret weapon,'" she said. "And it will be launched by week's end. Tell them we're still in this election to win. And, Margaret, can you call Andy? Tell him exactly the same thing."

The next call went to Ruth Silverton at the Women's Movement headquarters. "We're still out to win—we have a secret weapon to launch by the end of the week," Ms. Arnold said. "Keep working on the phone tree; close all the gaps, especially in Pennsylvania, Texas, and California." Ruth gave her Ellen's hotel phone number in Scranton, Pennsylvania.

Ms. Arnold caught Ellen just before she went down to a campaign breakfast meeting. "You're damn right we're still in to win," Ellen came back. "And we have one secret weapon you may not know about—the women I've talked to are mad as hell at Atwood, and the press too. Even the ones who were lukewarm on Katy because of her lack of emphasis on social programs, and the poor, and African Americans, are about ready to go to the polls and vote for her."

"You don't say? Ellen, that's good news! Maybe Mr. Atwood is in for a surprise."

"We're going to surprise the hell out of him."

Now she could call Andy. He was glad to hear from her. He enjoyed hearing Ellen's report from Scranton. Ms. Arnold assured him the campaign was on track and that Katy would emerge in a couple of days. "Disregard the news until then. We have a secret weapon to unleash later in week. Phone your workers in Pennsylvania and tell them we're still out to win."

The next call was to Harriett Landsdale in Santa Fe. Ellen's information gave Harriett renewed enthusiasm. "Don't pay any attention to the press the next two days," Ms. Arnold said. "They're beginning to reach the point of diminishing returns. Go ahead on the most enthusiastic newsletter you've ever published. It's the last letter of the campaign, so make it good! Push hard on getting out yard signs and all the campaign material on hand. Tell 'em to spend every dime they have left on local radio and newspaper ads. And, of course, wind up with a plea to get our people to the polls. Hell, what am I telling you? You're the best in the business on this sort of thing. And say, will you please call Clifford King and Elizabeth and tell them Katy is okay, and that she will be coming on strong later in the week. I'll call Maria and H.B., and I'll have the phone people here calling every state organization and as many local organizations as we can get to. I'll be in touch. Meanwhile stay tuned!"

The office meeting waited next on the agenda. Her phone calls, overheard by some of the staff, helped rally an eager assembly. Ms. Arnold made her best pitch, repeating all she had said on the phone calls.

After a quick lunch at her desk, Ms. Arnold called Carrie Brooks at LAND & SEA to confirm their appointment with the New York advertising agency the next morning. "Yes," said Carrie, "the appointment is at ten o'clock, and they're bursting with enthusiasm. John talked to them from London after he got the word from our Party Treasurer. You know what? Ms. Arnold, we're going to have a whole lot more money to spend the last week of the campaign than we expected! We're going to get millions in Federal funds because the polls prove we'll get over five percent of the popular vote. They won't give us the funds until after the election; that's the way the crazy law is written, but John has arranged with Bankcity to advance the money. Come on up as early as you can in the morning. We're going to spend eight or ten million dollars next week! The Agency says they have some good buys for us in the regions we want to hit."

* * *

John Van Dorn's call came shortly after noon on Thursday, the second day of her isolation. "Katy, honey, how are you?"

Katy's heart pounded. "I'm fine, John, but I blew it with Atwood. Ms. Arnold has me quarantined up here."

"I know. We got back yesterday; and I've had to dodge reporters ever since. I don't want to have a confrontation with them until tomorrow."

"Tomorrow? You'll confront them tomorrow?" Katy's voice trailed off as she asked the question.

"Mother and Ms. Arnold helped me set it up."

"Your mother? Ms. Arnold? Set up what?" The questions crowded on each other.

"I'm sorry, Katy," John said slowly. "So much has happened since we landed here yesterday that I'm not putting it in very good order for you. Let me start over. The Atwood thing came on London TV right after Mother and Ted and I finished our little family conference. We watched it together. From the reactions afterwards you would have thought we had watched different shows." He paused, "Are you there, Katy?"

"Yes, yes John, I'm here."

"Ted was angry at Atwood for badgering you. Mother became very defensive for you. And I never loved you so much in my life."

"John?" Katy murmured.

"Yes?"

"Are you sure any of you saw the show I was on?"

John chuckled. "It was you all right."

"And you still love me?"

"Very much!"

"And your mother? She was defensive about me?"

"You're going to like Mother, Katy. It was just fortunate that I told her about Johnny, and about our plans to be married, before TOWN HALL."

"John, when did you tell her? And what in the world did she think about Johnny?"

"I planned to tell her at the family meeting, but it worked out better at the reception on Sunday."

"The reception?"

"I didn't realize it at the time, but I suspect Mother planned the whole affair as kind of a 'coming out party' for me, the first big gathering of London friends since Stephanie's death. When I realized that half of the eligible women on the London social register were there, I took Mother to one side, and told her all about us."

"Oh, John."

"After the first shock wave when I told her we're getting married, and the second shock when I told her about Johnny, she felt sympathy for you for the first time.

"Mother suffered at the thought that I had fallen in love with a young girl in Albuquerque and left her pregnant. She said that if she had known, somehow we would have handled it differently."

"She did?"

"Yes, Katy. I explained to her that I hadn't known either, and that made a difference to her. She asked me if I am in love with you now. And I said, 'More than ever.' You know her response? She said, 'God bless you both.'"

"Oh, John..."

Katy detected some nervousness in John's next words. "Katy, can we 'go public' tomorrow?" He cleared his throat. "...at a luncheon for family and a few friends at the Westin Plaza?"

"Yes, John. Yes, we can." A lilt came into her voice. "I've been wondering how I'd get out of hiding."

John chuckled. "Oh? Well, you'll 'get out of hiding' in style! Ms. Arnold wants a press conference immediately following the luncheon. She has reserved the entire ballroom and is just waiting for me to call her back so she can advise the press. She thinks you and I should stand together and answer every question they can think of."

Katy became stern. "Well, you just tell Ms. Arnold to call me even if she has to go to a pay phone for privacy. I've got to tell her what to bring me to wear."

"I'll do it." John relaxed now. "See if the Scarboroughs can drive you down to New York early in the morning. I have a suite for you at the hotel. Mother is handling the luncheon arrangements."

"John, it all sounds like a fairy tale."

"Oh, one other thing. We were going to make it a surprise; but I have to tell you. I called your Uncle Clifford and Elizabeth. They're flying in tonight. They have a suite adjoining yours at the hotel."

"John, I love you."

38

"Is Katy Jenkins up there?" "And John Van Dorn?" "What's going on here?" The questions reverberated through the lobby of the Westin Plaza as reporters and photographers flocked in.

"They're at a private luncheon upstairs," advised the hotel manager. "They'll be down for the press party in the ballroom at one-thirty. You are all invited. Just present your credentials at the door."

Impatient reporters who managed to get on an elevator found out a key was required to open the elevator doors on the upstairs floors. Hotel security people turned back others who tried the stairways. With their attempts to crash the luncheon thwarted, the media people assembled at the entryway to the ballroom.

At one-fifteen a flurry of activity at the elevators announced the arrival of Katy and John's party. First off the elevator, a small cadre of Secret Service people unobtrusively took their positions, followed by Ms. Arnold, Carrie Brooks, Margaret Kincaid, Ruth Silverton, and Ellen Steele, who made straight for the ballroom entrance to welcome members of the press and get the press party underway. A table filled with champagne glasses and bottles of champagne in ice buckets greeted the media people as they entered the ballroom.

The second elevator arrived several minutes later. The Van Dorn and Barker families stepped out and made their way to the ballroom.

The elevator returned for Katy and John. Uncle Cliff, looking regal, and Elizabeth, radiating happiness, accompanied Katy. Henry Shaw of TODAY magazine, Tom Snelling from Bankcity, and Orville Jamison accompanied John. Jamison, a congenial elderly gentleman whom Katy had met for the first time at the luncheon, was an old family friend of both the Van Dorns and the Barkers. He was also chairman of the Republican National Committee.

Katy had felt loved at the luncheon from the beginning. Mrs. Van Dorn greeted her with a warm hug and whispered into her ear, "Katy, I'm glad you're becoming part of this family. I love your Uncle Clifford and Elizabeth, too."

The group Mrs. Van Dorn invited for the luncheon was perfectly selected to make me comfortable, thought Katy, and the luncheon itself was delightful! Now would come the hard part—facing the press again.

Katy and John walked into the ballroom through the gauntlet of reporters, ignoring their questions. At a signal from Ms. Arnold, Katy and John took their stances on a two-level platform at one end of the room. Security people flanked them on each side. John stood on the lower level of the platform. Katy, on the slightly higher level, fitted perfectly with John as he put his arm around her waist and cameras flashed.

Standing tall, his countenance firm and impressive, John signaled for quiet. His presence commanded respect. "I'm not accustomed to appearing with a dignitary for whom a ballroom full of media people would turn out," he began. "But I do have a happy announcement to make for Katy and myself. Upstairs awhile ago at a luncheon for some of our families and friends, Katy and I announced our plans to be married after the campaign is over. This is a very happy occasion for both of us. And we thank you for sharing it with us."

This sudden, casual announcement caught the media people by surprise. Some dashed for telephones; others stayed for details. When the commotion died down, a columnist for the New York Times offered his congratulations to the couple with a flourish, then asked, "John, you know you may be marrying the next president of the United States, don't you?"

"Oh sure. I'm counting on that. Should be interesting to be married to the first woman president."

Kitty Means of the Washington Post, a woman of slight build but with an aggressive personality, spoke up. "I have a question." She looked around expectantly. "Mr. Van Dorn, were you the secret father of Johnny Jenkins?"

"No question about that," John said easily.   "I was Katy's
full-time escort the summer Johnny was conceived. We were very
much in love; but I had to return to New York when my father
died suddenly—and I didn't know I had a son until a few weeks
ago when Katy told me."

"Didn't know?"   The question pierced the quiet that now
settled on the room.

"Communications breakdown," John answered.   But Katy
could see this answer wouldn't satisfy the press.

"Yes," she said thoughtfully, "there was a communications
breakdown. I came to New York twenty-eight years ago to tell
John; but when I saw New York, and LAND & SEA, and the Van
Dorn home, I was too overwhelmed to see John. I never told
him."

Katy hoped the simple truths John and she told would lay the
matter to rest. The next question came from the publisher of a
small, but influential daily newspaper in North Carolina.

"Miss Jenkins," he said condescendingly, "we still have an
unanswered question that stems from your carefree, we might even
say irresponsible, youth."

Katy tensed for the worst. Not only did her questioner have
the condescending, pious demeanor of Atwood—his short, stocky
build reminded her of Atwood, too.

"Would you mind telling us whom you aided and abetted to
have an illegal abortion in El Paso, Texas?"

"I certainly do mind," Katy shot back. "The question is totally
irrelevant."

Katy detected empathy for her among the press people. Some
glowered at her antagonist. This should have put an end to his
line of questioning; but it didn't. Aggressiveness replaced the
questioner's condescension.

"Wasn't it actually Elizabeth O'Connor?"

Katy recoiled from the question as if slapped across the face.
The shock she felt gradually turned to anger; she had an almost
uncontrollable urge to lunge at her inquisitor and knock the smirk
off his face. Somehow she managed to regain control. She
groped for an answer. Suddenly she felt Elizabeth's presence at
her side. Elizabeth's voice penetrated the now very quiet room.

"It was," she said quietly. "But Katy didn't aid and abet my 'crime.'" Elizabeth paused long enough for a deep breath. "I was raped; and I would rather have died—literally—than carry to term the pregnancy caused by the man who raped me."

Her gaze drifted to Katy and John. "It was at this critical time in their lives that Katy and John lost contact with each other.

"A few weeks later I realized I was in serious trouble—perhaps the ugliest thing a woman could ever have happen to her. I located the doctor in El Paso; and Katy helped me to live through it. That was a dreadful, sad time. Please, let's lay it to rest."

Elizabeth's countenance underwent a dramatic change. A warm smile lit up her face. "Let's celebrate the wonderful announcement John and Katy made." She stepped down alongside her dad.

"I'd like to propose a toast!" Clifford King stood tall and majestic, commanding attention. Already waitresses circulated through the crowd, trays loaded with sparkling champagne. Clifford waited until all the guests were served, then raised his glass:

> "To Katy and John I give this toast
> They are the ones we love the most.
> We wish for you a great success
> And all your life much happiness!"

"To Katy and John," echoed through the room as glasses clicked. Conversation erupted again. Katy felt boundless love for John and deep appreciation of what he did for her today.

When Katy and John stepped down off the platform, Katy rushed to Elizabeth and gave her a hug. John and Tom Snelling wandered toward the champagne table. Katy's heart sank as she saw several reporters descending on John, asking more questions. She made her way to John as fast as she could; but questions were coming at her, too. "Where did the big romance take place?" "How old were you at the time?" As she reached John's side she heard a question directed at him. "What were you doing in New Mexico at the time?"

His patience in answering, telling them about Frank Hibben in detail as if he were swapping yarns with some cronies, made friends of his questioners. He added some color, "I met Katy in a political science seminar. Apparently, Katy learned more than I did. She's a lot further along in the political world than I am."

Katy relaxed. *Let them ask their questions!* They would get answers—the tidbits they needed to enliven their stories. She realized that all the reporters were compelled to come up with their own stories; they needed new angles. The questions about Johnny still caused pain; but Katy spoke with candor, her love for the boy showing through in every answer. The demanding, prying press became a friendly press.

Staff photographers for TODAY asked Katy and John to pose for special pictures. Henry Shaw confided to John that a staff writer was making last minute revisions on the feature story for the next edition—next week, *before* the election.

Mrs. Van Dorn sought Elizabeth out and put her arm around her. "It's wonderful for Katy and John to have a friend like you. I hope we can be friends, too."

"What a lovely thing to say," Elizabeth said quietly. "I'm so glad we're going to be friends." John joined them, and although he hadn't heard their conversation, he sensed that they had hit it off well.

"Mother," he said, "next to you and Katy, I love Elizabeth the most of anybody I know."

"How many glasses of champagne have you had?" Elizabeth asked lightly. "Anyhow, it's nice to hear."

John's gaze followed Katy as he watched her chatting easily with a half dozen assorted individuals, all enjoying the conversation they exchanged with her. He turned back to his mother and Elizabeth. "New Mexico is the habitat of a very special breed of woman," he observed. "Elizabeth's gutsy handling of the press awhile ago is proof of that." His glance drifted back toward Katy. "And look at Katy. Even as she laughs and talks with everyone here today, she is carrying the heartbreak of Johnny's death."

Elizabeth's voice was subdued. "I know, John. And we're crying inside too."

John cleared his throat. "Excuse me," he said, "I want to get Katy together with Orville Jamison. Can't imagine what the old boy has on his mind."

39

Katy sized Orville Jamison up as a knowledgeable and shrewd old gentleman with so much political clout that he could do most anything he wanted to. What other chairman of a national party would invite Katy Jenkins, the woman candidate of an offbeat political party, to his home in Alexandria for a private conference? As she drove across the Potomac Saturday morning enroute to his place, she had one other thought: For a man of eighty, he has quite a sparkle.

His home was very much like she expected, old enough to be in the historical register, but comfortable in every respect. As he escorted Katy and Jean into his study off the entry hall, Katy advised, "Jean is Secret Service. All right if she stays?"

"Sure. I've been betrayed at one time or another by most everybody you can think of, but never by the Secret Service. You ladies sit down. I just sent for coffee."

Katy noticed the stack of disorderly newspapers scattered on the floor alongside Jamison's chair. Jamison observed her interest in them. "You got good press today. I guess John's coming forth and proposing to you struck them right. And not a malicious word in any of them about Elizabeth's confession. I liked her. I've always liked her father; except for backing you, Clifford has always been a hundred percent in the GOP camp. I'm glad his daughter turned out so nice; I hadn't met her before."

Katy felt the warmth in his words. "Thank you, Mr. Jamison. Elizabeth is one of the good people."

"Sure is," he confirmed, but Katy could see that he was already thinking ahead to something else. "Katy," he said, "could you get loose at four o'clock Monday afternoon to go over to the White House with me and talk to the President—and that dumb campaign manager of his?" Jamison caught the look of disbelief on Katy's face. He expected this and hurried on, "...and don't you tell anyone I said Gene Boggs is dumb. But the fact is, he's a better military man than politician."

Katy waited for more.

"Hell," he continued, "Boggs and the President think they're winning this election."

"I wouldn't bet any money on that," Katy said, still hedging.

"No, you're too smart to do that." He seemed to be carefully considering his next statement. "Katy, you may be in the middle of the biggest power play of the century. You know what I mean?"

"I think so."

"Well, if you don't now, you'll figure it out by Monday afternoon. You think you'll be free?"

"I'll make sure I am."

"Good!" He paused. "Maybe you had better come over here with your bodyguards. We'll go from here. I can get us into the White House without attracting too much attention. Could you be here about three?"

"I'll be here."

"And don't let the press get hold of this."

"You can be sure of that!"

* * *

Ms. Arnold had three secret weapons in place to unleash during the last week of the campaign. Four million pieces of mail sat ready to go, the biggest political mailing ever to be made to women only. Sponsored by the Women's Movement, it would go to every member of every women's organization. She scanned the banner headline, "MIRACLE in the MAKING!" Other headlines followed throughout: "Do We Want to Go Back to the Dark Ages?" "Second Class Citizens No More," "First Tuesday in November: Women's Bastille Day." Strong copy throughout.

The second arrow in Ms. Arnold's quiver was the "phone tree," a potential ten million phone calls if no one broke the chain. Strong links integrated throughout the three-level network ensured continuity. A backup system spotted weak links and got the calls going again. Millions of urgent phone calls would be made the week before the election.

The third weapon, an eight million dollar television and radio saturation campaign in Pennsylvania, Texas, and California, and spot announcements in other major areas, the announcements and TV videos carefully selected for each region.

Ms. Arnold, certain her secret weapons would all be launched with perfect precision, reflected on the busy week ahead. Meanwhile, Katy and Andy would blitz Pennsylvania, hitting a dozen cities in three days; then they would make a sweep together through California, after which Andy would return to Pennsylvania for a big push ending up in Philadelphia Monday night before the election. Katy would go from California to Phoenix for a state rally—and on to Texas. Her last big roundup would start in south Texas, working north up to Dallas on the Monday night before voting day—from there to Albuquerque to cast her vote in this election.

An unseen force would be with them on these final campaign sweeps, like a strong tailwind silently boosting a plane through the skies. Suddenly everybody wanted to see Katy Jenkins. They wanted to see the woman who was not only running for president, but also marrying her college sweetheart, with whom she had a somewhat naughty romance, and who was purported to be as rich as Croesus.

* * *

Orville and Katy sat facing the President across his desk in the oval office. Gene Boggs sat to one side, somewhat closer to the President. The President's greeting to Orville had been warm and friendly; Katy was included but detected some reserve. The President commented on the latest poll. "We're gaining in the last lap," he said. "And that's where races are won."

Katy watched Boggs; he seemed to concur.

The President continued. "I just can't believe the American people would elect a man with Mallory's tax-borrow-spend philosophy. Where would the money come from for all his spending schemes?"

"That's a good question," Orville Jamison said. "And I don't think the American people will elect him—but the House of Representatives very well may."

"What is that supposed to mean?" the President shot at him.

Jamison wasn't quick to answer. He waited for the President to grasp the full significance of what he said. When he spoke, he was very deliberate. "No one is going to win the election a week from Tuesday."

Katy wasn't as startled as Boggs and the President, but she hung on Jamison's words as he continued. "The pollsters are going to be dumbfounded. They may miss the vote Katy here will get by as much as a hundred percent."

Now the old man was enjoying himself. He had really shaken them up. And now they understood why he brought Katy Jenkins today. "I've been making some surveys of my own," he continued, "and I predict Katy will get enough of the popular vote so neither party will get a majority of the electoral votes; and that throws the election into the House." He paused for effect. "Who do *you* suppose those Democrats will elect?"

Katy saw the startled, uneasy look on the President's face, and Boggs' expression of disbelief. Her own mind whirred. Obviously, Jamison figured she was going to win some states! Some Electoral College votes! Enough to keep either major party from winning the election! *Could Jamison be right?* He wouldn't stick his neck out like this if he wasn't pretty sure of himself.

She hadn't attached much significance to Ms. Arnold's recent spurt of renewed optimism; but now she recalled her words Sunday as they pored over the newspapers. "You and John turned the tide," she said. "And now we're going to have a landslide." Even Ruth Silverton abandoned her usual reserve and stated: "Women are going to make their mark in this election." Steele went further. "The explosion from the women's vote in America is going to be heard around the world." And, the report Jimmy gave her from Texas, written on a post card mailed from McAllen, "They love us down here. We're going to get more votes in Texas than anyone ever dreamed of."

A FAX proof of Harriett Landsdale's final newsletter had arrived at the Headquarters Sunday. The headline proclaimed "GROUNDSWELL FOR JENKINS." The article flatly predicted that they would carry Pennsylvania. Bold print proclaimed, "The American Coalition party has eliminated the tired old status quo forever!"

Katy's heart pounded in exultation as she heard Orville Jamison's voice. "Katy isn't going to get ten percent of the vote as the pollsters predict."

"What do you predict?" asked the President nervously.

"Try twenty percent."

"Impossible," snorted Boggs.

"Come on now, Orville," said the President. "We know better than that."

Jamison disregarded them. "We're beat this time around," he stated flatly. "The Democrats are pulling together pretty well—except for an unknown number of women who will defect. But, we're losing women by the carloads. Goddammit! I tried to tell you guys at the Convention to get off the abortion issue. This isn't a Republican philosophy, but you've spouted off about it ever since."

"We had no choice," murmured the President. "We were committed to an important constituency."

"Oh, I know. But you're losing your women's constituency. Hell! We shouldn't let the fundamentalists run the government anyhow."

"They're not running this Government," the President said firmly.

"They packed the Supreme Court," Jamison snapped. "That's too much for me." Then his voice became conciliatory. "But, the reason I'm here today, I think Katy's people and the Republicans have some common cause in this election. As it stands today, neither of us has a chance to win."

Boggs' face lit up. More than anything else in the world, he wanted to put a coalition together to beat the Democrats. He leaned forward toward the President. "What Orville is saying makes some sense." That's as far as he dared go at this point.

The President fidgeted nervously. He never liked the idea of a woman running for president; he had tried to sweep her candidacy under the rug; he had made fun of her bid for the presidency: "Next thing you know, the Blue Room will be pink," he had scoffed. But he'd be willing to make almost any deal to beat Mallory. Yes, he would deal, even if he had to deal with a woman. "Orville," he said, "would you and Katy like to have a say in the selection of the next Supreme Court Justice, and see more cooperation on women's issues?"

Orville spoke up quickly before Katy could answer. "Oh, we haven't discussed anything like that."

A startling possibility loomed in Katy's mind. There might be a wild card here that would take the jackpot. She tried to conceal the excitement she felt. "There's no way I could change the direction or thinking of our people now," she said. "I'm locked in. But Mr. Jamison is right. We do seem to have a lot in common here. And I think he's right, too, about what the voters are going to do in this election; I don't know where he gets his crystal ball; but he's getting the same vibrations I am." Her next statement sounded casual. "There is an excellent possibility that if we could consolidate our votes, we could decide who wins this election. But we won't know for sure until election night, when the Electoral College votes will be calculated."

"Maybe there's still a way to beat the bastards," the President muttered.

Boggs caught what the President said. His countenance lit up. He turned to Katy. "Will you work with us?"

"I might make a deal," Katy's voice was steady, "on election night—if our combined electoral votes would give us enough to win."

"What kind of deal are you thinking about, Katy?" The President's words were matter-of-fact.

"It would have to be one that would work both ways."

"What do you mean?" questioned Boggs.

"The only way I can deal is if there is some chance for my party to win."

The President looked perplexed. "How could you possibly win?"

"Same way you could," Katy answered quickly, "By a consolidation of electoral votes."

Jamison watched quietly as Katy made her point with the President and Boggs. He leaned forward toward the President. "Now, we're getting somewhere," he said. "How about something like this," he began. "If Katy gets twenty percent, or more, of the popular vote, and at least a hundred electoral votes, we throw our electoral votes to her. But," he continued, "if Katy gets less than twenty percent of the popular vote or less than a hundred electoral votes, she throws her electoral votes to us. She would, however, need some assurances from us along the lines you mentioned to get her people to go along."

Jamison looked at Katy. "Is this acceptable to you?"

"It's acceptable," Katy stated without hesitation.

The President heaved a sigh of relief. No way she could get a hundred electoral votes. Or twenty percent of the popular vote, that'd be fourteen or fifteen million votes! Ridiculous on the face of it. The woman was daydreaming.

Boggs interrupted the President's thoughts. "Sounds like a reasonable proposition to me," he volunteered cordially. Obviously he shared the President's feelings; and maybe, just maybe, this would give him a chance to beat Mallory—and that damned David Wells.

Jamison sat impassively.

"All right," said the President. "It's a deal."

During the drive back to Jamison's house, the old man seemed quite happy. He talked about the Barkers, and Andy, and the Van Dorns, and about John. Katy listened politely and responded with her own stories. Jamison seemed especially interested when she mentioned John's dream of their living at Twin Oaks near London.

Driving back to Georgetown, with Jean in the front seat and Bert in the back seat, Katy wondered about Jamison. He had been careful not to divulge his real goal today. She liked him very much; and he was a power-house. But she knew they might be on a collision course. She would face that when the time came.

40

Buoyed by the terrific enthusiasm of the throngs who turned out for her and Andy on their final campaign swings together, Katy felt frequent surges of confidence that they were actually winning the election. On those gloriously wild days, she and Andy made four, five, or six campaign stops in a day. Well organized events in Pennsylvania and California—good crowds in both states.

Andy's new approach in Pennsylvania paid off; Katy thrilled at the enthusiasm of the crowds everywhere they appeared. And, in California, Lila Stanford and Beverly Hills Productions orchestrated sensational rallies.

But the blockbusters exploded on Katy's Texas blitz. From Corpus Christi to San Antonio to Austin, and across the state, the amplifiers carrying The Texans' up-beat music were strained to capacity.

Then came Dallas-Fort Worth! Monday evening before election day—the rally that would add another legend to Texas political history.

Katy knew Sam Pickens and Madge Bloomfield had spent weeks planning the "biggest barbecue ever held in Texas," but she couldn't believe her eyes when she and her entourage entered Texas Stadium. Located between Dallas and Fort Worth, the stadium, home of the Dallas Cowboys, seats 63,855 spectators. But there was no football game Monday evening. Instead, the tantalizing odor of roasting barbecue wafted through the arena from the giant, above-ground barbecue pits running diagonally across the entire field—over a hundred yards long. The wisps of smoke rose from the length of the pits into the Indian-summer evening air.

Katy could see thousands of people in lines on both sides of the pits loading tin plates with barbecue and pinto beans, and filling tin cups with black coffee, then making their way to the stands. At one end of the field, in front of the goal post, stood the largest speaker's platform Katy had ever seen, with colorful plastic arm-rest chairs that would seat a hundred dignitaries. Down in front were The Texans on their own platform, tuning their instruments and testing the amplifiers. Upon sighting Katy they broke into "The Eyes of Texas Are Upon You."

A lump came into Katy's throat as she was escorted to the speakers stand. How she wished Johnny were here to share this.

She hugged Marge, expressing her delight at the arrangements. "Your folks aren't here yet," Marge advised, "but J. Ross and Sam Pickens are here; that's the Governor with Sam."

"Everybody's going to be here tonight," enthused Katy.

Sam Pickens approached Katy; he greeted her warmly and presented her to the Governor of Texas. "How wonderful of you to come!" she exclaimed to the Governor.

"I couldn't have passed up an invitation from Sam Pickens—or this opportunity to meet you. A lot of Texans are going to vote for you for president tomorrow."

"I believe it," said Katy, "and I appreciate it."

In an aside to Katy, J. Ross said, "I'm happy for you and John."

A commotion at the top of the stairway to the platform distracted them. "Excuse me," Katy said quickly, "that's my Mom and Pop." She moved across to greet them, and was glad to see Gloria with them, and Jimmy.

"Half the people of the State of Texas must be here," observed Pop. "Never figured on anything this big."

"Not quite half," rejoined Katy, "but I've spoken to the rest of them in the last four days." Katy put her arm around Mom and guided them to seats next to the rostrum where she would be sitting.

People moved in around Katy; she greeted the State Chair for the Women's Movement, heads of the state organization for the Caucus of Women's Voters and the National Association of Business Women, and talked to county Coalition chairpersons from around the state, some of whom she had worked with in the last few days.   She noticed that Madge had gotten a few people together with Mom and Pop and Gloria, and that Jimmy was down talking with The Texans.

By the time Katy had visited with half a dozen of the Party Founders, some of whom came all the way from the West Coast to attend this rally, she saw that Sam Pickens was at the rostrum trying to get people's attention and start the meeting.

Sam welcomed the crowd and thanked the committee members who arranged the barbecue; the crowd responded with a standing ovation.   Sam then introduced everyone on the speakers' stand with eloquent fanfare, except Katy whose introduction he saved until later.   He then called on Madge Bloomfield to introduce the Governor, whose response was loaded with good-will.

Katy listened to the Governor's remarks with one ear.   Her mind raced with thoughts for her own speech.   She would be on shortly.   Not quite as quickly as she thought, however, because Sam's introduction of her became quite detailed and flattering, but he finally announced, "I present to you Katy Jenkins, the next president of the United States."

The Texans struck up "Happy Days Are Here Again" as the crowd rose cheering and applauding.   "Win, Katy, win!" resounded through the stadium.

Katy stood at the lectern feeling complete empathy with the crowd; moments like this overcame all of the hardships of campaigning.   "Thank you," she said simply as a semblance of order returned to the scene.

"What a glorious Texas evening! How wonderful that I can be here with so many of you on this election eve.   This is the most people we've ever had at a rally; and I understand there may be as many as eighty million people with us on the networks.   To all of you I say, 'Welcome.'"

A twinkle lit up her face as she spoke into the battery of cameras and microphones that would carry her message to the nation.   "I realize, of course, that some of you are here out of curiosity.   You want to see the woman who is making such a stir running for president, and at the same time is so thrilled about marrying her college sweetheart.   This must be the very best combination to make news, and I welcome all the newspeople here.   To me this combination of events is the happiest of circumstances.

"Whatever the reason you are listening, I am glad you're with me. I want to talk to you tonight not about affairs of the heart, but about affairs of the country.

"I am glad tonight that this country is pioneering so many new areas of human relationships. One of these is the opportunity for women to participate fully in the government of our nation. Within the next twenty-four hours, you may elect the first woman president. This is pioneering on a grand scale. Let's do it!"

Katy slowed her pace. "As I come into the final evening of my campaign to become president of this country, I am glad to be part of a bold, adventurous nation, that isn't afraid to allow its citizens freedom, that isn't afraid to try for new solutions to old problems, that isn't afraid to accept a leadership role in the world.

"I am glad to live in a nation that believes in the freedom and opportunity made possible by the free enterprise of its citizens. I believe in hundreds of thousands of individuals, businesses, and organizations handling the wealth of the nation, rather than one huge federal government controlling its capital—and its people!

"I have recently been accused of being pro-business," Katy stated thoughtfully. "I certainly am. Business is the source of our material blessings. Business makes it possible for the artisans and craftspeople and workers with their many skills to build the homes in which we live and the furnishings in them. Workers, management, and accumulations of capital produce the clothes we wear, the cars we drive, the planes we fly in, the books we read. The people of business grow, transport, and market the food we eat. Business enterprise, in its broadest sense, is the foundation of our cooperative society. When any part of business fails, especially management failure, but also labor failure or capital failure, we all lose. Let's get it all together and make our business environment the best in the world.

"Now, I want to tell you a few of the things I don't believe in! I don't believe we can solve our problems by the expedient of the Federal Government taxing more and spending more. Centralization of power in the Federal Government leads eventually to the loss of individual freedoms. Our tax laws should be made to raise money for legitimate requirements of the government, including whatever it takes to defend our country.

"I hasten to add, however, that I do not believe we need more taxes for defense. I think we have to get more for our money. Also, our people at the Pentagon must stop preparing for World War II, or war with Panama, or in the Persian Gulf. Instead, we must get ready for the new world of missile warfare; we must be first in building defenses against missiles which will wage the wars of the future.

"In this campaign we have dared to think out loud with the American people. We have dared to suggest that the taxpayers can get more for their money. We have dared to think that our country can pay its way, instead of borrowing against the future. We have dared to talk about freedom and opportunity, not only for the 'haves' but for the 'have-nots.' We have dared to believe that the Congress can represent the people instead of the special interests.

"For too long, Americans have tried to create prosperity by speculation instead of investment. We propose investing in people; developing our own energy, once again making our research the best in the world, retooling our industries, and creating millions of new jobs in the process.

"We have dared to suggest that we can renew America, that we can renew confidence in our Social Security system by investing our surpluses instead of spending the money as fast as it comes in; and at the same time give working Americans new hope by investing a part of this giant surplus in low-cost housing loans, making home ownership available to all. We have presented our plans to restore America's faith in our banking system, and in our handling of the national budget.

"Our energy plan will stabilize our energy industry and put thousands of Americans to work developing our own giant reserves of natural gas and building the necessary distribution systems. We will be spending our money in America instead of exporting it to the Middle East."

Her pace slowed, "Now we ask your approval of our plans to renew America, and renew faith in ourselves and our government.

"Thank you for the wonderful consideration and support you have given me. Now you can help renew America with your vote for Katy Jenkins and Andy Barker tomorrow."

Katy had told Sam Pickens that her speech would be short;

even so, he was surprised that it went so fast. But he knew what to do. He jumped to his feet and grabbed the microphone. "The party is just starting," he bellowed, "a lot of us haven't eaten yet, including all of us here on the speaker's platform. Come on! Let's eat!"

"Good speech," J. Ross said to Katy as he came up to renew friendships with Mom, Pop, Jimmy, and Gloria. "Good program," he said to Madge Bloomfield.

The Governor preceded them down the steps and soon they were all caught up in the crowd as The Texans music floated across the stadium, "This Land is Your Land ..."

* * *

"That was a barbecue to end all barbecues," commented Pop as the last stragglers departed. "There'll never be a better one than that."

Katy and her family would fly to Caprock in the GULFSTREAM and stay overnight. The Cessna would stay in Dallas for engine overhauls, which were due.

It was time to say "goodbye" to The Texans. Katy hugged them all in turn, thanking them for the supreme effort they had made. Jimmy presented personal thousand dollar bonus checks from the campaign fund to each of them.

Tex handed a neatly wrapped little package to Katy. "Here's something we put together for you." He explained that it was a tape they recorded of the campaign music. "And there's a couple of Johnny's speeches for you in there, too. We hope you like it." His voice faltered as he said the last part.

Katy tried to say something, but the words didn't come. Finally she whispered, "I'll love it."

Jimmy made a happy announcement, "The Texans will have their own television show starting next Saturday night. One year's contract to start, and a big name sponsor."

"Congratulations," said Katy, "and good luck."

"Good luck to you tomorrow," said Tex.

* * *

As the GULFSTREAM took off for Caprock after the rally, with her family aboard, Katy fell over on the sofa in exhaustion. Mom covered her with a blanket as she had done when she was a little girl, and Katy slept.

That evening Katy, Mom, and Pop sat around the kitchen table at the home place. For once Pop was the first to speak. "I'm glad you could come by here tonight, Katy. We're all mighty proud of you."

"I had to come." She spoke in almost a whisper. "Have to get used to coming home, and Johnny not being here."

"I know," Mom said quietly.

Again Pop started the conversation. "Your cows are doing good. Rains came just in time. As soon as the fall wheat is up, we'll move 'em in on the fields. They'll eat their fill."

"Pop?"

"Yeah?"

"If you want to keep furnishing some pasture, what would you think about me turning the cows over to my little nieces and nephews?"

Mom interrupted. "Katy, I don't know if anybody told you. Another one is on the way."

"I know. They don't keep news like that from me very long around here. We'd have to make arrangements for new ones to be taken in as partners as they come along."

Pop chuckled, then sobered. "I guess a partnership would be the way to go. But any time a kid wants to start his or her own herd, I'd say give 'em some starter stock out of the herd and let 'em go."

Katy remembered the pride of ownership she felt when Pop gave her the first heifer calf. "I understand what you're saying," she said quietly.

"I'll talk to Jack and Jimmy. We'll figure out the best way to handle it. Right now, I think maybe we should sell off some of the herd as soon as they're good and fat, and let Mom handle the proceeds for the grandkids—when they need it for school or something." Pop grinned. "Maybe one of them will be running for president some time."

"I love that idea!" Katy hugged Pop to her. "And the more I think about it, the better I like the proposition of each one having their own stock."

Pop rose and stretched. "You folks'll excuse me. It's past my bed time."

Katy and Mom talked and talked.

The next morning, hundreds of people showed up at the airport to wish Katy good luck. The many cars parked along the road didn't surprise Pop this time.

Mrs. Bayze presented Katy a dozen red roses on behalf of the Caprock County organization. Peter Barnes, arm resting comfortably in a sling, grinned happily as Katy accepted the roses and threw everyone a kiss. The chant, "Win, Katy, Win," resounded through the airport and drifted across the prairie.

41

Manuel met the GULFSTREAM at the general aviation terminal of Albuquerque Airport in Katy's Cadillac and immediately whisked Katy, accompanied by Bert and Jean, to the Albuquerque mid-school where she had voted so many times before. Friends in the voting line couldn't help but notice Bert and Jean's constant surveillance, which added a touch of excitement to the occasion.

Utter exhaustion enveloped Katy as she completed her selections and cast her vote. For once, she slipped quietly into La Posada, went straight to her suite, and fell across the bed into a sound sleep. Late in the afternoon she awakened, wondered where she was, oriented herself, and gradually pulled herself together for the evening ahead—the election night party!

First arrivals at the suite were Elizabeth and Uncle Clifford, followed soon by Dick Donovan, H.B. McGee, Harriett Landsdale, and finally Ms. Arnold who voted in D.C. and caught the next plane to Albuquerque.

The lobby bar at La Posada opened after the polls closed. Large TV screens played continuously in the lobby, in the ballroom, and on a platform outside the hotel facing Copper Street, where a crowd gathered. Ms. Arnold predicted that Katy's election party at the hotel would be one of the biggest parties in the nation.

Three phone lines had been added in Katy's suite, one of them direct to Andy at the Barker's home in Philadelphia. Another connected to LAND & SEA headquarters where John, Carrie Brooks, and the "Friends for Katy and Andy" staff watched the early returns, and the third one went to Lila Stanford's home in San Mateo.

As the party got under way, Katy picked up the Philadelphia line. "Hello, Madame President," Andy cheerfully answered. "We have a real party going on here; Margaret's here, some of the old Berkeley gang, and a bunch of friends. We have a direct line to the Women's Movement Organization in Washington; they have a mob there, too."

Let's hope we have something to celebrate," Katy joked. "How are we doing up there?"

"We'll carry Pennsylvania," Andy enthusiastically predicted. "Stay in touch."

With a smile, Katy set the receiver down and picked up the New York line. John answered.

"We're organized here," she said.

"You have time for me to say I love you?" he asked.

"I'll listen to that anytime," she said. Then she whispered, "I love you, too."

"Aw, for Chrissake, quit making love on the telephone, and listen to these returns." Katy laughed good-humoredly at H.B.'s gruffness.

H.B., obviously excited, exclaimed, "We've got those TV commentators scratching their heads. The East Coast returns are in no way conforming to expectations. The returns from New York and Pennsylvania are going crazy. And it looks like we are leading in New Hampshire, which is surprising, but what a boost! We're polling more votes in all three of these states than the Republicans. Pennsylvania looks especially good."

The soothsayer computer whizzes now looked at their screens in disbelief. For the first time in years, they couldn't call the winner before the polls closed in California.

Announcers on all three major television networks suddenly realized this was a whole new ball game. They talked about no candidate getting enough votes to win the election. They played it to the hilt. The Electoral College would decide the future president in December. If none of the three candidates won there, however, the decision fell to the House of Representatives. Conceivably the president wouldn't be elected until January of next year! "What will this uncertainty do to the world situation?" asked a commentator.

The networks brought on government history experts;

university professors sat squinting into the cameras, attempting scholarly explanations: this had happened before, in 1800, when the election was thrown into the House and Monroe was elected; it happened again in 1824 when the House of Representatives elected John Quincy Adams in a "corrupt bargain."

As the early returns came in from the southern states, the tempo of the newscasts slowed somewhat. The President led Democrats by small margins in these states, but Katy was still getting a solid ten or fifteen percent of the southern states' votes.

Cliff, Ms. Arnold, H.B. and Dick went across to the ballroom to get the election party going. They made their separate ways around the mezzanine shaking hands, talking confidentially, laughing at the jokes of friends.

Elizabeth and Katy, glad to be left alone in the suite, turned the television sets down low, and the two women sat quietly for awhile enjoying the lull before the storm that would engulf them as the night progressed.

Elizabeth spoke first. "Katy, remember that first evening we moved into our own little house over by the campus? I still remember how bold we felt."

"So do I, and how wicked we felt when we uncorked a bottle of real champagne to go with our first meal. Times like that are what make life worth living."

"And times like this," said Elizabeth. "I am thrilled to death about you and John."

"I guess no one in the world but you knew how much I loved him. And it's hard to believe, but I'm just as much in love today."

"I know, Katy." She paused, pensive, "What are you going to do if you're elected president?"

Katy laughed. "I am going to have my hands full. But I think we can handle it."

"'We can handle it.' You really are getting married! I love it. But I still hope you won't be elected. Becoming John's wife is a good enough project. I want you to be able to relish it, to enjoy it, to give it your all. You have more than done your bit for the country. After this you should take some time for yourself."

The statistics on the televisions changed little. The Democrats piled up early leads in Illinois. Katy was running well; that was the lead news item, a surprisingly close third. Apparently the Coalition party had cut much deeper into the Republican than into the Democratic vote. The first reports from the West Coast strongly favored the Democrats. Could the Democrats win this election tonight after all?

Elizabeth was bursting with eagerness to talk to Katy about wedding plans.

"Have you and John decided when?" she asked.

"We'll make plans after tonight. John wants to make it Thanksgiving, which doesn't give us much time."

"Thanksgiving, beautiful! We'll have a celebration." Elizabeth caught her breath. "Where's it going to be?"

"John would be happy to come to New Mexico. Maybe a small wedding. Just the families. Then a larger reception. Something like that."

"Albuquerque! Saint John's Cathedral! It's such a beautiful church! And John will meet all your Albuquerque friends. Oh, this is going to be a wonderful occasion! And Katy, you've got to have a honeymoon. The Brown Palace?"

Katy laughed. "You remember everything. No, John wants us to go to England—his country estate outside London. He loves it there."

"Ooh, Katy, I'm so happy for you I can't stand it."

Elizabeth rose, went to the door, and threw the bolt. She returned, and pulled her chair opposite Katy, close to her.

"What in the world...?"

"I can't wait," Elizabeth said. "I have to tell you now! I have the most wonderful, wonderful news you've ever heard. You and John are going to be...grandparents!"

"Elizabeth, what are you saying?"

"What I'm trying to say is—Gloria discovered she's pregnant by Johnny. It's for sure. She came over to the house Friday with the news. Could've been devastating for her—with Johnny gone—but she's as happy as a lark about it."

Katy gasped. "A little Johnny!"

"Or little Gloria. But Gloria is sure it's a boy."

Katy hugged Elizabeth. Someone was banging on the door. "Be right there," she yelled. Then, in a hushed, excited tone to Elizabeth, "We're going to be real grandparents!"

42

H.B. was the first one back to Katy's suite. He headed straight for one of the TV sets and tuned it in to Channel 2, Santa Fe, which was concentrating on New Mexico returns. Katy carried Albuquerque and Bernalillo County overwhelmingly, which didn't surprise H.B. any. Analyzing the early northern county returns, he shook his head in disbelief. Katy led in Taos and Rio Arriba Counties. She scored upsets everywhere the commentators looked. Early returns from Caprock County showed Katy winning by a landslide.

H.B. made a solemn pronouncement, "Katy, we've known for days that you'd carry New Mexico. But we underestimated by how much. It's possible that you will get more votes in New Mexico than the Republicans and Democrats combined. He looked perplexed, as if disbelieving his own prediction. "Wouldn't that be something?"

* * *

Puzzled as to why the switchboard would be ringing her, Katy picked up the phone. Ms. Arnold. "Guess who is here in the lobby, sitting at the bar, and acting like he owns the place?"

"I can't imagine," Katy answered.

"David Wells! What is the Democratic Campaign manager doing here?"

"I don't know," said Katy thoughtfully.

"It's strange that he would be down here in New Mexico tonight. You'd think he'd be in Chicago at the Democrats' election party."

"I think I know why he's here. He might come in handy

before this night is over. Get Uncle Clifford with him. Tell him
to make Wells feel muy importanto."

"Okay. But, remember, he can't be trusted."

"We won't put him in a position of trust. Make him happy,
though. Remember this is the Coalition party; we welcome
Democrats."

By ten o'clock Mountain Standard Time, the newscasters
regained their composure. Once again they knew it all. In their
wisdom, they declared the election an upset—a major upset.
Theories abounded: a larger than expected women's vote; the
Independent vote had gone for the Coalition party, shutting out the
Republican party—contrary to past elections.

Katy's popular vote was now estimated at twenty-five percent
of the total, a whopping fourteen million votes! The Coalition
party had New Hampshire almost for certain. And the ticket led
Pennsylvania with its big block of electoral votes. Early returns
from Texas, with another big block of votes, looked good. Same
in Oklahoma. New Mexico was certain for Katy, and possibly
Colorado and Arizona. It was too early to project California, but
early returns showed Katy running well there, too. "Amazing,"
said H.B.

Katy alerted Secret Service. She wanted to make a couple of
appearances before her 11:00 o'clock speech in the ballroom. The
first would be from her patio where she could talk to the people
out on Copper Street, the second from the mezzanine where she
could talk to the people down in the lobby, then to the ballroom
for the national television hookup. Secret Service questioned these
exposures, but Katy insisted. At ten minutes before 11:00 o'clock,
she appeared on the patio. A roar went up from the crowd in the
street when they saw her. A new chant went up, "Win, Katy,
Win." Harried camera men jockeyed their portable cameras in
position to catch it all. The voices rose in a crescendo, subsiding
only after Katy signalled for quiet, arms outstretched to the crowd.
"Thank you, thank you. Thank you!" She spoke briefly, her
enthusiasm thrilling her listeners. The chant resumed. "Win,
Katy, Win!" It echoed in her ears as she crossed to the sliding
doors and slipped inside. Jean mumbled to Bert, "It's going to be
a long night."

Elizabeth hugged Katy as she came through the door. "Katy,

it just came on the TV, you are projected to take Texas, with 32 electoral votes!"

H.B. was grinning from ear to ear. "Katy, you're making election history," he proclaimed.

Dick, looking dapper as ever, appeared unperturbed, but Katy could see the sparkle of excitement in his eyes. She knew her old partner, friend, and mentor was being rewarded tonight. The pulsing chant from outside flowed like electric energy through the suite.

Jean consulted Katy. "Do you still want to make the mezzanine appearance, or go straight to the Ballroom?"

"Let's stay on schedule," Katy said.

The crowd in the lobby burst with excitement over the Texas projection. They roared their approval when Katy appeared, saying, "Thank you! Thank you!" As she made her way along the mezzanine rail, the crowd took up the chant, "Win, Katy, Win!" Again Katy's speech kindled more enthusiasm.

Bert and Jean escorted Katy around the mezzanine to the ballroom. "We have it made now."

The crowd cheered wildly as Katy made her way to the platform with its battery of microphones. TV cameras surrounded the podium.

Ms. Arnold shoved a list of names in front of Katy. "Be sure to get them all. Except maybe David Wells. He may not want to be introduced at a Coalition meeting. Clifford arranged to get him into the ballroom."

Eleven o'clock. A signal from the TV coordinator. Katy was on the air. She took her time, waiting for the crowd to quiet down.

"Texas is ours!" she shouted. "They are projecting Texas for us." The crowd roared. Katy continued. "Who is really winning this election tonight? Neither the Democrats, nor the Republicans. The American Coalition party and all Americans win tonight regardless of the final outcome.

"If some of our ideas prevail in the long run, whether we go to the White House or not, we've won." The crowd quieted, as she continued. "We have surprised everyone tonight. But the surprises aren't over. Watch California! If we win in California, we're going to get the Electoral College votes to turn this election around. Watch California!

"And, thank you! The people here in this room and across the nation have made this evening possible." Katy cocked her head back with that look of challenge the Congress had seen so many times.

"Thank you!"

* * *

H.B., Dick, Uncle Cliff, and Katy got back to Katy's suite as soon as they could after the eleven o'clock broadcast. Ms. Arnold, Harriett Landsdale, and Maria joined them shortly thereafter. They all knew Katy planned to brief them on developments. Only Ms. Arnold and John knew about Katy's conference at the White House with the President. Now, she told the group assembled in her living room about the deal they made.

"The President was suspicious from the first sight of me," Katy said, "but feigned the usual cordiality. Orville Jamison, at his political best, explained the situation. But the President still denied that this wasn't the usual race between the Republicans and Democrats."

Maria Romero's eyes were popping with excitement as Katy talked. H.B. was almost as excited; Dick didn't seem to be paying much attention, but Uncle Cliff sat on the edge of his chair.

"At just the right time," Katy continued, "Jamison made a startling proposal. If I should get less than twenty percent of the popular vote and less than 100 electoral votes, I would throw all of my support to the Republicans. If, however, I should get twenty-percent or more, at least 100 electoral votes, the Republicans would throw all their support to me. The President agreed because he didn't think I could possibly do it. Jamison didn't think I could do it either, but he knew there was a possibility; the risk was worth taking because this was the only way the Republicans could win."

Maria was puzzled. "I don't understand how the Electoral College works," she admitted. "How could anyone win without getting the majority of the popular vote?"

Ms. Arnold explained. "When the American people vote for president, they're actually voting for 'electors.' Each party designates its own electors, so they're committed to cast their votes for their party candidate when they meet at the Electoral College. This is all set up in the Constitution, but the electors are not required to vote that way. Actually, they can vote for their choice even if the candidate is in another party."

"That's a funny way to work it," commented Maria.

"It is," agreed Ms. Arnold, "but when the Constitution was written, some of the founding fathers still weren't sure that the average voter would be qualified to elect the president, so they provided for him to vote for electors who in turn would elect the president."

Maria jumped up. "Don't you all see what this means? If we win in California, Katy is going to be elected president!"

Uncle Cliff put his arm around Katy's shoulders. "It looks like you may make it. The returns from California are looking better all the time."

Elizabeth had stayed in the background, but now she broke into tears. "I'm glad for you, Katy," she murmured. "I guess this was your destiny from the time you were born."

"Look everybody, I haven't won yet, the night's still young," Katy said.

H.B. still kept his optimism. "Well, gal, win California and you've got maybe 131 electoral votes. More than a hundred, that's for sure."

The LAND & SEA direct line rang. H.B. answered and handed the phone to Katy.

John said, "Katy, we've had the mainframe here analyzing California all evening. I checked the programming myself. I think it's giving us the right answers."

"Hey, don't keep me in suspense."

"Big Boy says you'll get thirty-six percent, Democrats thirty-two, Republicans twenty-eight. All other parties combined, less than four. I don't think it will be off over one or two percentage points on any of these projections. I think you've won California—and the deal with the President and Jamison."

Katy's mind whirred like the machine that made the projections.

"It will probaby be on the newscasts within an hour," John continued. "Jamison is on another phone in the next room; he knows these projections. And he's inviting Boggs over here. Boggs is close by—at the Sheraton—their victory party over there must be getting dull."

"John, thank you! I'm glad for the advance information. I'll call Lila Stanford, and Andy and Margaret, and Ellen and Ruth, and as many others as I can; then I'll be back with you."

By the time Katy made her calls, including one to Caprock, the TV announcers teased their audiences about an important projection on California to follow the next commercial break.

Shortly thereafter pandemonium broke out in the suite, reverberated through the hotel, and out into the street. Katy knew. She had carried California! And Pennsylvania! And New Hampshire! And Texas! And Oklahoma! With New Mexico, Colorado, and Arizona almost certain, she had the electoral votes required to win her proposition with the President and Jamison. Her popular vote was sure to be over the twenty percent required. The New York line rang furiously.

She answered it herself. Boggs and Jamison were on the line. "Katy," Boggs began in the most cordial tone, "I want to talk to you heart to heart."

"Yes?" said Katy.

"The American people won't go along with our little plan. We both know that. To try to throw the election to the candidate with the least votes would never work."

"Oh," said Katy.

"Now, here is my proposal: we can win this election if you throw your support to the President. It would make sense to the American people. After all, you voted with the Republicans on many issues in the Congress."

Orville Jamison broke in. "This is worth considering, Katy. The President has experience and a broader base for foreign affairs than you have. His proposition is logical. The American people are more accustomed to a man as their president."

Katy's blood boiled. Her inclination was to say: "Hell no!"

"I will have to get back to you, Gene," she said. "David Wells is here for Owen Mallory. I have an appointment with him right now. At least he seems eager to talk business."

"Katy, wait a minute!" Boggs tried to keep her on the line. But all he heard was the click as she hung up the phone.

* * *

Katy was glad she actually had agreed to see David Wells. She asked Maria to accompany her. David and his associate waited in the office around the corner of the mezzanine when Maria and Katy arrived. David offered his congratulations to Katy on winning California. She could see that he was impresssed with this victory. He seemed to look at her with new respect. "Let me come right to the point," he said. "The Coalition party has split the vote so no one wins tonight. If the election goes to the House of Representatives, as proscribed by the Constitution, the Democrats have a big edge. We win hands down. But you and I can make things much smoother if we combine forces." He hesitated, "Do you see what I mean?"

Katy nodded and David relaxed somewhat as he made his next statement. "You and John Van Dorn are getting married. I guess you know he has a beautiful estate outside London. He loves it there. It's public knowledge that he is turning the Operations Division of LAND & SEA over to his brother, Ted. John can be chairman of the board from one place as well as another."

"What are you getting at?" asked Katy.

"How would you like to be the United States Ambassador to England? This is one of the most prestigious jobs in the world." He didn't wait for a response from Katy. "And, we can give Andy Barker anything he wants, a Cabinet post, head of a Department, he can name it. His being a Democrat makes this all the more easy to do." He waited for Katy's response.

Katy was thinking—so this is what being a 'power broker' means.

"David," she said, "I will have to contact Andy, of course, and some of my people. Your offer is interesting." Her mind was filled with another thought. Should she consult with John? This would be very appealing to him.

David interrupted, "We need to know by midnight. All you will have to do is ask your delegates to consolidate their votes with ours. The networks could hook up so you and Andy could appear simultaneously. It would be a real victory for the Coalition party to team up with the winners."

"What room are you in, David?"

"1006."

"I will call you within an hour."

"Thank you, Katy; I'm sure you will be doing the right thing."

Katy sat thinking after David and his confederate left. Maria Romero sat quietly, too. She sensed that Katy needed the privacy that only this room could provide.

John would like that, Katy thought. A home at Twin Oaks outside London. She remembered him telling her about Twin Oaks. "I love the place almost as much as I love you," he said. "I'm certain you will like it just as much." He chuckled. "I can think, just offhand, of a dozen places I'm going to make love to you."

"All of them the first night of our honeymoon," she teased.

He kissed her. "No," he said mischievously, "I'm going to spread this out over an achingly long period of time. There's no hurry at Twin Oaks."

My God, it would be easy to take the post in London and live at Twin Oaks, she thought. And John would be delighted. No one ever expected me to win the election anyhow. Ambassador to England! Center stage on the International scene. What a wonderful life that could be for us!

43

Maria sat quietly as Katy put the new developments into perspective. Ambassador to England! Married to John and living at Twin Oaks! As compared to being president of the United States, fighting with the arrogant press, coping with politicians and their special interests and personal greed, and having the responsibility of a fiscally insolvent nation on her hands, moving to England with John would be pure heaven. Wasn't that what her heart had yearned for over the years? Wasn't that what she would like most of all?

Who could blame her? She had fought a good battle. She wasn't elected president anyhow. Twenty percent of the vote doesn't win an election, nor a hundred or so electoral votes; it takes two hundred and seventy to win.

She considered the scheme Orville Jamison cooked up. Sure, he wanted to beat the Democrats—that was his goal. She was only a pawn in his game of power politics. If the President and Boggs should honor the deal, and make an all-out effort to get the Republican electors to vote for her, it still might not work; once the electors were released, they could vote any way they pleased. Mallory and gang would go after them with every kind of bribe they could dream up. He would go to any length to win.

Her body trembled at a new thought. If she won the election, she could very well lose John in the process. She couldn't stand to lose John now. She remembered their night in Albuquerque, the comfort of his body against hers, the casual assurance when he said, "When this campaign is over, I think we should get married and live at Twin Oaks."

John isn't expecting me to win this election. No one is!

She wouldn't hold the President and Boggs to their deal. They never expected her to win. Let it go. Let the election take its course. Marry John. Accept the ambassadorship to England. She breathed a sigh of relief.

Katy turned to Maria. "Were you ever in love, Maria?"

Maria showed surprise at the question. "I'm a romantic, Katy. You know—the hot-blooded señorita? Yes, I'm afraid I have more heart sometimes than good sense. Tonight, though, my love isn't the romantic kind. It flames for you, Señora, the inspiration for women everywhere."

Katy caught her breath. This answer brought her back to reality. "Thank you, Maria. I love you, too. You put a lot of that heart of yours into this campaign."

"I'm so proud of Taos County. Even the women at the Pueblo voted for you; they kept it secret from the men."

Katy's thoughts focused.

She thought about Owen Mallory becoming president of the United States and the thought was repugnant to her. She thought about the President and felt no enthusiasm whatsoever for him.

Her thought flashed back to Margaret's first call of distress and the hope in her voice when she said, "Katy, you're the only one who can do it." She thought of Mom drawing out all of her personal savings to help her get started. She thought of Ellen Steele putting herself on the line, and Ruth Silverton quietly mustering her army of women for the cause, and Lila Stanford using all of her political skills to win California, and Ms. Arnold's steadfast loyalty.

She remembered Petie, his shoulder shattered by a bullet meant for her: "Ain't nothin' can keep you from being president, now." Johnny's happy, carefree voice rang in her ears, "Sis, go for it!"

"Maria," she said, "we'd better get back to the suite. I have a phone call to make."

* * *

All eyes were on Katy. Tension crackled in the air.

Dick Donovan's high-pitched voice pierced the room. "I hope you didn't let that Democrat talk you into anything."

"He wants to make me Ambassador to England."

"Like hell," growled Dick. "What he doesn't know is that you are going to be the next president."

Uncle Clifford was watching Katy for any signs of capitulation. He could detect none. He confidentially relayed his thoughts to Harriett Landsdale. She nodded agreement.

Katy went directly to the LAND & SEA line. She picked up the receiver and called.

"John here."

"Surprise—it's me again. Can you get Boggs and Jamison on the line together?"

"Sure...Orville is on. Here's Boggs."

Katy was deliberate. "Gene, I would like to have you consider being my Secretary of Defense."

There was silence at the other end of the line. Then Orville's voice came on. "Is that your decision, Katy?"

"That's it," said Katy. "The Coalition party stands pat!" Katy could feel the stunned silence at the other end of the line, but followed up quickly, "Can you ring the President and get him in on a conference call?"

"Well, yes, he's standing by at his home phone."

The President came on-line shortly. Boggs advised him Katy and Orville were on the line. He sounded weary. "Well, Orville, you were right; we lost this one."

"Katy wants to talk to you, Mr. President."

Katy spoke slowly. "The final round is still coming up in this campaign. The public knows you lost it to the Democrats. And you did. They peg me as a winner tonight. I honestly believe that I can come nearer holding your electoral votes than you could mine. Do you see what I mean?"

"Maybe." The President sounded hesitant. "But I'm not sure you're right." Then he added, "Katy, I can make the same offer the Democrats did. Wouldn't you like to be the Ambassador to England?"

"Well, you fellows still seem to have a 'good old boy' network going."

"Not really, Katy, we found out by accident. A leak by staff."

Katy sensed he was on the defensive now. This is the time to push, she thought. "Listen, Mr. President, you and Orville and Gene—forget about the little 'deal' we had. You're released from that." She paused long enough for this to sink in. "Instead, let's see where we are now. As it stands the Democrats will win in the long run. They control the House, and the election will be decided there—unless we head it off in the Electoral College. That will take our combined efforts. Follow me?"

Orville answered. "We follow, Katy. No other way you can figure it."

"Okay. Now, let's go a step further. Dissatisfaction with both Republicans and Democrats is what got me this far. And there still isn't much enthusiasm for either party. A majority of the electorate would be perfectly happy to see me win. Perhaps a big majority! And the press will stampede to me. You're hearing the television tonight. Just wait until you see the newspapers in the morning. I know they're as fickle as the wind, but right now I am the media's grand new toy. I'm the new kid on the block. You see what I mean?"

"I wish to hell I didn't," the President said with some conviction. "Yes, I can see you may be right about the whole thing."

"Where do we go from here, Katy?" Orville asked.

Boggs broke in. "There is still a crowd at the Park Sheraton; it's more like a wake over there than a party. But, the TV apparatus is still in place—waiting for a 'statement' from the President via satellite from his home. They can hook it up so the President can ask our electors to vote for you."

"Let's think about this for a minute," Katy said. "If we come on too fast, it will be quite a shock, not only to the electors but to the public. You can release your electors and ask them to vote for me, but at that point, you'd lose control. And the Democrats would yell 'foul.'"

"Katy, do you have a plan?" Orville sounded anxious.

"Yes, I do. We had better lay some groundwork. We have a battery of phones there at LAND & SEA and half a dozen of the best public relations phone people you could ever get together. The Electoral College list for every state is in the computer; it won't take long to sort out the states the Republicans have carried, together with the phone number of each elector. What you have to do is phone every Republican elector, the chairpeople first, and get them in on the act. We'll contact the Coalitionists from here."

Boggs had a question.   "What about the crowd at the Sheraton?"

"Thank them! Give them a pep talk! Go on the air pointing out that the election isn't over yet—that you will have an announcement sometime in the morning. Don't concede a thing. Thank your supporters again and again. Keep the press guessing. Tell them it doesn't look like anything will be decided before morning."

"That'll work.   Gives us some time.   Very good, but meanwhile the Democrats will be claiming victory."

"That's good too.   Let them go smugly off to bed tonight thinking they've won."

"Katy." Gene Boggs voice was cordial. "This will work, sure as hell, and I think I could work very well with you as Secretary of Defense."

As Katy replaced her receiver, a yell went up in the suite. "Katy, you did it!"   "You stood your ground!"   "We're going to win!"

Elizabeth came to Katy and put her arm around her, and none too soon.   Suddenly, Katy felt as if her knees were going to buckle. It dawned on her that she had made an irrevocable decision, and she hadn't consulted with John, the one person who was most concerned and the most important to her. The thought tormented her. *My God, what have I done?*

And who knows whether this will work out?   If some of the Republican electors go over to the Democrats, they'll be victorious after all.   Then I would be about the last person in the world they would appoint the Ambassador to England—even if John wanted me after tonight.

She sank down on the nearest sofa, her mind reeling, her heart racing. She scarcely heard Elizabeth say she'd bring some coffee.

She was grateful when Harriett and H.B. took over answering the phones, which rang incessantly. "No, Katy isn't conceding anything," they answered time and time again. "The final score isn't in yet."

Then Harriett handed her the phone. "It's David Wells."

Katy spoke into the phone. "David, I thank you for the offer.

Believe me, it was tempting. But my people won't go along."
She hung up.

"Look at this!" H.B. yelled at Katy, "the President is giving
his swan song. He's handling it well."

Katy listened as he spoke. "I thank the American people for
honoring me with their greatest trust. Tonight you have asked for
a change; and I accept that. But you haven't elected either of the
party candidates yet; this election is still to be decided. Tomorrow
is another day. Let's wait and see what happens. Meanwhile, I
thank you again for your support."

He's coming through, thought Katy.

Shortly after crying out, "We're going to win!" Ms. Arnold
had rushed from the suite. Now she reappeared and advised Katy
everything was set for her final appearances for the night. "Just
like before, talk to the people outside first, then from the
mezzanine to those in the lobby, then to the ballroom for the
national hookups."

Katy was glad she had heard the President first. In all three
appearances, she echoed some of his words. "Thank you! Thank
you for your support! The American people have asked for
change. But this election isn't settled yet. Right now it appears
no candidate will get enough votes to win." Then she added, "The
American Coalition party is the big winner tonight. No one
thought we could do what we did; let's celebrate the biggest upset
in American political history! I thank you all from the bottom of
my heart for your support."

After the final speech in the ballroom, Katy greeted as many
people personally as she could, shaking their hands, hugging,
calling them by name, thanking each one personally. Finally, the
crowd dispersed; the election party was over.

* * *

Katy had a few words for the group assembled in her suite.
Her voice had a lilt as she announced: "Ms. Arnold has been on
the phone to LAND & SEA in New York. Carrie advises the
phone calls to Republican electors are under way. So far the
response is a hundred percent in favor of going with us. Mr.

Jamison is talking personally to the big ones and Boggs to others, all in the name of the President. And the President is making some personal calls to key electors; they are determined to swing this election."

"Katy," Ms. Arnold boomed, "our next job is to select your cabinet."

All eyes focused on Clifford King as he rose and stood majestically. The room quieted as he spoke. "Good luck to you, Katy, as you ascend to the presidency. This country lucked out tonight beyond its happiest imaginings by selecting you—even if by sort of an accident. I feel tremendous excitement about having a ringside seat to watch you take over with a brand of democracy this country hasn't seen since the first Congress drew up the Bill of Rights." His pronouncement had a prophetic ring. He hugged Katy and dismissed himself with a cordial, "Good night; I'll be in the suite down the hall if you need me."

Dick announced it was past his bed time; he came to Katy and extended his hand. "Be seeing you around." H.B. had a bear hug for Katy as he took his leave. "Looks like you pulled it off. See you in the morning."

After everyone else left, Elizabeth had a private message from John for Katy. "John called just after you left for your final appearances. He said not to be influenced by the Democrats if they offered you all of England; and that you and he would make out, whatever happens."

The phone rang. Katy caught her breath as John came on the line. "Hey, lady president-elect, could you drop by the Park Plaza sometime soon?"

Katy's heart raced. *President-elect?* She knew the enormity of the job ahead of her, and that she would put her life on the line serving her country. She struggled to control the exhilaration coursing through her veins. But her voice was low, controlled, as she responded to John. She looked at the clock—2:00 A.M. "How about this evening?"

"Great." He chuckled the low, mirthful chuckle Katy loved so much. "I have the makings for some super coffee royals."

THE END

EPILOGUE

Katy and John were married at St. John's Cathedral in Albuquerque the day before Thanksgiving. The wedding reception at the Convention Center was the largest ever held in New Mexico. The Texans played their way into the hearts of the throng attending. The GULFSTREAM II-B and the crew that flew Katy a hundred thousand miles on the campaign trail stood by to whisk the honeymooners off to London after the reception.

The Electoral College gave Katy a solid win, and the Supreme Court promptly ruled that the election was in accordance with the provisions of the Constitution.

Katy and John's honeymoon at Twin Oaks is not recorded here. They enjoyed the privacy. Twin Oaks was their refuge many times during the years of Katy's presidency, the years in which her magnetic brand of leadership brought the American people together in the most dramatic political revolution in American history.